OXFORD MONOGRAPHS IN INTERNATIONAL LAW

General Editor

PROFESSOR ROGER O'KEEFE

Professor of International Law at Bocconi University, Milan

Regional and General International Law

OXFORD MONOGRAPHS IN INTERNATIONAL LAW

The aim of this series is to publish important and original pieces of research on all aspects of international law. Topics that are given particular prominence are those which, while of interest to the academic lawyer, also have important bearing on issues which touch the actual conduct of international relations. Nonetheless the series is wide in scope and includes monographs on the history and philosophical foundations of international law.

RECENT TITLES IN THE SERIES

Shades of Illegality in the Law Against War
Christian Marxsen

Recognition of States in International Law
Pavle Kilibarda

Overlapping Individual and Interstate Claims in International Law
Jessica Howley

Party Status to Armed Conflict in International Law
Alexander Wentker

The Identity of Governments in International Law
Niko Pavlopoulos

Access to Courts for Asylum Seekers and Refugees
State Obligations under the 1951 Refugee Convention
Emma Dunlop

Gravity at the International Criminal Court
Admissibility and Prosecutorial Discretion
Priya Urs

International Law Obligations on Climate Change Mitigation
Benoit Mayer

Coastal State Jurisdiction over Living Resources in the Exclusive Economic Zone
Camille Goodman

International Law and Corporate Actors in Deep Seabed Mining
Joanna Dingwall

The Concept of an International Organization in International Law
Lorenzo Gasbarri

Necessity and Proportionality and the Right of Self-Defence in International Law
Chris O'Meara

Neutrality in Contemporary International Law
James Upcher

Regional and General International Law

JANINA BARKHOLDT
Senior Research Fellow, Max Planck Institute for Comparative Public Law and International Law, Germany

OXFORD
UNIVERSITY PRESS

OXFORD
UNIVERSITY PRESS

Great Clarendon Street, Oxford, OX2 6DP,
United Kingdom

Oxford University Press is a department of the University of Oxford.
It furthers the University's objective of excellence in research, scholarship,
and education by publishing worldwide. Oxford is a registered trade mark of
Oxford University Press in the UK and in certain other countries.

Published in the United States of America by Oxford University Press
546 Fifth Avenue, New York, NY 10036, United States of America.

British Library Cataloguing in Publication Data
Data available

Library of Congress Control Number: 2026946376

ISBN 9780198953401

DOI: 10.1093/9780198953432.001.0001

Printed and bound by
CPI Group (UK) Ltd., Croydon, CR0 4YY

The manufacturer's authorized representative in the EU for product safety is
Oxford University Press España S.A. of Parque Empresarial San Fernando de Henares,
Avenida de Castilla, 2—28830 Madrid (www.oup.es/en or product.safety@oup.com).
OUP España S.A. also acts as importer into Spain of products made by the manufacturer.

MIX
Paper | Supporting responsible forestry
FSC™ C013604

General Editor's Preface

It is sometimes said that the future of international law is regional. It is not hard to see why. The European, Inter-American, and African human rights courts, the first two with their characteristic approaches to treaty interpretation, each exercise an authority and exert a wider influence of which the universal human rights treaty-monitoring bodies can only dream. In the realm of international trade, regional free-trade agreements vie for practical significance with the WTO covered agreements. In institutional terms, the EU and AU, the most highly developed and cohesive of the truly regional international organizations, assert here and there a normative priority, in effect, over the obligations arising for their member states in the latter's capacity as members of the United Nations and, for AU member states, as parties to the Rome Statute of the International Criminal Court. Alongside all this are the possibilities of regional customary international law. But the fundamental question raised by regional international law is how it relates to general international law, defined as international law of universal application, actual or potential.

Janina Barkholdt's overarching response in *Regional and General International Law* is that 'regional international law, as a distinct legal category, is central to the development of general international law, while general international law, comprising the rules applicable across all regions, is indispensable for protecting regional plurality'. On her way to this conclusion, Dr Barkholdt argues that regional international law is qualitatively different from other forms of particular international law and, as such, is not merely *lex specialis* to general international law. Her answer to the challenges posed by this distinctiveness is the 'common normative framework' furnished by the secondary rules of international law, in the sense of the rules of general international law 'govern[ing] the formation, identification, interpretation, and application of legal norms'. In extolling the promise of the secondary rules of international law, Dr Barkholdt promotes – in her own and Koskenniemi's words – 'the value of a "culture of formalism"'.

Regional and General International Law represents international legal scholarship of the highest order. It places deft, detailed technical analysis and lateral thinking at the service of insight. It is deeply researched and tightly written. It deserves to be read widely by scholars and practitioners of international law, both regional and general.

RO'K

Milan

September 2026

Acknowledgments

In completing this book, I often thought of Joan Didion's observation that '[i]t is easy to see the beginnings of things, and harder to see the ends'.[1] That the book has seen a beginning and, ultimately, an end owes much to the support and patience of many people who have stood by me along the way, and to whom I am grateful.

The book is a revised and updated version of my doctoral dissertation ('Regional and General International Law: Reconciliation through Secondary Rules'), which I defended at the Faculty of Law of Humboldt University Berlin in July 2022. I am grateful to Professor, now Judge, Georg Nolte, my doctoral supervisor and academic teacher, for his invaluable guidance, critical open-mindedness, and constant encouragement. His deep respect for regional plurality, and, above all, his commitment to general international law, guided by an acute sense of its fragility, influenced both this book and my thinking well beyond it.

I also thank Professor Matthias Ruffert for serving as the second examiner of my thesis, Professor Christian Tomuschat for presiding over its defence, and the *Absolventen und Freunde der Juristischen Fakultät der Humboldt-Universität zu Berlin Bibliotheksgesellschaft eV* for awarding the thesis the faculty prize for the best doctoral dissertation in public law in 2023. At Oxford University Press, I am grateful to Professor Roger O'Keefe and Professor, now Judge, Phoebe Okowa for accepting this book for the *Oxford Monographs in International Law* series, to the two anonymous reviewers for their constructive comments, and to Robert Cavooris, for his patient guidance in transforming the manuscript into a book.

The work on this book began in 2017 during my time as a research and teaching assistant at the Chair of Public International Law at Humboldt University Berlin, and as an associate researcher with the Berlin-Potsdam Research Group 'The International Rule of Law—Rise or Decline?'. I am grateful to Professors Heike Krieger, Georg Nolte, and Andreas Zimmermann for the many opportunities they gave me to explore and discuss my first ideas, as well as to the wonderful and supportive community affiliated with the chair and the research group. I would like to thank, in particular, Noora Arajärvi, Helmut Aust, Jonathan Bourguignon, Jan Philipp Cludius, Alfredo Crosato Neumann, Pierre d'Argent, James Devaney, Yuwen Fan, Chris Gutmann, Alicia Köppen, Malcolm Jorgensen, Balingene Kahombo, Liliya Khasanova, Apollin Koagne Zouapet, Nikolaus Koch, Julian Kulaga, Felix Lange, Hansong Li, Huw Llewellyn, Campbell McLachlan, Paolo Palchetti, Stefan Raffeiner, Alejandro Rodiles, Sabrina Schäfer, Sophie Schuberth,

[1] J Didion, 'Goodbye to all that' in *Slouching Towards Bethlehem* (4th edn, Harper Collins 2017) 225.

Alexander Silke, Artur Simonyan, Isabel Walther, and Lukas Willmer for inspiring discussions, which, in one way or another, found their way into this book. I am indebted to Juliane Brauer and Kerstin Schuster for their support and wise advice.

While the early drafts of the book were written in Berlin, the idea for it first took shape during my time as an assistant to Georg Nolte in his capacity as a member of the International Law Commission. In particular, the ILC sessions in Geneva left a lasting impression on me, shaping much of the thinking behind this book. I am especially grateful for many eye-opening discussions within the group of ILC assistants, some of whom became dear friends. Our conversations about the sources of international law and other secondary rules have continued ever since, and to them I owe particular thanks.

The work on this book has also greatly benefitted from the many exchanges I have had with other scholars over the years, in particular Congyan Cai, Valentin Jeutner, Claus Kreß, Huaxia Lai, Johann Ruben Leiss, Xuexia Liao, Lucas Carlos Lima, Yang Liu, Valentin Schatz, Christian Tams, and Yifei Wang. These include exchanges during several research stays generously funded by the German Academic Exchange Service (DAAD). I am especially grateful to Yifeng Chen for hosting me for six months at Peking University in 2019, to Paolo Palchetti for welcoming me for one semester at the *Institut de recherche en droit international et européen de la Sorbonne* (IREDIES), Paris I—Panthéon-Sorbonne, and to Samantha Besson for inviting me to her fantastic seminar series on regionalism in international law at the Collège de France in 2025, and whose thoughtful comments significantly strengthened the overall argument of the book.

I finalized the thesis and began transforming it into the present book while serving as an Associate Legal Officer at the International Court of Justice during four extraordinary years. It was a great privilege to assist and learn from the Court's Judges during this period and I am immensely grateful to many colleagues and friends at the Court, and beyond the Peace Palace, for stimulating discussions. I am particularly grateful to Hannes Jöbstl, Iñaki Navarrete-Arechavaleta, and Nikiforos Panagis for very kindly taking me under their wings upon my arrival at the Court, and for their cheerful and inspiring company over the years. My sincere thanks also go to my wonderful 'neighbours' in The Hague, Yateesh Begoore and Juliana Valle Pereira Guerra, as well as to Dean Rosenberg and Benjamin Salas Kantor, for many thought-provoking conversations and truly collegial collaboration on several projects. I am also indebted to the excellent library team of the International Court of Justice for their invaluable support. Particular thanks go to Gianina Merchez, who has been a constant source of good advice and inspiration over the years.

I finalized the book in the second half of 2025 in Berlin, at the newly established Institute of Public International Law and the Law of the European Union at Freie Universität Berlin, and I am grateful to all members of the Institute for their very warm welcome, in particular to Helmut Aust, Sophie Schuberth, and Felix Schott, who made me feel at home from the outset.

I am immensely grateful to Keilin Anderson, Helmut Aust, Céline Braumann, Jan Philipp Cludius, James Devaney, Valentin Jeutner, Hannes Jöbstl, Apollin Koagne Zouapet, Xuexia Liao, Justin Morris, Dean Rosenberg, Ashley Stanley-Ryan, Juliana Valle Pereira Guerra, and Lukas Willmer for generously reading and providing constructive feedback on individual chapters of this book. All errors remain my own. *During the preparation of this book, I used DeepL to assist with translating non-English quotations into English and consulted both DeepL and ChatGPT on an occasional basis for questions concerning grammatical accuracy. I take full responsibility for the content of the book.*

Finally, I would not have been able to write this book without the support of my family and friends. I am especially grateful to my mother, whom I cannot thank enough for her constant encouragement and inspiration, to my brothers, my father and Ulla, and to Daniel and Natalia. They not only listened patiently to all my worries along the way but also always knew exactly when to steer the conversation in a different direction. I dedicate this book to them.

Contents

Table of Cases

INTERNATIONAL COURTS AND TRIBUNALS

Permanent Court of International Justice

International Court of Justice

Arbitral Awards

International Tribunal for the Law of the Sea

World Trade Organization Dispute Settlement Body

Investor-State decisions

African Commission on Human and Peoples' Rights

African Court on Human and Peoples' Rights

East African Court of Justice

Court of the Eurasian Economic Union

European Court of Human Rights

Court of Justice of the European Union

Andean Court of Justice

Caribbean Court of Justice

Central American Court of Justice

Inter-American Court of Human Rights and Inter-American Commission on Human Rights

DOMESTIC COURTS

Abbreviations

ACJ	Advisory Committee of Jurists
AALCO	African Asian Legal Consultative Organization
AfCHPR	African Charter on Human and Peoples' Rights
AfrComHPR	African Commission on Human and Peoples' Rights
AfrCtHPR	African Court on Human and Peoples' Rights
AU	African Union
AUCIL	African Union Commission of International Law
ALBA	Alianza Bolivariana para los Pueblos de Nuestra América
ACHR	American Convention on Human Rights
CAN	Andean Community
ARIO	Articles on Responsibility of International Organizations
ARSIWA	Articles on Responsibility of States for Internationally Wrongful Acts
AIIB	Asian Infrastructure Investment Bank
ASEAN	Association of Southeast Asian Nations
BVerfG	Bundesverfassungsgericht (Federal Constitutional Court of Germany)
CARICOM	Caribbean Community
CCJ	Caribbean Court of Justice
CACJ	Central American Court of Justice
UN	Charter Charter of the United Nations
CSTO	Collective Security Treaty Organization
CAHDI	Committee of Legal Advisers on Public International Law
CIS	Commonwealth of Independent States
CoE	Council of Europe
CJEU	Court of Justice of the European Union
CIL	Customary international law
EACJ	East African Court of Justice
ECOWAS	Economic Community of West African States
EECC	Eritrea-Ethiopia Claims Commission
EAEU	Eurasian Economic Union
ECB	European Central Bank
ECHR	European Convention on Human Rights
ECtHR	European Court of Human Rights
CJEU	European Court of Justice
EFTA	European Free Trade Association
EU	European Union
GATT	General Agreement on Tariffs and Trade
GPL	General principles of law
IUU	Illegal, Unreported, and Unregulated
IDI	Institut de droit international
IAComHR	Inter-American Commission on Human Rights
IACtHR	Inter-American Court of Human Rights

IAJC	Inter-American Juridical Committee
CERD	International Convention on the Elimination of All Forms of Racial Discrimination
ICJ	International Court of Justice
ICC	International Criminal Court
ILO	International Labour Organization
ILA	International Law Association
ILC	International Law Commission
IO	International organizations
ITLOS	International Tribunal for the Law of the Sea
IsDB	Islamic Development Bank
LAS	League of Arab States
NAM	Non-aligned movement
NAFTA	North American Free Trade Agreement
NATO	North Atlantic Treaty Organization
OECD	Organisation for Economic Co-operation and Development
OECS	Organisation of Eastern Caribbean States
OIC	Organisation of Islamic Cooperation
OSCE	Organization for Security and Cooperation in Europe
OAU	Organization of African Unity
OAS	Organization of American States
PIF	Pacific Islands Forum
PCA	Permanent Court of Arbitration
PCIJ	Permanent Court of International Justice
RTA	Regional trade agreements
UNSC	Security Council
SCO	Shanghai Cooperation Organization
SADC	Southern African Development Community
SASP	Subsequent agreements and subsequent practice
TEU	Treaty on European Union
TFEU	Treaty on the Functioning of the European Union
UNCLOT	UN Conference on the Law of Treaties
UNCLOT-IO	UN Conference on the Law of Treaties between States and International Organizations or between International Organizations
UNGA	UN General Assembly
UK	United Kingdom
UN	United Nations
UNCIO	United Nations Conference on International Organization
UNCLOS	United Nations Convention on the Law of the Sea
UNGA	United Nations General Assembly
UNSC	United Nations Security Council
US	United States of America
VCCR	Vienna Convention on Consular Relations
VCDR	Vienna Convention on Diplomatic Relations
VCLT	Vienna Convention on the Law of Treaties
WHO	World Health Organization
WTO	World Trade Organization

1
Introduction

1.1 Regional and general international law: who(se) rules?

After the end of the Cold War, two premises came to dominate the discourse on regional and general international law. The first is that regional international law is no different from other forms of particular international law.[1] The second holds that the validity of regional international law is subject to, and determined by, general international law.[2] Whether these two premises ever accurately reflected practice is an open question.[3] While it would be premature to dismiss them as obsolete in a world allegedly moving from the post-World War II multilateral order toward regionally defined spheres of influence,[4] it is clear is that both premises have come under pressure in recent years.

Over the past three decades, State practice has repeatedly demonstrated the complex and inherently ambivalent character of regional international law. The end of the Cold War did not put an end to military interventions by regional organizations that arguably lack a justification under general international law. From the 1990s to the present, regional rules have been frequently invoked as a legal basis for such military interventions, notably by the Economic Community of West African States (ECOWAS), aimed at restoring peace, preventing mass atrocities, or protecting democracy.[5] While such interventions may pursue legitimate objectives, they also place pressure on core provisions of the United Nations Charter (UN Charter).

Furthermore, the tensions between the European courts and the UN in the context of targeted sanctions (notably in the so-called '*Kadi* saga') polarized and divided commentators in the first decade of the millennium. While some praised

[1] See eg ILC, 'Fragmentation of International Law: Difficulties Arising from the Diversification and Expansion of International Law: Report of the Study Group of the International Law Commission—Finalized by Martti Koskenniemi' (2006) UN Doc A/CN.4/L.682 (hereinafter 'Fragmentation Report') [216]; M Forteau, 'Regional International Law' in A Peters (ed), *Max Planck Encyclopedia of Public International Law* (OUP 2006) [24].

[2] See eg J Crawford, *Chance, Order, Change: The Course of International Law, General Course on Public International Law* (Brill 2013) 249 [434].

[3] See A Orford, 'Regional Orders, Geopolitics, and the Future of International Law' (2021) 74(1) Curr Leg Probl 149, 170–79.

[4] But see the assertions of the United States of America of a 'Trump Corollary' to the *Monroe Doctrine* 'to restore American preeminence in the Western Hemisphere' in National Security Strategy of the United States of America (November 2025), 5, 15–19; see also R Mitchell, 'Hegemony in a Multipolar World Order: Global Constitutionalism and the Großraum' (2019) 1 Jus Cogens 129, 148.

[5] See eg JJ Niyo, 'More Stick and Less Carrot: ECOWAS, the Use of Force to Restore Democracy, and the Contest between Regional and International Normative Regimes' (2025) 119 AJIL Unbound 254.

Regional and General International Law. Janina Barkholdt, Oxford University Press.
DOI: 10.1093/9780198953432.003.0001

the European courts as defenders of universal human rights, others criticized their approach as a form of European parochialism, highlighting the danger of undermining the authority of the UN Security Council (UNSC) and of opening a Pandora's box of regional exceptionalism.[6] Another example concerns the European Union's (EU) practice of adopting third-party countermeasures in response to alleged breaches of obligations *erga omnes*, regarded by some States and scholars as a 'trailblazer',[7] and by others as illegal.[8] Meanwhile, the controversy between member States of the African Union (AU) and the International Criminal Court (ICC) about the scope of head of State immunity played an important role in the AU member States' decision to establish an African Criminal Court under the 2014 Malabo Protocol.[9] The approach to immunity of sitting heads of State reflected in its Article 46A*bis* appears to constitute a counter-model to Article 27 of the Rome Statute and has been both hailed as a triumph of subsidiarity and criticized as a circumvention of the Rome Statute.[10]

Regional institutions have further repeatedly insisted on a reinterpretation or a differentiated application of universal treaties in light of regional particularities. Innovative provisions contained in regional trade agreements raise the question whether they complement or undermine the Covered Agreements of the World Trade Organization (WTO).[11] Regional organizations have adopted competing approaches to the regulation of cyberspace.[12] Climate change-induced sea-level rise has prompted the leaders of the Pacific Islands Forum (PIF) to advance the view that Article 5 of the 1982 United Nations Convention on the Law of the Sea (UNCLOS) permits States in the Asia-Pacific region 'specially affected' by climate change to fix their baselines—an interpretation that challenged the, at the time, prevailing interpretation of Article 5, but has since gained traction and acceptance across most regions.[13]

[6] See eg G Nolte and HP Aust, 'European Exceptionalism?' (2013) 2:3 Glob Const 407.

[7] See eg M Gestri, 'Sanctions Imposed by the European Union: Legal and Institutional Aspects' in N Ronzitti (ed), *Coercive Diplomacy, Sanctions and International Law* (Brill 2016) 70, 99.

[8] See eg A Hofer, 'Third-Party Countermeasures: Making Custom Out of Ambiguous Practice?' (2025) 74 ICLQ 287.

[9] See Protocol on Amendments to the Protocol on the Statute of the African Court of Justice and Human Rights ('Malabo Protocol') (adopted 27 June 2014 in Malabo, not yet in force). To date (15 November 2025), eight States have ratified the Protocol which requires the deposit of instruments of 15 ratifications to enter into force (art 11(1)). See for a comprehensive analysis of the reasons for establishing an African Criminal Court: A Abass, 'Historical and Political Background to the Malabo Protocol' in G Werle and M Vormbaum (eds), *The African Criminal Court: A Commentary on the Malabo Protocol* (Springer 2017) 11.

[10] See eg D Tladi, 'Of Heroes and Villains, Angels and Demons: The ICC-AU Tension Revisited' (2017) 60 GYIL 43, 58–59; 'Immunities (Article 46A*bis*)' in Werle and Vormbaum (n 9) 203.

[11] See eg MQ Zang, 'When the Multilateral Meets the Regionals: Regional Trade Agreements at WTO Dispute Settlement' (2019) 18 World Trade Rev 33.

[12] See eg L Khasanova and A Simonyan, '(Geo)politicizing International Law of Cyberspace in Post-Soviet Eurasia' (2025) 24 CJIL 1, 8; EEG Tan and B Ang, 'ASEAN Ambiguity on International Law and Norms for Cyberspace' (2022) 20 Balt Yearb Int Law Online 133.

[13] See Pacific Islands Forum, 'Declaration on Preserving Maritime Zones in the Face of Climate Change-related Sea-Level Rise' (12 August 2021); N Oral, 'Sea-Level Rise and Maritime Boundaries: From Uncertainty to Clarity?' (2025) 74 ICLQ 163, 175–77.

All these proclamations of parallel or even alternative regional norms across virtually all regions and in virtually all areas of international law provoke a critical question: how can we assess whether regional international law is being used by States to reform and actively shape general international law, or to circumvent and weaken it?

A classic response to this question has been given by James Crawford in his 2013 Hague Lecture. He emphasized that

> 'regional' claims can be accepted only if they can be accommodated within the ordinary framework of international law; there is no third, non-universal category in between general international law and the legal relations of specific States based on consent, acquiescence and recognition.[14]

Many international lawyers are likely to agree with this response. After all, there are good reasons for taking the existence of such an 'ordinary framework of international law' for granted. Numerous universal treaties have been concluded since 1945,[15] some of which are said to possess a 'constitutional character'.[16] Various international organizations (IOs) have been established to promote and implement community interests. The International Law Commission (ILC) has been tasked by the United Nations General Assembly (UNGA) to identify and progressively develop universally shared legal rules.[17] International expert bodies have been set up to ensure compliance with such rules, and international courts and tribunals are called upon to adjudicate disputes about their interpretation and application.[18]

[14] Crawford (2013) (n 2) 249 [434].

[15] See in particular the 'wave of codification' in the 1960s: Vienna Convention on Diplomatic Relations (adopted 18 April 1961, entered into force 24 April 1964) 500 UNTS 95; Vienna Convention on Consular Relations (signed 24 April 1963, entered into force 19 March 1967) 596 UNTS 261; International Covenant on Civil and Political Rights (adopted 19 December 1966, entered into force 23 March 1976) 999 UNTS 171; International Covenant on Economic, Social, and Cultural Rights (adopted 16 December 1966, entered into force 3 January 1976) 993 UNTS 3; Treaty on the Non-Proliferation of Nuclear Weapons (adopted 1 July 1968, entered into force 5 March 1970) 729 UNTS 161; Vienna Convention on the Law of Treaties (adopted 23 May 1969, entered into force 27 January 1980) 1155 UNTS 331.

[16] See eg United Nations Convention on the Law of the Sea ('UNCLOS') (adopted 10 December 1982, entered into force 16 November 1994) 1833 UNTS 3 (described as a 'constitution' by TB Koh in 'Remarks', reproduced in *UN The Law of the Sea: Official Text of the UNCLOS* (London 1983) xxxiii); Charter of the United Nations (adopted 26 June 1945, entered into force 24 October 1945) 1 UNTS XVI, art 13(1) (described as a 'constitution' by B Fassbender in *The United Nations Charter as the Constitution of the International Community* (Brill 2009)).

[17] Statute of the International Law Commission, UNGA Res 174 (II) (21 November 1947) annex, art 1(1).

[18] See eg the establishment of the International Tribunal for the Law of the Sea (ITLOS) in 1982 (Article 287 of UNCLOS); the permanent dispute settlement mechanism within the framework of the World Trade Organization in 1994 (Marrakesh Agreement Establishing the World Trade Organization (adopted 15 April 1994, entered into force 1 January 1995) 1867 UNTS 154, Annex 2 Dispute Settlement Understanding), and various international criminal courts and tribunals notably the International Criminal Court established under the Rome Statute of the International Criminal Court (adopted 17 July 1998, entered into force 1 July 2002) 2187 UNTS 3.

However, it has become increasingly difficult to identify a common understanding of these general rules. Proclamations of regional norms and institutions that claim to operate as alternatives or in parallel to general international law represent only one side of the coin. On the other side, these regional claims generate uncertainty and even disagreement about the scope and content of rules that are ostensibly general.

Over the past few years, (mainly) Western States and international organizations have on numerous occasions invoked the so-called 'rules-based order' to criticize what they consider to be a violation of the 'general rules'.[19] China and Russia, in turn, have emphasized their commitment to 'the international system with the UN playing a central coordinating role and [to] a world order based on international law'.[20] However, the context of such declarations, notably the fact that these States themselves often fail to adhere to the principles they proclaim (the problem of 'double standards'), makes it difficult to identify therein a coherent understanding of a shared set of rules.[21] It is also doubtful whether recourse to the term 'rules-based order' is helpful for the identification of the 'ordinary framework of international law'. As Michael Wood observed, '[a]s a favourite mantra, it [the term "rules-based order"] seems to be replacing "the rule of law in international affairs", but is even less clear. What rules? Whose order?'.[22]

These questions, 'What rules? Whose order?', highlight another source of uncertainty regarding the scope and content of the 'ordinary framework of international law': a (perceived) lack of 'normative authorship' by States from non-Western regions. Several authors have highlighted the asymmetric contribution of (some) regions to the creation of the various universal treaties and institutions that underlie traditional understandings of the term 'international legal order'.[23] Recent scholarship casts doubt on whether 'international law' indeed provides a common language.[24] Some even argue that international courts and tribunals should recognize

[19] See eg Statement between NATO Secretary General and the four Indo-Pacific partners in the context of the NATO Summit in The Hague (25 June 2025); The New Atlantic Charter 2021 (signed by the Prime Minister of the United Kingdom and the President of the United States of America on 10 June 2021).

[20] Joint Statement of the Russian Federation and the People's Republic of China on the Twentieth Anniversary of the Treaty of Good Neighbourliness and Friendly Cooperation between the Russian Federation and the People's Republic of China (28 June 2021) <https://www.rusemb.org.uk/fnapr/7007> (accessed 5 May 2026).

[21] See A Skordas, 'Authoritarian Global Governance? The Russian–Chinese Joint Statement of March 2021' (2021) 81 ZaöRV 293; JA Dugard, 'The Choice Before Us: International Law or a "Rules-based International Order"?' (2023) 36 LJIL 223; M Jorgensen, 'The Jurisprudence of the Rules-Based Order: The Power of Rules Consistent with but Not Binding Under International Law' (2021) 22 MJIL 221.

[22] M Wood, 'Method and Style in International Law, and the International Court of Justice's Contribution', in P Galvão Teles and M Almeida Ribeiro (eds), *Case-Law and the Development of International Law Contributions by International Courts and Tribunals* (Brill Nijhoff 2021) 14, 24.

[23] See eg GF Sinclair, *To Reform the World: International Organizations and the Making of Modern States* (OUP 2017); A Becker Lorca, *Mestizo International Law. A Global Intellectual History 1842–1933* (CUP 2014).

[24] A Roberts, *Is International Law International?* (OUP 2017).

distinct regional understandings of fundamental concepts of international law, such as statehood, sovereignty, and the sources of international law, in order to ensure a fair settlement of disputes.[25]

This leaves us with the question whether what James Crawford termed 'the ordinary framework of international law' (still) accommodates regional claims or whether this framework is itself subject to challenge, particularly at a time when some predict that the world is fragmenting into regionally defined spheres of influence.[26]

Is there indeed no separate category of 'regional' international law that claims and perhaps even deserves different treatment from 'other' special international law? Has the normative role of regional international law been underestimated? And have we taken the existence of 'general international law'—whatever meaning we attach to this expression—for granted?

More than three decades after the end of the Cold War, developments in State practice suggest revisiting the two premises which dominated the post-Cold-War thinking about regional and general international law. This book sets out to do that.

1.2 Central claim of the book

The claim advanced in this book is twofold. It contends that regional international law, as a distinct legal category, is central to the development of general international law, while general international law, comprising the rules applicable across all regions, is indispensable for protecting regional plurality.

To this effect, the book, firstly, challenges the view that regional international law is merely *lex specialis* in relation to general international law. Instead, it argues that certain forms of regional international law are qualitatively distinct from other types of particular international law. This distinctiveness is reflected in the way regional practice and rules shape the formation, identification, interpretation, and application of international law. In fact, regional international law represents a 'triple challenge' to general international law precisely because of the characteristics that sets it apart from other forms of particular international law. This triple challenge consists of the problem of distinguishing between constructive and corrosive forms of regional international law (analytical challenge), the difficulty of identifying a substantive common denominator shared across all regions

[25] See eg *Frontier Dispute (Burkina Faso/Niger)* [2013] ICJ Rep 134 (separate opinion of Judge Yusuf) [29]; see also TV Ananthavinayagan, 'Breaking Bad Customs: Involving the Idea of *Opinio Juris Communis* in Asian State Practice' (2018) 24 Asian YBIL 24; A Buss, 'The Preah Vihear Case and Regional Customary Law' (2010) 9 CJIL 111.

[26] See M Jorgensen, 'Equilibrium & Fragmentation in The International Rule of Law: The Rising Chinese Geolegal Order' (2018) 21 KFG Working Paper Series <https://papers.ssrn.com/sol3/papers.cfm?abstract_id = 3283626> (accessed 5 May 2026); GJ Ikenberry, 'Three Worlds: The West, East and South and the Competition to Shape Global Order' (2024) 100 Int Aff 121.

(normative challenge), and the problem of finding an approach by which common legal rules can be ascertained (methodological challenge).

Secondly, the book shows that the secondary rules of international law—a distinct type of general international law that governs the formation, identification, interpretation, and application of legal norms—provide a common normative framework that responds to this triple challenge posed by regional international law. This type of general international law has the methodological potential to reconcile regional and general international law, the normative potential to provide a common denominator and to confer 'normative ownership' to all States with respect to both regional and general international law, regardless of whether they belong to a certain region or not, and the analytical potential to distinguish between constructive and corrosive forms of regional international law.

1.3 Structure of the book

Chapter 2 demonstrates that the classification of regional international law as *lex specialis* does not fully capture its legal significance. It identifies three criteria that are used to identify a 'region' in legal practice. In this narrower sense, a region refers to a grouping of two or more States that (1) can be objectively identified by third parties, typically on the basis of geographic proximity (criterion of identifiability); (2) exhibits a minimum degree of normative cohesion (criterion of normative cohesion); and (3) is thereby distinguishable from other groups of States (criterion of distinctiveness). The term 'region[al]' defines a state of normative cohesion which typically arises from geographic proximity among a group of States, distinguishing it from third parties. 'Regional international law' describes rules of international law which arise from this form of normative cohesion. The Chapter then explains why these three defining features justify recognizing regional international law as a distinct legal category. It posits that regional international law poses a triple challenge to general international law precisely because of the characteristics that render it distinct from other forms of particular international law.

To overcome the triple challenge posed by regional international law, Chapter 3 argues that recourse to secondary rules as a distinct form of general international law provides a methodologically rigorous, yet inclusive approach for accommodating regional plurality within a common framework of international law, and thus a constructive and practicable way to overcome the triple challenge. To this effect, it introduces a 'three-step-approach' based on secondary rules as a method to assess the validity and effects of regional legal claims on the international legal system. The three-step-approach is further developed in Chapters 4 to 7.

The first step assesses under which conditions a regional rule or practice qualifies as regional international law and, accordingly, can, or even must, be recognized as such by third parties. Given the often idiosyncratic nature of regional rules and practices, it is frequently unclear to what extent they qualify as international law or merely as a regional legal tradition, overlapping domestic law, or merely a policy. The key question is thus to what extent the universal secondary rules governing the identification and interpretation of international law accommodate distinct regional approaches to the law of treaties (Chapter 4) and unwritten regional norms in the form of regional custom, regional general principles of law, and regional *jus cogens* (Chapter 5).

If a regional claim qualifies as regional international law, the second step involves determining which rule prevails when both a rule of regional international law and a rule of general international law apply to a specific situation (Chapter 6). The analysis focuses on the universal secondary rules governing the interpretation and application of international law, with particular attention to techniques for avoiding and resolving normative conflicts. If the regional rule successfully passes this second step—meaning that it may be applied despite competing rules under international law—the entity asserting the regional legal claim is entitled to demand recognition of its validity and applicability as a rule of international law from third parties.

If the regional claim fails either the first or second step, the analysis proceeds to the third step, which involves evaluating whether the regional practice nonetheless constitutes a constructive contribution to the development of general international law (Chapter 7). The focus here is on the universal secondary rules governing the formation, identification, and interpretation of international law. Specifically, the analysis considers which conditions must be met for regional practice to contribute to the interpretation of a multilateral treaty over time, the formation of a general rule of customary international law, the emergence of a general principle of law, or of a peremptory norm under general international law (*jus cogens*).

Chapter 8 concludes that at a time when the 'normative authorship' of many supposedly universal rules and institutions is being challenged by regional practice, general international law can only be preserved if the specific nature and the distinct challenge of regional international law is taken seriously. Secondary rules of international law impart 'normative ownership' to all States in relation to both regional and general international law, whether or not they belong to a particular region. Secondary rules are thus key in keeping the framework of general international law both responsive and resilient over time.

1.4 Contribution and scope of the book

Given the abundance of literature on regionalism in international law, it may be useful to briefly outline what this book offers and what not.

The book seeks to examine the normative role of regionalism in international law from a positivist perspective, focusing on the practice of States and international organizations. Unlike other works on this topic,[27] it does not confine the analysis to regional international organizations but also considers the legal significance of normative claims arising from a region independently of institutional frameworks. To date, legal scholars seem hesitant to engage with the role of regionalism as a normative project. *Anne Orford* criticized in 2021 that '[i]nternational lawyers still largely treat the centrality of regionalism to the normative ordering of space as if it operated outside international law'.[28] This reluctance to address regionalism from the perspective of positivist legal scholarship may be explained by several conceptual, methodological, and normative challenges associated with the topic. The book engages with these challenges and thus seeks to make three principal contributions.

Firstly, the book offers a definition of the term 'region' as a legal concept. While the phenomenon of statehood has eventually found acceptance as a central concept of international law, scholars have been reluctant to define the 'region' as a legal concept.[29] It has been claimed, not without reason, that any attempt to define a 'region' runs the risk of becoming either tautological, arbitrary, or essentialist.[30] However, this book argues that a 'region', similar to the 'State', is a social phenomenon with legal implications. Based on the practice of States and IOs, the jurisprudence of courts and tribunals, the work of expert bodies, as well as scholarly writings, the book distils several defining features of the concept of a 'region', proposes a definition of the term 'region' as a legal concept, and identifies three criteria that typically characterize regions and, accordingly, regional international law.

Secondly, the book shows that regional practice and rules meeting these three criteria play a distinctive role in the formation, identification, interpretation, and application of international law, often creating a 'triple challenge' to general international law that sets them apart from other forms of particular international law. This conclusion is grounded in a comprehensive analysis of practice and doctrine.

Thirdly, the book proposes an overarching general legal framework based on secondary rules that not only accounts for the complex relationship of regional

[27] See for a comprehensive analysis of the role of regional organizations: ILA Study Group, 'The International Law of Regional Organizations: Final Report' (Athens 2024) and the special issue on 'The International Law of Regional Organizations' (2024) 21 IOLR.

[28] See Orford (n 3) 190.

[29] Orford (n 3).

[30] The spatial connotation of the term 'region' and its potential normative implications may inadvertently evoke associations with the concept of *Großraumordnung* ('greater spatial order'), which was developed by Carl Schmitt during the period of National Socialist rule in Germany C Schmitt, *Völkerrechtliche Großraumordnung mit Interventionsverbot für raumfremde Mächte* (3rd edn in the 1941 version, Duncker & Humblot 2009). Schmitt himself claimed to have been inspired by the *Monroe Doctrine* formulated by the United States in 1823 (22–33). The way in which Schmitt's scholarship, including his concept of *Großraumordnung*, sought to legitimise Nazi tyranny should urge caution with regard to his writings, see J Weiler, 'Cancelling Carl Schmitt?' (EJILTalk! 13 August 2021 <https://www.ejiltalk.org/cancelling-carl-schmitt/> (accessed 5 May 2026)). This book limits its references to his works where these are useful to understand potential risks arising from regional normative claims. It considers the theory of the *Großraumordnung* to be incompatible with the principle of the sovereign equality of States.

international law vis-à-vis general international law but is also applicable to different types of regional law.[31] This book engages with the concern that any concept of an overarching legal framework is inherently biased, Eurocentric, and thus doomed to fail.[32] It posits that common legal rules are indispensable in a legal community that recognizes and protects regional plurality. The book focuses on the 'secondary rules of international law' as a set of common rules that accommodate the very diverse forms of international law, from supranational regional IOs, especially the EU, to less dense forms of regional institutionalization. It develops a 'three-step-approach' based on secondary rules as a means to deconstruct regional exceptionalism, rectify regional imbalances and give States within and outside the region 'normative ownership' of international legal rules.

In making these three contributions, the book bases its findings on a representative analysis of the practice of States and IOs and of scholarly writings from all regions. Acknowledging that such an approach has its limitations, efforts are made to reduce regional imbalances resulting from differences in accessibility of regional practices as much as possible.[33] Moreover, the book does not claim that the challenge posed by regional international law to general international law is a novel challenge. Rather, the history of international law is shaped by the tension between regionalism and universalism. Although the book ultimately does not include a separate chapter on the history of regionalism in international law due to space constraints, it is informed by a historical analysis of the interplay between regional and general international law, particularly the oscillation of regional international law between policy-based (functionality-driven) and polity-based (identity-driven) approaches.[34]

This book aims to offer a constructive and practical approach to navigating the relationship between regional and general international law, while acknowledging that this will remain a topic of enduring scholarly debate.

1.5 Terminology

It may be useful, at the outset of this book, to clarify a few key terms, as the analysis of regional phenomena in international law is often complicated by terminological ambiguities.

[31] See on the objection that regional organizations are too diverse for being studied as a single object of research: S Besson and E Kassoti, 'The International Law of Regional Organizations—Mapping the Issues' (2024) 21 IOLR 1, 5.

[32] See eg C Miéville, 'The Commodity-Form Theory of International Law: An Introduction' (2004) 17 LJIL 271, 302.

[33] See also ILC, 'Memorandum by the UN Secretariat, Ways and means for making the evidence of customary international law more readily available' (2018) UN Doc A/CN.4/710/Rev.1.

[34] See GF Sinclar, 'Between Functionalism and Hegemony: Regional International Organizations in the History of International Law' (2024) 21 IOLR 65.

Unless stated otherwise, the terms 'international law', 'international legal order', and 'international legal system' are used interchangeably. These terms refer to the entire body of rules and principles that are binding on subjects of international law. The term 'universal' describes rules, principles, and institutions which are accepted as legally binding by almost all States.[35] This definition does not exclude the possibility that States can, under certain conditions, modify or terminate 'universal' obligations under international law,[36] which distinguishes 'universal' norms understood in this broad sense from 'peremptory norms of general international law'.[37] While universal rules and *jus cogens* norms often overlap, only *jus cogens* norms are non-derogable.

The term 'general international law' has received many definitions in international law scholarship and practice which are discussed in depth in Chapter 3. 'Secondary rules of international law' are understood as a specific type of general international law that determines the formation, identification, interpretation, and application of rules under international law.

The terms 'region', 'regionalism', and 'regional international law' are defined in detail in Chapter 2, whereas the term 'regional practice' is defined in Chapter 7. 'Particular international law' describes those norms the scope of application of which is limited *ratione materiae, ratione personae,* and/or *ratione loci.* As a generic term, 'particular international law' encompasses both 'regional' international law and other, 'non-regional', forms of 'particular international law'. These 'non-regional' forms of 'particular international law' are also described as 'special', 'thematic', or 'functional' international law and include rules which pertain to a specific subject-matter. The term 'corrosive' refers to regional practice that may undermine the existing framework of rules common to all States, whereas 'constructive' describes regional conduct that contributes to the development of legal rules shared across regions.

[35] See eg *Application of the International Convention on the Elimination of All Forms of Racial Discrimination (Qatar v United Arab Emirates)* [2021] ICJ Rep 71 [87] ('CERD, whose universal character is confirmed by the fact that 182 States are parties to it . . . ').

[36] For example, by submitting a reservation to a universal treaty, by concluding an *inter se* agreement, or by withdrawing from a universal treaty in accordance with the rules set out in the VCLT. With respect to customary international law, States may deviate from general custom based on a rule of regional customary international law.

[37] See VCLT, arts 53 and 64.

2
What is regional international law?

2.1 Regional international law as *lex specialis*?

For much of the post-Cold War era, the normative role of regionalism in international law was neglected or even explicitly dismissed, particularly by doctrinal-positivist scholarship.[1] In keeping with the *zeitgeist* at the turn of the millennium,[2] a study group established by the International Law Commission (ILC) in the early 2000s for the purpose of examining the 'difficulties arising from the diversification and expansion of international law' stated that the role of 'geographical regions' as 'the moving forces behind international law' was a relic of the past.[3] Accordingly, the study group's 2006 'Fragmentation Report' asserted that 'any specific normative (in contrast to historical, sociological or legislative-technical) debate about regionalism [is] superfluous'.[4] The challenge posed by regional international law, it concluded, was 'no different from the general problem of the applicability and limits of *lex specialis*'.[5]

The present chapter seeks to determine the extent to which the classification of regional international law as *lex specialis* does full justice to its legal significance. Based on the characteristics attributed to 'regions', both in practice and scholarship, this chapter seeks to develop a definition and three criteria for identifying a 'region' and 'regional international law' (2.2) before explaining why regional international law qualifies as a distinct legal category (2.3). The chapter explores how the challenge presented by regional international law to the international legal order differs in nature from that posed by other forms of particular international law (2.4). The chapter concludes that regional international law cannot be simply equated with other forms of particular international law (2.5).

[1] A Orford, 'Regional Orders, Geopolitics, and the Future of International Law' (2021) 74(1) Curr Leg Probl 149, 190.
[2] See eg M Forteau, 'Regional International Law' in A Peters (ed), *Max Planck Encyclopedia of Public International Law* (OUP 2006) [6]–[11].
[3] ILC, 'Fragmentation of International Law: Difficulties Arising from the Diversification and Expansion of International Law: Report of the Study Group of the International Law Commission—Finalized by Martti Koskenniemi' (2006) UN Doc A/CN.4/L.682 (hereinafter 'Fragmentation Report') [204].
[4] Fragmentation Report (n 3) [215].
[5] Fragmentation Report (n 3) [216].

Regional and General International Law. Janina Barkholdt, Oxford University Press. © Janina Barkholdt 2026.
DOI: 10.1093/9780198953432.003.0002

2.2 The identification of a region

States and international institutions attach legal consequences to 'regional' practices, rules, and institutions across all regions and fields of international law.[6] States frequently incorporate references to 'regions' in regional[7] and quasi-universal treaties.[8] Most member States of the United Nations (UN) are party to at least one intergovernmental regional organization.[9] States from all continents have invoked the regional character of a rule in proceedings before the International Court of Justice (ICJ), arguing that such a rule qualifies or modifies the general rules otherwise applicable to the case.[10] The ICJ has, in turn, responded to such arguments—either by accepting[11] or rejecting[12] the latter. Regional international law is further frequently considered by domestic courts.[13]

This ubiquity of regional elements in practice thus suggests that States have some idea of the underlying concept of a 'region' to which they seem to attribute certain normative qualities. Still, defining a 'region' in legal terms remains notoriously difficult,[14] if not impossible.[15]

[6] But see J Klabbers, 'The Soft Phenomenology of the Regional International Organization' in E Kassoti, T Cabrita, and N Idriz (eds), *The European Union and Regionalism: Conceptual and Contextual Perspectives* (Brill 2025) 21, 22: 'the law does not attach legal consequences to the quality of being a regional international organization.'

[7] See eg Inter-American Treaty of Reciprocal Assistance (adopted 2 September 1947, entered into force 12 March 1948) 21 UNTS 77, arts 3(3) and 4; African Charter on Human and Peoples' Rights (adopted 27 June 1981, entered into force 21 October 1986) 1520 UNTS 217, arts 60 and 61.

[8] See eg Charter of the United Nations (adopted 26 June 1945, entered into force 24 October 1945) 1 UNTS XVI, arts 33, 52–54; General Agreement on Tariffs and Trade (adopted 30 October 1947, entered into force 1 January 1948) 55 UNTS 187, arts V and XXIV; Treaty on the Non-Proliferation of Nuclear Weapons (adopted 1 July 1968, entered into force 5 March 1970) 729 UNTS 161, art VII.

[9] For an overview, see ILA Study Group, 'The International Law of Regional Organizations: Final Report' (Athens Conference 2024) 8–12.

[10] See eg *Sovereignty over Pedra Branca/Pulau Batu Puteh, Middle Rocks and South Ledge (Malaysia/Singapore)*: Counter-Memorial of Singapore (25 January 2005) [3.2]–[3.42]; *Fisheries Jurisdiction (United Kingdom v Iceland)*: Memorial of the United Kingdom (31 July 1973), in particular [182], [243], and [257].

[11] *Dispute regarding Navigational and Related Rights (Costa Rica v Nicaragua)* [2009] ICJ Rep 213 [141].

[12] *Asylum (Colombia/Peru)* [1950] ICJ Rep 266, 276–78.

[13] See eg German Federal Constitutional Court, Order of 23 July 2024 (2 BvR 557/19); *ZN v Secretary for Justice and ors* (Hong Kong Court of Final Appeal, 10 January 2020) ILDC 3189 (HK 2020) [57]–[63]; *Law Society of South Africa and Others v President of the Republic of South Africa and Others* [2018] ZACC 51.

[14] See eg L Boisson de Chazournes, *Interactions Between Regional and Universal Organizations—A Legal Perspective* (Brill 2017) 8; A Hurrell, *On Global Order—Powers, Values, and Institutions of the International Society* (OUP 2008) 241; A Anghie, 'Identifying Regions in the History of International Law' in B Fassbender and A Peters (eds), *The Oxford Handbook of the History of International Law* (OUP 2012) 1058, 1077; Klabbers (n 6) 22.

[15] Fragmentation Report (n 3) [212]; ILC, 'Fourth report on peremptory norms of general international law (*jus cogens*) by Dire Tladi, Special Rapporteur' (2019) UN Doc A/CN.4/727 (hereinafter: ILC, 'Fourth report on *jus cogens*') [29]; A Koagne Zouapet, 'States and Regional International Organizations' (2024) 21:1 IOLR 147, 156.

2.2.1 Characteristics of a region

Despite the absence of a generally agreed definition of 'region' in legal practice, certain characteristics recur both in practice and scholarship to delineate the contours of a given 'region'.

2.2.1.1 Size

'Non-universality' is a widely accepted characteristic of a region.[16] In the context of the World Trade Organization (WTO), for example, 'regional trade agreements' are understood to include 'agreements that are bilateral as well as those that are not regional in a geographic sense'.[17] As a result of this negative understanding, the term 'regional' extends to virtually all forms of international rules and institutions aside from a limited number of universal international organizations (IOs) and agreements. It is thus questionable whether this criterion by itself is sufficient to meaningfully determine what constitutes a region. Although some scholars have adopted this broad understanding of 'region' beyond the WTO context,[18] it is usually regarded as insufficient for characterizing a 'region' in a meaningful way.[19]

Still, the question remains whether regions are to be defined by reference to their size. Indeed, the fact that occasionally a difference is made between bilateral, local, sub-regional, and continental relations, on the one hand, and regional relations on the other, suggests that an implicit numerical threshold may underlie the concept of a region.[20] To distinguish 'regional' from 'bilateral' forms of co-operation, some scholars thus propose a minimum number of three States for the purpose of identifying a region,[21] while others argue that '[c]onceptually it makes no difference whether the "region" consists of 2 States or 22'.[22]

[16] See eg S Besson and E Kassoti, 'The International Law of Regional Organizations—Mapping the Issues' (2024) 21:1 IOLR 1, 3, 5, 6–7; H Kelsen, *The Law of the United Nations. A Critical Analysis of Its Fundamental Problems* (Steven and Sons Limited 1951) 319–20.

[17] See eg L Bartels, 'Regional Trade Agreements' in A Peters (ed), *Max Planck Encyclopedia of Public International Law* (OUP 2013) [1].

[18] See eg Besson and Kassoti (n 16) 3, 5.

[19] See subsequent sections.

[20] See eg draft conclusion 16(1) of the ILC's 'Draft conclusions on identification of customary international law, with commentaries' (2018) UN Doc A/73/10 (hereinafter: ILC Report 2018 (CIL)) 112–13, which seems to consider 'regional', 'local', and 'bilateral' custom as different forms of 'particular' custom; *Asylum (Colombia/Peru)* [1950] ICJ Rep 290 (Diss Op Álvarez) 294, who differentiated between 'continental and regional law'.

[21] See eg TA Börzel and T Risse, 'Introduction: Framework of the Handbook and Conceptual Clarifications' in TA Börzel and T Risse (eds), *The Oxford Handbook of Comparative Regionalism* (OUP 2016) 7; A Cuyvers, 'Comparing Regional Law' in M Siems and PJ Yap (eds), *The Cambridge Handbook of Comparative Law* (CUP 2024) 649, 652.

[22] See J Crawford, 'Universalism and Regionalism from the Perspective of the Work of the International Law Commission' in *International Law on the Eve of the 21st Century* [1997] (UN Publication (No E/F 97.V.4) 99, 116 fn 83.

Determining a numerical criterion for identifying a region is, however, difficult and easily becomes somewhat arbitrary. At what point, for example, do local rules become regional, and when do regional rules evolve into continental ones? Thus, unsurprisingly, the use of these terms in practice remains inconsistent. In the context of customary law, for instance, the ICJ has referred to a potential customary rule between only two States as 'local' custom in the *Right of Passage* case.[23] In other cases, the ICJ has used 'regional' and 'local' interchangeably, or favoured one over the other without providing a clear rationale.[24] Similarly, it is doubtful whether a maximum number of States can be identified, beyond which regional co-operation automatically transforms into universal forms of co-operation.[25]

Consequently, both legal scholarship and practice tend to move beyond purely quantitative criteria, relying instead on more substantive elements to define and delineate a region.

2.2.1.2 Geographic proximity

In addition to non-universality, a central characteristic of a region is, consistent with its literal meaning, the geographic proximity among a group of States.[26]

The UN regional groups are based largely on geographic proximity.[27] Several quasi-universal treaties, such as the Constitution of the World Health Organization (WHO),[28] as well as IOs with a more limited membership, including the North Atlantic Treaty and the 'Rio Treaty',[29] explicitly provide for such an understanding. Moreover, the practice under Article VII of the Nuclear Non-Proliferation Treaty with respect to 'regional treaties' is characterized by a remarkably high degree of geographic cohesion.[30] Similarly, the references to 'regional agreements' in Article 282 of the United Nations Convention on the Law of the Sea (UNCLOS) are interpreted as being 'open only to States in a geographically defined part of the world'.[31]

It is unclear, however, how much geographic proximity is necessary for establishing a region and whether this criterion is indeed sufficient to characterize

[23] *Right of Passage over Indian Territory (Portugal v India)* [1960] ICJ Rep 6, 39.

[24] But see Chapter 5, section 5.2.3.

[25] See S Scott, 'Universalism and Title to Territory in Antarctica' (1997) 66 NJIL 33, 37 pointing out that '[v]irtually all international law is "regional" in the sense of having been developed by a sub-set of the international legal community'; see also Klabbers (n 6) 23–24.

[26] See Fragmentation Report (n 3) [211]; ILC Report 2018 (CIL) (n 20), Conclusion 16, 155; F Bordin and J Odermatt, 'International Law of Regional Organizations: A Comparative Perspective' (2024) 21:1 IOLR 19, 22–23; Kelsen 1951 (n 16) 319; JS Nye (ed), *International Regionalism* (Boston, Little, Brown and Co 1968) vii; Klabbers (n 6) 39.

[27] See <https://www.un.org/dgacm/en/content/regional-groups> (accessed 5 May 2026).

[28] Constitution of the World Health Organization (adopted 22 July 1946, entered into force 7 April 1948) 14 UNTS 148, art 44(a).

[29] See eg 1947 Rio Treaty, art 3(3); North Atlantic Treaty (adopted 4 April 1949, entered into force 7 September 1949) 34 UNTS 243, art 5.

[30] See K Davenport, *The Nuclear Nonproliferation Treaty* (Morgan & Claypool Publishers 2019) 2-21-23.

[31] See A Serdy, 'Article 282' in A Proelss (ed), *United Nations Convention on the Law of the Sea: A Commentary* (CH Beck/Hart/Nomos, 2017) 1827 [7].

a region in the legal sense. One prominent example that casts doubt on the centrality of 'geographic proximity' for characterizing a 'region' is the reference to 'regional arrangements and agencies' in Articles 33, 52, and 53 of the UN Charter.[32] According to the *travaux préparatoires* of the 1945 San Francisco Conference, Egypt proposed defining them as

> organizations of a permanent nature grouping in a given geographical area several countries which, by reason of their proximity, community of interests or cultural, linguistic, historical or spiritual affinities, make themselves jointly responsible for the peaceful settlement of any disputes which may arise between them and for the maintenance of peace and security in their region, as well as for the safeguarding of their interests and the development of their economic and cultural relations.[33]

Here, geographic proximity is treated as a necessary, but not sufficient condition. Egypt's proposal was ultimately rejected as being both 'unnecessary' and too narrow, although the reasons were not clearly specified.[34]

Over time, it became evident that the criteria employed for identifying 'regional arrangements' were not as clear cut as had been assumed when the relevant provisions in the Charter were drafted. Some scholars and judges understood the element of 'regional' very broadly, defining the term negatively as 'non-universal'[35] or in contrast to 'continental systems of law'.[36] Some would go so far as to assert that the definition of a region 'has no obvious legal or practical significance' for the purpose of applying the respective provisions in the UN Charter.[37] These overly inclusive approaches do not seem to be shared by the ICJ, which appears inclined to require geographic proximity as a necessary characteristic of a 'region'.[38] This aligns with subsequent practice under Chapter VIII, most of which involved institutions whose membership is characterized by geographically proximate States.[39]

[32] See for the various definitions of 'regional' under Chapter VIII: A Abass, *Regional Organisations and the Development of Collective Security: Beyond Chapter VIII of the UN Charter* (Hart 2004) 9–20.

[33] See Documents of the United Nations Conference on International Organization (San Francisco 1945) (hereinafter: 'UNCIO') vol xii, 857.

[34] UNCIO (n 33).

[35] See Kelsen 1951 (n 16) 319–20; FJ Krezdorn, *Les Nations Unies et les Accords Régionaux* (Jägersche Buchdruckerei 1954) 106; A Ross, *Constitution of the United Nations* (Rinehart 1950) 166; R Pernice, *Die Sicherung des Weltfriedens durch regionale Organisationen und die Vereinten Nationen. Eine Untersuchung zur Kompetenzverteilung nach Kapitel VIII der UN-Charta* (Hansischer Gildenverlag 1972) 26–29.

[36] *Asylum (Colombia/Peru)* (n 20) (Diss Op Álvarez) 294.

[37] See C Gray, *International Law and the Use of Force* (4th edn, OUP 2018) 415, for further references.

[38] *Land and Maritime Boundary between Cameroon and Nigeria (Cameroon v Nigeria)* [1998] ICJ Rep 275 [67].

[39] See E de Wet, 'Regional Organizations and Arrangements: Authorization, Ratification, or Independent Action' in M Weller (ed), *The Oxford Handbook of the Use of Force in International Law* (OUP 2015) 315–16; Nye (n 26) xii. See also more generally Bordin and Odermatt (n 26) 22–23. See, however, Walter, who includes the Organization for Islamic Cooperation and the Commonwealth

Nevertheless, while a minimum level of geographic cohesion—whether through geographic proximity or a common geographic reference point—may serve to prevent a 'diffuse and unmanageable' use of the term,[40] this alone is unlikely to suffice for defining a region.[41] As Egypt's proposal indicates, and as the subsequent controversy in practice and scholarship confirms, geographic proximity provides only limited guidance. After all, all States are ultimately geographically connected, making it difficult to delineate precisely where one region ends and another begins.

Moreover, the question is not merely whether geographic proximity is invariably sufficient, but also whether and to what extent it is necessary. In some instances, geographic proximity appears to serve rather as a 'placeholder',[42] pointing to the presence of a more substantive, shared characteristic among a group of States. In such cases, the requisite degree of geographic proximity is assessed in relation to the underlying factor which constitutes the core of the bond uniting a group of States.

2.2.1.3 Social cohesion

Indeed, only few definitions of the term 'region' reduce it to the existence of geographic proximity among a non-universal group of States. Additionally,[43] or even alternatively,[44] both practice and scholarship refer to other shared characteristics, such as historical experience, economic interdependence, ideological alignment, legal traditions, or religious ties as criteria for delineating a region, insofar as these elements signify a certain level of social cohesion among the States in question.

The critical role of social cohesion in defining a region is often explained by the function attributed to a regional institution. With respect to 'regional arrangements' as used in Chapter XIII of the United Nations Charter, for example, Christian Walter argues that 'the decisive factor (. . .) is a stable and pre-existing enduring bond among its members, a bond which justifies the expectation that the organization can contribute to the maintenance of international peace and security'.[45] This bond, he notes, 'can be based on geographical proximity, but also other factors, such as history or culture'.[46] According to Walter, 'regional' refers to arrangements which reflect a pre-existing bond, 'close and reliable ties' among its

of Nations (C Walter, 'Article 52' in B Simma and others (eds), *The Charter of the United Nations: A Commentary, Volume II* (4th edn, OUP 2024) 1845 [12]).

[40] See Hurrell (n 14) 241; M Prost, *The Concept of Unity in Public International Law* (Hart 2012) 36 fn 14.

[41] See Boisson de Chazournes, *Interactions* (n 14) 8; J-C Gautron, 'Le fait régional dans la société internationale' in Société Française pour le Droit International (ed), *Colloque de Bordeaux, Régionalisme et universalisme dans le droit international contemporain* (Pedone 1977) 4, 9–14.

[42] Besson and Kassoti (n 16) 7.

[43] See eg Nye (n 26), who also refers to 'mutual interdependence'.

[44] See eg the ILA Study Group (2024) (n 9) 13.

[45] Walter (n 39) 1846 [16].

[46] Walter (n 39) 1845 [12].

members which 'must lead to the expectation that the organization can provide specific contributions'.[47]

The difficulty with such non-geographic characteristics, however, lies in determining the requisite permanence and degree of social cohesion that permits the assumption of such 'close and reliable ties' and thereby justifies the expectation of a distinct form of solidarity within a given group of States. Compared to geographic criteria, these non-geographic characteristics tend to be less clear cut and exclusive, potentially giving rise to overlapping regional groupings and loyalties. From the perspective of third parties, as well as judicial bodies tasked with assessing the applicability of regional rules, their potentially elusive nature poses a particular challenge in identifying a region with the necessary level of legal certainty.

Formal legal structures grounded in shared characteristics, such as the establishment of a treaty or an IO with limited membership, may readily justify the assumption of a certain degree of social cohesion that distinguishes one particular group of States from another. Yet, such formalization cannot be regarded as a necessary condition for identifying a region. In practice, several examples illustrate that regional groups or alliances which do not meet the formal criteria of an IO exhibit a significant degree of internal social cohesion that translates externally to a non-negligible normative impact.[48] Such a requirement would also be incompatible with the concept of regional custom, which may develop independently of any institutional framework.[49] Identifying the necessary cohesion among States by pointing solely to the existence of legal relations under international law risks becoming tautological, emptying the concept of a 'region' of all meaning.

Similarly, some form of political commitment at the international level, for instance, in the form of an 'arrangement' (Articles 52 to 54 of the UN Charter) may be evidence for requisite social cohesion but cannot constitute a necessary requirement for the constitution of a 'region'. Should this be the case, the inclusion of the term 'arrangement' in Articles 52 to 54 would be superfluous—the reference to a 'region' would be enough.[50]

Thus, a formal legal framework is not constitutive, but, at most, indicative of a 'region' and can facilitate the identification and formation of regional rules. Other forms of evidence objectively indicating the existence of cohesion among a group of States include the existence of shared legal traditions at the domestic level

[47] Walter (n 39) 1449 [12]; see, for a similar view, Abass (n 32) 9, 20.

[48] See eg C O'Hara and V Vázquez Guevara, '"We, the Peoples of the Earth": ALBA, Populism and the Making of an Alternative International Law' (2025) 13(2) Lond Rev Int Law 201–23, discussing, for example, ALBA's influence at COP15 and on the Preamble of the Paris Agreement (8–9).

[49] See Chapter 5, section 5.2.

[50] The fact that the ICJ rejected the application of 'regional arrangements' to the Contadora process in *Military and Paramilitary Activities in and against Nicaragua (Nicaragua v United States of America)* [1984] ICJ Rep 392 [107] was not motivated by the absence of a 'regional' group, but rather the lack of an 'arrangement' (see eg Walter (n 39) 1847 [21]).

arising, for example, from the same historical experience,[51] shared religious reference point,[52] or mutual regulatory need arising from managing a shared natural resource.[53] Much like geographical factors, these characteristics reflect a normative bond between the States, endowed with a degree of permanence that sets them apart from other States.

2.2.1.4 Subjective element

The characteristics examined thus far share a common feature: they are objective in nature. This raises the question as to whether—and if so, to what extent—the existence of a region also depends on the subjective understanding of States of themselves as a group linked by shared characteristics.

While some treaties confer authority on an organ of the respective IO to ultimately define the region for the purpose of admitting new members,[54] such examples are relatively rare and, for the most part, limited to the constituent instruments of regional development banks.[55] Furthermore, even these regional instruments take objective criteria, such as geographic proximity or a geographically defined field of operation, as points of departure.[56]

Thus, practice does not support the view that a group of States' self-understanding as a 'region' is sufficient to characterize a region in a legal context. This is not to suggest, however, that such self-understanding is devoid of legal relevance. The subjective self-understanding of a group of States may help identify a region in a broader, political sense. It is thus indicative of a certain cohesion[57] and certainly necessary for the construction of regional institutions[58]. However, in a legal context, particularly when the 'region' serves as the controlling criterion in the application of a legal rule, understandings of regions grounded exclusively in the self-understanding of a group of States lack objective identifiability, permanence, and stability. Conversely, objective criteria, such as geography or social cohesion, have the potential to endure throughout the shifting alliances, occasional non-compliance with regional rules, ad hoc coalitions, and the polemics of everyday politics, thereby providing the requisite legal certainty.

[51] For example, the experience of occupation by France (and the introduction of the *Code Napoléon*), having been part of the British Empire (and the subsequent establishment of the Commonwealth of Nations), dissolution of the Soviet Union (and membership in the Commonwealth of Independent States (CIS) and Collective Security Treaty Organization (CSTO)), or (de-) colonization.

[52] See eg the Organisation for Islamic Cooperation (OIC) and the Islamic Development Bank (IsDB).

[53] See eg the establishment of river commissions.

[54] See eg Articles of Agreement on the Asian Infrastructure Investment Bank (adopted 29 June 2015, entered into force 25 December 2015) 3217 UNTS 1, art 1(2).

[55] See ILA Report (2024) (n 9) 11–12 for further examples.

[56] See eg AIIB Agreement, art 1(2).

[57] Besson and Kassoti (n 16) 7.

[58] See in this direction: Boisson de Chazournes, *Interactions* (n 14) 22.

It is a different question if such a self-understanding is *necessary* for the constitution of a region and for a State to be considered part of it. Practice indicates that the lack of self-identification of a regional organization as 'regional', be it for political or legal reasons, does not necessarily deprive it of this quality provided that the States in question form an objectively cohesive group.[59] The issue, however, is whether a State can be disassociated from a region—either through its own unilateral declaration or as a result of exclusion by a regional IO—despite possessing the objective characteristics common to that group of States. Ultimately, this seems to depend on the way in which such acts result in the dissolution of any meaningful cohesion between the State and the group and thereby undermine any expectation of regional solidarity or similarity. This could occur, for example, through the consistent rejection of a cohesive group of States to consider another State as a part of their region, as has happened in the case of Morocco's application to join the European Communities in 1987,[60] or through the severance of institutional, ideological, economic, or political ties, as exemplified by the proclamation of the *Monroe Doctrine* (1823)[61] or the aftermath of the Russian Revolution (1917),[62] which led to the emergence of new regional legal blocs. Thus, practice suggests that the subjective element is legally significant for characterizing a region only insofar as it manifests objectively.[63]

2.2.2 Definition and criteria

The analysis of State practice and scholarship reveals a range of characteristics used to delineate a 'region'. While broader understandings of the concept of a 'region' exist, in particular outside the legal context, practice generally supports a narrower conception of the term where legal consequences hinge on the classification of a practice, rule, or institution as 'regional'. Three core, cumulatively applicable criteria emerge from the discussion above, embodying the common, narrow understanding of a 'region' in international law. In this narrower sense, a region refers to a grouping of two or more States that: (1) can be objectively identified by third parties, typically on the basis of geographic proximity (criterion of identifiability); (2) exhibits a minimum degree of normative cohesion (criterion of

[59] On this: C Brölmann, 'Regional Organizations in International Law: Exploring the Function-Territory Divide' (2024) 21:1 IOLR 132, 137–38 on NATO.

[60] See ILA Report (2024) (n 9) 9.

[61] US President James Monroe, 'Seventh Annual Message of the President to Congress' (2 December 1823), available at: https://www.oas.org/sap/peacefund/VirtualLibrary/MonroeDoctrine/Treaty/MonroeDoctrine.pdf(accessed 5 May 2026).

[62] See eg L Mälksoo, 'International Legal Theory in Russia: A Civilizational Perspective, or Can Individuals be Subjects of International Law?' in A Orford and F Hoffmann (eds), *The Oxford Handbook of the Theory of International Law* (OUP 2016) 257, 264.

[63] See on the 'persistent objector' in the context of regional custom, Chapter 5.

normative cohesion); and (3) is thereby distinguishable from other groups of States (criterion of distinctiveness).[64] The expression 'region[al]' defines a state of normative cohesion which typically arises from geographic proximity among a group of States, thereby distinguishing it from third parties. 'Regional international law' describes rules of international law arising from this form of normative cohesion. 'Regionalism' refers to claims to a different legal treatment based on the affiliation with a 'region' defined in this narrow sense.

2.2.2.1 Identifiability

The characteristic of geographic proximity[65] points to the first criterion for defining a region, namely the criterion of identifiability, that is, the capacity of a group of States to be identified as such by third parties. Support for identifiability as a criterion for defining a region is found, for instance, in the Memorial submitted by the United Kingdom (UK) in the *Fisheries Jurisdiction (United Kingdom v Iceland)* case before the ICJ, in which it addressed the potential existence of regional custom. The UK argued that

> [t]here are certainly situations in which local customs, as exceptions to the general rule, are applicable .... But these situations arise either in a geographically defined area or within identifiable State-relationships where the departure from the general rule is consented to by all the States concerned, expressly or tacitly.[66]

This quotation suggests that geographic proximity is typically an important, but not a constitutive feature of a 'region'. Rather, the decisive criterion is the identifiability of 'State-relationships'. Geographic proximity usually serves as a point of departure for identifying a cohesive group of States. However, geographic proximity alone neither enables third parties to determine the boundaries of a given region nor fully captures the reality that certain States may, from the perspective of third parties, be regarded as part of a group of States despite having only a tenuous geographic connection to it. The delineation of such a group therefore depends on additional factors that enable the objective identification of a group of States and complement geographic proximity, such as consistent and enduring forms of social cohesion, including shared institutional, historical, political, or religious ties. This view is supported by practice demonstrating that geographic proximity alone is not decisive and may, in some instances, even be absent, provided

[64] See also A Paasi, 'The Institutionalisation of Regions: A Theoretical Framework for Understanding the Emergence of Regions and the Constitution of Regional Identity' (1986) 164:1 Fennia 105, 115: '[a] region is commonly regarded as a part of the earth's surface which possesses a quality of cohesion derived from a consistent relationship between associated features . . . that distinguishes [the region] from the concept of area which usually contains no implication of homogeneity or cohesion.'

[65] See section 2.2.1.2.

[66] *Fisheries Jurisdiction (United Kingdom v Iceland)*, Memorial of the United Kingdom (31 July 1973) 242.

that the states concerned are bound by a sufficiently stable and enduring bond capable of generating the expectation that they constitute a socially cohesive group.[67] The criterion of identifiability is further supported by practice suggesting that the self-identification as a region is insufficient to characterize a group of States as a region.[68]

2.2.2.2 Normative cohesion

The second criterion for defining a region in the legal sense is the presence of a minimum degree of normative cohesion among a group of States. Normative cohesion may arise from both geographic proximity or social cohesion, explaining why neither provides a fully adequate definition of a region and instead functions merely as a 'placeholder' or presumption indicating, ultimately, the presence of such normative cohesion.[69]

The criterion of normative cohesion requires a shared normative approach to orienting, ordering, and organizing State conduct that is reflected in consistent practices within the group of States. Nonetheless, comprehensive normative uniformity across all areas in which States exercise their sovereign functions is not required to fulfil the criterion of normative cohesion for the purpose of identifying a region. Instead, such normative cohesion may be present even where it is limited to certain areas, for example, similar regulatory approaches or policy frameworks relating to a specific geographic area, notably for the purpose of maintaining regional peace and security[70] or the management and use of shared natural resources located therein.[71]

While normative cohesion typically arises from geographic proximity,[72] it may also stem from social cohesion originating in shared historical experiences, economic interdependence, religious ties, or ideological alignment. However, since practice typically treats geographic proximity as a key criterion for defining a region, States with only minimal geographic proximity, or lacking it entirely, would need to meet a high evidentiary threshold to demonstrate a sufficient degree of normative cohesion to be regarded as forming or belonging to a region. Such evidence includes, for example, the existence of institutions at the regional or domestic level

[67] See section 2.2.1.3.

[68] See section 2.2.1.4.

[69] The relationship between geographic, social, and normative cohesion and their implications for the distinct significance of regional international law are addressed extensively in section 2.3.2.

[70] For example, the Antarctic Treaty (adopted 1 December 1959, entered into force 23 June 1961) 402 UNTS 71 or the Organization for Security and Co-operation in Europe (OSCE).

[71] For example, States in the Arctic region, notably those that are members of the Arctic Council, have very different domestic legal systems and political traditions. Still, on certain questions regarding the management of the Arctic Ocean and the role of indigenous people, member States co-ordinate their regulatory approaches: Declaration on the Establishment of the Arctic Council (Ottawa, 19 September 1996).

[72] See on the link between geographic proximity and normative cohesion section 2.3.2 below.

that explicitly aim to guide State conduct in accordance with a shared normative approach within that group of States.[73]

The criterion of normative cohesion poses a particular problem for identifying large groups of States as 'regions' in the *legal* sense, especially ideologically diverse ones such as the UN regional groups, which may, however, serve as starting points for identifying legally relevant regions in the narrow sense. The criterion of normative cohesion, furthermore, does not privilege 'integrationist' oriented groups of States in form or in substance. Groups of States that are only loosely institutionalized, such as the Pacific Islands Forum (PIF) aligned to protect their interests when facing a sea-level rise,[74] or those that are particularly protective of State sovereignty, such as the Association of Southeast Asian Nations (ASEAN),[75] are still normatively cohesive in the sense that their practices relating to a specific subject-matter correspond to a shared normative approach. Finally, this criterion does not require proof of compliance with a certain set of rules or values by all States within the region. At most, non-compliance may affect the outer limits of the region to the extent that consistent non-compliance translates into a complete severance of any normative bonds and an erosion of normative cohesion.[76]

2.2.2.3 Distinctiveness

Thirdly, the identifiable normative cohesion must also objectively distinguish one group of States from third parties.[77] Given that the criterion of distinctiveness underlies all of the characteristics analysed in section 2.2.1, a group of States satisfying identifiability and normative cohesion does not, on that basis alone, constitute a 'region' in the narrow legal sense. It must also fulfil this third criterion. The criterion of distinctiveness is particularly important to identify the scope *ratione personae* and *loci* of sub-regions and regions bound by geographic proximity in the absence of formal institutional structures given that all States are—to some extent—bound by geography.

[73] See eg with respect to the Commonwealth of Nations (RY Jennings, 'The Commonwealth and International Law' (1953) 30 BYBIL 320), the OIC and the IsDB (A Jahbri, 'ILA Study Group Questionnaire: Middle East & Arab World' <https://www.ila-hq.org/en/study-groups/international-law-of-regional-organisations> (accessed 5 May 2025)). See also Walter (n 39), who considers the Commonwealth of Nations and the OIC as 'regional' in the context of Chapter XIII of the UN Charter.

[74] See GF Sinclar, 'Questionnaire answers on Pacific Islands Forum and Pacific Community' (14 January 2022) <https://www.ila-hq.org/en/study-groups/international-law-of-regional-organisations> (accessed 5 May 2025).

[75] See D Chalmers, 'Questionnaire answers on Association of South East Asian Nations (ASEAN)' (10 March 2022) <https://www.ila-hq.org/en/study-groups/international-law-of-regional-organisations> (accessed 5 May 2025).

[76] See with respect to Russia: I Aral, 'Russia's Expulsion: The Council of Europe as the Guardian of European Imperialism' (2025) 38(2) LJIL 113–130.

[77] See also E Kassoti, 'The European Union and Other Regional International Organizations: Tales of Solidarity' (2024) 21:1 IOLR 190, 191.

The criterion does not require that States within a given region see themselves as belonging exclusively to one region. It may well be that membership in several groups overlaps. The decisive factor is that their internal normative cohesion on a specific issue sets them apart from their neighbouring States. The Bolivarian Alliance for the peoples of our America (ALBA), for example, a sub-regional group of States in Latin-America, formed an ideological alternative to 'neoliberal' regional institutions in the Latin American region partly overlapping with larger regional groups, such as the Organization of American States (OAS), and, accordingly, met the criterion of distinctiveness.[78]

2.3 Regional international law as a distinct legal category

It is true that international law originating from regions defined in a broad sense (ie, as based on non-universality or the self-understanding of a group of States) does not necessarily differ in any significant way from other forms of particular international law. The key question, however, is whether legal rules and institutions emerging from regions defined in a narrower sense constitute a distinct legal category.[79] This section argues that such a distinct category may indeed exist where the distinct legal significance of a practice or rule is not only asserted by a State or a group of States within a given region but also accepted by third parties precisely because of the *regional* character of that practice or rule.

To illustrate this point, one may draw a parallel with statehood.[80] Just like States, regions can be considered as social phenomena with legal implications. Just as statehood and the legal consequences resulting from statehood cannot be established by self-assertion of a political entity alone, the special or even *sui generis* nature of a particular regional rule likewise cannot depend solely on a region's own proclamation. Instead, the decisive question is whether practice shows that, in certain cases, both the entity itself (here: the members of a given region) and third parties agree on attributing distinct legal consequences to a social phenomenon (here: practices and rules arising from a region).

In the context of statehood, the dynamic between an entity's asserted status and the recognition or non-recognition it receives from other States has brought about

[78] See JM Díaz de Valdés and S Verdugo, 'The ALBA Constitutional Project and Political Representation' (2019) 17:2 ICON 479–88 on the specificities and distinctiveness of 'ALBA constitutionalism'.

[79] On this, see also D Chalmers, 'The Distinctiveness of Regional International Organization Law' (2024) 21:1 IOLR 43, 44.

[80] See also on the parallels between Statehood and regionhood: S Besson, 'The Politics of Regional International Organizations: A New Dawn for the Political Legitimacy of International Law' (2024) 21:1 IOLR 87, 96–104; L Van Langenhove. 'What is a Region? Towards a Statehood Theory of Regions' (2013) 19:4 Contemporary Politics 474–90.

a convergence on the criteria for statehood, ultimately crystallizing these criteria in customary international law.[81] For regions, however, no equivalent criteria have been established yet. The question, then, is whether the criteria identified above might serve a comparable function—that is, to help identify a category of regional law with distinct legal implications, notably with respect to the formation, identification, interpretation, and application of international law.

This section prepares the ground for analysing the role of regional practices and rules in Chapters 4 to 7. To this end, it examines the parameters that influence whether third parties are likely to recognize the distinct legal nature of regional international law. It first considers the legal risks that claims based on regional particularity may pose to third parties (2.3.1) and then explores the legal grounds on which third parties recognize the distinct legal significance of the defining criteria of regions in international law (2.3.2–2.3.4).

The section demonstrates that regional affiliation gives rise to a presumption of distinct normative qualities inherent in legal claims originating from regions that meet the three above-mentioned criteria. This presumption functions not as a source of specific rights or powers, but as an interpretive lens through which legal claims are understood and assessed.[82] It is precisely the defining attributes of regions and regional law that may give rise to a convergence between a distinct normative claim asserted by one part of the legal community (the region) and the acceptability of that claim from the perspective of third parties. This convergence facilitates the transformation of a claim or practice—originating within a particular group—into legal rules recognized as such by the broader legal community.[83] Accordingly, this section shows that belonging to a region (regional affiliation) entails a presumption of acceptable legal distinctiveness that bears on the identification, interpretation, application, and formation of international law.

2.3.1 Risks posed by particular international law to third parties

To understand the factors motivating third parties to accept the distinct legal consequences of regional rules, it is essential to first recall the risks inherent in particular international law from the perspective of third parties. These risks may help

[81] On the three elements of statehood: G Jellinek, *Allgemeine Staatslehre* (3rd edn, Verlag von O Haring 1914) 394–434. See further: R Nicholson, *Statehood and the State-Like in International Law* (OUP 2019) 92–145.

[82] See also in the context of statehood: J Crawford, *The Creation of States in International Law* (2nd edition, OUP 2007) 44–45: 'the exclusive attributes of States do not prescribe specific rights, powers or capacities that all States must, to be States, possess: they are presumptions as to the existence of such rights, powers or capacities, rules that these exist unless otherwise stipulated. . . . The legal concept of statehood provides a measure for determining whether in a given case rights have been acquired or lost.'

[83] See also J Brunnée and S Toope, 'International Law and the Practice of Legality: Stability and Change' (2018) 49:4 Vic Univ Wellingt Law Rev 429–45.

explain their reluctance to recognize the legal significance of regional law. There are indeed sound reasons for third parties to be wary of particular international law. This is because particular international law, including its regional forms, may entail significant disadvantages for third parties. As Andrew Hurrell notes:

> [f]or those outside the region, regionalism is politically significant to the extent that it can impose costs on outsiders: whether through the detrimental impact of preferential regional economic arrangements (so-called malign regionalism that diverts trade and investment) or through causing a shift in the distribution of political power. It is also politically significant when outsiders are forced to define their policies towards individual regional states in regionalist terms. For those inside the region, regionalism matters when exclusion from regional arrangements imposes significant costs, both economic and political (such as loss of autonomy or a reduction in foreign policy options) and when the region becomes the organizing basis for policy within the region across a range of important issues.[84]

Hurrell's observations about the political costs of regional international law are mirrored in the potentially adverse effects on the legal position of third parties.[85] Third parties are certainly formally protected from being bound by regional rules to which they have not consented by virtue of the *pacta tertiis* principle.[86] They are nevertheless confronted with the existence of such regional rules as these shape the conduct of other States and IOs on the international plane and thus the normative environment in which they operate. Third parties' freedom of action may, at least indirectly, be curtailed without their consent by normative spill-over effects. Such effects may be (incidentally) adverse or unfavourable, but do not necessarily amount to obligations *stricto sensu* and thus fall outside the scope of the *pacta tertiis* principle.[87] Where a regional organization imposes third-party countermeasures on a State in response to alleged breaches of obligations *erga omnes* on the basis of regional rules, for instance, this may contribute to the emergence, or confirm the existence, of a corresponding right under general customary international law. Such practice therefore arguably implicates the position of all States that might become targets of such countermeasures in the future.[88] Moreover, legal relations between limited groups of States represent *prima facie* a threat to legal certainty given

[84] See Hurrell (n 14) 243.

[85] See eg ILC, 'Fourth report on *jus cogens*' (n 15) [29]; Fragmentation Report (n 3) [212].

[86] See Chapter 4, section 4.4 and Chapter 7, section 7.2.3.

[87] A Proelss, 'Article 34', in O Dörr and K Schmalenbach (eds), *Vienna Convention on the Law of Treaties: A Commentary* (2nd edn, Springer 2018) [15]. See section 4.4.

[88] A Hofer, 'Third-Party Countermeasures: Making Custom Out of Ambiguous Practice?' (2025) 74 ICLQ 287, 306; see also: MT Veber, 'The Notion of Regionalism in the Context of Sanctions Adopted by Regional International Organizations in the Defence of the General Interest' in E Kassoti, T Cabrita, and N Idriz (eds), *The European Union and Regionalism: Conceptual and Contextual Perspectives* (Brill 2025) 142.

that special rules—and the implications they may have for members of a given region with which third parties interact—are often difficult to identify from the outside.[89] Finally, where obligations under particular international law are created, interpreted, and applied based on regional 'meta-rules' different from those at the universal level, third parties may fear that regional deviations circumvent generally applicable rules, threatening the coherence of the common legal framework.[90] Hence, the risk associated with particular international law, from the perspective of third parties, essentially consists in a loss of control over their normative environment. While regional international law, as defined here, is not exempt from posing such risks, it nonetheless responds to them differently from other forms of particular law, *precisely* because of the three criteria defining a 'region'.

2.3.2 Identifiability of regional affiliation as the basis of a presumption

Although geographic proximity is not sufficient to define a region, it typically serves as a starting point for its identification.[91] It is here where we come back to the 'placeholder' function attributed to geographic proximity,[92] asking whether third parties attribute any legal consequences to it. While the 2006 Fragmentation Report asserted that '[t]he fact that the States come from the same region is only a factual ingredient of their relationship',[93] this section shows that geographic proximity among a group of States does not only facilitate the identification of a group of States, but also the identification of a common normative approach shared among them from the perspective of third parties due to a correlation of geographic, social, and normative cohesion (2.3.2.1), giving rise to a (rebuttable) presumption of normative cohesion arising from geographic proximity (2.3.2.2).

2.3.2.1 Correlation of geographic, social, and normative cohesion

According to *Thomas Franck* and *Peter Prows*, 'presumptions are a guess about causality or correlation based on the common experience of a community of law'.[94] Both practice and scholarship are replete with such 'guesses' about the correlation of geographic proximity and the existence of a shared normative approach among a given group of States. The presumption that geographic regions represent 'the main forms of civilization and of the principal legal systems of the world' is, for

[89] On this, see eg the discussion in the ILC on whether an error about regional law constitutes a relevant error under the law of treaties, see section 2.4.2.2. See also Klabbers (n 6) 35.

[90] See also Boisson de Chazournes, *Interactions* (n 14) 325. See further the discussion on regional *jus cogens* and its effects on third parties, Chapter 5, section 5.4.

[91] Section 2.2.2.1.

[92] Section 2.2.2.1.

[93] Fragmentation Report (n 3) [212]; see also C Schreuer, 'Regionalism v. Universalism' (1995) 6 EJIL 477, 498; see also Brölmann, 'Divide' (n 59) 143.

[94] T Franck and P Prows, 'The Role of Presumptions in International Tribunals' (2005) 4:2 Law Pract Int Courts Trib 197, 200.

example, reflected in the way in which judges of the ICJ and ILC members are elected in practice, namely based on their affiliation with one of the geographically defined regional groups of the UN.[95] A presumption of normative cohesion among geographically proximate States also underlies the work of the ILC on the topic of 'General principles of law'.[96] The text of draft Conclusion 5(2) as adopted on second reading in 2025 indicates that a principle may be presumed to be common to the main legal systems of the world if it is shared across 'regions'.[97] Similarly, the 2018 report by an ILA study group on 'the use of domestic law principles in the development of international law' noted that

> [i]t is also not enough to 'identify' a general principle among the main legal systems if there is not enough geographical representation, e.g. a general principle shared by Civil Law countries in Europe should also be identified in other Civil Law countries located in different geographical areas and belonging to different civilizations.[98]

The understanding of geographic proximity as giving rise to a presumption of normative cohesion seems to be shared by *Christopher Borgen* who considers 'regions' as 'physical (geographic) space, but also (. . .) areas of normative similarity'.[99] Along similar lines, *James Crawford* observed that

> [t]he matters that most Governments spend most time on and which can affect them most tend to relate to their neighbours or their region. Indeed even when States focus on questions of apparently universal concern, their approach is likely to be influenced by regional postures and implications—and not only in such matters as minority rights or the use of international watercourses.[100]

These 'guesses' in practice and scholarship about the correlation of geographic proximity and normative cohesion are rooted in the functional and ideological interdependence typically arising from geographic proximity.[101]

[95] Statute of the International Court of Justice, annexed to the UN Charter (adopted 26 June 1945, entered into force 24 October 1945) 1 UNTS XVI, art 9; Statute of the International Law Commission, GA Res 174 (II), 21 November 1947, annex, art 8.

[96] See also Chapter 7, section 7.4.2.

[97] ILC, 'General principles of law: texts and titles of the draft conclusions adopted by the Drafting Committee on second reading' (2025) UN Doc A/CN.4/L.1018, draft conclusion 5(2).

[98] ILA, 'Report of the Study Group on the use of domestic law principles in the development of international law' Report of the Seventy-Eighth Conference (Sydney 2018) 1170–242 [214].

[99] CJ Borgen, 'Treaty Conflicts and Systemic Fragmentation' in DB Hollis (ed), *The Oxford Guide to Treaties* (2nd edn, OUP 2020) 432, 435.

[100] J Crawford, *Chance, Order, Change: The Course of International Law, General Course on Public International Law* (Brill 2013) 243 [424].

[101] Nye (n 26); Boisson de Chazournes, *Interactions* (n 14) 12; GF Sinclar, 'Between Functionalism and Hegemony: Regional International Organizations in the History of International Law' (2024) 21:1 IOLR 65, 80.

Geographic proximity is not only conducive to co-operation among neighbouring States in the pursuit of shared interests, giving rise to postal, telecommunication, and sanitation organizations, military alliances, or regional free trade zones. It may even render co-operation necessary where those interests are inextricably linked to a shared territorial, maritime, or other natural feature, thereby generating and consolidating legal regimes governing transit rights, fisheries, or river systems (functional interdependence).[102]

Geographic proximity further gives rise to and entrenches normative cohesion in relation to (political) self-organization among neighbouring States (ideological interdependence). The link between geography and ideological cohesion can stem from a shared historical experience or political past of the States in question, for example, as former administrative units of another State or as colonies of the same colonial power. It may also arise from the establishment of regional institutions based on the idea that the realization, preservation, perhaps even survival of a certain political identity may depend on adherence to it by neighbouring States ('Domino theory'), as notably illustrated by the combination of geography-based admission criteria and shared political principles in various instruments establishing regional organizations.[103] Such regional institutions may entrench ideological cohesion in two ways. They can foster convergence in the choice of domestic political systems, as defining features of a shared political order are projected onto the regional plane and sovereign functions and competences are transferred to regional institutions, as is particularly evident in regional integration organizations. Regional institutions may also serve to protect a shared understanding of what forms the *domaine réservé* of States at the regional level, ie what should not become subject to international regulation.[104]

2.3.2.2 Consequences of the presumption

Owing to the correlation between geographic, social, and normative cohesion, the identification of regional legal rules is generally more accessible to third parties than other forms of specialized law.[105] Unlike other particularistic legal regimes,

[102] See eg Convention on the Law of the Non-Navigational Uses of International Watercourses (adopted 21 May 1997, entered into force 17 August 2014) 51 UNTS 49, art 8(2); *Fisheries (UK v Norway)* [1951] ICJ Rep 116, 133; *Right of Passage* [1960] (n 23) 39; *Eritrea/Yemen—Second stage of the proceedings between Eritrea and Yemen (Maritime Delimitation)* (1999) 22 UNRIAA 335 [92]–[94]. See also Boisson de Chazournes, *Interactions* (n 14) 10.

[103] See eg Charter of the Association of Southeast Asian Nations (adopted 20 November 2007, entered into force 15 December 2008) 2624 UNTS 223, art 6; Treaty on European Union (adopted 13 December 2007, entered into force 1 January 2009) (Consolidated version 2016–OJ C 202 (2016)), art 49; Constitutive Act of the African Union (adopted 11 July 2000, entered into force 26 May 2001) 2158 UNTS 3, art 29(1); Charter of the Organization of American States (adopted on 30 April 1948, entered into force 13 December 1951) 119 UNTS 3, art 2.

[104] See eg AV Obydenkova and A Libman, *Authoritarian Regionalism in the World of International Organizations: Global Perspective and the Eurasian Enigma* (OUP 2019) 263; T Ginsburg, 'Authoritarian International Law?' (2019) 114:2 AJIL 221–60; Besson, 'The Politics of RIOs' (n 80) 113.

[105] See eg Memorial of the UK, in *Fisheries Jurisdiction (United Kingdom v Iceland)* (n 66) 242.

the normative cohesion that stems from geographically-induced interdependence tends to exhibit greater permanence and stability.[106] One of the key reasons for this lies in its intersubjective non-disposability: whereas parties to other special legal regimes retain broad discretion to renegotiate or redefine their shared interests and values *inter se*, regional arrangements are often constrained by enduring geographic realities and deeply rooted domestic interdependencies, which limit the scope for such flexibility.[107]

Regional affiliation thus allows for a convergence of *perceived* normative cohesion from States within the region arising from the interdependence created by geographic proximity, and *perceivable* normative cohesion from outside the region, that is, by third parties, through the identifiability of such regional law. As a result, the presumption of normative cohesion arising from geographic cohesion may entail, inter alia, a more prominent role of implicit forms of consent, notably in the form of inaction, both with respect to States within the region and third States. With respect to States within the region, their functional and ideological interdependence compels them to decide between different regulatory approaches and, in particular, to decide whether to follow the approach adopted by its neighbours. Therefore, States within the region may generally be expected to react to the adoption of a certain normative approach in their immediate environment should they wish to remain outside the scope of that specific legal arrangement.[108] At the same time, rules affiliated with regions defined by geographic proximity (or a comparable form of cohesion) are easier to accept for third parties than other forms of particular law. For one, the risk for legal certainty is reduced by their external identifiability. Moreover, this identifiability also fulfils an important ordering function in that it facilitates the identification of international law.[109]

The presumption of normative cohesion arising from geographic proximity is, however, rebuttable. This notably concerns 'outliers' in the region that do not, for historical or political reasons, partake in the normative approach adopted by a geographically linked group of States. This outlier status is, for example, visible by the fact that a State is, exceptionally, allocated to a different regional group in the UN system, a member State (only) to regional integration organizations in the neighbouring region, not a member to any regional integration organization in the region, or has a very different legal tradition compared to its neighbours. Such presumption of normative cohesion in relation to a State within the region is further rebuttable with respect to a specific issue to the extent that that State in question has unambiguously opted not to participate in the normative approach prevalent

[106] See also *Territorial Dispute (Libya/Chad)* [1994] ICJ Rep 6, 37 [73]: 'territorial regime established by treaty achieves a permanence which the treaty itself does not necessarily enjoy following its termination.'

[107] Boisson de Chazournes, *Interactions* (n 14) 10.

[108] See also Chapter 5, section 5.2.

[109] See also Chapter 7, section 7.2.2.

in the region, for example by joining a regional institution that explicitly deviates from that approach or by adopting specific domestic laws to this effect.

Treating geographic proximity as a presumption rather than a definitional factor is also consistent with the idea that geography is not a necessary condition for the existence of a region. Rather, geographic proximity serves as an indicator for identifying normative cohesion among a group of States. As such, it functions as an evidentiary tool, not a conceptual constraint. This allows for the existence of regional 'exclaves' or even entirely non-contiguous regional groupings, provided that the relevant States are identifiable as a region through shared normative or social characteristics.

2.3.3 Normative cohesion of regional law as the basis of a privilege

The criterion of normative cohesion may justify a privileged role of regional rules and practices in the formation of international law. This has also been recognized by the ILC Study Group in the 2006 Fragmentation Report, which maintained that

> regionalism is [...] a privileged forum for international lawmaking. It is often assumed that international law is or should be developed in a regional context because the relative homogeneity of the interests or outlooks of actors will then ensure a more efficient or equitable implementation of the relevant norms. The presence of a thick cultural community better ensures the legitimacy of the regulations and that they are understood and applied in a coherent way.[110]

At the same time, the Study Group did not view this as a distinctly regional phenomenon, but rather as one stemming from functional diversification.[111] The next subsection challenges this view. It shows that regional practices and rules are typically embedded in existing normative relations among States (2.3.3.1) and, for this reason, enjoy a privileged status in international law (2.3.3.2).

2.3.3.1 Embeddedness of regional law

Unlike other forms of particular international law, regional international law typically arises from and reflects existing normative relations among a group of States (normative cohesion). Such embeddedness of regional rules and practices is largely due to geographically induced interdependence, whereby their mutual relations are continuously redefined, re-equilibrated, renegotiated, juridified, and institutionalized. The 'region' is thus a source of existing and constantly evolving communal relations which incrementally mature and solidify into legal obligations, or,

[110] Fragmentation Report (n 3) [205], see also [206]–[210].
[111] Fragmentation Report (n 3) [209].

in the words of Hersch Lauterpacht, regional rules 'grow[n] up together in that part of the world as appropriate to its needs, traditions and legal conceptions'.[112]

Furthermore, (regional) international law is 'typically the product of the dissolution of empires, of federal or centralised States' with the result that '[t]he former experience of a common collectivity creates a series of bonds between the peoples concerned. These bonds also feed their relationships after the dissolution of the collectivity, and thus continue in the international space.'[113] Hence, 'RIOs are unlike UIOs and come closer to States.'[114] Indeed, regional rules often resemble domestic legal rules in that they tend to be embedded in a holistic or all-embracing legal order characterized by normative completeness. This embeddedness also renders them distinct from other specialized legal rules that 'only establish law for the single functional sector of society to which they are connected'.[115]

This particularity of regional law matters to third parties because such communal relations represent the connecting link, the 'hinge' between stable legal rules and their adaptation to social realities, the structural coupling of law and politics, which is the source of social trust that keeps a legal order as a whole resilient to changes over time.[116] Regional law may provide the 'nexus between civilization and international law' which, according to Georg Schwarzenberger, 'is a basic question of international law (. . .) a current legal problem of the first order'.[117] Regional law facilitates consensus-building by way of combining the subsidiarity of law-making processes and the forging of similar understanding of legal concepts.[118] It also releases the universal community from the need to balance competing interests insofar as an equivalent solution has already been conceived at the regional level.[119] Accordingly, regional law serves both as a source of, and a driving force behind, the juridification of international relations.[120]

Owing to the above reasons, we find deference towards, or at least legal recognition of, subcutaneously existing communal relations in legal orders, as reflected, notably, in the principle of subsidiarity[121] and in the notion of *quieta non*

[112] H Lauterpacht, *The Development of International Law by the International Court* (Steven & Sons 1958, reprinted by Grotius Publications Ltd Cambridge 1982) 382.

[113] R Kolb, *Theory of International Law* (Hart 2016) 11; Besson, 'Politics of RIOs' (n 80) 101.

[114] Besson, 'Politics of RIOs' (n 80) 100.

[115] G Teubner, *Constitutional Fragments: Societal Constitutionalism and Globalization* (OUP 2012) 156.

[116] See also LM Dellmuth and J Tallberg, 'Why National and International Legitimacy Beliefs are Linked: Social Trust as an Antecedent Factor' (2020) 15 Rev Int Organ 311–37; Kolb (n 113) 11; Besson, 'Politics of RIOs' (n 80) 103.

[117] G Schwarzenberger, 'The Standard of Civilization in International Law' (1955) 8 Curr Leg Probl 212.

[118] N Luhmann, *Das Recht der Gesellschaft* (Suhrkamp 1995) 577.

[119] Luhmann (n 118) 582.

[120] See also R Wolfrum, 'Sources of International Law' in A Peters (ed), *Max Planck Encyclopedia of Public International Law* (OUP 2011) [45].

[121] A Føllesdal, 'The Principle of Subsidiarity as a Constitutional Principle in International Law' (2013) 2:1 Glob Const 37–62; A Acharya, 'Norm Subsidiarity and Regional Orders: Sovereignty, Regionalism, and Rule-Making in the Third World' (2011) 55:1 Int Stud Q 95–123.

movere.[122] This is not only the case for the domestic legal orders of many States.[123] It has also found expression at the international level, for instance, in the recognition of transboundary relations arising from geographically induced interdependence[124] and the principle of self-determination.[125] Many treaties refer to a 'given region', thus presupposing and not creating a community.[126] Other treaties recognize the analogous application of their provisions to regional integration organizations; thus expressing the view that a certain level of legal integration—one comparable to that of States—would only be found in specifically regional IOs.[127]

In short, regional rules often reflect more than a legal technique adopted to advance a common goal, as is typical of non-regional particular international law. They arise from pre-existing and, in many ways, inescapable normative relations that already structure interactions before any specific common legal interests crystallize at the international level.

2.3.3.2 Consequences of the privilege

The privilege arising from the embeddedness of regional law may entail heightened regulatory autonomy. This means that third parties may recognize regional rules as valid within the region, even if the processes by which they emerge differ from those applicable under general international law—for example, due to the presence of distinct regional sources of law. Similarly, third parties may defer to region-specific interpretive approaches—even if these are not expressly found in the general law of treaties—when applied by regional bodies to regional agreements and the approach finds recognition within the region.

However, this privilege is not absolute. It is treated as an exception, with the burden of justification resting on those asserting idiosyncratic regional claims. The scope and limits of regional regulatory autonomy is derived from its underlying rationale, the analogy between regional legal orders and domestic legal systems, respect for the principle of self-determination, and the reliance of the international legal order on the decentralized formation and implementation of international law. Accordingly, the extent to which third parties are willing to acknowledge a

[122] *The Grisbådarna Case (Norway v Sweden) (Award)* PCA Case 1908-01 (23 October 1909) 6.

[123] In the majority of domestic legal systems, at least some forms of communal relations located at the level between the individual and the State are recognized in the respective domestic law (S Choudhry, 'Group Rights in Comparative Constitutional Law: Culture, Economics, or Political Power?' in M Rosenfeld and A Sajó (eds), *The Oxford Handbook of Comparative Constitutional Law* (OUP 2016) 1100–28).

[124] L Boisson de Chazournes and D Campanelli, 'Neighbor States' in A Peters (ed), *Max Planck Encyclopedia of Public International Law* (OUP 2006) [6].

[125] It may even be said that regional law is an expression of the principle of self-determination at the international level, see also Besson, 'Politics of RIOs' (n 80) 99.

[126] See above Chapter 2, section 2.2.

[127] See eg United Nations Framework Convention on Climate Change (adopted 9 May 1992, entered into force 21 March 1994) 1771 UNTS 107, art 22(1); United Nations Convention against Corruption (adopted 31 October 2003, entered into force 14 December 2005) 2349 UNTS 41, art 67.

degree of regulatory autonomy depends on several factors, namely, the normative nexus between the regional rule and a cohesive, almost complete legal order, the general acceptance of the regulatory approach by the members of the regional system; and on the condition that the rule either emerged through a process functionally equivalent to a recognized source of international law or concerns a subject-matter falling within the *domaine réservé* of States—making the regional rule a 'trailblazer' and not a normative competitor at the international level.

2.3.4 Distinctiveness of regional law as the basis of (non-)opposability

The criterion of distinctiveness corresponds to the limited generalizability of regional approaches beyond the region itself (2.3.4.1). This, in turn, can render alternative regional approaches more acceptable to third parties as the risks of incidentally unfavourable spill-over effects is considerably lower (2.3.4.2).

2.3.4.1 Non-generalizability of regional law

A parallel may be drawn between regional international law and the rationale underlying the (controversial) concept of 'objective regimes'. This concept has been discussed as an exception to the *pacta tertiis* rule (Article 34 VCLT).[128] According to Gerald Fitzmaurice, the legal basis of 'objective regimes' is either 'implied consent' (this would apply for States within the region) or derives from

> a general duty for States [. . .] to respect, recognize and, in the legal sense, accept, the consequences of lawful and valid international acts entered into between other States, which do not infringe the legal rights of States not parties to them in the legal sense.[129]

The non-universal character of a rule or institution *ratione personae* plays a decisive role for the non-generalizability of its legal effect.[130] While this more quantitative factor, its limited effect *ratione personae*, is shared by both regional and non-regional international law, what renders certain forms of regional law distinct is their 'qualitative[] or substantive[] non-universal[ity]'.[131] Many regional rules

[128] See also Chapter 4, section 4.4.2.

[129] See ILC, 'Fifth Report of the Special Rapporteur, Sir Gerald Fitzmaurice, 12th session of the ILC (1960)' (1960) YBILC II, UN Doc A/CN.4/130, 91, 93, 97, and 98 [71]; Proelss, 'Article 34' (n 87) [36].

[130] As an *argumentum e contrario* based on *Reparation for Injuries Suffered in the Service of the United Nations* (Advisory Opinion) [1949] ICJ Rep 174, 185: 'the Court's opinion is that fifty States, representing the vast majority of the members of the international community, had the power, in conformity with international law, to bring into being an entity possessing objective international personality, and not merely personality recognized by them alone, together with capacity to bring international claims.'

[131] See PC Jessup, 'Non-Universal International Law' (1973) 12:3 Columbia J Transnatl Law 415, 419; this claim is also supported—to some extent—by the recognition that the practice of 'specially

arise from, are based on, or pertain to a specific geographic situation or the activities of a regional organization relating to that region.[132] In the latter case, it may even be said that regional norms often express a congruent understanding of political self-organization relating to the areas and functions which form a common concern of all States within the region, and about what is to remain in the *domaine reservé* of the respective States.[133] The personal and territorial scope of these regional rules is thus more confined, inward-looking and closed. Consequently, the threat of normative 'spill-over' effects is lower with respect to these regional rules than in other forms of particular international law whose subject matter is functionally determined and thus potentially generalizable beyond the confines of the region.[134]

2.3.4.2 Consequences of non-opposability

Due to their lack of generalizability, regional rules are not only not opposable to third parties,[135] but, in the absence of any rule regulating the subject-matter at the level of general international law, such rules also do not even affect the interpretation or application of legal rules applicable beyond the region. The characteristic distinctiveness of regional rules is precisely what may render them more acceptable to third parties.

Conversely, the level of acceptance on the part of third parties tends to decrease where regional rules either replicate or substantively deviate from rules established under general international law—particularly in areas such as international human rights law or provisions diverging from the collective security framework enshrined in the UN Charter. In such cases, regional rules risk producing normative spill-over effects and may be perceived as circumventing legal standards agreed upon at the universal level.

2.4 The difference between regional and other particular law: a triple challenge

The legal category of regional international law differs from other forms of particular international law not only in its distinct significance for the formation,

affected States' deserves particular normative significance (see ILC Report 2018 (CIL) (n 20) 136 [4]); see on this Chapter 7, section 7.4.1.2.

132 See eg *European Commission of the Danube* (Advisory Opinion) [1927] PCIJ Series B, No 14, 17; *Right of Passage* (n 23) 39–40; *Navigational and Related Rights* (n 11) [141].

133 On this, see N Luhmann, *Die Gesellschaft der Gesellschaft, Vol I* (Suhrkamp 1997) 166.

134 See also the example given by Jessup (n 131) 420: 'The neutralization of Switzerland is uniquely non-universal but surely it is not objectionable to the Third World.'

135 See on this generally: E Bjorge, 'Opposability and Non-opposability in International Law' (2021) BYIL 1, 20–21.

identification, interpretation, and application of international law. It also poses a 'triple challenge' to the international legal order, which differs significantly from the challenge arising from non-regional particular international law. This 'triple challenge' arises from its ambivalent legal effects (analytical challenge), its elusive legal nature (methodological challenge), and the challenge of identifying a substantive common denominator shared across all regions (normative challenge).

2.4.1 The analytical challenge: ambivalent legal effects

The 'dual, ambivalent character of regionalism',[136] along with the ambiguous motivations driving States to pursue it,[137] its opaque relation to (universal) international institutions,[138] and its double-edged impact on those institutions,[139] has been examined extensively by more critical strands of international law scholarship and international relations theory. By contrast, the Janus-faced nature of regionalism, that is, its simultaneous constructive and corrosive potential, has received little, if any, attention by doctrinal-positivist scholars since the end of the Cold War.[140] This section demonstrates that the three above-mentioned criteria that render regional international law normatively distinct also give rise to an analytical challenge. The analytical challenge posed by regional law stems from its inherent tension between legal exclusion and integration: States accept being integrated into a (regional) legal order while, and not infrequently *because* others are excluded from it.[141] The double-edged nature of the identity claim, autonomy claim, and alternativity claim inherent in certain forms of regional international law makes it difficult to distinguish between its constructive and corrosive forms.

2.4.1.1 Between identifiability and identity?

It is precisely the defining feature that renders regional rules identifiable, namely the normative cohesion arising from geographically induced interdependence, that also give rise to assertions of exclusive rules based on a regional identity.[142]

[136] Anghie, 'Identifying Regions' (n 14) 1059.

[137] See eg Obydenkova and Libman (n 104).

[138] See eg H Bull, *The Anarchical Society. A Study of Order in World Politics* (3rd edn, Palgrave 2002) 294–99; Hurrell (n 14) 239–40, 247–61; Nye (n 26).

[139] See eg Acharya (n 121); A Cooley and M Schaaf, 'Grounding the Backlash: Regional Security Treaties, Counternorms, and Human Rights in Eurasia' in S Hopgood, J Snyder, and L Vinjamuri (eds), *Human Rights Futures* (CUP 2017) 159–88.

[140] See also Orford (n 1).

[141] See also Special Rapporteur L Diaz Gonzalez (ILC, 'Fourth report on relations between States and international organizations' (1989) YBILC II(1), UN Doc A/CN.4/424, 159: 'organizations of a universal character are founded on the principle of inclusion, whereas organizations of limited membership are founded on the principle of exclusion.'). See also: Koagne Zouapet (n 15) 156; Kassoti (n 77) 191.

[142] See Boisson de Chazournes, *Interactions* (n 14) 8, 325; Hurrell (n 14) 28; Kassoti (n 77) 191.

Membership criteria based on non-disposable criteria, such as geographic proximity, the form of political self-organization, or both, facilitate the identification of a normative 'bloc'. Yet, this facilitation depends on the exclusionary nature of such criteria, which cut across the community of States by including some and excluding others. These forms of 'closed' memberships rarely occur in non-regional agreements but frequently in regional instruments.[143] The entrenchment of a certain identity is further shown by the way in which some regional provisions refer to, and draw legitimacy from, the respective constitutions and legislation of member States,[144] and incorporate intra-regional duties of loyalty.[145] These forms of regional institutions are thus considerably more 'inward-turned' than functional IOs.[146]

The way in which regional identity claims are institutionally entrenched varies among regional IOs.[147] Groups of States that seek to project their shared understanding of political self-organization onto the regional level reinforce their normative distinctiveness by 'pooling' sovereignty at the regional level, for example through the transposition of exclusive competences on regional bodies,[148] or the direct effect and applicability of regional law.[149] Conversely, regional institutions that serve to protect a shared understanding of what is to remain within the *domaine réservé* tend to establish institutional and normative frameworks that mirror the constitutional structures of their member States[150] and resist any external encroachment on member sovereignty.[151] Yet, despite their differences, both forms

[143] Exceptions include regional development banks, and 'open-ended regionalism' established based on regional interests aiming at universality (Boisson de Chazournes, *Interactions* (n 14) 13–14, 20–21).

[144] See eg Consolidated version of the Treaty on European Union (2016) 59 Official Journal C 202, 13 (TEU), art 6(3).

[145] See eg TEU, art 4(3) TEU; Treaty of the Southern African Development Community (concluded 17 August 1992, entered into force 5 October 1992) (1993) 32 ILM 120 (amended by the 2001 Agreement Amending the Treaty of the Southern African Development Community), art 6.

[146] See on 'finalité extravertie' and 'finalité introvertie': M Virally, 'Les relations entre organisations régionales et organisations universelles' in *Régionalisme et universalisme* in Société Française pour le Droit International (ed), *Colloque de Bordeaux, Régionalisme et universalisme dans le droit international contemporain* (Pedone 1977) 147, 154–55.

[147] Koagne Zouapet (n 15) 151–52 distinguishes between offensive and defensive strategies adopted by regional institutions. See also section 2.3.2.

[148] See Boisson de Chazournes, *Interactions* (n 14) 324–25.

[149] See apart from the Court of Justice of the EU (CJEU): Central American Court of Justice (CACJ) of the Central American Integration System (SICA) and the Caribbean Court of Justice (CCJ) of the Caribbean Community (CARICOM). See eg S Caserta, 'Regional Integration Through Law and International Courts—The Interplay Between De Jure and De Facto Supranationality in Central America and the Caribbean' (2017) 30:3 LJIL 579, 588–91.

[150] See eg Z Kembayev, 'Eurasian Economic Union (EAEU)' in A Peters (ed), *Max Planck Encyclopedia of Public International Law* (OUP 2018) [36].

[151] Some of these forms would be considered as 'false regionalism' due to a lack of intra-regional commitment by Boisson de Chazournes, *Interactions* (n 14); see also M Salter and Y Yin 'Analysing Regionalism within International Law and Relations: The Shanghai Cooperation Organisation as a Grossraum?' (2014) 13 Chin J Int Law 819, 862; CPR Romano, 'Mirage in the Desert Regional Judicialization in the Arab World' in I de la Rasilla and JE Viñuales (eds), *Experiments in International Adjudication: Historical Accounts* (CUP 2019) 169, 185–86.

share a reliance on ideological idiosyncrasies of member States seeking to justify deviations from universal international law.[152] Unlike specialized regimes, where exceptions to general international law are justified based on effectiveness (*effet utile*), deviations from general international law contained in regional treaty rules tend to be based on identity claims, in particular, by reference to the community itself and notions of *ordre public*.[153]

Accordingly, the flipside to the greater identifiability of regional law may entail a more limited openness toward general international law, the non-negotiability of certain normative positions grounded in claims of exceptionalism,[154] and the potential for evasion, isolation, or disintegration from the broader international legal order through identity-based justifications, which undermines legal compliance.[155]

2.4.1.2 Between cohesion and autonomy?

The very factors that foster greater normative cohesion underlying regional law simultaneously fuel assertions of legal autonomy understood as the capacity to adopt special rules which deviate from or set aside general international rules.[156] In some instances, these claims to legal autonomy go so far as to assert that the regional legal order does not even qualify as international law.[157]

Historically, claims of regional legal autonomy have been most prominently, though not exclusively, articulated by the European Union (EU).[158] Practices reflecting such assertions predate the establishment of the EU; one of the earliest and most notable examples being the *Monroe Doctrine* of 1823.[159] Today, claims for autonomy are found across many regions and are particularly common in regional

[152] See already W Friedmann, *The Changing Structure of International Law* (Steven & Sons 1964) 62–63.

[153] See eg *Loizidou v Turkey* App 15318/89 (ECtHR, 23 March 1995) [75].

[154] See eg UNCLOT II, 72: 'Costa Rica, like other Latin American countries, formed part of a legal system that was more developed than many rules of international law . . . in any conflict that might arise between a customary rule of international law and the principles of inter-American law, Costa Rica could not accept the authority of the former.'

[155] See J Klabbers, 'Contending Approaches to International Organizations: Between Functionalism and Constitutionalism' in J Klabbers and A Wallendahl (eds), *Research Handbook on the Law of International Organizations* (Edward Elgar Publishing 2011) 3, 9; Besson, 'Politics of RIOs' (n 80) 112–13

[156] See further M Karliuk, *The Emerging Autonomous Legal Order of the Eurasian Economic Union* (CUP 2023) 17–37; B de Witte, 'European International Law' in R Schütze (ed), *Globalisation and Governance: International Problems, European Solutions* (CUP 2018) 227, 236–37.

[157] Bordin and Odermatt (n 26) 25 pointing to the EU, European Free Trade Association (EFTA), Andean Community (CAN), and Eurasian Economic Union (EAEU).

[158] See eg *Flaminio Costa v ENEL* Case 6/64 (ECJ, 15 July 1964) 593; J Odermatt, 'Unidentified Legal Object: Conceptualising the European Union in International Law' (2018) 33:2 Conn J Int Law 215–47; A Skordas, 'Supranational Law' in A Peters (ed), *Max Planck Encyclopedia of Public International Law* (OUP 2014) [39].

[159] US President James Monroe (n 61).

integration organizations equipped with a regional court,[160] though not limited to them.[161] While it is true that claims to autonomy in the form of 'self-contained regimes' have also emerged in the context of functional fragmentation,[162] autonomy claims rooted in normative regionalism possess a distinct character. While specialized regimes are still perceived as 'inter-connected islands'[163] within the realm of public international law, claims of regional autonomy are often framed in constitutional language.[164] Moreover, they are occasionally accompanied by assertions that the regional legal order is distinct from public international law and that the latter requires a separate act of recognition before it can be considered valid and applicable within the region.[165]

Assertions of regional autonomy are also reflected in recourse to distinct sources of law,[166] and the primacy of regional community law.[167] Moreover, some regional orders confer a distinct legal status to entities under regional international law, notably individuals,[168] or nature,[169] which is not universally recognized.

Accordingly, the same factors that lead to normative cohesion within a region as a building block for the development of general international law may also lead to an institutionalization of normative difference, the establishment and encapsulation of distinct legal spaces.

[160] Bordin and Odermatt (n 26) 26 pointing to the EU, EFTA, CAN, EAEU, East African Community (EAC), Organisation of Eastern Caribbean States (OECS), and Mercosur.

[161] See eg for the SCO and AIIB: Y Chen, 'Questionaire answers on Shanghai Cooperation Organization (SCO) & Asian Infrastructure Investment Bank (AIIB)' (13 April 2022) <https://www.ila-hq.org/en/study-groups/international-law-of-regional-organisations> (accessed 5 May 2026).

[162] See A Marschik, 'Too Much Order? The Impact of Special Secondary Norms on the Unity and Efficacy of the International Legal System' (1998) 9 EJIL 212, 214.

[163] J Pauwelyn, 'Bridging Fragmentation and Unity: International Law as a Universe of Inter-Connected Islands' (2004) 25:4 Mich J Int Law 903–16.

[164] See eg *Al-Dulimi and Montana Management Inc v Switzerland* App 5809/08 (ECtHR, 21 June 2016) [145]; *Kadi and Al Barakaat International Foundation v Council and Commission* C-402/05 P and C-415/05 P (CJEU, 3 September 2008) [281].

[165] See eg Andean Court of Justice: *Acción de incumplimiento planteada por Caracol Televisión SA y RCN Televisión SA contra la República de Colombia*, Cases 1 and 2-AI-2018 (ACJ, 1 February 2024) [3.1.2] confirming a long line of jurisprudence since its decision in ACJ, Case 89-AI-2000 (28 September 2001). See de Witte, 'European International Law' (n 156) 235–41 with references to the jurisprudence of the CJEU.

[166] See eg *Frontier Dispute (Burkina Faso/Niger)* [2013] ICJ Rep 134 (separate opinion of Judge Yusuf) [26] and [29]; A Jabri, 'Questionnaire answers on the Middle East & Arab World' <https://www.ila-hq.org/en/study-groups/international-law-of-regional-organisations> (accessed 5 May 2026) 1–3, 12, 17.

[167] See eg *Myrie v Barbados* App No OA 002 of 2012, CCJ 3 (OJ) (CCJ, 4 October 2013) [51]–[54].

[168] See eg PJ Neuvonen, 'Transforming Membership? Citizenship, Identity and the Problem of Belonging in Regional Integration Organizations' (2019) 30:1 EJIL 229.

[169] See Bolivia ('Ley de Derechos de la Madre Tierra' Ley 071 (December 2010)), Brazil (Municipality of Linhares (Brazil) Law on the Rights of the Waves (12 August 2024)), Colombia (Constitutional Court of Colombia, Judgment T-622 (10 November 2016)), Ecuador (Articles 10 and Chapter 7, Articles 71–74 of the Ecuadorian Constitution, amended in 2008), Panama (Ley No 287 (24 February 2022)), and Peru (*Federación Huaynakana Kamatahuara Kana v Petroperú SA, Ministry of the Environment and others*, Civil Chamber of the Superior Court of Justice of Loreto, 00010-2022-0-1901-JM-CI-01 (29 August 2024) recognizing the legal rights of the Marañon River) in the Latin American region.

2.4.1.3 Between distinctiveness and alternativity?

The characteristic non-generalizability of regional law facilitates its acceptance by third parties, to the extent that such legal claims are not presented as universally applicable but are instead rooted in specific geographic and political contexts.[170] This inherent limitation of scope, however, can be accompanied by a claim to normative alternativity, grounded in a region's distinct geographical circumstances or its divergent approach to political self-organization.[171] Whereas functional fragmentation within international law typically asserts speciality—distinguishing itself from general international law by focusing on particular subject areas—regional international law does not primarily rest on a claim to speciality. Rather, it articulates a claim of alternativity or complementarity. Regional legal orders are not merely derivative or specialized subsets of the general international legal framework; they represent qualitatively distinct normative projects. They are not 'more of the same', but rather 'different from the rest'. This alternativity goes beyond the protection of identity or mere insulation from general international law. Instead, it involves an active effort to establish and institutionalize normative divergence within the broader international legal order. It manifests itself through deliberate counter-norming,[172] by the introduction of a special status for (certain) regional organizations,[173] region-specific legal concepts,[174] reservations,[175] limitations and exceptions,[176] and the establishment of alternative institutions.[177]

2.4.2 The methodological challenge: elusive legal nature

The question is whether criteria exist by which the analytical challenge posed by regional law can be addressed, allowing us to understand at what point regional exclusivity does not 'help to bring international law home'[178] but rather undermines

[170] But see Chapter 7 on the extent to which regional practice shapes international law beyond the region.

[171] See HL Buxbaum, 'Territory, Territoriality, and the Resolution of Jurisdictional Conflict' (2009) 57:3 AJCL 631, 635.

[172] See on this: Cooley and Schaf (n 139) 159–88.

[173] See eg the practice of insisting on disconnection clauses by the EU.

[174] See eg the reference to Islamic law in the Convention on the Rights of the Child (adopted 20 November 1989, entry into force 2 September 1990) 1577 UNTS 3, art 20(3).

[175] See eg reservations on the Convention on the Elimination of All Forms of Discrimination Against Women (adopted 18 December 1979, entered into force 3 September 1981) 1249 UNTS 13 by members of the OIC and League of Arab States.

[176] See eg Constitutive Act of the AU (done 11 July 2000, entered into force 26 May 2001) 2158 UNTS 3, art 4(h); Preamble of the Charter of the Organization of the Islamic Conference (adopted 14 March 2008, entered into force 3 September 2009).

[177] Romano (n 151) 181–83; see further the establishment of the Bolivarian Alliance for the Peoples of Our America ('ALBA'), the AIIB, and the African Criminal Court.

[178] See HP Aust, 'The Rules of Interpretation as Secondary Rules: The Perspective of Domestic Courts' in M Heupel and T Reinold (eds), *The Rule of Law in Global Governance* (Palgrave Macmillan 2016) 59, 60 on a similar question regarding domestic courts.

the common framework of international law. One (perhaps intuitive) approach would be to examine regional law by drawing on well-established doctrinal categories of particular law, in order to understand the extent to which these provide a transposable method for regulating relations between general international law and regional law. However, as this section demonstrates, such an approach offers only limited guidance. This is because, unlike non-regional particular international law, the legal character of regional law is elusive, oscillating between legal forms that resemble non-regional particular international law and more idiosyncratic manifestations.[179]

2.4.2.1 Particular international law

For the most part, regional law is understood as a form of particular international law.[180] No distinction is made between particular international law with a regional scope of application, and legal regimes which deal with a specific area of law.[181] Yet, regional law challenges the framework envisaged for particular international law in at least two respects.

Firstly, the secondary rules on 'particular international law' are tailored to 'particular treaties'. Article 38(1)(a) of the ICJ Statute refers to 'particular' in addition to 'general conventions'. The 2006 Fragmentation Report barely touched upon unwritten particular law and focussed on conflicts arising from treaties. Yet, claims regarding the existence of unwritten regional law are more common than proclamations of unwritten sectorial law.[182] The existence of unwritten regional law, and its recognition under Article 38(1)(b) and (c) of the ICJ Statute as well as Articles 53 and 64 VCLT, however, remain obscure; most likely because of the ostensible tension between the respective wording of the provisions ('general', 'international community as a whole') and the regionally limited character of such rules. Secondly, not all forms of regional law can be conceived of as 'special' in the sense of 'sectorial' law.[183] Many regional regimes do not deal with a specific area but, on the contrary, claim normative completeness and autonomy.[184]

2.4.2.2 Domestic law

The claim of normative completeness and autonomy has traditionally evoked comparisons of regional law with domestic law (instead of international law). Certain forms of regional law are characterized by a dense interweaving of international law with domestic law. Historically, the status of the Soviet Republics and the relationship between the members of the British Commonwealth are particularly striking

[179] See also Besson and Kassoti (n 16) 5–6.
[180] Fragmentation Report (n 3) [216].
[181] Fragmentation Report (n 3).
[182] See section 5.1.
[183] See examples in sections 2.4.1.1 and 2.4.1.2.
[184] See JHF Van Panhuys, 'Regional or General International Law? A Misleading Dilemma' (1961) 8:2 Neth Int Law Rev 146, 162–63.

examples,[185] whereas the EU offers contemporary practice in this regard.[186] In the ILC, the question of the relationship of regional law to municipal law arose as early as 1963, when the Commission debated what was to later become Article 48 VCLT (Error).[187] Mustafa Kamil Yasseen questioned the distinction between an error of fact and an error of law precisely by pointing to the hybrid nature of regional law:

> Admittedly, the Permanent Court of International Justice had tended to regard municipal law as a fact; but what was the status of regional international law? If, for example, a Latin-American country concluded a treaty with an Asian country and the latter committed an error with regard to Latin-American international law, should that error be regarded as an error of law? Ignorance of the law was no excuse, but an Asian country could hardly be expected to know Latin-American law.[188]

This question divided the ILC as well as States at the Vienna Conference.[189] Eventually, a compromise was struck by the formulation 'error relat[ing] to a fact or a situation'. According to this compromise, an error of law is exceptionally relevant (namely, a State may invoke it in order to invalidate its prior consent to a treaty) so long as it is based on facts, which arguably encompasses an error about regional law by a non-regional State.[190]

The curious character of regional law has also been pointed out in several decisions of international courts and tribunals. In its 1980 Advisory Opinion on the *Interpretation of the 1951 Agreement between the WHO and Egypt*, the ICJ seemed perplexed by the question as to whether the Alexandria Sanitary Bureau was a regional IO in the sense of Article 54 of the WHO Statute or an organ of the Egyptian State.[191] A number of arbitral tribunals addressed the 'dual' legal nature of EU law in the aftermath of the CJEU's *Achmea* decision.[192] Another such example relates to a recent debate between the EU and the UN concerning the General Data Protection Regulation (GDPR)—on whether to apply Articles 30 and 41 VCLT,

[185] *Sovereignty over Pedra Branca/Pulau Batu Puteh, Middle Rocks and South Ledge (Malaysia/Singapore)* [2008] ICJ Rep 133 (Diss Op Judge ad hoc John Dugard) 138–39 (nature of *inter se* agreements).

[186] See also J Crawford, 'Continuity and Discontinuity in International Dispute Settlement: An Inaugural Lecture' (2010) 1(1) J Int Dispute Settl 3, 4.

[187] ILC, 'Summary records of the fifteenth session from 6 May to 12 July 1963' (1963) YBILC I, UN Doc A/CN.4/SER.A/1963, 44–45, 44–45.

[188] ILC (n 187) 44 [70].

[189] See ILC, 'Documents of the fifteenth session including the report of the Commission to the General Assembly' (1963) YBILC II, UN Doc A/CN.4/SER.A/1963/ADD.1, 196 44–45 [71]–[75].

[190] T Rensmann, 'Article 48' in O Dörr and K Schmalenbach (eds), *Vienna Convention on the Law of Treaties: A Commentary* (2nd edn, Springer 2018) [21]–[22].

[191] *Interpretation of the Agreement of 25 March 1951 between the WHO and Egypt* (Advisory Opinion) [1980] ICJ Rep 73 [14].

[192] *Eskosol SpA v Italy* (Decision on Termination Request and Intra-EU Objection) ICSID Case No ARB/15/50 (7 May 2019) [173]; *AES Summit Generation Limited and AES-Tisza Erömü Kft v The Republic of Hungary* (Award) ICSID Case No ARB/07/22 (23 September 2010) [7.6.6].

ie provisions dealing with particular international law, or rather Article 27 VCLT, which concerns domestic law, to such EU law.[193]

Are these forms of regional law to be treated as domestic law or as international law? The practical consequences of such a distinction become clear when comparing the way in which Article 38(1) of the ICJ Statute, the VCLTs of 1969 and 1986, and also the Articles on Responsibility of States for Internationally Wrongful Acts (ARSIWA) treat the legal effects of (particular) international law and domestic law for third parties, respectively. In contrast to particular international law, domestic laws are 'merely facts' on the international plane.[194] Since a State cannot be expected to know the domestic law of another State—which is highly particular—the universal secondary rules protect that State from any adverse effects of this asymmetry.[195] However, to regard regional law as either forming part of particular international law or as resembling domestic law is an oversimplification. Over the past decades, several other doctrinal categories have emerged to capture the characteristic aspects of regional law.

2.4.2.3 Institutional law

A high degree of autonomy is granted to regional law to the extent that it qualifies as internal institutional law of a given regional organization.[196] Throughout the VCLT, its provisions reserve a special role for the 'competent organ of the IO' leaving unaltered 'relevant rules of the organization'[197] for the interpretation of its constituent instrument.[198] Without going further into the debate about the legal nature of the 'rules of the organization' at this point,[199] their legal effect has been aptly described as 'to some extent closed off from general international law'.[200] The reason for this separation from general international law, that is, from the rules

[193] See eg 'Comments of the United Nations Secretariat on behalf of the United Nations System Organizations on the "Guidelines 2/2020 on articles 46(2)(a) and 46(3)(b) of Regulation 2016/679 for transfers of personal data between EEA and non-EEA public authorities and bodies" adopted by the European Data Protection Board on 18 January 2020' (14 May 2020) 17 [47].

[194] See also *Certain German Interests in Polish Upper Silesia (Germany v Poland)* (Merits) [1926] PCIJ Series A, No 7, 19.

[195] Domestic law is not applicable before the ICJ (Article 38(1) ICJ-Statute) and internal law cannot be invoked as a justification for non-performance of an international obligation (Article 27 VCLT and Article 32 of the ILC, 'Articles on the Responsibility of States for Internationally Wrongful Acts' (2001) YBILC II(2) UN Doc A/56/10). Provided that the violation is not manifest and does not concern a rule of fundamental importance, a lack of competence does not invalidate consent given to a treaty (Article 46 VCLT). The error of a third party about the domestic law of its treaty partner may amount to a relevant error about facts (Article 48 VCLT).

[196] On this, see Bordin and Odermatt (n 26) 24–27.

[197] 1969 VCLT, art 5.

[198] 1986 VCLT, arts 20(3) (Reservations) and 77(2) (Depositary).

[199] See on the question on whether it is part of public international law or rather comparable to the internal law of States: the commentary on Article 10, ILC, 'Draft Articles on the Responsibility of International Organizations, with commentaries' (2011) YBILC II(2), UN Doc UN Doc A/66/10, 52, 99–100. See also Chapter 7, section 7.3.2.4.

[200] C Brölmann, 'Typologies and the "Essential Juridical Character" of Treaties' in MJ Bowman and D Kritsiotis (eds), *Conceptual and Contextual Perspectives on the Modern Law of Treaties* (CUP 2018) 79, 91.

shared by members and non-members of the institution, is simply that they 'do not have legal effects in relation to third subjects'.[201] While member States of the respective regional IO can thus expect third parties to recognize their regulatory autonomy, they cannot expect third parties to know about their internal law: for this reason, various provisions in the 1986 VCLT equate the legal effects of internal institutional law with that of the domestic law of States.[202]

2.4.2.4 Supranational law

Forms of regional law characterized by 'normative completeness' and claims to legal autonomy are often associated with yet another doctrinal category: supranational law.[203] Being mostly defined by an entanglement of domestic and public international law,[204] this form of regional law has been characterized as

> a hybrid constantly moving across the international and the domestic, never fully abandoning the former, and never fully mutating into the latter; its distinctiveness is materialized through this non resolvable tension.[205]

Supranational law is frequently—but not exclusively—associated with the law on European integration. The Court of Cartago, established in Central America in 1907, could be understood as the first supranational court.[206] Other, more contemporary examples outside the context of EU-integration include CARICOM and its Caribbean Court of Justice,[207] the Andean Tribunal,[208] the Eurasian Economic Union,[209] Islamic law,[210] the AU legal order,[211] and a number of supranational courts in Africa.[212]

[201] P Palchetti, 'Halfway Between Fragmentation and Convergence: The Role of the Rules of the Organization in the Interpretation of Constituent Treaties' in M Andenas and E Bjorge (eds), *A Farewell to Fragmentation—Reassertion and Convergence in International Law* (CUP 2015) 486, 493.

[202] See 1986 VCLT, arts 27(2) and 46.

[203] See for that terminology: Brölmann 2018 (n 200) 89–91; Karliuk (n 156) 37–42.

[204] See R Schütze, *From Dual to Cooperative Federalism: The Changing Structure of European Law* (OUP 2009) 3.

[205] Skordas (n 158) [58].

[206] F Baetens, 'First to Rise and First to Fall The Court of Cartago (1907–1918)' in I de la Rasilla and JE Viñuales (eds), *Experiments in International Adjudication: Historical Accounts* (CUP 2019) 211.

[207] *In the matter of a request for an Advisory Opinion by the Caribbean Community pursuant to Article 212 of the Revised Treaty of Chaguaramas and Rule 11.3(1) of the Caribbean Court of Justice (Original Jurisdiction) Rules 2019* App No AOOJ2019/001 (CCJ, 18 March 2020) [58].

[208] See eg infringement proceedings (Treaty Creating the Court of Justice of the Cartagena Agreement (signed 28 May 1979, entered into force 19 May 1983) 18 (1979) 5 ILM 1203, arts 17 and 18).

[209] See Protocol on the Eurasian Economic Commission, Annex 1 to the Treaty on the Eurasian Economic Union (signed 29 May 2014, entered into force 1 January 2015), art 1(13) (authorizing the Commission to take binding decisions which 'shall be a part of the contractual legal basis of the EAEU and be subject to direct application on the territories of the member States.').

[210] H Thirlway, *The Sources of International Law* (2nd edn, OUP 2019) 32.

[211] O Amao, *African Union Law. The Emergence of a Sui Generis Legal Order* (Hart 2018) 18–22, 26, 45.

[212] See R Murray and K Oteng Kufuor (eds), 'The Judicial Power of Africa's Supranational Courts' (2020) 28 AJICL 1–158.

Yet, supranational law poses a challenge for third States and IOs in that it deviates from other forms of particular international law in substance and form. From a substantive point of view, supranational law typically 'internationalizes' areas of law that have traditionally been part of the *domaine réservé* of States. At the same time, supranational organs are often endowed with (exclusive) competences of an adjudicative, legislative, or executive nature. Thus, the assumption of 'structural similarity', which underlies the universal secondary rules on 'particular international law', reaches its limits in the face of the highly complex and allegedly *sui generis* character of supranational law. Third parties face considerable difficulties when trying to predict the potential legal effects of supranational law and to identify the respectively competent organ.

2.4.2.5 Transnational law

The category of 'particular international law' further reaches its limits when turning to regional law involving non-State entities across territorial borders in a certain geographic area. The ILC has refrained from attributing an independent role to non-State actors in the formation of international law. The latter are largely understood to play only an indirect role in the identification and interpretation of international law to the extent that they reflect or initiate State practice.[213]

The practice of international courts and tribunals—while by and large concordant with the above approach—seems to be more liberal when it comes to 'traditional rights' or 'local custom' involving non-State actors that pertain to territorial rights or the use of a certain geographical feature. The nature of this form of localized law was addressed in the *Western Sahara* Advisory Opinion of 1975, where the Court noted the existence of

> certain ties of a legal character between the tribes of the territory and those of neighbouring regions. . . Furthermore, the relations between all the tribes of the region in such matters as inter-tribal clashes and the settlement of disputes were also governed by a body of inter-tribal custom. Before the time of Western Sahara's colonization by Spain, those legal ties neither had nor could have any other source than the usages of the tribes themselves or Koranic law. . . They were ties which knew no frontier between the territories and were vital to the very maintenance of life in the region.[214]

Case law reflects three main ways in which these forms of local law can be translated to the international level. Firstly, the conduct of private actors can be understood,

[213] ILC Report 2018 (CIL) (n 20), Conclusion 4(3), 132; ILC, 'Draft Conclusions on Subsequent Agreements and Subsequent Practice in relation to the Interpretation of Treaties, with Commentaries' (2018) UN Doc A/73/10, Conclusion 5(2).

[214] *Western Sahara (Advisory Opinion)* [1975] ICJ Rep 12 [152].

under certain circumstances, as having been adopted by the respective State as its own.[215] Courts, secondly, have assessed whether the respective States recognized the entity as being capable of entering into legal obligations with another State.[216] Thirdly, a local practice involving non-State entities may be recognized by courts as binding on the respective States under what is called the principle of traditional, acquired, or vested rights.[217]

In recent years, courts have been increasingly confronted with transnational law in the form of indigenous peoples' rights. In 2007, the General Assembly adopted a resolution on the rights of indigenous people which recognizes, inter alia, their 'right to promote, develop and maintain their institutional structures and their distinctive customs, spirituality, traditions, procedures, practices and, in the cases where they exist, juridical systems or customs'.[218] It remains to be seen whether courts will treat indigenous peoples' rights as a form of traditional right or as yet another category of (international) law.[219]

2.4.3 The normative challenge: contested common denominator

In the absence of a transposable methodological taxonomy, the analytical challenge posed by regional international law shifts to its normative dimension. To distinguish the potentially corrosive from constructive effects of regional legal claims, it is essential to identify a normative reference point—a common denominator—whereby which regional practices, rules, and institutions can be meaningfully evaluated. Yet, the three possible candidates for a common denominator, namely, universal community interests (2.4.3.1), the international rule of law (2.4.3.2), and State sovereignty (2.4.3.3), tend to be either too rigid to respond to regional claims to identity, autonomy, and alternativity, or too abstract and indeterminate to base an analytical distinction on it.

[215] *Navigational and Related Rights* (n 11) [141]; but see *Eritrea/Yemen (Territorial Sovereignty and Scope of the Dispute)* (1998) 22 UNRIAA 209, 288 [340]; *Kasikili/Sedudu Island (Botswana v Namibia)* [1999] ICJ Rep 1045 [74]–[75].

[216] *Western Sahara* (n 214) [95] and [107] (Sherifian State); *Land and Maritime Boundary between Cameroon and Nigeria (Cameroon v Nigeria: Equatorial Guinea intervening)* [2002] ICJ Rep 303 [203] (agreements concluded with local rulers).

[217] *Frontier Dispute (Burkina Faso/Mali)* [1986] ICJ Rep 554 [116]; *Land, Island and Maritime Frontier Dispute (El Salvador/Honduras; Nicaragua intervening)* [1992] ICJ Rep 351 [66]; *Government of Sudan v Sudan People's Liberation Movement/Army (Abyei Arbitration) (Final Award)* PCA Case 2008-07 (22 July 2009) [759]; *Certain German Interests* [1926] (n 194) 42; see also separate opinion of Judge Sepúlveda-Amor, *Navigational and Related Rights* (n 11) 280 [28]; *Alleged Violations of Sovereign Rights and Maritime Spaces in the Caribbean Sea (Nicaragua v Colombia)* [2022] ICJ Rep 266 [201]–[221].

[218] UNGA, 'United Nations Declaration on the Rights of Indigenous Peoples' (13 September 2007) UN Doc A/RES/61/295, art 34, was adopted by a majority of 143 states in favour, 4 votes against, and 11 abstentions.

[219] See *Alleged Violations (Nicaragua v Colombia)* (n 217) 435 (dissenting opinion Judge ad hoc McRae) [50]–[70].

2.4.3.1 Universal community interests or imposition?

In seeking a common standard, international lawyers typically assess regional conduct against 'universal' rules. Yet, recurrent abuses of the language of 'universality' have been grist to the mills of those who criticize such invocations as a hegemonic imposition.[220] Without subscribing to the often-cited cynical adage that 'whoever invokes humanity wants to cheat',[221] identifying genuinely universal rules is still a difficult task, not least because the very notion of universality is itself far from settled.[222]

'Universal' may refer to rules which have a universal scope *ratione personae* insofar as they have been consented to by a large number of States.[223] Such a quantitative understanding of 'universality' includes a wide array of treaties, such as the UN Charter, but also various international copyright agreements.[224] It is doubtful whether the rules set out in the UN Charter and in the agreements on copyrights are of an equally fundamental nature. Furthermore, the fact that rules are accepted by many States does not mean per se that these rules are set in stone. States may submit reservations, conclude modifying agreements *inter se*, withdraw from agreements, arguably persistently object to being bound by customary international law, or adopt a treaty or special custom that prevails over a general custom.[225]

'Universal' legal rules could also designate rules which are universal *ratione materiae*, reflecting 'community interests'.[226] One possible approach to identifying such rules is to focus on norms the normative intensity of which is such that all States regard them as constituting a substantive legal minimum.[227] In recent decades, three groups of such rules have emerged in the practice of States: peremptory norms of general international law (*jus cogens*),[228] obligations *erga omnes*,[229]

[220] See eg E Jouannet, 'Universalism and Imperialism: The True-False Paradox of International Law?' (2007) 18:3 EJIL 379, 382–85; see also P Weil, 'Towards Relative Normativity in International Law' (1983) 77:3 AJIL 413, 422–30.

[221] C Schmitt, *The Concept of the Political*, G Schwab, trans (University of Chicago Press 2007) 54.

[222] See B Simma, 'Universality of International Law from the Perspective of the Practitioner' (2009) 20:2 EJIL 265, 267–68.

[223] See eg the ICJ in *Application of the International Convention on the Elimination of All Forms of Racial Discrimination (Qatar v United Arab Emirates)* [2021] ICJ Rep 71 [87] ('CERD, whose universal character is confirmed by the fact that 182 States are parties to it . . . ').

[224] See eg Convention Establishing the World Intellectual Property Organization (signed 14 July 1967, entered into force 26 April 1970) 828 UNTS 3 (193 member States).

[225] See ILC, Report 2018 (CIL) (n 20) 152–54, Conclusion 15 ('Persistent Objector'); *Right of Passage* (n 23) 44; Fragmentation Report (n 3) [84].

[226] F Hoffmeister and T Kleinlein, 'International Public Order' in A Peters (ed), *Max Planck Encyclopedia of Public International Law* (OUP 2019) [2]–[3].

[227] B Simma, 'From Bilateralism to Community Interests in International Law' (1994) 250 RdC 217, 233.

[228] See VCLT, arts 53 and 64; see also F Lange, 'Challenging the Paris Peace Treaties, State Sovereignty, and Western-Dominated International Law—The Multifaceted Genesis of the Jus Cogens Doctrine' (2018) 31:4 LJIL 821–39.

[229] See eg *Barcelona Traction, Light and Power Co Ltd (Belgium v Spain)* [1970] ICJ Rep 3 [33]; *East Timor (Portugal v Australia)* [1995] ICJ Rep 90 [29]; *Legal Consequences of the Construction of a Wall in the Occupied Palestinian Territory* (Advisory Opinion) [2004] ICJ Rep 136 [155]–[157].

and rules which protect the 'common heritage of mankind'.[230] However, this approach offers only limited practical guidance in identifying a concrete set of rules as a common denominator in the face of regional plurality in that it merely shifts the problem to another level, namely to the challenge of determining the specific content of the purportedly universal rule.[231]

2.4.3.2 Rule of law or hypocrisy?

The 'international rule of law' presents another potential candidate for a common denominator in the context of regional international law, as references to the 'rule of law' frequently appear in the constituent instruments of regional IOs, where it is often designated as a core value.[232] Yet, once again, the content of this concept is deeply contested.[233] It is often seen, moreover, as a 'Trojan Horse' by means of which powerful States promote their own values, only to disregard those same values when it suits their interests.[234]

It is neither feasible nor necessary to provide an exhaustive discussion of the various approaches to the 'international rule of law' here.[235] Yet, even were one to adopt a minimalist definition—grounded in three core elements, namely, equality before the law, legal certainty, and legality, which commonly appear as the baseline components of the 'international rule of law'[236]—then the limitations of the concept as a common denominator in the face of regional plurality become readily apparent.

Equality before the law, prominently embodied in the sovereign equality of States, finds itself in tension with regional international law which frequently claims special legal treatment based on regional affiliation ('regional exceptionalism'). Claims of regional particularity not only affect third States but may also result in the formation of 'geolegal' spheres of influence which deprive weaker States

[230] See eg the Deep Seabed: UNGA, 'Declaration of Principles Governing the Sea-Bed and the Ocean Floor, and the Subsoil Thereof, beyond the Limits of National Jurisdiction' (17 December 1970) UN Doc A/RES/2749(XXV); UNCLOS, arts 136 and 311(6).

[231] See eg the controversies on *jus cogens*: UNGA, 'Topical summary of the discussion held in the Sixth Committee' (2018) UN Doc A/CN.4/724 [17] (effect on resolutions of IOs) [24] (universal jurisdiction) and [25] (immunity).

[232] See EU (Art 2 TEU), the Council of Europe (Statute of the Council of Europe (adopted 5 May 1949, entered into force 3 August 1949) 87 UNTS 103, art 3); the OAS (Protocol of Washington (14 December 1991), OEA/Ser.A/2 Add. 3), AU (Article 4(m) of the Constitutive Act of the African Union); ASEAN (Art 2(h) of the 2007 ASEAN Charter); ECOWAS (Protocol relating to the Mechanism for Conflict Prevention, Management, Resolution, Peace-Keeping and Security (signed and provisionally entered into force 10 December 1999)) ('Lomé Protocol'), ECOWAS Doc A/P10/12/99 (1999); International Conference on the Great Lakes Region (Pact on Security, Stability and Development in the Great Lakes Region (adopted 15 December 2006, entered into force 21 June 2008) 46 ILM 175, art 6).

[233] See eg S Chesterman, 'An International Rule of Law?' (2008) 56:2 AJIL 331–62, 341–43.

[234] See eg S Pahuja, *Decolonizing International Law* (CUP 2011) 172–253; JA Dugard, 'The Choice Before Us: International Law or a "Rules-based International Order"?' (2023) 36:2 LJIL 223–32.

[235] On these discussions: Chesterman (n 233) 333–42.

[236] Chesterman (n 233) 359–60.

within the region of equal rights vis-à-vis more powerful States.[237] And yet, regionalism does not necessarily undermine (sovereign) equality. It also serves to counter the *de facto* existing inequality between States by uniting smaller States and allowing them to pursue their normative projects at eye-level vis-à-vis more powerful States.

Legal certainty is put under pressure by the establishment of parallel or even alternative regional norms and institutions: the emergence of regional norms and institutions often goes unnoticed by third parties, unfamiliar as the latter are with regional norm-setting processes and despite being—at least indirectly—affected by it. The interpretation of overlapping rules by competing authorities further complicates the understanding of the scope of legal rights and obligations. Finally, States are induced to engage in 'cherry-picking' between diverging regional and non-regional international law. At the same time, regional institutions also contribute to 'vernaculariz[ing]' and thus to stabilizing the application of rules, as well as to adapting them to changes, which is particularly important in the decentralized international legal system.[238]

Finally, regional conduct could also be measured against the element of legality understood as the supremacy of law as an ordering mechanism.[239] However, regional initiatives also set incentives to disengage from existing forms of universal legal co-operation, block emerging rules, or suggest the withdrawal from judicial third-party dispute settlement.[240] At the same time, whether a 'reduction' of legal obligations as such has a corrosive effect remains doubtful. Collective withdrawal from a legal institution can also be a form of productive protest against a lack of representation therein, a means to push forward an overdue reform process, or may even be the result of establishing a new organization.

2.4.3.3 Sovereignty or hegemony?

Another potential candidate for a common denominator that could serve as a basis for deriving common legal rules is sovereignty and the 'set of minimal legal rules governing the interactions between a plurality of sovereign institutions'.[241] Following a classic understanding of international law, it is 'State sovereignty' which is 'the fundamental principle [. . .] on which the whole of international

[237] See M Jorgensen, 'Equilibrium & Fragmentation in The International Rule of Law: The Rising Chinese Geolegal Order', *KFG Working Paper Series, No 21* (November 2018).

[238] See eg Prost (n 40) 36.

[239] Highlighting the 'intrinsic value which law offers (Eigenwert des Rechts) in comparison to other normative orders' (H Krieger and G Nolte, 'The International Rule of Law—Rise or Decline?—Approaching Current Foundational Challenges' in H Krieger and others (eds), *The International Rule of Law: Rise or Decline?* (OUP 2019) 3, 7).

[240] G Werle and M Vormbaum, 'African States, the African Union, and the International Criminal Court: A Continuing Story' (2018) 60(1) Ger Yearb Int Law 17–42.

[241] Besson, 'Politics of RIOs' (n 80) 96.

law rests'.[242] 'Sovereignty' is usually understood as 'supreme political authority of a given public institution, usually a State'.[243] State sovereignty has two main implications, namely, that States cannot be bound to any legal obligation without their consent,[244] and their sovereign equality.[245]

Yet, treating State sovereignty as a normative benchmark against which regional acts could be measured is not free from difficulties. Regional international law often reflects a claim of representation which often coincides, but sometimes also challenges that embodied by the respective States.[246] Certain regional political orders, such as local communities connected by religious bounds or personal allegiance, have successfully claimed a legal status comparable to that of States when it comes to the validity of territorial agreements.[247] Concepts such as 'limited' or 'hybrid' sovereignty, or the *Monroe Doctrine* according to which States pertaining to a region (allegedly) submit to a regional hegemon, have been adopted both by the Soviet Union and the US vis-à-vis formally independent States within their region. Finally, supranational legal orders, not only the EU, claim to constitute a 'legal order *sui generis*',[248] being

> a new legal order of international law for the benefit of which the states have limited their sovereign rights, albeit within limited fields and the subjects of which comprise not only member states but also their nationals.[249]

Each of these examples has inspired scholars from otherwise widely opposing ideological camps to criticize what, in their eyes, amounts to inadequate subjugation of regional political orders under the concept of State sovereignty. From a critical perspective, the focus on State sovereignty is an expression of Western hegemony which unduly excludes other forms of collective political self-organization, such as tribes or religious communities,[250] as well as 'civilizations'.[251] Carl Schmitt,

[242] *Military and Paramilitary Activities in and against Nicaragua (Nicaragua v United States)* (Merits) [1986] ICJ Rep 14 [263].

[243] Besson, 'Politics of RIOs' (n 80) 93–96, in particular 93.

[244] *The Case of the SS 'Lotus'* (Judgment) [1927] PCIJ Series A, No 10, 18–19.

[245] *Military and Paramilitary Activities in and against Nicaragua (Nicaragua v United States)* (Merits) [1986] ICJ Rep 14 [202].

[246] See MS McDougal and HD Lasswell, 'The Identification and Appraisal of Diverse Systems of Public Order' (1959) 53:1 AJIL 1, 19.

[247] See eg *Right of Passage* (n 23) 37; *Western Sahara* (n 214) 39; *Cameroon v Nigeria: Equatorial Guinea intervening* (n 216) [203].

[248] See eg *SP v Commission* Case T-27/03 (Court of First Instance of the EC, 25 October 2007) [58]; see also for examples other than the EU: ILA Report (2024) (n 9) 12–13.

[249] *Van Gend & Loos v Netherlands Inland Revenue Administration* Case 26/62 (ECJ, 5 February 1963) 12.

[250] A Anghie, *Imperialism, Sovereignty, and the Making of International Law* (CUP 2004) 103–105; BS Chimni, 'International Institutions Today: An Imperial Global State in the Making' (2004) 15:1 EJIL 1, 17–19; Pahuja (n 234) 5–6, 46.

[251] Y Onuma, *International Law in a Transcivilizational World* (CUP 2017) 58–63.

analogizing the *Monroe Doctrine*, argued that the concept of the State did not reflect the reality of political self-organization as a concrete unity of political idea and space.[252] Dismissing the concept of the State as obsolete[253] and sovereign equality as fictitious,[254] he suggested replacing an order based on State sovereignty by one based on spatial orders, realms, and peoples.[255] From yet a different angle, Jürgen Habermas points to the role played by individuals which would transcend the regulatory capacity of States requiring supranational—regional—approaches to 'global governance'.[256] Even from a doctrinal-positivist perspective the central role of States has been criticized as taking insufficient account of regional institutions. While otherwise defending the focus on the State as 'the most comprehensive law-based organisation within its domain', Joseph Raz also admits that 'regional organisations are the most likely to absorb and replace the states as we know them'.[257] More recently, Samantha Besson proposed to abandon the idea that sovereignty is exclusive to States and suggests recognizing 'a shared and partial' sovereignty of regions.[258]

Still, State sovereignty has, to date, not been replaced by sovereignty arising from 'regionhood'.[259] Regional communities at the sub-national level have either been treated as 'State[s] of a special character'[260] or their recognition was based on an act of recognition on the part of the States with whom they interacted.[261] The same applies to the EU, many idiosyncrasies of which have been traced back to the consent of member States.[262] The underlying reasons for the continued adherence to sovereignty as arising from statehood are twofold. From the perspective of third parties, this formal concept offers legal certainty—a presumption regarding the existence of specific powers vested in a unit claiming to realize the self-determination of a people—particularly given that the notion of the 'region' has so far been lacking criteria as clear and as established as those that define statehood. From the

[252] C Schmitt, *Völkerrechtliche Großraumordnung mit Interventionsverbot für raumfremde Mächte* (3rd edn in the version of 1941, Duncker & Humblot 2009) 29 and 51.
[253] Schmitt (n 252) 55.
[254] Schmitt (n 252) 54.
[255] Schmitt (n 252) 51 and 62.
[256] J Habermas, 'Making Sense of the EU: Toward a Cosmopolitan Europe' (2003) 14:4 J Democr 86, 95–99.
[257] J Raz, 'Why the State?' in N Roughan and A Halpin (eds), *In Pursuit of Pluralist Jurisprudence* (CUP 2018) 136, 155.
[258] Besson, 'Politics of RIOs' (n 80) in particular 96–104.
[259] See on the concept of 'regionhood': Van Langenhove (n 80).
[260] *Western Sahara* (n 214) 44 [95]. See, in contrast, Singapore's assertion of a 'traditional Malay concept of sovereignty' based on personal allegiance which was briskly rejected by the ICJ observing 'that sovereignty comprises both elements, personal and territorial' (*Sovereignty over Pedra Branca/Pulau Batu Puteh, Middle Rocks and South Ledge (Malaysia/Singapore)* [2008] ICJ Rep 12 [79]).
[261] See eg *Western Sahara* (n 214) 39 [80]); see further K Schmalenbach, 'Article 3' in O Dörr and K Schmalenbach (eds), *Vienna Convention on the Law of Treaties: A Commentary* (2nd edn, Springer 2018) [56]–[58].
[262] See B de Witte, 'European International Law' (n 156) 228–31.

perspective of States within a given region, the principles of State consent and sovereign equality—as expressions of State sovereignty—serve to safeguard the plurality of political self-organization and to protect the self-determination of peoples who meet the criteria of statehood from encroachment by regional hegemons.

Yet, while State sovereignty, for the time being, represents a substantive common denominator, three caveats are necessary. First, the exclusive character of sovereignty must not be misunderstood to mean exclusive legal personality for States. Second, to the extent that 'regionhood' is at all identifiable in a way that is equivalent to statehood while ensuring free and equal political representation and internal self-determination, it then becomes necessary to ask whether the continued primacy of State sovereignty is still justified.[263] Thirdly, the concept of sovereignty, even if extended to regions, may offer a measure of normative guidance, but its broad and abstract nature still does not furnish a concrete method for assessing whether a specific regional act is constructive or corrosive with respect to sovereignty.

2.5 Conclusion

Three key conclusions emerge, each indicating that regional international law should not be equated with other forms of particular international law.

Firstly, the term 'regional' is, for the most part, understood as describing the normative distinctiveness of a cohesive group of States from the perspective of States both within and outside the region. While broader understandings of the concept of a 'region' exist outside the legal context, practice generally supports a narrower conception of the term, particularly where legal consequences hinge on the classification of a practice, rule, or institution as 'regional'. Defined in this narrower sense, a region refers to a grouping of two or more States that: (1) can be objectively identified by third parties, typically based on their geographic proximity (criterion of identifiability); (2) exhibit a minimum degree of normative cohesion (criterion of normative cohesion); and (3) are thereby distinguishable from other States (criterion of distinctiveness).

Secondly, although the defining features of regions do not entitle them to claim exceptionalism, they do create a presumption of distinct normative qualities in legal claims arising from regions that satisfy the three criteria above. This presumption influences the identification, application, and development of international law and supports recognizing regional law as a separate legal category.

Thirdly, the defining features of regional law present a triple challenge to international law. To the extent that international law is to play a constructive role in

[263] See on this: Besson, 'Politics of RIOs' (n 80) 96–104; Van Langenhove (n 80).

addressing this challenge, it requires a methodological framework sufficiently determinate to distinguish corrosive from constructive forms of regional international law, while striving to remain as value neutral as possible. Whether the concept of 'general international law' can provide such a framework is the focus of the next chapter.

3

How does general international law accommodate regional plurality?

3.1 Regional or general international law?

An important reason for the relative lack of concern about regional fragmentation among international lawyers has been a robust trust in general international law's capacity to address and resolve any fragmentation tendencies within the 'system' of international law.[1] Speaking at the 2006 annual conference of the European Society of International Law, Michael Wood, for example, emphasized that 'there is, and can only be, one system of international law in today's world. International law is universal—or it is nothing.'[2] With respect to regional rules, he added that '[a]ll that needs to be said here is that such [regional] rules derive their authority from general international law.'[3]

Whether this is indeed 'all that needs to be said' about the relationship between regional and general international law is open to doubt. A markedly different view had been expressed roughly sixty years earlier by Haro van Panhuys in his 1959 inaugural lecture at the University of Leiden. Noting that 'the phenomena of international law are too complex to be explained by simply making a choice between regional or general international law',[4] he even suggested that given 'the controversial character of general international law (as an objective system of law) there would be every reason for preferring any other theory' for explaining the binding force of regional international law.[5]

We may dismiss van Panhuys' scepticism as hopelessly outdated given the profound transformation of international law in the seventy years following his

[1] R Jennings, 'Universal International Law in a Multicultural World' in M Bos and I Brownlie (eds), *Liber Amicorum for Lord Wilberforce* (OUP 1987) 39, 41.

[2] M Wood, 'A European Vision of International Law: For what Purpose?' in H Ruiz Fabri, E Jouannet, and V Tomkiewicz (eds), *Select Proceedings of the European Society of International Law (2006)* (Hart 2008) 151, 152.

[3] Wood (n 2) fn 3.

[4] This inaugural lecture was published in: HF Van Panhuys, 'Regional or General International Law? A Misleading Dilemma' (1961) 8:2 NILR 146–64, 162.

[5] Van Panhuys (n 4) 147. See also A de Hoogh, 'Regionalism and the Unity of International Law from a Positivist Perspective' Conference Paper No 3/2012 of the ESIL 5th Biennial Conference (Valencia, 13–15 September 2012), 25: 'rules of regional international law do not necessarily depend on the system as a whole for their validity.'

Regional and General International Law. Janina Barkholdt, Oxford University Press. © Janina Barkholdt 2026.
DOI: 10.1093/9780198953432.003.0003

remark. Still, the precise meaning of the term 'general international law' remains unsettled.[6] In its 2006 Fragmentation Report, the ILC study group noted that there was 'no well-articulated or uniform understanding of what this might mean'.[7] Indeed, the findings of Chapter 2 indicate that the idea of 'one system of international law' with an overarching body of 'general international law' is difficult to reconcile with assertions of autonomously operating regional legal systems, including distinct regional sources of law.[8] How then can general international law accommodate the centrifugal forces of regional plurality?

This chapter seeks to answer this question in two steps. It first examines the three most common understandings of 'general international law' (3.2) before then turning specifically to secondary rules of international law as a distinct form of general international law. It argues that secondary rules have the methodological (3.3), normative (3.4.), and analytical potential to respond to the triple challenge posed by regional international law identified in Chapter 2 (3.5).

3.2 What is 'general international law'?

Like the concept of a 'region', the term 'general international law' is both ubiquitous and notoriously difficult to define. Just like its predecessor,[9] the ICJ frequently relies on 'general international law' in its decisions.[10] Several multilateral treaties, notably the 1961 VCDR,[11] the 1969 VCLT,[12] and the 1982 UNCLOS,[13] refer to 'general international law'. Yet, international law lacks a uniform definition of the term. As pointed out in the 2022 commentaries on the ILC 'Draft conclusions on identification and legal consequences of peremptory norms of general international law (*jus cogens*)', '[t]he meaning of general international law will always be context-specific'.[14] This is true in the sense that there are at least three—partly overlapping—definitions of the term.[15]

[6] See also M Wood, 'The International Tribunal for the Law of the Sea and General International Law' (2007) 22 Int'l J Marine and Coastal Law 351, 354.

[7] ILC, 'Fragmentation of International Law: difficulties arising from the Diversification and Expansion of International Law: Report of the Study Group of the International Law Commission—Finalized by Martti Koskenniemi' (2006) UN Doc A/CN.4/L.682 (Fragmentation Report) [500].

[8] See Chapter 2, section 2.3.

[9] See eg *The Case of the SS 'Lotus'* (Judgment) [1927] PCIJ Series A, No 10, 16–17.

[10] See eg *Legal Consequences arising from the Policies and Practices of Israel in the Occupied Palestinian Territory, including East Jerusalem* (Advisory Opinion) [2024] ICJ [250]–[251], [267].

[11] Vienna Convention on Diplomatic Relations (18 April 1961) 500 UNTS 95, art 41(3).

[12] VCLT, arts 53, 64, and 71.

[13] UNCLOS, preamble.

[14] ILC, 'Draft conclusions on identification and legal consequences of peremptory norms of general international law (*jus cogens*), with commentaries' (2022) UN Doc A/77/10, commentary on draft conclusion 5, 31 (ILC Report 2022 (*Jus cogens*)).

[15] See also S Besson, 'Sources of International Human Rights Law: How General is General International Law?' in J d'Aspremont and S Besson (eds), *The Oxford Handbook of the Sources of International Law* (OUP 2017) 839.

3.2.1 International law generally applicable *ratione personae*

'General international law' is often understood as referring to the scope *ratione personae* of a set of rules and describes 'international law as it is applied between all nations belonging to the community of States'.[16] It comprises customary international law and general principles of law as reflected in Article 38(1) of the ICJ Statute[17] and, arguably, also includes the content of certain provisions contained in multilateral treaties.[18] This understanding of 'general international law' thus strongly resembles the definition of 'universal(ly applicable) international law'.[19]

However, when it comes to the way in which general international law can provide a framework that is sufficiently determinate for distinguishing between corrosive and constructive forms of regional law, such a quantitative understanding is, without more, unsatisfactory. While general international law, understood in this sense, applies to all States by default,[20] they are generally free to adopt regional rules *inter se* that deviate from it.[21]

3.2.2 International law generally applicable *ratione materiae*

A second way of understanding 'general international law' refers to the scope *ratione materiae* of a set of rules. It describes those rules whose application is not limited to a specific subject-matter of international law,[22] but which govern the formation, interpretation, and application of legal obligations across the various fields of international law, such as the principles of *pacta sunt servanda*,[23] good faith, *lex specialis*, and systemic integration.[24]

[16] Lotus (n 9) 16–17; *North Sea Continental Shelf (Federal Republic of Germany/Denmark)* [1969] ICJ Rep 3 [63];ILC Report 2022 (*Jus cogens*) (n 14) 31; A Gourgourinis, 'General/Particular International Law and Primary/Secondary Rules: Unitary Terminology of a Fragmented System' (2011) 22:4 EJIL 993, 1011.

[17] Fragmentation Report (n 7) 254.

[18] Different views exist whether this depends on the extent to which these codify customary international law or their quasi-universal ratification. In the direction of the first view: ILC Report 2022 (*Jus cogens*) (n 14) conclusion 5(2), 33–34; A Kulick and M Waibel, 'General International Law in International Investment Law' in *General International Law in International Investment Law: A Commentary* (OUP 2024) 5 [11]. For an inclusion of treaties: K Schmalenbach, 'Article 53' in Ö Dörr and K Schmalenbach (eds.), *Vienna Convention on the Law of Treaties: A Commentary* (2nd edn, Springer 2018) 979–80; GI Tunkin, 'Co-existence and International Law' 1958 (95) RdC 5, 21–22. Ambiguous: Wood (2007) (n 6) 355.

[19] G Abi-Saab, 'Cours général de droit international public' (1987) 207 RdC 198. But see GP Buzzini, 'La "généralité" du droit international général: réflexions sur la polysémie d'un concept' (2004) 2 RGDIP 381, 395–97.

[20] G Fitzmaurice, 'The General Principles of International Law Considered from the Standpoint of the Rule of Law' 1957 (92) RdC 92.

[21] See eg *Right of Passage over Indian Territory (Portugal v India)* Merits [1960] ICJ Rep 6, 44.

[22] Buzzini (n 19) 386, 391; R Mackenzie-Gray Scott, 'Due Diligence as a Secondary Rule of General International Law' (2021) 34 LJIL 343, 344.

[23] See eg *Nuclear Tests (Australia v France) (Judgment)* [1974] ICJ Rep 253, 268 [46].

[24] See on these: *Obligations of States in Respect of Climate Change* (Advisory Opinion of 23 July 2025) ICJ [165]–[166] and [303].

Still, given the level of abstractness of these principles, it is doubtful that they can be operationalized as a tangible standard for assessing normative claims at the regional level.

3.2.3 Fundamental rules of international law

'General international law' has also been understood as a synonym for 'fundamental' rules of international law, ie as referring to the substantive content or rank of the rules in the international legal order.[25]

However, unless 'fundamental' rules are effectively equated with peremptory norms (*jus cogens*) (which, as was discussed in Chapter 2, brings about its own challenges[26]), this approach inevitably raises the question how 'fundamental' rules are identified and distinguished from other, 'mundane' rules. 'Fundamental' means different things to different people. On one end of the spectrum, very narrow conceptions of 'fundamental' rules essentially seek to ensure peaceful co-existence between powers (not even necessarily 'States'), including the principle of non-intervention as the only shared rule among different regional regimes[27] or the five principles of peaceful coexistence.[28] Somewhat broader, but very much 'State-centric' approaches aim at providing a set of rules that facilitates co-ordination and co-operation among States, notably by proposing catalogues of 'fundamental rights and duties of States'.[29] Some sets of 'fundamental' rules additionally include certain principles protecting human and peoples' rights, such as the ten Bandung principles (1955),[30] and the seven principles enshrined in the Friendly Relations Declaration (1970).[31] Other, more 'eclectic' sets of fundamental rules comprise 'certain general and well-recognized principles' as identified by the ICJ,[32] including obligations *erga omnes*.[33] On the other side of the

[25] Buzzini (n 19) 386, 391; Abi-Saab (n 19) 198.

[26] Section 2.3.3.1.

[27] See eg C Schmitt, *Völkerrechtliche Großraumordnung mit Interventionsverbot für raumfremde Mächte* (3rd edition in the version of 1941, Duncker & Humblot 2009). Carl Schmitt introduced the concept of a Grossraumordnung consisting of geopolitical spheres of influence, which is incompatible with the principle of sovereign equality among States.

[28] See Agreement on Trade and Intercourse between Tibet Region of China and India 299 UNTS 70, preamble.

[29] See eg Convention on Rights and Duties of States (signed 26 December 1933, entered into force 26 December 1934) 165 LNTS 19; UNGA, 'Draft Declaration on Rights and Duties of States, prepared by the International Law Commission' (1949) UN Doc A/RES/375(IV) Annex.

[30] Final Communiqué of the Asian-African Conference of the Non-Aligned Countries (24 April 1955).

[31] UNGA, 'The Declaration on Principles of International Law concerning Friendly Relations and Co-operation among States' (24 October 1970) UN Doc A/RES/2625(XXV); see eg GI Tunkin, 'International Law in the International System' (1975) 147 RdC 44, 55, 71–72.

[32] See eg *Corfu Channel Case (United Kingdom v Albania)* [1949] ICJ Rep 4, 22.

[33] See eg *Barcelona Traction, Light and Power Company, Limited (Belgium v Spain)* [1970] ICJ Rep 3, 33 [33]–[34].

spectrum, we find approaches that put human dignity at the core of fundamental rules of international law.[34]

In addition to the challenge of determining how broadly or narrowly the fundamental rules should be defined, many of the suggested principles are formulated in broad and open-ended terms allowing for different regional interpretations and raising doubts as to whether this understanding offers a sufficiently determinate framework for overcoming the challenge posed by regional international law.

In sum, these three understandings of 'general international law' converge in a single idea: they designate the rules that are shared by, and which are applicable to, all subjects across all regions. Yet, none of these three most common understandings of 'general international law' proves to be entirely satisfactory as a set of rules that could help in overcoming the triple challenge posed by regional international law.[35] A fourth, more narrowly defined type of general international law, however, provides a more tangible standard: the so-called 'secondary rules of international law'.

3.2.4 Secondary rules as a distinct form of general international law

The secondary rules of international law, understood here as the rules that determine the creation, identification, interpretation, application, and enforcement of international law,[36] represent a fourth, more narrowly defined understanding of general international law.[37] The category of secondary rules is characterized by a triple generality, effectively combining the three previously discussed understandings of general international law:

Firstly, the scope *ratione personae* of secondary rules extends, by default, to all subjects of international law given that secondary rules typically comprise the law of sources, the rules on interpretation, the law of State responsibility, and the law on State succession, which are rooted in customary international law or general principles of law.[38]

[34] MS McDougal and HD Lasswell, 'The Identification and Appraisal of Diverse Systems of Public Order' (1959) 53:1 AJIL 1–29; E de Wet, 'The Emergence of International and Regional Value Systems as a Manifestation of the Emerging International Constitutional Order' (2006) 19:3 LJIL 611, 612; B Fassbender, 'The United Nations Charter as Constitution of the International Community' (1998) 36:3 Columbia J Transnatl Law 529–619.

[35] See on the triple challenge Chapter 2, section 2.3.

[36] See on the controversial content of the concept of 'secondary rules' section 3.5.1 below.

[37] Considering 'secondary rules' as 'general international law': Kulick and Waibel (n 18) [11]; C McLachlan, 'On the Interface Between Public and Private International Law' (2025) 446 RdC 275–76 [569]–[570].

[38] Kulick and Waibel (n 18) [11]; McLachlan (n 37) [569]–[570].

Secondly, as international law's 'common grammar',[39] their scope *ratione materiae* is not limited to a specific field or type of conduct but covers all fields of international law.[40]

And, thirdly, their content is also of 'fundamental' importance. One could even say that the existence of secondary rules is peremptory for the international legal order; however, in a different sense than *jus cogens*. While 'peremptory norms of general international law' are characterized by their non-derogability, it is still possible to imagine international law without the concept of *jus cogens*.[41] However, this is different for secondary rules. It is arguably difficult to imagine a legal system without unwritten 'rules' that determine how rules are formed, recognized, interpreted, applied, and enforced.[42] In other words, secondary rules are rules that are indispensable for a legal system.[43] Unlike peremptory norms, however, their indispensability does not entail their non-derogability.[44] Decisive is the existence as such of those rules, not their specific content. Accordingly, they can be abrogated if they are replaced by a functionally equivalent rule,[45] as will be elaborated in detail below.

The central claim this chapter makes is that recourse to secondary rules as a distinct form of general international law provides a rigorous, yet inclusive approach for accommodating regional plurality within a common framework of international law, and thus a constructive and practicable way out of the triple challenge posed by regional international law.

This book does not claim to (re-) invent the concept of secondary rules. That concept lies at the core of some of the work which perceives international law as a 'system' and has also—at least implicitly—featured in the way in which the ILC has sought to integrate regional plurality.[46] Notably, its potential to reconcile domestic and international law has been explored.[47] Yet, the potential of secondary rules when confronting challenges arising from regional international law has so far never been systematically examined. As we will see in this chapter, secondary rules of international law have the methodological

[39] Kulick and Waibel (n 18), citing P-M Dupuy, 'A Doctrinal Debate in the Globalisation Era: On the "Fragmentation" of International Law' (2007) 1 Eur J Leg Stud 1, 4.

[40] Mackenzie-Gray Scott (n 22).

[41] But see R Kolb, 'Peremptory Norms as a Legal Technique Rather than Substantive Super- Norms' in D Tladi (ed), *Peremptory Norms of General International Law (Jus Cogens)* (Brill 2021) 21, 33–39 on 'logical jus cogens', such as the principles of *pacta sunt servanda* and good faith.

[42] Abi-Saab (n 19) 122.

[43] See below section 3.4.1.

[44] Abi-Saab (n 19) 150.

[45] See below section 3.5.2.

[46] See J Barkholdt, 'Is the International Law Commission Taking Regionalism Seriously (Enough)?' (2022) 12 GoJIL 155–88.

[47] See A Nollkaemper, 'The Power of Secondary Rules to Connect the International and National Legal Orders', in T Broude and Y Shany (eds), *Multi-Sourced Equivalent Norms in International Law* (Hart 2011) 45–68.

potential to respond to the elusive legal nature of regional law (3.3), the normative potential to provide a common denominator and to confer 'normative ownership' to all States with respect to both regional and general international law, regardless of whether they belong to a certain region or not (3.4), and the analytical potential to distinguish between constructive and corrosive forms of regional law (3.5).

3.3 The methodological potential of secondary rules

In Chapter 2, we saw that one of the differences between regional law and other particular international law is its distinct, yet elusive, legal nature.[48] Regional affiliation entails a presumption of acceptable legal distinctiveness that bears on the identification, application, and creation of international law.[49] Yet, some forms of regional law are not only legally distinct, but also highly idiosyncratic (sometimes called *sui generis*),[50] making it difficult to determine the extent to which these forms can still be considered international law without suppressing or privileging a particular regional legal tradition.[51] Methodologically, the central challenge is thus to develop an approach that delineates the scope of normative idiosyncrasy within international law that is both acceptable to third parties and does not suppress regional legal diversity.[52]

This section argues that recourse to secondary rules is a well-established method in international legal practice for balancing legal plurality with the need to distinguish law from non-law which can be transposed to the specific challenge posed by regional plurality.

After introducing the concept and function of 'secondary rules' as developed by HLA Hart, it shows that the concept of 'secondary rules' is deeply ingrained in the theory and practice of international law as a method to establish shared rules which apply across different legal fields and systems (3.3.1) and engages with the criticism articulated by scholars and practitioners with respect to the role played by secondary rules in international law (3.3.2). It then explains why this recourse to secondary rules offers a methodological approach that is transposable to regional plurality (3.3.3).

[48] Section 2.4.2.
[49] See Chapter 2, section 2.3.
[50] See eg for examples for the alleged '*sui generis*' nature of regional organisations across various regions: ILA Study Group, 'The International Law of Regional Organizations: Final Report' (Athens Conference 2024) 12–13.
[51] See Chapter 2, section 2.4.2.
[52] See Chapter 2, section 2.3.

3.3.1 The trajectory of secondary rules in international law: from doctrine to practice

The distinction between 'primary' and 'secondary' rules of law is commonly associated with HLA Hart's 1961 monograph *The Concept of Law*.[53] The differences between these two types of rules have been described by Hart as follows:

> Under rules of the one type, which may well be considered the basic or primary type, human beings are required to do so or abstain from certain actions, whether they wish to or not. Rules of the other type are in a sense parasitic upon or secondary to the first; for they provide that human beings may by doing or saying certain things introduce new rules of the primary type, extinguish or modify old ones, or in various ways determine their incidence or control their operation. Rules of the first type impose duties; rules of the second type confer powers, public or private. Rules of the first type concern actions involving physical movement or changes; rules of the second type provide for operations which lead not merely to physical movement or change, but to the creation or variation of duties or obligations.[54]

For Hart, secondary rules as 'rules (. . .) about (. . .) rules' operate on a different level than primary rules and 'specify the ways in which the primary rules may be conclusively ascertained, introduced, eliminated, varied, and the fact of their violation conclusively determined'.[55] Importantly, Hart did not consider the existence of secondary rules a necessary requirement for having 'binding [legal] rules'.[56] Instead, he insisted that rules are 'binding' if they are 'thought of, spoken of, and function as such'.[57]

Why then are secondary rules indispensable for a legal system? According to Hart, the 'simple social structure of primary rules' encounters three 'defects': 'uncertainty' as to the existence and scope of a rule, their 'static character' and lack of means to adapt the rules; and the 'inefficiency of the diffuse social pressure by which the rules are maintained'.[58] Secondary rules, he argued, are 'remedies' to these three defects. He identified three inter-connected types of secondary rules, each of which remedies one of the respective defects: the 'rule of recognition' as 'a rule for conclusive identification of the primary rule of obligation' as a remedy for uncertainty;[59] the 'rules of change' which prescribe ways in which a rule can be

53 HLA Hart, *The Concept of Law* (3rd edn, OUP 2012).
54 Hart (n 53) 81.
55 Hart (n 53) 94.
56 Hart (n 53) 213–14, 235.
57 Hart (n 53) 231, 234.
58 Hart (n 53) 92–93.
59 Hart (n 53) 94–95.

changed or terminated as a remedy to the static character of primary rules;[60] and 'rules of adjudication', as a remedy to the inefficiency of the enforcement of primary rules, which define the entity and procedure according to which a determination about a potential violation of the primary rule is made.[61] Hart accorded particular importance to the 'rule of recognition' as an 'ultimate rule'[62] which introduces 'in embryonic form, the idea of a legal system'.[63]

The question is whether the concept of secondary rules is transposable to the international level. As is well known, *Hart* rejected the existence of secondary rules in international law, arguing that international law

> not only lacks the secondary rules of change and adjudication which provide for legislature and courts, but also a unifying rule of recognition specifying 'sources' of law and providing general criteria for the identification of its rules[64]

To Hart, international law 'resembles (. . .) a simple regime of primary or customary rules'[65] 'which are not united in this manner'.[66] However, Hart's view of international law is not particularly relevant to the role of secondary rules therein. Although the concept of secondary rules seems to be inextricably linked to his name and his work prominently informed the academic debate in international law scholarship, the terminological and conceptual distinction between primary and secondary rules in international law long predates the publication of *The Concept of Law*.[67]

Charles de Visscher, for example, noted in this 1925 Hague Lecture the existence of

> . . . une distinction qui, à notre avis, est absolument fondamentale. C'est la distinction, formulée si magistralement par M. Duguit, entre les règles primaires ou normatives et les règles secondaires, constructives ou technique.[68]

Yet, de Visscher employed this terminology, inspired by *Léon Duguit*'s work from 1911, to distinguish between the basis or foundation of international law (primary rules), such as the independence of States, freedom of States, equality of States (the

[60] Hart (n 53) 95–96.
[61] Hart (n 53) 96–97.
[62] Hart (n 53) 105–10.
[63] Hart (n 53) 95.
[64] Hart (n 53) 214 and further 233–34, 236.
[65] Hart (n 53) 232 and further 227, 233, 236.
[66] Hart (n 53) 233.
[67] See also P-M Dupuy, 'L'unité de l'ordre juridique international: Cours général de droit international public' 297 (2000) RdC 74–79, who argues that already Jhering distinguished between rules of conduct, addressed to the citizens, and rules on sanctions, addressed to judges (74).
[68] C de Visscher, 'La codification du droit international' (1925) 6 RdC 325, 341–48, referring to L Duguit, *Traité de droit constitutionnel, Tome 1* (Paris 1911).

'fundamental rights of States', as he puts it), and *pacta sunt servanda*,[69] and the body of law derived from it (secondary rules). He defined primary rules as those rules which exist independently from the will of States, and which are transposed from fundamental notions of law existent in all domestic legal systems,[70] whereas secondary rules, according to him, form the body of positive law which concretizes these primary rules.[71] This understanding of secondary rules, while using the same terminology as *Hart*, is thus conceptually very different.

However, the term 'secondary rules' became most prominent in international law practice in the context of what comes closest to Hart's 'secondary rules of adjudication': the rules concerning State responsibility. Earlier works on the enforcement of international law, notably the Commentaries to the 1929 Harvard Draft Convention on International Responsibility, preceded Hart in distinguishing primary and secondary international legal rules.[72] In the ILC, it was *Roberto Ago* who, first in the 'Sub-Committee on State Responsibility' in 1963, then in his first report in 1969, introduced a 'horizontal' distinction

> between the rules of substance laying down the international rights and duties of States in the various fields and the aspects and consequences of the violation, by States, of the obligations deriving from these rules.[73]

By doing so, Ago broke with the, in his words, 'vertical' approach taken by the first Special Rapporteur on the topic, Francisco Garcia-Amador, who had focussed on different 'sectors', notably on responsibility for injuries to aliens and related questions of diplomatic protection.[74] This 'vertical' approach had two major shortcomings: firstly, it led to controversies about the substance of rules for the violation of which responsibility was invoked. Secondly, the sectorial focus brought about a lack of generalizability for other fields of international law. Still, the terminology of 'secondary' and 'primary' was not used in the early statements of Ago. It was most likely Arnold Tammes, who, in his statement on Ago's first report, suggested that

> For want of a better terminology, the distinction which was being adopted could be described as a distinction between primary, material or substantive rules of international law, on the one hand, and secondary or functional rules, on the

[69] de Visscher (n 68) 341–42.

[70] de Visscher (n 68) 341–42.

[71] de Visscher (n 68) 343–45.

[72] Harvard Law School, 'Draft Convention and Comments on Responsibility of States for Injuries to Aliens' (1929) 23:2 Supplement to AJIL 133, 141.

[73] ILC, 'Report in the Sub-Committee on State Responsibility' (1963) YBILC II, UN Doc A/CN.4/152, 252–53; ILC, 'First report on State responsibility by Mr. Roberto Ago, Special Rapporteur' (1969) YBILC II, UN Doc A/CN.4/217, 139 [90].

[74] See on its earlier works: ILC, 'First report on State responsibility by Mr. Roberto Ago, Special Rapporteur' (1969) YBILC II, UN Doc A/CN.4/217, in particular 133–37 [47]–[81].

> other. Primary rules were intended to influence the conduct of States directly; secondary rules, which were those of State responsibility proper, were intended to promote the practical realization of the substance of international law contained in the primary rules.[75]

The ILC retained the distinction between secondary and primary rules for the project on State responsibility until its conclusion in 2001 upon which it stated in the accompanying commentaries:

> The emphasis is on the secondary rules of State responsibility: that is to say, the general conditions under international law for the state or an international organization to be considered responsible for wrongful actions or omissions, and the legal consequences which flow therefrom.[76]

The ILC has referred to 'secondary rules' in several other projects dealing with the enforcement of international law over the last decades.[77] This was not uncontroversial among ILC members. John Dugard, when commenting on the project 'The obligation to extradite or prosecute (*aut dedere aut judicare*)', warned in 2007 that

> the Commission [should] not [] become too involved in distinctions between primary and secondary rules, given that it was uncertain whether reference was being made to the formulation of Roberto Ago or that of H.L.A. Hart.[78]

However, the Commission's approach based on the distinction between primary and secondary rules generally met with support by States in the UNGA Sixth Committee[79] and played a central role in the more recent proposals for the topics 'Compensation for the damage caused by internationally wrongful

[75] ILC, 'Summary record of the 1012th meeting' (1969) YBILC I, UN Doc A/CN.4/SR.1012, 109 [5]. The distinction between secondary and primary 'obligations' was briefly alluded to by Briggs in 1963 (ILC, 'Report on the fifteenth session' (1963) YBILC II, UN Doc A/5509, 231) as highlighted in E David, 'Primary and Secondary Rules' in J Crawford and others (eds), *The Law of International Responsibility* (OUP 2012) 27, 28.

[76] ILC, 'Report of the International Law Commission on the work of its fifty-third session' (2001) YBILC II(2), UN Doc A/56/10, 31.

[77] See eg ILC, 'Draft Articles on most-favoured-nations clauses' (1978) YBILC II (2), UN Doc A/CN.4/309, Commentary on draft article 27, 71; ILC, 'International liability for injurious consequences arising out of acts not prohibited by international law' (1980) YBILC I, UN Doc A/CN.4/SR.1631; ILC, 'Draft Articles on the Responsibility of International Organizations, with commentaries' (2011) YBILC II(2), UN Doc UN Doc A/66/10, 46; ILC, 'Fourth report on succession of States in respect of State responsibility' (2020) UN Doc A/CN.4/713 [99].

[78] ILC, 'Summary record of the 2945th meeting' (2007) YBILC I, UN Doc A/CN.4/2945, 210 [26].

[79] See eg ILC, 'Topical summary of the debate held in the Sixth Committee' (2001) UN Doc A/CN.4/513, 10 [14]; ILC, 'Topical Summary of the debate held in the Sixth Committee' (2017) UN Doc A/CN.4/713 [67] (succession of States in respect of State responsibility).

acts' and 'Due Diligence in International Law' for the purpose of delineating the scope of the projects, which were included by the ILC in its programme of work in 2025.[80]

Since the adoption of ARSIWA in 2001, this distinction has also been increasingly invoked in judicial practice. In recent years, the term 'secondary rules' was explicitly used to refer to the rules on State responsibility, notably in the 2025 Advisory Opinion of the ICJ on *Obligations of States in respect of Climate Change*,[81] several arbitral awards,[82] and in individual opinions of ICJ judges.[83] States have also resorted to the distinction in their pleadings before international courts and tribunals.[84]

But does international law recognize the concept of secondary rules beyond the context of State responsibility? Unlike Hart, who claimed that secondary rules do not exist in international law, several international lawyers, in the attempt to prove Hart wrong,[85] have pointed to various candidates for the 'rule of recognition',[86]

[80] ILC, 'Report of the International Law Commission to the General Assembly on the work of its seventy-fifth session' (2024) UN Doc A/79/10, Annex 1 (Compensation for the damage caused by internationally wrongful acts by Mārtiņš Paparinskis) [7] and Annex 2 (Due Diligence in International Law by Penelope Ridings) [21] and [28].

[81] *Climate Change* (Advisory Opinion 2024) (n 24) [104].

[82] *The Arctic Sunrise Arbitration (Netherlands v Russia) (Award on the merits)* PCA Case 2014-02 (14 August 2015) [190]; *The Duzgit Integrity Arbitration (Malta v São Tomé and Príncipe) (Award)* PCA Case 2014-07 (5 September 2016) [208].

[83] See eg *Application of the Convention on the Prevention and Punishment of the Crime of Genocide (Croatia v Serbia)* (Judgment) [2015] ICJ Rep 3 (separate opinion Judge ad hoc Kreća) 450 [76]–[78] and [105] arguing that the rules on State succession were—in contrast to the rules of State responsibility—primary rules); *Questions relating to the Obligation to Prosecute or Extradite (Belgium v Senegal)* (Judgment) [2012] ICJ Rep 422 (Declaration Judge Donoghue) 584 [13]; *Jurisdictional Immunities of the State (Germany v Italy: Greece intervening)* (Judgment) [2012] ICJ Rep 99 (dissenting opinion Judge Cançado Trindade) 179 [121] and [294]; *Application of the Interim Accord of 13 September 1995 (the former Yugoslav Republic of Macedonia v Greece)* (Judgment) [2011] ICJ Rep 344 (separate opinion Judge Simma) 695 [20]–[21] and [27].

[84] See eg in the *Appeal Relating to the Jurisdiction of the ICAO Council under Article 84 of the Convention on International Civil Aviation (Bahrain, Egypt, Saudi Arabia and United Arab Emirates v Qatar)*, ICJ Verbatim Record 2019/13 (2 December 2019) 63 [26]; Germany and Italy referred to it in their written submissions in *Jurisdictional Immunities of the State* (Memorial of Germany (12 June 2009) 55 [89]; Reply of Germany (5 October 2010) 40 [67]; Counter-Memorial of Italy (22 December 2009) 64–65 [4.67]); Memorial of Panama, *The M/V 'Norstar'* Case (Panama v Italy), ITLOS, (11 April 2017) [150].

[85] Abi-Saab (n 19) 119–22; PM Dupuy, 'The Danger of Fragmentation or Unification of the International Legal System and the International Court of Justice' (1999) 31:4 NYU J Int'l L & Pol 791, 793; TM Franck, 'Legitimacy in the International System' (1988) 82:4 AJIL 751–59; M Payandeh, 'The Concept of International Law in the Jurisprudence of H.L.A. Hart' (2010) 21:4 EJIL 967–95; T Reinold and M Zürn, '"Rules about Rules" and the Endogenous Dynamics of International Law: Dissonance Reduction as a Mechanism of Secondary Rule-making' (2014) 3:2 Glob Const 236, 242; KC Wellens, 'Diversity in Secondary Rules and the Unity of International Law: Some Reflections on Current Trends' (1994) 15 NYIL 3–37; J Waldron, 'International Law: 'A Relatively Small and Unimportant' Part of Jurisprudence?' in L Duarte d'Almeida and others (eds), *Reading HLA Hart's 'The Concept of Law'* (Hart 2013) 209–23.

[86] Many writers would point to the doctrine of sources as reflected in Article 38(1) ICJ Statute (JI Charney, 'Universal International Law' (1993) 87:4 AJIL 529, 533–34; Payandeh (n 85) 989–93; Wellens (n 85) 9 who also mentions the VCLT provisions on validity; ambiguous: S Yee, 'Article 38 of the ICJ Statute and Applicable Law: Selected Issues in Recent Cases' (2016) 7 J Int Dispute Settl 472, 475).

'rules of change',[87] and 'rules of adjudication'[88] at the international level. More recent scholarship on the ILC's work on the sources of international law,[89] but also on that topic generally[90] uses this terminology.

Still, the meaning and relevance of a distinction between secondary and primary rules in legal practice outside the context of State responsibility has remained obscure.

This appears to be partly rooted in terminological and conceptual ambiguities of the distinction. For example, the ICJ's distinction between 'procedural law' and 'substantive law' in its *Jurisdictional Immunities* judgment of 2012[91] has been interpreted by Pierre-Marie Dupuy as corresponding to the distinction between primary and secondary rules,[92] whereas Stefan Talmon argued that the distinction adopted by the Court was 'not identical with so-called "secondary rules"'.[93] Until today, the ICJ has not used the term 'secondary rules' outside the context of State responsibility. Judge Simma in his 2011 separate opinion on the *Interim Accord* judgment designated the law of treaties codified in the VCLT, which according to Hart's understanding clearly qualifies as 'secondary rules', as 'primary rules' which he juxtaposed to the 'secondary rules' on State responsibility.[94]

Nevertheless, an expansion of the term 'secondary rules' can be observed in legal practice. ILC special rapporteurs increasingly refer to 'secondary rules' to designate rules on the identification of rules under international law, for example, in the 2006 Fragmentation Report,[95] as well as in the projects on the identification of customary international law,[96] and *jus cogens*.[97] In 2025, the ILC even adopted

[87] Payandeh (n 85) 982–85; Waldron (n 85) 216–18.

[88] Pointing to 'norms of adjudication' in the law of State responsibility: Dupuy (n 85) 793. Emphasizing international courts: Payandeh (n 85) 985–88 (who also mentions the law of state responsibility); Waldron (n 85) 214–16.

[89] M Wood, 'International Law in Practice. Courses of the Summer School on Public International Law' (2022) XI International and Comparative Law Research Center 99–100; D Azaria, '"Codification by Interpretation": The International Law Commission as an Interpreter of International Law' (2020) 31:1 EJIL 171, 172.

[90] G Kajtár, B Çalı, and M Milanovic, 'Introduction' in *Secondary Rules of Primary Importance in International Law* (OUP 2022) 4; Kulick and Waibel (n 18); McLachlan (n 37); D McRae, 'Treaty Interpretation by the WTO Appellate Body: The Conundrum of Article 17(6) of the Anti-Dumping Agreement', in E Cannizzaro (ed), *The Law of Treaties Beyond the Vienna Convention* (OUP 2011) 179.

[91] See eg *Jurisdictional Immunities of the State (Germany v Italy: Greece intervening)* (Judgment) [2012] ICJ Rep 99, 124 [58]; 140 [93]; 141 [95]; *Armed Activities on the Territory of the Congo (New Application: 2002) (Democratic Republic of the Congo v Rwanda)* (Jurisdiction and Admissibility: Judgment) [2006] ICJ Rep 6 [64] and [125]; *Arrest Warrant of 1 April 2000 (Democratic Republic of the Congo v Belgium)* (Judgment) [2002] ICJ Rep 25 [60].

[92] P-M Dupuy, '2000–2020: Twenty Years Later, Where Are We in Terms of the Unity of International Law?' (2020) 9 Camb Int Law J 6, 12–13 and in fn 49.

[93] S Talmon, '*Jus Cogens* after Germany v. Italy: Substantive and Procedural Rules Distinguished' (2012) 25:4 LJIL 979, 982.

[94] Separate opinion Judge Simma (n 83) 704 [20]–[21], [27].

[95] Fragmentation Report (n 7) [27].

[96] ILC, 'First report on the formation and evidence of customary international law by Sir Michael Wood, Special Rapporteur' (2013) UN Doc A/CN.4/663 [38]: 'But as in any legal system, there must in public international law be rules for identifying the sources of the law.'; ILC, 'Summary records [of the debate on the first report on CIL]' (2013) UN Doc A/CN.4/3181 (Wood, 82), (Forteau, 84).

[97] ILC, 'Fourth report on peremptory norms of general international law (*jus cogens*) by Dire Tladi, Special Rapporteur' (2019) UN Doc A/CN.4/727, 23.

on second reading Draft Conclusion 10 of the project on 'General principles of law' which states that general principles of law serve 'as a basis for substantive rights and obligations, as well as for secondary and procedural rules'.[98] At closer inspection, however, the debate surrounding Draft Conclusion 10 demonstrates that uncertainty about the scope of 'secondary rules' persist.[99]

Still, States in the Sixth Committee have also started to use the term 'secondary rules' for referring to the 'rules about rules'.[100] For example, France stated in 2019 on the topic of *jus cogens* that

> the mandate of the Commission on *jus cogens* covers only secondary rules, that is, how a rule would attain the status of a *jus cogens* norm and the legal effects that would be attached to that status.[101]

Furthermore, arbitral awards and pleadings have put forward an understanding of 'secondary rules' which encompasses the law of treaties.[102]

In sum, in international legal practice, the concept of secondary rules has developed autonomously from the concept shaped by Hart. Hart's claim that secondary rules are absent in international law is even less convincing today than it was in 1961. The last twenty years have rather seen a convergence of the concept of 'secondary rules' in the sense put forward by Hart and the way in which recourse is made to it in the practice of international law: while earlier practice referred to secondary rules exclusively in the context of State responsibility, this understanding was incrementally extended to include the doctrine of sources and rules on interpretation, thus 'rules of recognition' and 'rules of change'.

3.3.2 The limits of secondary rules: working method or window dressing?

Hart's argument that secondary rules do not exist in international law is even less tenable today than it was back in 1961. As the previous section demonstrated, the concept of secondary rules is not alien to, but an established element in the

[98] ILC, 'General principles of law: texts and titles of the draft conclusions adopted by the Drafting Committee on second reading' (2025) UN Doc A/CN.4/L.1018.

[99] Statement of the Chair of the Drafting Committee on 'General principles of law', Mr. Mario Oyarzábal (27 May 2025) 12.

[100] See the statement of Belarus in the UNGA 6th Committee (2–3 November 2022) 2: 'General principles of law should also not be limited to "secondary rules", so-called rules about rules, if we were to use the terminology of Herbert Hart.'

[101] Statement of France UNGA 6th Committee (28 October 2019) 4 [translation by the author].

[102] *Arctic Sunrise Arbitration* (n 82) 190; *The Duzgit Integrity Arbitration* (n 82) 208; position of the UK as cited in *Chagos Marine Protected Area Arbitration (Mauritius v United Kingdom) (Award)* PCA Case 2011-03 (18 March 2015) [185]; *The Eurotunnel Arbitration (Partial Award)* PCA Case 2003-06 (30 January 2007) [107].

practice of international law. But this does not yet explain its precise role in the discourse, notably its methodological potential. For Hart himself, 'secondary rules' formed part of a classification of legal rules. He neither conceived of secondary rules as a 'working method' for the purpose of codifying and progressively developing (international) law, nor as a 'method' in the more general sense, understood here as a systematic procedure that is consistently applied to pursue a specific objective, which typically consists in the resolution of a problem.[103]

Some practitioners have indeed dismissed the concept as a purely 'academic distinction'[104] and as 'inadequate and unpersuasive'.[105] Several scholars, in turn, seem reluctant to attest any methodological role to secondary rules in international law. Instead, the distinction in secondary and primary rules is described as a popular, but rather functionally (some may say arbitrarily) employed tool of legal policy to exclude controversial legal issues (in projects on codification and progressive development of international law) and to avoid an undesirable legal result (in judicial practice).[106] Others, notably Monica Hakimi, would even go so far as claiming that the concept of secondary rules is incompatible with the 'inconstant and contingent nature of customary international law'.[107] Arguing that 'global actors do not consistently use the discursive moves [to argue about and justify particular decisions in CIL], as they would secondary rules',[108] Hakimi has sharply attacked the 'rulebook conception' of the ILC Conclusions on CIL based secondary rules.[109]

It is doubtful whether these different points of criticism from both practitioners and scholars are justified. The overview given in the previous section shows that recourse to secondary rules is neither a purely theoretical construct nor arbitrary, but a procedure that is consistently used to ensure generality across different legal fields and jurisdictions.

Since the 1960s—when 'secondary rules' made their debut in the practice of international law as a pragmatic way to overcome a deadlock in the ILC's work on State responsibility—the distinction between 'primary' and 'secondary rules' has

[103] See similarly S Vogenauer, 'Sources Of Law and Legal Method in Comparative Law' in M Reimann and Zimmermann (eds), *The Oxford Handbook of Comparative Law* (2nd edn, OUP 2019) 890.

[104] *Impregilo SpA v Argentine Republic (I)* (Award) ICSID Case No ARB/07/17 (21 June 2011) (concurring and dissenting opinion Professor Brigitte Stern) [29]–[30].

[105] *Jurisdictional Immunities of the State* (dissenting opinion Judge Cançado Trindade) (n 83) [294].

[106] J d'Aspremont, 'The Idea of Rules in International Law' (2014) 84 BYBIL 103, 108; but see his changed view in response to Hakimi below (n 107). See also J Crawford, 'The ILC's Articles on Responsibility of States for Internationally Wrongful Acts: A Retrospect' (2002) 96:4 AJIL 874, 879.

[107] M Hakimi, 'Making Sense of Customary International Law' (2020) 118:8 Mich Law Rev 1487, 1516.

[108] Hakimi (n 107) 1506–507.

[109] Interestingly, Hakimi's piece provoked d'Aspremont to publicly declare that he changed his formerly sceptical view on the existence of secondary rules (J d'Aspremont, 'Customary International Law Symposium: Rules Everywhere and At All Times (Whether You Like It or Not)' *OpinioJuris* (8 July 2020) <http://opiniojuris.org/2020/07/08/customary-international-law-symposium-rules-everywhere-and-at-all-times-whether-you-like-it-or-not/> (accessed 10 May 2026)).

not only become ingrained in the practice of international law but also extended to those rules which serve to identify common legal rules. The growing attention devoted to secondary rules can be understood as a response to the increasing normative plurality which the international legal order has started to face since the second half of the twentieth century. The very introduction of the term 'secondary rules' into the work of the ILC occurred against the background of decolonization.[110] The projects on treaty law were warranted by the explosion of multilateral treaty-making. The Fragmentation Report represented a reaction to the proliferation of international courts and tribunals, whereas the project on customary international law was inspired by 'differing approaches to the formation and identification of customary international law' 'in the context of a world of nearly 200 States and numerous and varied international organizations, both regional and universal',[111] uncertainty about the role of non-State actors in its formation, and the claim about different forms of custom in the various fields of international law.

This suggests that recourse to secondary rules represents a 'methodological vehicle'[112] for ensuring generality, even generalizability, in the enforcement, but also in the formation, interpretation, application, modification, and termination of international law.[113]

3.3.3 Secondary rules as a method to approach regional plurality

The challenge posed by regional international law can be understood as a variant of the challenges to which both Hart's concept of secondary rules as well as the distinction employed in international law respond.

While the challenge posed by regional international law stems from spatial, instead of sectorial plurality, the dilemma is structurally similar to the one that traditionally inspired the development of the distinction between primary and secondary rules in international law, that is the identification of rules that have a general scope *ratione materiae* and *ratione personae* the very purpose of which consists in ensuring generality in the identification, application, and enforcement of international law. The question here is thus to what extent such common rules (ie, universal secondary rules) can be identified, potentially

[110] See G Nolte, 'From Dionisio Anzilotti to Roberto Ago: The Classical International Law of State Responsibility and the Traditional Primacy of a Bilateral Conception of Inter-state Relations' (2002) 13:5 EJIL 1083, 1097.

[111] ILC, 'Report of the International Law Commission to the General Assembly on the work of the sixty-third session' (2011) UN Doc A/66/10, Annex 1 ('Formation and evidence of customary international law' by Michael Wood) 183 [2]–[3].

[112] Gourgourinis (n 16) 1018.

[113] See also Abi-Saab (n 19) 121.

extrapolated from the various regional legal orders, which will be discussed below.[114]

Moreover, the challenge posed by regional international law mirrors the three defects that Hart attributes to primitive legal orders and to which secondary rules respond. Regional international law, too, provokes three questions, or—in Hart's language—three defects, which may be remedied by shared secondary rules: firstly, claims to special legal treatment based on a regional affiliation point to the defect of uncertainty: to what extent can an idiosyncratic claim be recognized as regional international law and where does it merely amount to a regional policy without legal quality? Regional international law raises, secondly, the question of which rule prevails when both a regional rule and a rule under general international law are applicable. Finally, which requirements must be met for regional practice to change general international law?

These three questions underlie the 'three-step-approach' which this book proposes, based on secondary rules, in order to overcome the analytical challenge posed by regional international law and which will be addressed in detail below and in Chapters 4 to 7. Before turning to the analytical use of the recourse to secondary rules, the next section explores how this approach can address the normative challenges posed by regional international law—that is, why it not only represents a practicable, but also an equitable method for reconciling regional and general international law.

3.4 The normative potential of secondary rules

The fact that recourse to secondary rules is an established mechanism to address normative plurality in international law does not explain why it is also an equitable approach for doing so. In this vein, an arbitral tribunal has stated that

> [i]t may be that some international lawyers reflexively adopt the dichotomy of primary/secondary obligations made familiar by the International Law Commission . . . Perhaps this idea merges into that of a substance/procedure distinction. Yet there is nothing normative about the primary/secondary dichotomy; it has simply been the classification by which the ILC determined its field of work on State responsibility.[115]

[114] See on extrapolation as a method for identifying secondary rules: Mackenzie-Gray Scott (n 22) 349–54. See also on the identification of secondary rules section 3.5.1.

[115] *Quasar de Valores SICAV SA, Orgor de Valores SICAV SA, GBI 9000 SICAV SA and ALOS 34 SL v The Russian Federation* (Award on Preliminary Objections) SCC Case No 24/2007 (20 March 2009) [99].

This section argues that secondary rules serve an indispensable function in any legal order, including the international legal order, and thus qualify as the (lowest) common normative denominator (3.4.1) that is also relatively best-suited to addressing the normative challenge posed by regional international law (3.4.2), before engaging with the potential objections that the concept represents a normative imposition of its own or, conversely, downplays the existence of international law's substantive import (3.4.3).

3.4.1 The indispensable function of secondary rules in (international) law

The first reason why recourse to secondary rules provides an appealing approach for overcoming the normative challenge posed by regional international law—consisting in identifying a sufficiently determinate common denominator that does not carry the risk of imposing the values of one region on the others—is that the secondary rules of international law arguably represent the lowest common denominator in international law.

Every legal system develops rules to identify, change, and enforce the rights and obligations set out in that system.[116] There may be different views about whether these rules should be called 'rules',[117] whether secondary and primary rules can always be neatly distinguished,[118] whether these two categories need to be supplemented by 'tertiary rules',[119] and, naturally, about the content of these rules.[120] But unless one shares Hart's view from 1961 that international law is not a legal system, secondary rules are in fact indispensable for the functioning of the international legal system.[121] In this regard, secondary rules differ from other categories of rules in international law, perhaps including even norms of *jus cogens* that are non-derogable but the existence of which is, strictly speaking, not indispensable for the functioning of the international legal system. This becomes clear when

[116] See Hart (n 53); R Kolb, 'Le Droit International Comme Corps de Droit Privé et de Droit Public' (2021) 419 RdC 59; Y Onuma, 'A Transcivilizational Perspective on International Law' (2010) 342 RdC 156 fn 55; Vogenauer (n 103) 884. But see I Saunders, *General Principles as a Source of International Law* (Hart 2021) 244, pointing out that chthonic legal systems do not necessarily contain 'rules of change'.

[117] See d'Aspremont (n 106).

[118] See N Bobbio, 'Nouvelles réflexions sur les normes primaires et secondaires', *Essais de théorie du droit* (Librairie générale de droit et de jurisprudence 1998) 168.

[119] R Michaels, 'Tertiary Rules' in N Krisch (ed), *Entangled Legalities Beyond the State* (CUP 2021) 424, 447: 'These are the rules with which a legal system organizes its own relation to other legal systems and also designates those other legal systems' normative space with regard to itself.'

[120] See section 3.5.1 below.

[121] See also KJ Heller, 'Customary International Law Symposium: The Stubborn Tenacity of Secondary Rules' (*OpinioJuris*, 7 July 2020); d'Aspremont (n 109).

looking at the list of *jus cogens* rules annexed to the ILC's work on the topic.[122] Before 1919, several norms mentioned therein would arguably not have met the standard set out by the ILC for the identification of *jus cogens* in Conclusion 4 of its 2022 Conclusions.[123] Still, the international legal system long predates that date.[124]

The fact that the terminology and concept of secondary rules were not used in scholarship and practice until roughly 100 years ago does not undermine the claim relating to their indispensability. As Georges Abi-Saab observed in his 1987 General Course

> It is true that historically, secondary rules were only gradually perceived, at an advanced stage of reflection on primary rules, when this reflection transcended the content of these rules or attempted to better understand it through a second-degree reflection on the structures and patterns underlying the functioning and evolution of the rules as such. This does not mean, however, that these secondary rules did not exist from the outset and before their express formulation, even if they had remained latent in the primary rules, which could not have existed without such implicit anchoring.[125]

It is true that some scholars, including van Panhuys and Hakimi, have criticized the assumption that international law is formed, identified, and applied pursuant to a commonly shared set of rules, proposing alternatives to universal 'secondary rules'.

Van Panhuys, for example, observed that the validity of regional international law might be based on five different explanations. Apart from general international law, it could derive from the municipal law of one State, from coinciding rules of the 'external municipal laws', from a legal order established ad hoc, or from a pre-existing rule of international law that is only applicable among the States concerned, in other words, particular secondary rules.[126] Indeed, the question is how can we tell whether allegedly universal secondary rules are really 'accepted' in the Hartian sense or just coincidentally converging 'habits of obedience' stemming from several autonomous regional secondary rules.

However, van Panhuys' observations from 1959 that the rules determining the formation of international law may also stem from (coinciding) domestic law or ad

[122] ILC Report 2022 (*Jus cogens*) (n 14), Annex, 89.

[123] ILC Report 2022 (*Jus cogens*) (n 14), Conclusion 4. See on the genesis of *jus cogens* in international law: F Lange, 'Challenging the Paris Peace Treaties, State Sovereignty, and Western-Dominated International Law—The Multifaceted Genesis of the Jus Cogens Doctrine' (2018) 31:4 LJIL 821.

[124] Which is not to suggest that this system was either just or universally accepted. As scholars have noted, international law at the time was largely shaped by European powers and has itself contributed to injustices. See, for example, for a critical analysis of the current framework on reparations for colonial injustices: A Anghie, 'The Injustices of Reparation' (2025) 119(3) AJIL 423.

[125] Abi-Saab (n 19) 122 fn 74 [translation by the author].

[126] Van Panhuys (n 4) 147–50.

hoc arrangements among groups of States is less convincing in light of subsequent developments in State practice. Since then, as we will see, such practice has largely and consistently adhered to, confirmed, and entrenched commonly shared criteria for identifying, interpreting, and applying international law. The extent to which secondary rules may deviate from such universal secondary rules at the regional level is a different question and will be addressed below.

Hakimi, for her part, argues that practice in the 'real-world', as she puts it, shows that the identification of customary international law 'is not determined by secondary rules. The status of a given normative position within CIL depends instead on how global actors interact with it over time.'[127] Others have demonstrated in detail that her view is not substantiated by practice from the 'real-world', in particular in light of the overall agreement among States in the 6th Committee about the premise underlying the various ILC works on the secondary rules of international law, namely that rights and obligations under international law are to be identified, interpreted, applied, and enforced pursuant to common secondary rules.[128]

In this sense, one cannot but agree with Heller's observation that 'states uniformly embrace the idea that CIL consists of valid and binding primary rules produced by identifiable secondary rules—they simply disagree about how the secondary rules should be understood and applied'.[129] The indeed controversial issue about the identification of the content of these universal secondary rules is addressed below.[130]

3.4.2 Normative ownership through secondary rules

The second reason why recourse to secondary rules can overcome the normative challenge of regional international law is that these rules, through their characteristic dual function, ensure the 'normative ownership' of all subjects of international law with regard to both universally applicable and regionally limited legal rules.

Unlike other candidates for 'common denominators', secondary rules perform two seemingly contradictory functions: they establish and stabilize a common understanding of the existing law, while at the same time allow all subjects of international law, from any region, to contest, transform, or even dismantle that understanding, provided the criteria laid down in the secondary rules are met. Secondary rules thus constitute both the scaffolding of the common framework and, simultaneously, the instruments for changing that framework.[131]

[127] Hakimi (n 107) 1510.
[128] Hakimi (n 107); J d'Aspremont (n 109).
[129] Heller (n 107).
[130] Section 3.5.1.
[131] Similarly: N Krisch, 'International Law in Times of Hegemony: Unequal Power and the Shaping of the International Legal Order' (2005) 16:3 EJIL 369–408 (arguing that international law fulfils two

As a common framework, secondary rules set the minimum conditions for a sufficient degree of stability and normative consolidation without which law would not be able to fulfil its determinative function and independent role vis-à-vis politics. Secondary rules allow for 'snapshots' of the common legal *acquis* which are taken in the moment when law needs to be applied to a concrete case. In the context of regional international law, secondary rules demarcate the frame in which regional claims to legality converge with the respective expectations of third parties. By doing so, they may provide for sufficient 'normative equidistance' in the sense that they protect the legal framework from ideological usurpation.

At the same time, secondary rules provide devices to express and recognize different legal views, thus allowing for what may be called a certain 'normative empathy'. In this regard, secondary rules have an 'empowering' function by representing 'facilities for realizing their [the author: the members of a legal community] wishes, by conferring legal powers upon them ... within the coercive framework of law'.[132] As Scott Shapiro notes '[p]ower-conferring rules are tools that enable members of the community to realize their plans and projects'.[133] The dynamic potential of secondary rules is the key element when encountering regional claims to identity or representation, alternativity, and autonomy.[134] Concerns about a petrifying common denominator become groundless as secondary rules render the common *acquis* sufficiently inclusive, opposable, malleable, contestable, and revisable. Regarding regional claims to identity or representation, secondary rules provide for an alternative to disengaging from or violating general international law. They set out the requirements—generalizable across all regions—according to which regional legal claims can be recognized under international law, how normative impositions which contravene a certain regional identity can be opposed by legal means, and how general international law can be shaped and changed to include different regional identities equally. Claims to alternativity are translatable through 'secondary rules of change' as these set out the conditions under which general international law can be contested, changed, or deviated from by regional practice. Finally, secondary rules determine the extent to which claims of regional autonomy can be recognized by third parties.

interdependent functions, namely as an instrument of dominance and a means of resistance to it). See also: S Yee, 'The Role of Law in the Formation of Regional Perspectives in Human Rights and Regional Systems for the Protection of Human Rights: The European and Asian Models as Illustrations' (2004) 8 SYBIL 157, 159 ('constitutive'/'instrumental').

132 Hart (n 53) 27–28 and 48.

133 SJ Shapiro, *Legality* (The Belknap Press of Harvard University Press 2011) 79.

134 Chapter 2, section 2.4. See also J d'Aspremont, 'The International Court of Justice and the Irony of System-Design' (2017) 8 J Int Dispute Settl 366, 374–75; Yee (n 131) 159. See also L Obregón, 'Regionalism Reconstructed: A Short History of Latin American International Law' ESIL Conference Paper No 5/2012, 14.

The dual function inherent in secondary rules avoids, on the one hand, normative impositions and, on the other hand, legal indeterminacy. Instead, secondary rules allow, in the words of Norberto Bobbio, to maintain a 'dynamic equilibrium' (or, in Sundhya Pahuja's words and with a different emphasis, 'critical instability'[135]) within a legal order marked by the tension between regional plurality and the centripetal forces of universality.[136] Secondary rules prevent either of them from ever prevailing over the other.

In sum, secondary rules afford 'recognition' in a double sense.[137] They enable third parties to identify and 'recognize' regional claims, while also allowing legal subjects within a region to demand recognition from third parties and to see themselves reflected and represented in the body of international law.[138] In this way, secondary rules safeguard the 'normative ownership' of subjects from all regions not only with respect to universally applicable primary rules, but also—crucially—with respect to primary rules binding only within a particular region. This is because the determination of which forms of regional law qualify as international law, through the content of the secondary rules, remains the responsibility of all members of the international legal community.

3.4.3 The limits of secondary rules: a normative imposition or devoid of import?

The proposed approach based on secondary rules is neither a *panacea* nor free from preconceptions. It is based on the premise that contradictions between different regional approaches or between a regional and a universal set of rules occur in practice, that a legal reconciliation is both possible and preferable to leaving the issue to the free play of power politics, and that a solution based on law ultimately requires making a determination. Still, as a middle-ground approach, it, by its very nature, attracts criticism from both sides. For some, the role of secondary rules in ensuring the unity of international law is not only over-emphasized but also oversimplified and reductionist.[139] Others have highlighted that 'the claim of neutrality of secondary rules obscures the organic historical relationship between primary and secondary rules, which were shaped in the colonial era', in other words, that

[135] S Pahuja, *Decolonizing International Law* (CUP 2011) 42.

[136] Bobbio (n 118) 168.

[137] On the rule of recognition in the context of conflicts between State law and indigenous law, see: N Roughlin, 'Plurality of Laws and Conflict of Laws: Reconciling through Recognition?' in MS Green, R Michaels, and R Banu (eds), *Philosophical Foundations of Private International Law* (OUP 2024) 217.

[138] On this: See BS Chimni, 'Is There an Asian Approach to International Law? Questions, Theses and Reflections' (2008) 14 AYIL 249, 260.

[139] See eg M Prost, *The Concept of Unity in Public International Law* (Hart 2012) 81–83; see more generally for criticism of Hart's distinction between primary and secondary rules: R Dworkin, 'The Model of Rules I', in *Taking Rights Seriously* (Harvard University Press 1977).

secondary rules themselves may be—and have frequently been—used for normative impositions.[140]

None of these critiques is fully convincing. Those who criticize the lack of substantive content in the secondary-rules approach may wish to recognize the resilience it instils in the international legal system; resilience that is itself a precondition for the more ambitious functions international law is often expected to perform. As for the critique concerning the origins or alleged abuse of secondary rules by European or Western powers, much of the criticism relating to abuse concerns the scope and content of specific secondary rules, rather than the concept of secondary rules as such. This brings us to the next section.

3.5 The analytical potential of secondary rules

This section explains how the method based on secondary rules can be operationalized in practice to overcome the triple challenged posed by regional law to general international law.[141] It argues that a 'three-step approach' grounded in secondary rules offers a relatively neutral yet practicable framework for addressing the analytical challenge posed by regional international law, namely, the difficulty of distinguishing between its constructive manifestations ('regional trailblazing') and its corrosive forms ('regional trespassing').

To this end, it first examines the complex question of how the scope and content of universal secondary rules is identified (3.5.1) and then considers the extent to which these rules allow for regional secondary rules (3.5.2), before introducing the proposed 'three-step approach' (3.5.3) which will then be explained, 'step by step', in Chapters 4 to 7.

3.5.1 The identification of universal secondary rules

The preceding sections of this chapter suggested that many objections against recourse to secondary rules to overcome the triple challenge posed by regional international law are rooted in the difficulty of identifying the scope and content of universal secondary rules.

Despite its differences from the concept of secondary rules at the international level, Hart's concept of secondary rules still provides an insightful point of departure and comparison in this regard. According to Hart, the content of the rule of recognition is 'not stated, but [] shown in the way in which particular rules

[140] BS Chimni, 'The Articles on State Responsibility and the Guiding Principles of Shared Responsibility: A TWAIL Perspective' (2020) 31:4 EJIL 1211, 1213; see also Saunders (n 116).
[141] See Chapter 2, section 2.4.

are identified by courts or other officials or private persons or their advisers'.[142] Transposing this understanding to the international level, the existence and content of the rule of recognition 'may be inferred from the conduct and belief (*opinio juris*) of states'.[143] While Hart then considered the rule of recognition to be a 'social practice', international law scholars mostly understand secondary rules as unwritten legal rules, be it customary international law or general principles of law.[144] Both Hart and international lawyers thus seem to agree that secondary rules are rooted in practice. Hence, the fact that some secondary rules are codified in treaty provisions does not mean that these treaty provisions constitute the ultimate legal basis for the secondary rules of recognition and change. Moreover, these treaty provisions are often rather broad and do not necessarily provide specific guidance.

For this reason, the ascertainment of the precise content of secondary rules in international law is anything but straightforward. Secondary rules are rarely explicitly addressed but mostly implicitly applied. Exchanges about rules in practice tend to focus on primary rules, ie, whether a certain right or obligation exists or not, and not on the criteria of validity of a rule, ie why this right or obligation exists or not. A certain understanding of secondary rules is rather tacitly assumed; it motivates a certain conduct or legal view concerning these primary rules of international law. The challenge of ascertaining secondary rules is, moreover, rooted in the unwillingness of some actors to elucidate and codify the content of secondary rules.[145] Fearing a loss of flexibility, many actors tend to avoid pronouncing on their respective views in explicit terms beyond the concrete case.

The question, then, is how we can identify the scope and content of these universal secondary rules in a way that comprehensively and representatively reflects the practice of the subjects of international law. In its work on secondary rules concerning the identification, interpretation, and application of international law, the ILC has adopted a methodological approach comprising three steps. First, it identifies widely ratified treaty provisions that are regarded as codifications of these secondary rules. Second, it analyses how these provisions have been interpreted and applied by States, international courts and tribunals, as well as by scholarly doctrine, and formulates proposals for the concretization of the rules based on that analysis. Third, it submits these proposals to States and international organizations

[142] Hart (n 53) 101.

[143] TM Franck, *The Power of Legitimacy Among Nations* (OUP 1990) 187. See further at 190.

[144] See eg CJ Tams, 'Meta-Custom and the Court: A Study in Judicial Law-Making' (2015) 14 LAPE 51–79 on 'meta-custom'.

[145] See, for instance, the initial scepticism of some delegations in the Sixth Committee towards the ILC's decision to include the projects on 'Treaties over time' (ILC, 'Topical summary of the debate held in the Sixth Committee' (2009) UN Doc A/CN.4/620, 18; on CIL (ILC, 'Topical summary of the debate held in the Sixth Committee' (2013) UN Doc A/CN.4/657, 12. See also Memorandum submitted by the Secretary-General, 'Survey of International Law in Relation to the Work of Codification of the International Law Commission: Preparatory work within the purview of article 18, paragraph 1, of the International Law Commission' (1949) UN Doc A/CN.4/1/Rev.1, 1, 22 [33].

through the Sixth Committee of the United Nations General Assembly, subsequently revising its conclusions and commentaries in light of the comments received. Although this book cannot fully replicate the methodology employed by the ILC, it seeks, as far as possible, to draw inspiration from its 'trialogic' approach.[146]

Turning to the treaties that may serve as a starting point for identifying universal secondary rules on the identification, interpretation, and application of international law, Article 38(1) of the ICJ Statute (ratified by 193 States) and the 1969 VCLT (with 116 parties, and many of its provisions widely recognized as customary international law) provide a suitable point of departure. However, despite their broad ratification, the critical question remains to what extent these provisions were intended to reflect—exhaustively and exclusively—a shared understanding among States concerning the rules of recognition and legal change. The answer to this question has significant consequences for the degree to which these provisions are open for the recognition of regional sources of law and rules on interpretation.

Starting with Article 38 of the PCIJ Statute—which was adopted in 1920 and almost identically incorporated into Article 38(1) of the ICJ Statute in 1946—we may recall that this provision was never meant to represent the 'source of sources', the 'rule of recognition', of international law.[147] In 1920, its purpose was more modest, yet still revolutionary: Article 38 specified the applicable law on the basis of which the PCIJ was to decide international disputes. By proposing such a provision, the Advisory Committee of Jurists (ACJ), which was entrusted with the preparation of a draft statute for the PCIJ in 1919, hoped to convince States to accept the PCIJ's compulsory jurisdiction. While the proposal for compulsory jurisdiction of the PCIJ was rejected, the draft of what became Article 38 of the PCIJ Statute and later of the ICJ Statute was retained in its entirety.[148] But does this drafting history mean that Article 38 is no more than a 'repressive construction'[149] designed for a specific purpose and institution without any bearing on the larger question of sources in international law?

This view was taken by some scholars and practitioners in the inter-war and post-World War II period.[150] However, already the members of the 1920 ACJ

[146] See also on the interplay between the ILC and the ICJ: O Sender, *International Law-Making by the International Court of Justice and International Law Commission* (CUP 2024).

[147] H Thirlway, *The Sources of International Law* (2nd edn, OUP 2019) 3.

[148] The content of Article 38 of the PCIJ Statute and the ICJ Statute was proposed as Article 35 of the draft by the Advisory Committee of Jurists.

[149] J d'Aspremont, 'The International Court of Justice as the Master of the Sources' in C Espósito and K Parlett (eds), *The Cambridge Companion to the International Court of Justice* (CUP 2023) 165, 171–73.

[150] See G Fitzmaurice, 'Some Problems Regarding the Formal Sources of International Law' in FM van Asbeck and others (eds), *Symbolae Verzijl* (Martinus Nijhoff 1958) 153, 173–74 and 176. See also *Lotus* (n 9) (dissenting opinion Judge Weiss) 43–44 ('In reality the only source of international law is the *consensus omnium*.').

discussed what became Article 38 not merely as the applicable law for the Court, but in terms of the 'sources' of international law.[151] As observed by Hugh Thirlway:

> the drafting of Article 38 of the PCIJ Statute was not an act of creation, but of recording… International law as it had developed, and as it then stood, derived from the relations built up among States (including, but not limited to, what could be classified as 'State practice' for purposes of custom), and Article 38 reflected what was, in the view of those who drafted it, already there.[152]

After World War II, Article 38 gradually emerged as the authoritative definition of the sources of international law.[153] As early as 1949, the UN Secretariat observed in a survey with respect to the 'Sources of International Law' that

> [t]he codification of this aspect of international law has been successfully accomplished by the definition of the sources of international law as given in article 38 of the Statute of the International Court of Justice. That definition has been repeatedly treated as authoritative by international arbitral tribunals.[154]

During the Vienna Conference on the Law of Treaties, notably when discussing what became Article 38 of the VCLT, delegations frequently invoked Article 38(1) of the ICJ Statute as an authoritative reflection of the sources of international law.[155] Commenting on the Vienna Conference in 2014, Abdulqawi Yusuf highlighted that

> [t]he newly independent African States also expressed resistance towards some elements of the sources of international law as outlined in Article 38 of the Statute of the ICJ. They did not contest the sources themselves as such.[156]

[151] Advisory Committee of Jurists, *Procès-verbaux of the Proceedings of the Committee June 16th to July 24th, 1920, with Annexes* (The Hague: Van Langenhuysen, 1920) 295 (de Lapradelle); 318, 336, 337 (Descamps); 332, 336 (Ricci-Busatti), 333 (Phillimore).

[152] Thirlway (n 147) 10; see also Abi-Saab (n 19) 191 calling Article 38(1) PCIJ Statute 'un reflet fidèle' of the understanding of sources at that time.

[153] See also Article 10 of the 1958 *Model Rules on Arbitral Procedure* which mirrors the text contained in Article 38 (ILC, 'Model Rules on Arbitral Procedure, with commentaries' (1958) YBILC II, UN Doc A/CN.4/SER.A/1958/Add.l, 83).

[154] Memorandum, 'Survey of International Law in Relation to the Work of Codification of the International Law Commission' (1949) (n 145) 22 [33].

[155] See UN Conference on the Law of Treaties, First Session: 26 March–24 May 1968, Official Records: Summary Records of the Plenary Meetings and of the Meetings of the Committee of the Whole, UN Doc A/Conf.39/11 (hereinafter: 'UNCLOT I'), 198 [2] (Turkey); 198 [6] (Greece); 199 [19] (Trinidad and Tobago); 200 [34] (Colombia); 200 [39] (Iraq); UN Conference on the Law of Treaties, Second Session: 9 April–22 May 1969, Official Records: Summary records of plenary meetings and of the meetings of the Committee as a whole, UN Doc A/CONF.39/SR.13 (hereinafter: 'UNCLOT II'), 69 [38] (Argentina); 95 [25] (Federal Republic of Germany); 172 [37] (Uruguay); 295 [25] (Guatemala); 329 [3] (Ecuador).

[156] AA Yusuf, *Pan-Africanism and International Law* (Brill 2014) 108.

Nowadays, it is uncontested that Article 38(1) is an authoritative reflection of the sources of international law,[157] a position that has also been adopted by the ICJ.[158] Instead, the debate has shifted to another question, ie, whether the list contained in Article 38(1) is exhaustive.

This debate ensued primarily against the background of the increasing legislative activities of IOs,[159] but also in light of several ICJ decisions in which the Court recognized the binding character of unilateral acts.[160]

Many scholars have emphasized the non-exhaustive character of Article 38(1) with varying lines of argument.[161] Alain Pellet and Daniel Müller even go so far as to describe Article 38(1) as 'a useful directive, [which] has not prevented the Court from deciding on the basis of other sources of international law'.[162] Others seem more reluctant to view Article 38(1) as non-exhaustive.[163] Pointing to the drafting history, Sienho Yee, for instance, argues that

> [t]he struggles in the Committee of Jurists at The Hague in 1920 that resulted in the final text of the article evinced an intention for the list of applicable law to be a closed one.... the non-listed 'sources' can be applied if they are somehow brought within the framework of Article 38 (1) (a), (b) or (c).[164]

In a similar vein, yet less categorical than Yee, Gennadij Danilenko cautions that 'while Article 38 may not contain a closed list of sources, it is still possible that at this stage it is an exhaustive one'.[165] He suggests to approach this issue on the basis of a 'strong presumption of completeness' underlying Article 38(1); exceptions from which required 'a careful examination of the contemporary practice of States and international law-applying agencies'.[166] In his view, official statements of States declaring Article 38 to be exhaustive, treaty provisions—such as Articles 74 and 83 UNCLOS—referring exclusively to Article 38, and the absence of 'any serious movement towards official revision of the basic article on sources' demonstrate

[157] See also R Jennings and A Watts, *Oppenheim's International Law, Vol I* (9th edn, OUP 2008) 24.

[158] See eg *Military and Paramilitary Activities in and against Nicaragua (Nicaragua v United States)* (Merits) [1986] ICJ Rep 14 [56].

[159] See eg Yusuf (n 156) 108–109: 'The newly independent African States . . . wanted . . . to complement the enumerated sources through the recognition of a role for the declaratory resolutions of the united nations General Assembly.'

[160] See *Nuclear Tests (Australia v France)* (n 23) [43]; *Nuclear Tests Case (New Zealand v France) (Judgment)* [1974] ICJ Rep 457 [46]; *Frontier Dispute (Burkina Faso/Republic of Mali) (Judgment)* [1986] ICJ Rep 554 [40].

[161] Thirlway (n 147) 3; A Pellet and D Müller, 'Article 38' in A Zimmermann and others (eds), *The Statute of the International Court of Justice: A Commentary* (3rd edn, OUP 2019) [81] for further references.

[162] Pellet and Müller (n 161) 76.

[163] See M Shaw, *International Law* (8th edn, CUP 2017) 52.

[164] Yee (n 86) 475.

[165] GM Danilenko, *Law-Making in the International Community* (Martinus Nijhoff Publishers 1993) 40.

[166] Danilenko (n 165) 40–41.

that the 'presumption of completeness' still holds valid.[167] On closer inspection, the difference between these three positions—considering Article 38(1) as non-exhaustive, a closed list, or as containing a 'presumption of completeness'—is marginal. All three assume that Article 38(1) and the meaning given to it may change over time.[168]

In contrast to Article 38 of the ICJ Statute, several provisions contained in the 1969 VCLT clarify that the Convention does not *exhaustively* cover the law of treaties.[169] What is unclear, however, is to what extent the provisions in the VCLT claim to prescribe how issues addressed by the VCLT must be approached, possibly excluding diverging regional rules on interpretation. Once again, we are confronted with the question to what extent the codification of secondary rules does not only 'record', but also 'freezes' them. To avoid such a freezing effect, the third Special Rapporteur, Gerald Fitzmaurice, suggested the adoption of a 'code on the law of treaties' instead of a 'treaty on the law of treaties' in 1956:

> First, it seems inappropriate that a code on the law of treaties should itself take the form of a treaty; or rather, it seems more appropriate that it should have an independent basis. In the second place, much of the law relating to treaties is not especially suitable for framing in conventional form. It consists of enunciations of principles and abstract rules, most easily stated in the form of a code; and this also has the advantage of rendering permissible the inclusion of a certain amount of declaratory and explanatory material in the body of the code, in a way that would not be possible if this had to be confined to a strict statement of obligation. ... Finally, reference may be made to certain inherent difficulties in drafting any code on treaty law, arising out of the attempt to give a unified treatment to the subject.[170]

The ILC chose not to follow this line of argument and rather drafted what became the 1969 VCLT. But why did the ILC codify something that, according to Danae Azaria, 'was not necessary', given their nature as 'secondary rules of recognition (and change)'?[171] Was the VCLT indeed meant as an 'attempt to give a unified treatment to the subject', excluding any scope for idiosyncratic approaches?

[167] Danilenko (n 165) 40–42. In footnote 91 at 41 he refers to statements made by Brazil and Japan in the 6th Committee in 1974 declaring Article 38 to be exhaustive.

[168] This also seems to be the position taken by Sir Michael Wood who 'observed that Article 38 was drafted with a degree of openness that was able to accommodate changes to the international legal system' (A Keene (ed), 'Outcome Paper for the Seminar on the International Court of Justice at 70: In Retrospect and in Prospect' (2016) 7 J Int Dispute Settl 238, 257).

[169] See eg Articles 3, 4, and 5 of the VCLT. See also F Berman, 'Why Do We Need a Law of Treaties?—Inaugural Lecture' (2017) 385 RdC 19, 24.

[170] ILC, 'First Report on the Law of Treaties, by Sir Gerald Fitzmaurice, Special Rapporteur' (1956) YBILC II, UN Doc A/CN.4/101, 107 [9]–[10].

[171] D Azaria, 'The International Law Commission's Return to the Law of Sources of International Law' (2019) 13:6 FIU Law Review 989, 991.

The choice of the treaty form can be understood as the strongest 'antidote' to the risk of a fragmentation of the law of treaties into different variations. At the time of the elaboration of the law of treaties, the 1950s and 1960s, the international legal order faced significant transformations and an increasingly pluralist community of States following the decolonization process, as well as the ideological cleavage between East and West. As reflected in the ILC's explanation of 1962, the form of a treaty was not meant to create new rules or to impose a certain approach to treaty law but rather to maintain the existing rules' equilibrating function.[172]

The two reasons given by the ILC effectively reflect the two normative functions of secondary rules that were discussed in the previous section. The envisaged treaty was to consolidate the secondary rules on the law of treaties (in line with the 'framing function' of secondary rules discussed above).[173] Moreover, the ILC emphasized the 'empowering function' of secondary rules when arguing that the form of a multilateral treaty 'would give all the new States the opportunity to participate directly in the formulation of the law if they so wished'.[174] During the subsequent Vienna Conference, the ideologically diverse assembly of States ensured that the VCLT would be drafted in a way that no specific approach to treaty law would prevail over others, but would be broad enough to give space to different regional practices.[175]

It is thus difficult to describe the VCLT as aiming to be 'exclusive'. Instead, it may be more appropriate to describe it as being 'conditionally permissive': while the VCLT indeed leaves considerable leeway for pursuing idiosyncratic approaches, it also provides for certain 'outer limits' on which States across all regions agreed.[176]

We can draw four conclusions: firstly, Article 38(1) of the ICJ Statute and the rules contained in the 1969 VCLT are not constitutive but rather declaratory with respect to universal secondary rules. Secondly, these treaty rules are neither exhaustive nor exclusive. Instead, they can be compared to 'snapshots' taken in 1920, 1946, and 1969, which recorded a certain understanding of the 'rules of recognition' and 'rules of change'. Universal secondary rules as reflected in Article 38(1) of the ICJ Statute and the VCLT are thus not set in stone. Rather, and thirdly, the treaty rules that codified the universal secondary rules have been serving as a common starting point for the identification and interpretation of international law by States, IOs, and international courts and tribunals. However, it is, fourthly,

172 ILC, 'Report of the International Law Commission covering the work of its fourteenth session, 24 April–29 June 1962' (1962) YBILC II, UN Doc A/5209, 160 [17].

173 ILC (n 172).

174 ILC (n 172).

175 See Chapter 4.

176 See also Berman (n 169), who points, on the one hand, to the 'freedom of contract' as the 'overall guiding principle of the Convention' (21–23) with 'virtually no area in which the negotiating States cannot, by agreement, disapply the general rule' (25), but also argues that the reasons for invoking invalidity were exhaustive and exclusive (25); D Peat, 'Disciplining Rules? Compliance, the Rules of Interpretation, and the Evaluative Dimension of Articles 31 and 32 of the VCLT' (2022) 69 NILR 221, 237.

not clear how far we can diverge from that common point of departure when it comes to the accommodation of more idiosyncratic regional legal claims.

3.5.2 The limits of codified secondary rules

While the existence of universal secondary rules is indispensable, the subjects of international law are generally free to adopt distinct secondary rules *inter se*. The residual nature of universal secondary rules is illustrated, for example, by Article 55 ARSIWA.[177] At the heart of the challenge posed by regional law thus lies the question about the extent to which universal secondary rules accommodate not only regional primary rules, but also distinct regional secondary rules, notably regional sources and rules of interpretation.[178]

This section discusses how we can identify the conditions under which third parties are obliged, in accordance with universal secondary rules, to recognize a claim based on regional law as international law, and conversely, when they may treat such claims, like domestic law, as mere factual assertions.

Taking Hart as a point of departure, he essentially argued that regional and universal secondary rules form part of the same legal system if they share the same rule of recognition. Yet, Raz criticized in his 1971 article 'The Identity of Legal Systems' that Hart failed to clarify '[w]hat changes [to the rule of recognition] are consistent with the continued existence of the same rule, and what changes compel the admission that a new rule has replaced the old one?'.[179] Raz' critique, however, could have acknowledged that Hart had indeed addressed this aspect, even if briefly.[180] In fact, Hart pointed to the transition of domestic law to (regional) international law: taking the history of the British Commonwealth as an example for the 'embryology of legal systems', Hart described the process in which 'a new legal system emerges from the womb of an old one' by developing a new rule of recognition with a 'local root'.[181] In other words, the mere fact that a regional legal system relies on distinct regional sources or interpretative rules that do not align neatly with Article 38 of the ICJ Statute or the VCLT does not, in itself, deprive it of its character as international law as long as we can ascertain that these regional secondary rules do not replace the universal rule(s) of recognition in international law. But how can this be determined? Three methodological premises inform the way in which this Chapter and the following ones will examine this question.

[177] See also Kajtár, Çalı, and Milanovic (n 90) 3.
[178] See also N Krisch, 'The Dynamics of International Law Redux' (2021) 74 Curr Leg Probl 1, 18–19.
[179] J Raz, 'The Identity of Legal Systems' (1971) 59 Calif L Rev 795, 812.
[180] Hart (n 53) 102–103, and 147–54 (entitled 'Uncertainty in the Rule of Recognition') in particular at 152.
[181] Hart (n 53) 120–21.

Firstly, we may recall the findings made in Chapter 2, ie, that belonging to a region entails a presumption of tolerable legal distinctiveness that bears on the identification, application, and creation of international law and justifies recognizing regional law as a distinct legal category.[182] For this reason, the first premise is that the extent to which universal secondary rules accommodate idiosyncratic regional claims depends on the extent to which these conform to the defining features of regions and regional law, namely normative cohesion, identifiability, and distinctiveness.[183]

Secondly, drawing on the methods of comparative international law, it may be presumed that the closer a regional secondary rule aligns in methodology and function with a universal secondary rule, the less likely it is intended to supplant the latter.[184]

Thirdly, these conceptual considerations must be substantiated through empirical analysis of practice. This involves, inter alia, comparing the conduct and claims of States within a given region with the responses of States and international organizations outside that region; compiling and systematizing relevant case law from international courts and tribunals; evaluating statements made by States and international organizations in the Sixth Committee concerning regional dimensions; and synthesizing the perspectives articulated within the ILC and academic scholarship. Accordingly, the third premise holds that a regional secondary rule may be deemed consistent with universal rules of recognition insofar as it emerges from a congruent practice among subjects of international law both within and beyond the region.[185]

3.5.3 Regional trespassing or trailblazing: the 'three-step-approach'

The three-step approach developed in this section provides a framework to assess the validity and effects of regional claims on the international legal system. It is based on the premise that a legal claim articulated at the regional level, whose alleged legal consequences do not correspond to the legal significance accorded to it by universal secondary rules, may be considered detrimental to the international legal system if that regional claim is further upheld.[186] The three steps reflect the three 'defects' resulting from regional law and their corresponding secondary rules:

[182] See Chapter 2, section 2.3.
[183] See Chapter 2, section 2.2.
[184] See also A Cuyvers, 'Comparing Regional Law' in M Siems and PJ Yap (eds), *The Cambridge Handbook of Comparative Law* (CUP 2024) 649, 666–73 on the merits of functionalism and methodological options for corrections.
[185] See section 2.3.
[186] See similarly: R Kolb, *Theory of International Law* (Hart 2016) 96: 'In technical terms: the density and configuration of the primary rules of a legal order cannot outweigh by too much the maximum limit allowed by the infrastructure of the secondary rules of the system, ie its institutional setting. The two must grow together, with a certain harmony. An excessive proliferation of primary rules, which the secondary level is not equipped to digest, will lead to the regression, the weakening and sometimes the destruction of the legal order.'

The first step addresses whether regional law can be considered international law and, accordingly, can—or even must—be recognized as such by third parties. This first step responds to, in Hart's words, the 'defect' of uncertainty: given the often idiosyncratic nature of regional law, it is frequently unclear to what extent they qualify as international law or merely as a regional legal tradition, overlapping domestic law or merely a policy. At this stage, the key question is how far the universal secondary rules governing the identification and interpretation of international law accommodate a regional 'law of treaties' (explored in Chapter 4) and unwritten sources of regional law in the form of regional custom, regional general principles of law, and regional *jus cogens* (examined in Chapter 5).

If a regional claim qualifies as international law, the second step involves determining which rule prevails when both a rule of regional international law and a rule of general international law apply to a specific situation (as analysed in Chapter 6). This step addresses the defect of inefficiency that arises when two or more potentially conflicting legal rules threaten to neutralize each other. The analysis focuses on the universal secondary rules governing the interpretation and application of international law, with particular attention to techniques for avoiding and resolving normative conflicts. If the regional rule successfully passes this second step—meaning it may be applied despite competing rules under general international law—the analysis ends on the conclusion that the entity asserting the claim is entitled to demand recognition of its validity and applicability from third parties.

If the regional claim fails to succeed either at the first or second step, the analysis proceeds with the third step, ie with evaluating whether the regional practice nonetheless represents a constructive contribution to the development of international law (as explored in Chapter 7). This third step addresses the defect of *stasis*—a condition particularly pronounced in an international legal system that lacks a central legislator. The focus here is on the universal secondary rules governing the formation and evolution of international law. Specifically, the analysis considers what requirements must be met for regional practice to qualify as a 'building block'—whether by contributing to the interpretation of a multilateral treaty over time, the formation of a general rule of customary international law, the emergence of a general principle of law, or of a peremptory norm under general international law.

3.6 Conclusion

Returning to our point of departure, one must agree with van Panhuys that the question—regional *or* general international law—does not seem particularly helpful in overcoming the challenge posed by regional law. Given that regional law latently claims to arise from a distinct polity, such a query is hardly more productive than the question 'domestic or international law'. It is thus much more interesting to ask how regional *and* general international law can be reconciled in a way that is neither too rigid nor repressive towards regional plurality, nor too indeterminate to serve as a basis for legal definition.

This chapter argued that the 'three-step-approach', based on secondary rules as a distinct category of general international law, provides a method by which the international legal order can be kept both responsive and resilient vis-à-vis regional legal diversity. In times of increasing normative plurality and crumbling consensus on the *acquis* of primary rules, secondary rules can provide for a common grammar, a common denominator, and thus preserve a minimum of universality in the international legal order. Ultimately, the limits of their integrative capacity contribute to the analytical distinction between constructive and corrosive forms of regionalism. So, in this sense, we also see the claim confirmed that regional rules derive their authority from general international law understood as the secondary rules of international law.

4

Does a 'law of regional treaties' exist?

4.1 A law of regional treaties?

Regional treaties hold a distinctive place in international law for at least four reasons. First, their provisions frequently serve as trailblazers or blueprints for universal treaties.[1] Second, within universal treaties, regional treaties are commonly granted a privileged status.[2] Third, in the day-to-day practice of international law, they regularly constitute the decisive legal framework.[3] Finally, and rather unsettlingly considering the preceding points, the legal status, content, and effects of regional treaties often remain obscure, both for their parties and for third parties.[4]

It is true that the differences between regional and other treaties should not be artificially overstated. The point of departure for their application is certainly the same. Once concluded, regional treaties, as any other international agreement, 'acquire[] a life of their own'.[5] Their application, like that of any other treaty, almost invariably requires some form of interpretation of their text that may give rise to divergent views.[6] Yet, there is a significant difference between regional and

[1] See eg the Treaty on the Non-Proliferation of Nuclear Weapons (adopted 1 July 1968, entered into force 5 March 1970) 729 UNTS 161, which was preceded, and some of its provisions inspired by the Treaty for the Prohibition of Nuclear Weapons in Latin America and the Caribbean (adopted 14 February 1967, entered into force 22 April 1967) 634 UNTS 281. See also Chapter 7, section 7.2.

[2] See eg Covenant of the League of Nations (adopted 28 June 1919) 225 CTS 195, art 21; Charter of the United Nations (adopted 26 June 1945, entered into force 24 October 1945) 1 UNTS XVI, arts 33(1), 47(4), 52, 53, and 54; General Agreement on Tariffs and Trade (adopted 30 October 1947, entered into force 1 January 1948) 55 UNTS 187, arts V and XXIV.

[3] Apart from regional trade agreements, human rights treaties, and constituent instruments establishing regional integration organizations, regional treaties play a significant role in cases before the ICJ, eg, in: *Alleged Violations of Sovereign Rights and Maritime Spaces in the Caribbean Sea (Nicaragua v Colombia)* (Preliminary objections) [2016] ICJ Rep 3 [26]–[46] (Pact of Bogotá); *Maritime Dispute (Peru v Chile)* [2014] ICJ Rep 3 [71]–[95]. See also on the way in which regional agreements in Africa complement general international law: M Wiebusch, *A Theory on Africanizing International Law* (Pretoria University Law Press 2024) 1–3, 102–103, 146–48; T Maluwa, 'Reassessing Aspects of the Contribution of African States to the Development of International Law Through African Regional Multilateral Treaties' (2020) 41:2 Mich J Int Law 327–415.

[4] See CD Gaver, 'What are the Riyadh Agreements?' (*EJILTalk!*, 1 July 2020) <https://www.ejiltalk.org/what-are-the-riyadh-agreements/> (accessed 8 May 2026). The term 'third parties' is defined in line with Article 2(1)(h) 1969 VCLT and 1986 VCLT as subjects of international law that are not party to the treaty.

[5] See *Reservations to the Convention on the Prevention and Punishment of Genocide* (Advisory Opinion) [1951] ICJ Rep 49, 53 (Diss Op Judge Álvarez).

[6] On the distinction between 'interpretation' and 'application': R Gardiner, *Treaty Interpretation* (2nd edn, OUP 2015) 26–30.

Regional and General International Law. Janina Barkholdt, Oxford University Press. © Janina Barkholdt 2026.
DOI: 10.1093/9780198953432.003.0004

other treaties. For third parties, it is often difficult to discern whether distinctive approaches to the interpretation and application of regional treaties are owed to different legal traditions, established practices, or even region-specific secondary rules, or whether they instead amount to attempts to circumvent or undermine the general law of treaties.[7] The result is a practice replete with hard cases.

For example, the way in which regional treaties have evolved through the jurisprudence of regional bodies has been increasingly invoked, whether as a genuine explanation or a convenient pretext, to justify non-compliance and even withdrawal by member States from those regional dispute settlement mechanisms.[8] Powerful regional hegemons occasionally ascribe a content or effect to a provision contained in a regional treaty that aligns with their own normative preferences and which is not necessarily shared by the other parties.[9] Parties to a regional instrument sometimes even disagree whether they have concluded a binding regional agreement in the first place.[10] In addition, third parties at times raise concerns about the normative 'spillover effects' of regional treaties, notably from the European region, commonly referred to as the 'Brussels effect' and the 'Strasbourg effect'.[11]

At the same time, the regional character of a treaty may not only give rise to a distinct way of interpreting or applying it but might also justify such a distinct approach. Given the presumption of acceptable legal distinctiveness arising from regional affiliation,[12] the acceptance by both parties to the regional treaty and third parties may be greater for regional deviations from the general rules of the law of treaties. The challenge thus consists in identifying the permissible range of such variations and deviations.

There are principally three possible ways or degrees in which such legal distinctiveness arising from regional affiliation could play out in the law of treaties: in the development of a set of universal secondary rules governing all regional treaties (a 'law of regional treaties'), the emergence of regional secondary rules applicable to treaties concluded within a particular region (a 'regional law of treaties'), or simply the accommodation of distinct regional approaches to treaty law under the

[7] See Chapter 2, section 2.4.

[8] See eg Joint letter of nine governments of CoE member States to the ECtHR (22 May 2025) <https://www.governo.it/sites/governo.it/files/Lettera_aperta_22052025.pdf> (accessed 29 April 2026) 2.

[9] See eg the way in which the Soviet Union interpreted the provisions of the Warsaw Pact to justify its interventions in Hungary and Czechoslovakia: UNSC, 754th Meeting (4 November 1956) UN Doc S/PV.754 [53]; UNSC, 1441st Meeting (21 August 1968) UN Doc S/PV.1441 [90]–[92].

[10] See eg *The South China Sea Arbitration (The Republic of Philippines v The People's Republic of China) (Award on Jurisdiction and Admissibility)* PCA Case 2013-19 (29 October 2015) 212–19 on the (non-) bindingness of the 2002 Declaration on the Conduct of Parties in the South China Sea.

[11] A Bradford, *The Brussels Effect: How the European Union Rules the World* (OUP 2020); B Saul, 'The Council of Europe's Proposed Definition of Terrorism Infringes Human Rights' EJILTalk! (18 February 2025) <https://www.ejiltalk.org/the-council-of-europes-proposed-definition-of-terrorism-infringes-human-rights/> (accessed 29 April 2026).

[12] See Chapter 2, section 2.3.

universal secondary rules on the law of treaties (a 'general law of treaties regionally accommodated').

To understand the extent to which a distinct legal regime applies—or may apply—to regional treaties, this chapter first analyses whether specific legal rules for regional treaties were considered during the drafting of the 1969 and 1986 Vienna Conventions on the Law of Treaties (4.2). It then examines the limits for regional approaches to treaty interpretation (4.3), before analysing the extent to which the application of regional treaties is constrained by the legal interests of third parties (4.4).

Before doing so, two clarifications regarding the scope of this chapter are in order.

Firstly, it is of course inaccurate to assume that the relations among States within regions are exclusively governed by regional treaties. Apart from unwritten regional law—the subject of Chapter 5—States also organize their relations through non-legally binding instruments—commonly referred to as 'soft law'.[13] This chapter addresses non-legally binding instruments only indirectly. Its focus is on regional treaties that meet the definition set out in Article 2(1)(a) of the 1969 and 1986 VCLT respectively, ie that are an 'international agreement in written form and governed by international law . . . whatever its particular designation'.[14] Yet, to do so, non-legally binding agreements must be incidentally addressed. The reason for this is that a key difficulty for determining the applicable legal rules for interpreting and applying regional instruments stems from the fact that their legal nature is not always clear.[15] Moreover, non-legally binding instruments may still produce significant legal effects which will be analysed when discussing their role in the interpretation of regional treaties,[16] in the formation of unwritten regional law,[17] and in the identification of general international law.[18] At both the regional and universal level, expert bodies have proposed criteria for the identification of non-legally binding agreements based on an analysis of practice and the case law of courts and tribunals.[19] And while there may be regional variations in the way

[13] T Hsien-Li, 'No Longer Hard Law's "Poor Relative": The Growing Respect for Soft, Non-Binding Legal Instruments in the International Order' EJILTalk! (6 June 2025) <https://www.ejiltalk.org/no-longer-hard-laws-poor-relative-the-growing-respect-for-soft-non-binding-legal-instruments-in-the-international-order/> (accessed 29 April 2026); H Mahaseth, 'Binding or Non-binding: Analysing the Nature of the ASEAN Agreements' (2021) 21 ICLR 100–23.

[14] Vienna Convention on the Law of Treaties (23 May 1969) 1155 UNTS 331; Vienna Convention on the Law of Treaties between States and International Organizations or between International Organizations (21 March 1986, not yet in force) UN doc A/CONF.129/15. See also Y Onuma, 'A Transcivilizational Perspective on International Law' (2010) 342 RdC, 269–70 arguing that the definition of a 'treaty' in the 1969 VCLT is a valuable point of departure.

[15] See also A Cuyvers, 'Comparing Regional Law' in M Siems and PJ Yap (eds), *The Cambridge Handbook of Comparative Law* (CUP 2024) 655–58.

[16] Section 4.3.

[17] See Chapter 5.

[18] See Chapter 7.

[19] See eg ILC, 'Second report on non-legally binding international agreements' (2025) UN Doc A/CN.4/784, 21–60; Inter-American Juridical Committee, 'Guidelines on Binding and Non-Binding

in which non-legally binding agreements are drafted and used,[20] the common denominator in practice largely converge on the view that a written instrument is considered binding if this is either expressly stated in its text or, where the text is silent, the instrument's actual terms and the circumstances in which it was drawn up indicate that the parties intended it to have legal effect at the time of its adoption.[21] It is this understanding of legally binding written instruments that defines the term 'regional treaty' for the purpose of this book.

Secondly, as this chapter cannot cover all issues relating to the law of treaties, its focus is limited to the interpretation and application of regional treaties—that is, the rules that keep a treaty 'alive' over time, rather than those governing its formation or termination.

4.2 Regionalism in the preparation of the VCLT

Neither the 1969 VCLT nor the 1986 VCLT contains any explicit reference to *regional* treaties or IOs. However, during the drafting process leading up to their adoption, considerable attention was given to accommodating the particularities of regional treaties.

4.2.1 'General' vs 'restricted multilateral treaties'

The closest the drafting process of the 1969 VCLT ever came to a 'law of regional treaties' was when France introduced a proposal envisaging special rules in eight draft articles for 'restricted multilateral treaties' during the Vienna Conference in 1968.[22] According to France, it was

> necessary to refer specifically to restricted multilateral treaties because of the very special nature of that type of agreement. Restricted multilateral treaties represented a special category of regional treaties, in that they established between the participating States obligations and advantages which were so balanced that any

Agreements' (7 August 2020) Resolution CJI/RES. 259 (XCVII-O/20) <https://www.oas.org/en/sla/iajc/docs/Guidelines_on_Binding_and_Non-Binding_Agreements_publication.pdf> (accessed 5 May 2026), Guideline 3.

[20] See eg ILC, 3682nd Meeting (11 July 2024) UN Doc A/CN.4/SR.3682, 16 (Patel); 3683rd Meeting (16 July 2024) UN Doc A/CN.4/SR.3683, 4 (Paparinskis).

[21] On this, see also the ILC Special Rapporteur, 'Second Report (2025)' (n 19) [21].

[22] See the proposals A/CONF.39/C.1/L.24 and A/CONF.39/C.1/ L.46, introduced in UN Conference on the Law of Treaties 'Official Records: Summary Records of the Plenary Meetings and of the Meetings of the Committee of the Whole (First Session)' (26 March–24 May 1968) UN Doc A/CONF.39/11 (UNCLOT I), 22–23, 205. The proposed amendments related to Articles 2, 8, 17, 36, 37, 55, and 66.

> change in the contribution of a party, or a party's failure to ratify the treaty, would upset the whole structure of the instrument.[23]

By way of examples, France referred to treaties

> establishing very close co-operation between several States, such as treaties of economic integration, treaties between riparian States relating to the development of a river basin or treaties relating to the building of a hydroelectric dam, scientific installations, or the like.[24]

By introducing this proposal, France intended to build on and supplement drafts based on works of the ILC on special rules for treaties between 'a limited number of negotiating States' in the context of reservations.[25] Yet, the French proposal went even further and argued for a comprehensive set of special rules that provided for a higher threshold—unanimous consent—for the conclusion, amendment, modification of, and reservations to such treaties.[26]

This proposal triggered a considerable debate. Curiously, it has not received much attention in scholarship, despite the fact that it was, according to Shabtai Rosenne, one of five major controversies during the whole drafting process.[27] Some States, such as Argentina and the USSR, expressed themselves favourably towards the category of 'restricted multilateral treaties'.[28] Others, including Ecuador, Nigeria, and the US, rejected it outright.[29] Eventually, the debate was deferred to the second session of the Vienna Conference, at the beginning of which France, having 'come to the conclusion that it was not essential', withdrew its proposal.[30] What remained as a faint trace of the proposal on 'restricted multilateral treaties' is Article 20(2) of the VCLT, which had, however, already been part of the initial draft proposed by the ILC. Interestingly, the UK, despite having earlier expressed its scepticism vis-à-vis the French proposal,[31] reacted rather cryptically to this withdrawal by stating that

[23] UNCLOT I, 80 [2] (France).

[24] UNCLOT I, 22–23 [16] (France).

[25] ILC, 'Draft Articles on the Law of Treaties with commentaries (1966)' UN Doc A/CN.4/SER.A/1966/Add.1, 207 [19].

[26] UNCLOT I, 22–23 [17] (France).

[27] S Rosenne, *The Law of Treaties: A Guide to the Legislative History of the Vienna Convention* (AW Sijthoff 1970) 79.

[28] At UNCLOT I: Expressing support for the French amendment: Argentina (29 [71]); USSR (30 [90]). In favour of defining 'restricted multilateral treaty': Syria (25 [6]); Italy (26 [23]); Guinea (32 [6]); Mali (33 [23]).

[29] At UNCLOT I: Ecuador (25 [12]); Nigeria (25 [18]); US (165–66 [20]–[22]); UK (203 [74]).

[30] UN Conference on the Law of Treaties 'Official Records: Summary Records of the Plenary Meetings and of the Meetings of the Committee of the Whole (Second Session)' (9 April–22 May 1969) UN Doc A/CONF.39/11.Add.1 (UNCLOT II), 213 [3].

[31] UNCLOT I, 203 [74] (UK).

> [t]he fact that the French delegation had agreed to withdraw its amendments relating to restricted multilateral treaties, because of the difficulty of formulating special rules for that category of treaties, did not mean that no such category existed.[32]

One reason why France withdrew its proposal may have been the fact that the debate on different categories of treaties had shifted to what later became Articles 5 and 20(3) of the VCLT (the distinction between 'constituent instruments' of IOs and other treaties) as well as to the distinction between interdependent or integral and other treaty obligations (Articles 41(1)(b) and 60(2)(c) of the VCLT). These provisions responded, to some extent, to the concerns that had initially motivated the French proposal.

4.2.2 Inspiration by and accommodation of regional treaty practice

Although the proposal for special rules on 'regional treaties' failed, it would be inaccurate to conclude that the drafters of the VCLT did not take regional particularities seriously. Inspiration drawn from regional treaty practice is, for instance, visible with regard to the regime on reservations.[33] The need to accommodate regional treaties and their often idiosyncratic construction in the draft convention also played a significant role in drafting the provisions relating to the 'rules of the organization' (Article 5),[34] conflicts between successive treaties (Article 30),[35] invalidity subsequent to an 'error' (Article 48),[36] and peremptory norms of general international law (Articles 53 and 64 of the VCLT).[37]

During the 1986 Conference, several States and international organizations submitted comments to ensure that what became the 1986 VCLT would not be shaped based on the practice of just one particular regional IO (the European Economic

[32] UNCLOT II, 239 [69] (UK).

[33] See eg ILC, 'Resolutions of the General Assembly concerning the law of treaties: memorandum prepared by the Secretariat' (1963) YBILC II, UN Doc A/CN.4/SER.A/1963/ADD.1, 20 [17] ('The practice of the Pan American Union was strongly advocated by many delegations.').

[34] UNCLOT I, 53–54 [4] (Senegal): '[T]hat the codification of principles hitherto derived from customary law should not entail the establishment of excessively rigid criteria which might paralyse the development of regional law. Inter-African law was a case in point.'

[35] UNCLOT I, 206 [42] (Uruguay): 'Regional arrangements, for which the United Nations Charter itself made specific provision in articles 52 to 54, were an important example of *inter se* agreements to vary, as between some of the parties, the provisions of the main treaty. Frequently a number of States bound by close historic and other ties would be able, in their *inter se* relations, to go further than the other parties in the direction of progress marked by the main treaty.'

[36] ILC, 'Summary records of the fifteenth session from 6 May to 12 July 1963' (1963) YBILC I, UN Doc A/CN.4/SER.A/1963, 44–45 [70]–[78].

[37] See debate triggered by the proposal of the US to identify *jus cogens* on the basis of regional legal systems: UNCLOT I, 295–326. See also Chapters 5 and 7.

Communities),[38] but would also leave scope for the distinct treaty practice that had been emerging in their respective regions.[39] For example, the Australian delegate emphasized that

> [i]n his region there was a fast-developing body of regional treaty practice whose procedures were characterized by a large degree of informality, so much so that it had become known as the 'Pacific way'. His delegation would like the draft convention to provide scope for procedures of that kind to expand, particularly in the case of organizations.[40]

Given the drafters' awareness of regional particularities, and their insistence on accommodating them in the texts of the 1969 and 1986 VCLT, it is difficult to see why later, in practice, States would have felt the need to develop a separate law of regional treaties. Still, recalling the statement by the UK that 'the difficulty of formulating special rules for that category of treaties, did not mean that no such category existed',[41] it does not seem far-fetched to assume that States and regional organizations may have agreed to a general law of treaties and, in practice, developed more specific secondary rules, a 'law of regional treaties' or, in the case of a regionally confined law of treaties, a 'regional law of treaties', that diverge from the secondary rules codified in the 1969 and 1986 VCLT. In any event, the boundary between regional approaches accommodated within the general law of treaties and regional rules that depart from it is often difficult to delineate.

Since the adoption of the 1969 VCLT, much attention has been focused on identifying distinct approaches to the law of treaties in various sub-fields of international law, particularly in relation to human rights treaties or economic integration. By contrast, the question of whether regional variations and deviations from the rules set out in the 1969 VCLT exist has, if at all, been raised only in passing and rarely examined in depth.[42] This is only one of the symptoms of the almost obsessive pre-occupation with functional fragmentation rather than regional fragmentation by scholars in recent decades. It is true that the two phenomena are

[38] See in particular the debate on the ILC's draft Article 36*bis* which provided that member States of an IO may, in certain cases, be bound by the treaties concluded between that IO and a third party: UN Conference on the Law of Treaties between States and International Organizations or between International Organizations, 'Official Records: Documents of the Conference (Vol I)' (18 February–21 March 1986) UN Doc A/CONF.129/16/Add.1 (UNCLOT-IO I), 150–51 [47] (USSR); 145, [49] (Cameroon).

[39] See eg UN Conference on the Law of Treaties between States and International Organizations or between International Organizations, 'Official Records: Documents of the Conference (Vol I)' (18 February–21 March 1986) UN Doc A/CONF.129/16/Add.1 (UNCLOT-IO I), 76 [8] (Australia).

[40] UNCLOT-IO I, 76 [8].

[41] UNCLOT II, 239 [69] (UK).

[42] See eg the very concise treatment in the 2024 ILA Report: ILA Study Group, 'The International Law of Regional Organizations: Final Report' (Athens Conference 2024) 33.

not easily disentangled.[43] In other words, it is not always clear if a regional body adopts a certain approach to the law of treaties because of a treaty's subject-matter or because of its regional character.[44] However, as noted in Chapter 2, the motivation of the entity that interprets and applies a regional treaty constitutes only one dimension of qualifying a certain practice.[45] Equal attention must be given to the reactions of other actors to that conduct, particularly other parties to the regional treaty (4.3) as well as third parties (4.4).

4.3 Within the region: the limits for regional approaches to treaty interpretation

Contrary to certain concerns voiced during and after the drafting process,[46] the interpretative framework of the VCLT, as set out in Articles 31 to 33 and now recognized as reflecting customary international law,[47] does not prescribe a particular approach or a fixed hierarchy of interpretive methods.[48] As Michael Waibel points out, these provisions are 'far from being an interpretive straightjacket, flexibility is a built-in feature of the VCLT's interpretive armoury'.[49] Such flexibility 'left substantial leeway for idiosyncratic approaches to interpretation within the bounds staked out by the VCLT's broad interpretive principles'.[50] In addition to the flexibility provided by Articles 31 to 33, Article 5 contains a 'general reservation clause'[51] regarding the interpretation of constituent instruments of IOs, which provides that 'any relevant rules of the organization' are *lex specialis* vis-à-vis the rules contained in the VCLT.[52]

[43] See also ILC, 'Fragmentation of International Law: Difficulties Arising from the Diversification and Expansion of International Law: Report of the Study Group of the International Law Commission—Finalized by Martti Koskenniemi' (2006) UN Doc A/CN.4/L.682 [204].

[44] See also F Bordin and J Odermatt, 'International Law of Regional Organizations: A Comparative Perspective' (2024) 21:1 IOLR 19, 42.

[45] See Chapter 2, section 2.3.

[46] MS McDougal, 'The International Law Commission's Draft Articles upon Interpretation: Textuality Redivivus' (1967) 61:4 AJIL 992; A Orakhelashvili, *The Interpretation of Acts and Rules in Public International Law* (OUP 2008) 309: 'the rules of treaty interpretation are fixed rules.'

[47] *Question of the Delimitation of the Continental Shelf between Nicaragua and Colombia beyond 200 Nautical Miles from the Nicaraguan Coast (Nicaragua v Colombia)* (Preliminary Objections) [2016] ICJ Rep 100 [33].

[48] R Gardiner, 'The Vienna Convention Rules on Treaty Interpretation' in DB Hollis (ed), *The Oxford Guide to Treaties* (2nd edn, OUP 2020) 459, 487; D Peat, *Comparative Reasoning in International Courts and Tribunals* (CUP 2019) 39.

[49] M Waibel, 'Uniformity Versus Specialization (2): A Uniform Regime of Treaty Interpretation?' in CJ Tams, A Tzanakopoulos, and A Zimmermann (eds), *Research Handbook on the Law of Treaties* (Edward Elgar Publishing 2014) 375, 410–11.

[50] M Waibel, 'Demystifying the Art of Interpretation' (2011) 22:2 EJIL 571, 575.

[51] K Schmalenbach, 'Article 5' in O Dörr and K Schmalenbach (eds), *Vienna Convention on the Law of Treaties: A Commentary* (2nd edn, Springer 2018) 99 [1].

[52] See also Chapter 7, section 7.3.2.4.

Practice confirms that the secondary rules on interpretation reflected in the VCLT are generally accepted as a common framework that reconciles regional particularity with generality. The ICJ frequently interprets regional treaties based on the rules reflected in the VCLT without having recourse to special rules of interpretation.[53] Regional bodies explicitly refer to Articles 31 and 32 VCLT when interpreting regional treaties.[54]

The true challenge to these rules' integrative capacity, however, arises in cases where it is unclear whether regional practice conforms to the rules reflected in the VCLT. As we will see, the secondary rules on treaty interpretation reflected in the VCLT simultaneously limit (4.3.1) and enable (4.3.2) the recognition of regional claims to identity, alternativity, and autonomy.[55] While it remains difficult to delineate a distinct set of interpretive rules for regional treaties, the distinct characteristics of regional law, outlined in Chapter 2, often support a more generous recognition of regional approaches to interpretation.

4.3.1 The 'outer limits' of treaty interpretation: three elements

The rules reflected in the VCLT are flexible, but they do set certain 'outer limits' for treaty interpretation. It is true that some scholars have argued that Articles 31 to 33 contain no more than a 'convenient set of guidelines that can be twisted at will'.[56] This scepticism has its roots in a traditional uneasiness about codifying and speaking of 'rules' of interpretation which had already emerged during the drafting process of the VCLT and has persisted ever since.[57] Jan Klabbers, for instance, argues that interpretation rules 'do not fit the regular pattern of rules' and are but 'methodological devices . . . One cannot, in any meaningful way, violate

[53] See eg the detailed interpretation of the 1948 Pact of Bogotá in *Alleged Violations (Nicaragua v Colombia)* (n 3) [26]–[46].

[54] *Golder v The United Kingdom* App No 4451/70 (ECHR, 21 February 1975) [29]–[30]; *Mapiripán Massacre v Colombia* (Merits, Reparations, and Costs) (15 September 2005) IACHR Series C No 134 [106]; *The Attorney General of the Republic of Uganda v Tom Kyahurwenda* (Judgment) Case No 1 of 2014 (EACJ, 31 July 2015) [33]; *Advisory Opinion concerning the Interpretation of Article 29 of the Treaty on the EAEU ('Internal Market Exceptions')* Case SE-2-2/2-17-BK (Court of the Eurasian Economic Union, 30 October 2017), 3; *In the matter of a request for an Advisory Opinion by the Caribbean Community pursuant to Article 212 of the Revised Treaty of Chaguaramas and Rule 11.3(1) of the Caribbean Court of Justice (Original Jurisdiction) Rules 2019* App No AOOJ2019/001 (CCJ, 18 March 2020) [44].

[55] See Chapter 2, section 2.4.1.

[56] See for criticism of this approach: *Right to Strike under ILO Convention No. 87* (Advisory Opinion of 21 May 2026) ICJ (separate opinion of Judge Nolte) [59]–[64], who argues, in para 60 that the purpose of the VCLT rules on interpretation is 'to reduce the risk that arbitrariness or the interpreter's personal preferences will prevail'.

[57] See ILC, 'Sixth Report on the Law of Treaties, Special Rapporteur Sir Humphrey Waldock' (1966) YBILC 1966 II, UN Doc A/CN.4/186, 94 [1]: 'The Commission was fully conscious . . . of the undesirability—if not impossibility—of confining the process of interpretation within rigid rules (. . .)'. See also J Crawford, *Brownlie's Principles of Public International Law* (9th edn, OUP 2019) 366.

them'.[58] However, Klabbers' argument that a violation of Articles 31 to 33 of the VCLT does not constitute a wrongful act under the law of State responsibility does not preclude that the rules contained therein impose constraints on the way in which treaties are interpreted.[59] The flexibility afforded by the VCLT should not be interpreted as permitting an 'anything goes' approach. Due to their character as secondary rules, the constraining effect of the rules on treaty interpretation simply manifests itself differently (a possibility that Klabbers acknowledges).[60] In this regard, it is important not to conflate the mandatory character of the VCLT rules, ie, the requirement of having recourse to them,[61] with an obligation to achieve a certain result or an 'explicit "show your workings" requirement'.[62] The VCLT rules are not even 'exclusive in a way that they prevent the interpreter from applying other principles that are compatible with the general rule laid down in Art 31'.[63] Yet, the question is how to assess 'whether the proposed rule of interpretation is in fact one that lies outside the Convention's system or whether it is encompassed by the latter's provisions'.[64]

This issue is unproblematic in cases which are characterized by what we may call 'substantive equivalence'. As Helmut Aust notes, 'if the result is correct, it does not matter whether interpretation according to the Vienna rules took place, or according to some other method'.[65] Far more challenging, however, are the likely majority of cases in which the 'correctness' of the meaning given to a certain term is called into question.

This problem has arisen in the context of annulment proceedings under Article 52(1)(b) of the ICSID Convention.[66] The respective ad hoc committees in the 2007 *Lucchetti* and 2010 *Fraport* annulment decisions indicated that an 'untenable' interpretation may amount to a 'manifest excess of power' under this provision.[67]

[58] J Klabbers, 'Virtuous Interpretation' in M Fitzmaurice, O Elias, and P Merkouris (eds), *Treaty Interpretation and the Vienna Convention on the Law of Treaties: 30 Years On* (Brill Nijhoff 2010) 17, 29–31.

[59] See even from a critical perspective: F Zarbiyev, 'The "Cash Value" of the Rules of Treaty Interpretation' (2019) 32 LJIL 33, 43–45.

[60] Klabbers (n 58) 29–30, fn 55.

[61] See HP Aust, 'Between Universal Aspiration and Local Application: Concluding Observations' in HP Aust and G Nolte (eds), *The Interpretation of International Law by Domestic Courts* (OUP 2016) 333, 340; J d'Aspremont and R Gardiner, 'Methodological Observations on Interpretation in International Law' in ILA, 'Final Report of the Study Group on the Content and Evolution of the Rules on Interpretation' (Kyoto 2020), Annex, 7–8.

[62] Gardiner (n 6) 40.

[63] O Dörr, 'Article 31' in O Dörr and K Schmalenbach (eds), *Vienna Convention on the Law of Treaties: A Commentary* (2nd edn, Springer 2018) 577 [32]; see also Gardiner (n 6) 40: '[T]he Vienna rules are not exclusive of other compatible principles and techniques for treaty interpretation.'

[64] Dörr (n 63).

[65] Aust (n 61) 340.

[66] Convention on the settlement of investment disputes between States and nationals of other States (adopted 18 March 1965, entered into force 14 October 1966) 575 UNTS 159.

[67] *Empresas Lucchetti, SA and Lucchetti Peru, SA v The Republic of Peru* (Decision on Annulment) ICSID Case No ARB/03/4 (5 September 2007) [112]; *Fraport AG Frankfurt Airport Services Worldwide v The Republic of the Philippines* (Decision on Annulment) ICSID Case No ARB/03/25 (23 December

Regarding the identification of an 'untenable' interpretation, the ad hoc committees applied a high threshold. In their view, an interpretation is not yet untenable if it 'does not reflect all relevant aspects of treaty interpretation according to the Vienna Convention' or is 'summary and somewhat simplified in relation to the Vienna Convention'.[68] However, this threshold would have been crossed had the tribunal 'disregarded any significant element of the well-known and widely recognised international rules of treaty interpretation'.[69] This prompts the question of what, precisely, qualifies as a 'disregard of a significant element' of the rules of treaty interpretation.

Three 'significant elements' can be distilled from the preparatory works of the ILC, the debate during the Vienna Conference, and the jurisprudence of the ICJ.

Firstly, as emphasized by both the ILC and the ICJ, the essential purpose of the VCLT rules ultimately consists in ascertaining the meaning of a text 'in accordance with the intentions of its authors'.[70] In this regard, the structure of Articles 31 and 32 of the VCLT is an important indication: this structure channels and controls the consideration of sources extrinsic to the treaty itself by distinguishing between 'authentic' (Article 31) and 'supplementary' (Article 32) means for establishing the intention of the parties.[71] Any interpretive approach that makes no attempt to identify the meaning of a text on the basis of the (presumed) intention of the parties to the treaty at the time of its conclusion but either relies solely on extrinsic sources, or even casts aside the intentions of the parties by referring to a collective value, goal, or identity is incompatible with the basic thrust of the VCLT rules.

A second significant element of the VCLT rules is that they accord a central role to the text of the treaty. According to the ILC, the text

> must be presumed to be an authentic expression of the intention of the parties; . . . in consequence, the starting point of interpretation is the elucidation of

2010) [112]: 'As long as the interpretation arrived at by the Tribunal is a tenable one, it is not open to the Committee to conclude that the Tribunal manifestly exceeded its powers.'

68 *Lucchetti* (n 67) [116].

69 *Lucchetti* (n 67) [116]. In his dissenting opinion, Sir Franklin Berman found the interpretation to justify an annulment, pointing out that 'the actual evidence of their Award does not sustain the supposition that the Tribunal did diligently and systematically apply the Vienna Convention rules at all' (*Lucchetti* (n 67) (Diss Op Sir Franklin Berman) 12). See d'Aspremont and Gardiner (n 61) 8–9.

70 *Dispute regarding Navigational and Related Rights (Costa Rica v Nicaragua)* [2009] ICJ Rep 213 [48]; *Land and Maritime Boundary between Cameroon and Nigeria (Cameroon v Nigeria: Equatorial Guinea intervening)* [2002] ICJ Rep 303 [59]; *Legal Consequences for States of the Continued Presence of South Africa in Namibia (South West Africa) notwithstanding Security Council Resolution 276 (1970)* (Advisory Opinion) [1971] ICJ Rep 16 [53]; see also as underlying the second and third reason for codifying the rules on interpretation given by Waldock in his third report (ILC, 'Third Report on the Law of Treaties, by Sir Humphrey Waldock, Special Rapporteur' (1964) YBILC II, UN Doc A/CN.4/167 and Add.1–3, 54 [8]).

71 ILC, 'Documents of the sixteenth session including the report of the Commission to the General Assembly' (1964) YBILC II, UN Doc A/CN.4/SER.A/1964/ADD.1, 204–205.

> the meaning of the text, not an investigation *ab initio* into the intention of the parties.[72]

However, this second element is not disregarded if a meaning is attributed to the treaty that goes beyond the ordinary meaning of the text, nor is it disregarded if the interpretation does not start with the text. Yet, an interpretation is arguably untenable, for instance, where an interpretation is adopted that prima facie contradicts the ordinary meaning of the wording, and no attempt is undertaken to explain this result in terms of the rules of interpretation.[73]

Thirdly, the Vienna rules are based on the premise that in order to properly respect the 'intention of the authors'

> the application of the means of interpretation in the article would be a single combined operation. All the various elements, as they were present in any given case, would be thrown into the crucible, and their interaction would give the legally relevant interpretation.[74]

This view was confirmed in 2017 and subsequently by the ICJ[75] and in Conclusion 2(5) of the 2018 project on 'Subsequent agreements and subsequent practice in relation to interpretation of treaties' (SASP).[76] An interpretation is not untenable just because the interpreter does not deal with all methods in depth or puts a particular emphasis on one method.[77] However, the line is crossed in those cases, in which interpretive methods, notably 'authentic' means of interpretation, point to a meaning that differs from the one eventually adopted, but are, nonetheless, entirely disregarded in the interpretive process.[78]

Failure to take account of any of these three elements signals that the broad discretion afforded under the VCLT has been overstepped. What remains to be addressed are the consequences of such non-compliance.

Unlike primary rules, where non-compliance typically engages the responsibility of the acting entity, the breach of secondary rules raises issues of legal validity

[72] ILC, 'Draft Articles on the Law of Treaties with commentaries' (1966) YBILC II, UN Doc A/CN.4/SER.A/1966/Add.1, 220 [11].

[73] Peat (n 48) 21: 'The text of the treaty, for example, cannot be ignored in a free-ranging search for the intentions of the parties (. . .)'.

[74] ILC (1966) YBILC II (n 57) 219–20 [8]; Gardiner (n 6) 9.

[75] *Maritime Delimitation in the Indian Ocean (Somalia v Kenya)* (Preliminary Objections) [2017] ICJ Rep 3 [64]: 'These elements of interpretation—ordinary meaning, context and object and purpose—are to be considered as a whole.'; confirmed in *Arbitral Award of 3 October 1899 (Guyana v Venezuela)* (Preliminary Objections) [2020] ICJ Rep 455 [71].

[76] ILC, 'Draft Conclusions on Subsequent Agreements and Subsequent Practice in relation to the Interpretation of Treaties, with Commentaries' (2018) UN Doc A/73/10 (ILC Report 2018 (SASP)), Conclusion 2(5).

[77] See eg *Territorial Dispute (Libya/Chad)* [1994] ICJ Rep 6 [41]: 'Interpretation must be based above all upon the text of the treaty.'

[78] Peat (n 48) 21.

instead. This means that the frame set by the universal secondary rules reflected in the VCLT protect individual States parties to a regional treaty from normative impositions by regional hegemons as well as from excessively activist organs of a regional IO entrusted with the interpretation and application of a regional treaty. To the extent that procedures, such as appeal or annulment proceedings, are available to the State, it can raise objections as to the legality of the act in question.[79] If such procedures do not exist, non-compliance with the test established above gives that State a justification for its non-recognition of the interpretation in question.

The shockwaves resulting from such a scenario are illustrated by the controversy between the German Constitutional Court (BVerfG) and the CJEU concerning the *Public Sector Asset Purchase Programme* (PSPP) of the European Central Bank (ECB).[80] In its judgment of 5 May 2020, the BVerfG recognized that different rules of interpretation apply to the interpretation of the EU treaties when stating that

> The particularities of EU law give rise to considerable differences with regard to the importance and weight accorded to the various means of interpretation.... as long as the CJEU applies recognised methodological principles and the decision it renders is not arbitrary from an objective perspective...The mandate, conferred upon the CJEU in Art. 19(1)...necessarily entails that the CJEU be granted a certain margin of error....[81]

At the same time, the BVerfG stated that the Court's mandate 'is exceeded where the traditional European methods of interpretation or, more broadly, the general legal principles that are common to the laws of Member States are manifestly disregarded'.[82] After having invested a considerable effort in demonstrating that the CJEU's approach 'contradicts the methodological approach taken by the CJEU in virtually all other areas of EU law',[83] the BVerfG came to the conclusion that 'the interpretation undertaken by the CJEU is not comprehensible from a methodological perspective'[84] and that '[t]he CJEU thus acted *ultra vires*, which is why,

[79] See eg the establishment of the Tribunal Permanente de Revisión under the Olivos Protocol for the Settlement of Disputes in MERCOSUR (signed 18 February 2002, entered into force 1 January 2004) 2251 UNTS 243 which, according to Article 17, is mandated as a court of appeal for legal questions considered by a previous arbitral tribunal; see further: Treaty for the Establishment of the East African Community (signed 30 November 1999, entered into force 7 July 2000) 2144 UNTS 255, which provides for the possibility of an appeal in Article 35 A before an appellate division; in the EU context: Articles 263, 264, and 266 TFEU pursuant to which Member States can seek judicial review of the legality of the acts of EU institutions, bodies, offices, and agencies by the CJEU. See also Article 256(1) TFEU, according to which appeals against decisions of the EU General Court may be brought before the EU Court of Justice.

[80] *Public Sector Asset Purchase Programme* (German Federal Constitutional Court, Judgment of the Second Senate of 5 May 2020) 2 BvR 859/15; *Weiss and Others* C-493/17 (CJEU, 11 December 2018).

[81] *Public Sector Asset Purchase Programme* (n 80) [112].

[82] *Public Sector Asset Purchase Programme* (n 80) [112].

[83] *Public Sector Asset Purchase Programme* (n 80) [133] and [146].

[84] *Public Sector Asset Purchase Programme* (n 80) [153].

in that respect, its Judgment has no binding force in Germany'.[85] The decision of the BVerfG evoked harsh criticism by scholars.[86] Moreover, the European Commission instituted infringement proceedings against Germany 'for violation of fundamental principles of EU law, in particular the principles of autonomy, primacy, effectiveness and uniform application of Union law, as well as the respect of the jurisdiction of the European Court of Justice under Article 267 TFEU' on 9 June 2021.[87] Such proceedings were, however, discontinued on 2 December 2021.[88]

While it is unnecessary to go in-depth into this case, it should be noted that the BVerfG's own reasoning is not entirely free from contradictions when applying its standard of review (on whether 'the CJEU applies recognised methodological principles and the decision it renders is not arbitrary from an objective perspective'). On the one hand, the BVerfG recognizes the competence of the CJEU to determine its own methodological standards for the interpretation of the EU treaties and acknowledges the existence of a wide margin of error. On the other hand, it argues that it may find the CJEU's interpretation to exceed its mandate 'even where this finding derives only from a careful and meticulously reasoned interpretation'.[89] Yet, it appears difficult to reconcile such a 'seek and you shall find'-approach with the allegedly exercised judicial self-restraint.[90] Without taking a stance on this particular case, it illustrates that, although States allow regional treaties to be interpreted with some flexibility because of their specific characteristics, interpretations by regional courts that stray beyond accepted interpretive methods can lead to non-compliance and disengagement. At the same time, the allegation that 'activist' regional courts exceeded their mandate may serve merely as a pretext for States to justify their non-compliance or withdrawal from such a treaty. The distinction between pretextual and justified criticism of the interpretation of a regional treaty is thus often difficult to draw.[91] The test outlined above can help address this challenge.

85 *Public Sector Asset Purchase Programme* (n 80) [163].

86 See eg FC Mayer, 'Auf dem Weg zum Richterfaustrecht. Zum PSPP-Urteil des BVerfG' (*Verfassungsblog*, 7 May 2020) <https://verfassungsblog.de/auf-dem-weg-zum-richterfaustrecht/> (accessed 29 April 2026).

87 Press Release of the European Commission (9 June 2021) <https://ec.europa.eu/commission/presscorner/detail/en/inf_21_2743> (accessed 29 April 2026).

88 Press Release of the European Commission (2 December 2021) <https://ec.europa.eu/commission/presscorner/api/files/document/print/de/inf_21_6201/INF_21_6201_DE.pdf> (accessed 29 April 2026).

89 *Public Sector Asset Purchase Programme* (n 80) 113. See also A Nußberger, 'Was ist Willkür? Auf der Suche nach europäischen Standards' (2021) 76 Juristenzeitung 965, 973.

90 *Public Sector Asset Purchase Programme* (n 80) [112] ('exercised with restraint, giving effect to the Constitution's openness to European integration').

91 See eg A Donald and A Forde, 'Reinforce, Reform or Rupture? The Future of the European Convention on Human Rights' (EJILTalk!, 29 October 2025) <https://www.ejiltalk.org/reinforce-reform-or-rupture-the-future-of-the-european-convention-on-human-rights/> (accessed 29 April 2026); N De Silva and M Amadi, 'Renewed State Backlash Against the African Court: Tunisia is the Fifth State to Withdraw Individual and NGO Access' (EJILTalk!, 23 May 2025) <https://www.ejiltalk.

4.3.2 Regional challenges to secondary rules on interpretation

Despite the permissive character of the VCLT, certain regional practices, emanating from claims to identity, alternativity, and autonomy,[92] test the outer limits of treaty interpretation. Still, it is precisely recourse to and translation through these universal secondary rules that allow them to be recognized within and beyond the region.

4.3.2.1 Regional values and identity

A particular feature of the interpretation of regional treaties is the frequent reference to the underlying values, experiences, and particularities of the respective region. In numerous decisions, international courts and tribunals have pointed to regionally 'shared values' when interpreting regional treaties.[93] In that vein, the African Commission in *Constitutional Rights Project and Another v Nigeria* stated that

> [t]he African Charter should be interpreted in a culturally sensitive way, taking into full account the differing legal traditions of Africa and finding expression through the laws of each country.[94]

Two examples from the jurisprudence of the ICJ—one being one of its first decisions, the second a more recent one—illustrate that the general rules on treaty interpretation are not averse to considerations of regional identity and sensitivities. The first example is the 1950 *Asylum case* between Colombia and Peru. In this case, the ICJ referred to regional 'considerations' and the 'firmly established traditions' of the Latin-American republics when interpreting the 1928 Pan-American Havana Convention on Asylum.[95] Sixty-four years later, in the *Maritime Dispute* case between Peru and Chile, Peru relied heavily on 'regional solidarity vis-à-vis third States' when interpreting the regional instruments applicable among the parties,[96] an interpretation that was, save for the consequences resulting from it, shared by Chile,[97] and eventually reflected in the Court's judgment.[98]

org/renewed-state-backlash-against-the-african-court-tunisia-is-the-fifth-state-to-withdraw-individual-and-ngo-access/> (accessed 29 April 2026).

[92] See Chapter 2, section 2.4.1.

[93] *Mapiripán Massacre v Colombia* (n 54) [104]; *Demir and Baykara v Turkey*, App 34503/97 (ECHR, 12 November 2008) [85].

[94] *Constitutional Rights Project and Another v Nigeria* Comm No 143/95, No 150/96 (ACHPR, 15 November 1999) [26].

[95] *Asylum (Colombia/Peru)* [1950] ICJ Rep 266, 285.

[96] *Maritime Dispute (Peru v Chile)* Memorial of Peru (20 March 2009) [4.89], [4.92], [8.5].

[97] *Maritime Dispute (Peru v Chile)* Counter-Memorial of Chile (9 March 2010) [3.138].

[98] *Maritime Dispute (Peru v Chile)* [2014] ICJ Rep 3 [75]–[77], [125], and [150]–[151].

These decisions illustrate threes way in which considerations of regional identity may play a role in the interpretive process. Firstly, 'regional traditions' that attain the status of unwritten regional law, notably as regional custom, 'shall be taken into account' under Article 31(3)(c) of the VCLT.[99] If they do not qualify as unwritten regional law, they may, secondly, be translated into the interpretive process as the 'object and purpose' of the treaty under Article 31(1).[100] Thirdly, they may be considered as 'circumstances of [the treaty's] conclusion' under Article 32 of the VCLT.[101] Both decisions thus demonstrate that considerations of regional identity are not a 'trump card', but one element of the interpretive process whose weight depends on whether they are classified as 'authentic' or 'supplementary' means of interpretation.

4.3.2.2 Alternative regional rules of interpretation

The outer limits of treaty interpretation have also been challenged by alternative principles or rules of treaty interpretation at the regional level.

Some regional treaties either explicitly provide for special interpretive approaches, or such rules have been developed by the respective treaty organs. This includes the '*pro homine* approach' in the Inter-American system,[102] the principle of '*effet utile*' developed by the CJEU,[103] and doctrines such as the 'autonomous interpretation' and the 'living instrument approach' employed by the ECtHR.[104] There is neither a requirement to cite the VCLT nor to adopt its terminology.[105] To the extent that these interpretive approaches are functionally equivalent to the method contained in the VCLT, they are compatible with the VCLT framework.[106]

[99] Contrary to the assessment by Dörr, there are good reasons to understand the example from the Asylum case as a case of systemic integration of a (regional) customary rule.

[100] As was done with the argument relating to 'regional solidarity', *Maritime Dispute (Peru v Chile)* [2014] ICJ Rep 3 [63] and [77].

[101] See O Dörr, 'Article 32' in O Dörr and K Schmalenbach (eds), *Vienna Convention on the Law of Treaties: A Commentary* (2nd edn, Springer 2018) 625 [22].

[102] American Convention on Human Rights (adopted 22 November 1969, entered into force 18 July 1978) 1144 UNTS 123, art 29; see also L Lixinski, 'Treaty Interpretation by the Inter-American Court of Human Rights: Expansionism at the Service of the Unity of International Law' (2010) 21:3 EJIL 585–604.

[103] See eg *Van Duyn v Home Office* Case 41-74 (ECJ, 4 December 1974) [12] ('useful effect').

[104] See on 'Other methods of interpretation developed by the ECtHR': Council of Europe, Committee of Ministers, Steering Committee for Human Rights (CDDH) (2020), 'Report on the Place of the European Convention on Human Rights in the European and International Legal Order' (Strasbourg, 26–29 November 2019) 33–35 [84]–[90] with extensive references to case law.

[105] Gardiner (n 6) 40.

[106] Such approaches are usually understood as variants of the 'object and purpose' (eg J-M Sorel and V Boré Eveno, 'Article 31' in O Corten and others (eds), *The Vienna Conventions on the Law of Treaties* (2nd edn, OUP 2025) 948–49 [54] and fn 266); Dörr, 'Article 31' (n 63) 577 [30]. Some consider them as falling in the scope of Article 31(3) VCLT or Article 5 VCLT (eg P Palchetti, 'Halfway Between Fragmentation and Convergence: The Role of the Rules of the Organization in the Interpretation of Constituent Treaties', in M Andenas and E Bjorge (eds), *A Farewell to Fragmentation: Reassertion and Convergence in International Law* (CUP 2015) 486, 492–93). See also the examples cited in 'ILA, 'Final Report of the Study Group on the Content and Evolution of the Rules on Interpretation' (Kyoto 2020) 7, where the ICJ referred to interpretive methods not explicitly listed in the VCLT.

However, the issue becomes more complicated if such idiosyncratic methods of interpretation imply an application or effect that is different from a comparable method contained in the VCLT. Controversies about the limits in the application of interpretive methods have notably arisen in the context of the taking into account of subsequent practice under Article 31(3)(b) and the integration of other 'relevant rules' under Article 31(3)(c).

The ECtHR, for instance, adopts a more liberal understanding of Article 31(3)(b) of the VCLT than the ILC, in the sense that 'the Court often referred to the subsequent practice of not all but only a majority of the States Parties of the ECHR'.[107] This broad understanding has also been adopted by the Inter-American Court of Human Rights in its 2012 judgment on the legality of *in vitro* fertilization, as well as by the East African Court of Justice in an advisory opinion issued in 2015 outside the context of human rights law.[108] Divergences have also arisen with regard to the role of 'soft law' in the interpretation of the ECHR which, according to Oliver Dörr, has been introduced into the interpretive process by application of Article 31(3)(c) —'[n]otwithstanding the fact that "rules" would imply that only legally binding instruments can play a role under lit c.'[109]

Do these examples cross the threshold to an untenable interpretation? Even though—as the ILC has recently emphasized—the interpreters are not 'more or less free to choose how to use and apply the different means of interpretation',[110] two observations should be made before drawing any conclusions.

Firstly, practice under Article 31(3)(b) has traditionally been marked by divergence, as notably illustrated by the practice of domestic courts.[111] It was only in 2018 that the ILC adopted its Conclusions, which may explain a certain inconsistency up until then. Notably, as the ILC acknowledged in Conclusion 10(2) and the commentary, '[t]he number of parties that must actively engage in subsequent practice in order to establish an agreement under article 31(3)(b), may vary', which makes it possible to subsume some of the examples mentioned under Article 31(3)(b).[112] Practice under Article 31(3)(c) had been scarce until about twenty years ago, which is why it is equally difficult to speak of a settled understanding in this regard.[113]

[107] CAHDI, Report of the Steering Committee 2020 (n 104) [55] citing the ECtHR decisions in: *Demir and Baykara* (n 93) and *Hassan v the United Kingdom* App 29750/09 (ECHR, 16 September 2014). See, in contrast, ILC (1966) YBILC II (n 57) 221–22, and ILC Report 2018 (SASP) (n 76) 74 [2] 'all the parties'.

[108] *Artavia Murillo et al v Costa Rica* (Preliminary Objections, Merits, Reparations, Costs) (28 November 2012) IACHR Series C No 257 [256] and fn 416; *Request by the Council of Ministers of the East African Community* Advisory Opinion No 1 of 2015 (EACJ, 1 November 2015) [88] (on the approach by the ECtHR) and [93].

[109] Dörr, 'Article 31' (n 63) 608–609 [100] with further references to the case law of the ECtHR.

[110] ILC Report 2018 (SASP) (n 76) 22 [14].

[111] ILC Report 2018 (SASP) (n 76) 22 [14] fn 51, 26 [8], 36 [33].

[112] ILC Report 2018 (SASP) (n 76) Conclusion 10 (2), 79–82.

[113] But see: *Right to Strike under ILO Convention No. 87* (Advisory Opinion of 21 May 2026) ICJ [90]–[99], where the Court stated, in para

Secondly, and even more importantly, the scope of both Article 31(3)(b) and (c) tends to overlap with Article 32. In most of the cases mentioned by Dörr, the 'soft law' provisions could thus arguably be subsumed under Article 32. As illustrated by the 2020 judgment in the *Immunities and Criminal Proceedings* case and subsequent decisions, even the ICJ has had recourse to the subsequent practice of only a few States. While cryptically stating that this practice 'does . . . not necessarily establish "the agreement of the parties" within the meaning of a rule codified in Article 31, paragraph 3 (b)',[114] the Court still relied significantly on this practice—probably as a supplementary means of interpretation under Article 32. This means that the framework established by the VCLT is respected so long as the interpretative weight accorded to a 'subsequent practice' or a 'relevant rule' does not exceed what is permissible under Article 32.

4.3.2.3 Modification of regional treaties through interpretation

Regional practice is further replete with examples in which the respective treaty has been given a meaning over time which seems to overstep the threshold from interpretation to modification. For example, the ECtHR's case law on the death penalty[115] and detention[116] goes in this direction. Moreover, the interpretation of the North Atlantic Treaty in light of subsequently adopted strategies comes close to a modification of the original text[117] as does the interpretation of the 'minimum standard of treatment' in Article 1105 of the North American Free Trade Agreement (NAFTA) by NAFTA's Free Trade Commission.[118]

The rules reflected in the VCLT offer three main avenues that allow for interpretations that *prima facie* overstep the original intention of the parties as expressed in a treaty's text.

The first avenue, often called 'evolutionary interpretation', is not a separate interpretive method but rather requires the interpreter 'to answer the question of whether parties can be presumed to have intended, upon the conclusion of the

90, that Article 31(3)(c) 'does not necessarily require all parties to the treaty under interpretation to be bound by the "relevant rules of international law" in order for those rules to be taken into account.' This position, however, provoked several individual opinions of judges expressing diverging views on the correct understanding of Article 31(3)(c) (see in particular separate opinion of President Iwasawa [2]–[14]; dissenting opinion of Judge Tomka [65]–[72]; declaration of Judge Bhandari [7]–[8]; separate opinion of Judge Nolte [23]–[30]).

[114] *Immunities and Criminal Proceedings (Equatorial Guinea v France)* [2020] ICJ Rep 300 [69]; *Right to Strike* (n 113) [113]–[115].

[115] Eg *Al-Saadoon and Mufdhi v UK* App 61498/08 (ECHR, 2 March 2010) [120].

[116] Eg *Hassan v the United Kingdom* App 29750/09 (ECHR, 16 September 2014) [101].

[117] *NATO Strategic Concept Case* (German Federal Constitutional Court, Judgment of 19 June 2001) Application 2 BvE 6/99 [148].

[118] See I Buga, *Modification of Treaties by Subsequent Practice* (OUP 2018) 281–85. It has to be noted that Article 1105 of NAFTA has been replaced by Article 30.2(2)(f) of the Agreement between the United States of America, the United Mexican States, and Canada (signed 30 November 2018, entered into force 1 July 2020).

treaty, to give a term used a meaning that is capable of evolving over time'[119] on the basis of a careful application of the 'crucible-approach'.[120] This approach has notably been adopted in practice with regard to terms that are 'generic', contained in a treaty 'designed to be of "continuing duration"', or 'by definition evolutionary'.[121]

The second avenue is reflected in Article 31(3)(a) of the VCLT, on the basis of which subsequent agreements by all the parties as 'authentic means' of interpretation 'may even go beyond the ordinary meaning of the terms of the treaty'.[122] As emphasized by the ILC, '[a]n agreement to modify a treaty is thus not excluded [given that Article 39 of the VCLT explicitly addresses this option], but also not to be presumed'.[123]

It is the third avenue that is arguably the most difficult when it comes to the dividing line between interpretation and modification: the effect of a subsequent practice under Article 31(3)(b). After an extensive analysis of the practice of international courts and tribunals and the relevant literature, the ILC concluded in its 2018 commentaries on Conclusion 7(3) of SASP that

> while there exists some support in international case law that, absent indications in the treaty to the contrary, the agreed subsequent practice of the parties theoretically may lead to modifications of a treaty, the actual occurrence of that effect is not to be presumed, and the possibility of amending or modifying a treaty by subsequent practice has not been generally recognized.[124]

The reasons for this reluctance are probably best reflected in the debate that took place fifty years earlier at the Vienna Conference about what was then draft article 38 providing for a modification by subsequent practice (as a 'twin' to what became Article 39) and which was eventually discarded. States particularly invoked the risk of circumventing the requirements for formal treaty amendments, 'serious constitutional problems', and the loss of legal certainty and stability when admitting unlimited informal treaty modifications.[125]

However, State practice has exceptionally acknowledged the modifying effect of subsequent practice in two categories of cases. In each of these categories, we observe the very characteristics identified in Chapter 2 that are typical of regional law.[126]

This concerns, firstly, treaties that are inextricably linked to a geographic feature, thus arising from 'geographic interdependence' among a group of States. Several examples confirm that the understanding of terms contained in these

[119] ILC Report 2018 (SASP) (n 76) Conclusion 8, 67 [9].
[120] ILC Report 2018 (SASP) (n 76) 66 [8].
[121] ILC Report 2018 (SASP) (n 76) 65 [6] with further references to case law.
[122] ILC Report 2018 (SASP) (n 76) 59 [24].
[123] ILC Report 2018 (SASP) (n 76).
[124] ILC Report 2018 (SASP) (n 76) 63 [38].
[125] UNCLOT I, 207–15.
[126] Sections 2.3.2 and 2.3.3.

treaties has been significantly changed by the subsequent practice of the parties. Although this is usually framed as acquiescence or estoppel,[127] Article 31(3)(b) was mentioned in an *obiter dictum* in the most recent example, the *Navigational and Related Rights* case.[128] Another pertinent example is the PCIJ's 1927 advisory opinion on the powers of the *European Commission of the Danube*.[129] In this case, the Court held that a regional treaty had been significantly modified by 'by usage having juridical force simply because it has grown up and been consistently applied with the unanimous consent of all the States concerned'.[130]

Secondly, the presumption formulated by the ILC against modification through subsequent practice seems to have been rebutted in those cases that are characterized by 'ideological interdependence', ie where a normative bond outside the treaty itself exists that holds the States together. In these cases, the modified understanding did not only arise from a subsequent practice among the parties in the sense of Article 31(3)(b) but was simultaneously 'backed up' by either a consistent domestic practice of the States parties, notably in the ECtHR cases on capital punishment, or by a relevant rule at the international level—leading often to a parallel invocation of Article 31(3)(b) and (c)—as it had occurred in the *Namibia* case and in the detention cases before the ECHR.

These two categories, regional treaties relating to a territory or geographic feature, and those that reflect a normative consensus of States that is also entrenched in their domestic laws or at the universal level, have in common that they mitigate many of the concerns which were raised against draft Article 38 during the drafting process of the VCLT. In particular, the risk of States within the region being subjected to an informal change in a treaty regime without their consent is reduced. As to the first group, the identifiability inherent in territorial regimes—and, accordingly, changes therein—affords a high degree of legal certainty. Regarding the second category, the fact that the normative change is also grounded in yet another source equally protects them from normative impositions, notably those that would create conflicts with their domestic law. As they are bound by rules from this other source anyway, the modification does not represent an additional limitation to their scope of manoeuvre.

However, these two avenues for unusually broad interpretations have limits.[131] An evolutionary interpretation becomes untenable if the interpreter entirely

[127] *Temple of Preah Vihear (Cambodia v Thailand)* (Merits) [1962] ICJ Rep 6, 32–33; *Kasikili/Sedudu Island (Botswana v Namibia)* [1999] ICJ Rep 1045 (Diss Op Judge Parra-Aranguren) 1212–13; *Cameroon v Nigeria* (n 70) 353 [68].

[128] *Navigational and Related Rights* (n 70) 242 [64]; see also the separate opinion of Judge Skotnikov [10].

[129] *European Commission of the Danube* (Advisory Opinion) [1927] PCIJ Series B, No 14, 6, 17.

[130] *European Commission of the Danube* (n 129).

[131] See also Report of the Steering Committee 2020 (n 104) [96]: '(. . .) the traditional rules of treaty interpretation and the consensual nature of international law, as well as the need to avoid fragmentation of the latter, place limits on such approaches. It is important therefore that the Court explains its methods of interpretation within these limits and that the outcomes reached are predictable and understandable for the Contracting States (. . .)'.

ignores the 'ordinary meaning' of the terms at the time of conclusion. The consideration of subsequent practice and agreements crosses the threshold to an impermissible modification if it substitutes the original object and purpose of the treaty,[132] if it creates new rights and obligations,[133] or if it cannot be assumed that the suggested interpretation was encompassed by the presumed intention of the authors at the conclusion of the treaty.[134]

4.3.2.4 Exclusion of interpretive rules reflected in the VCLT by regional bodies

Given that the 'crucible-approach' forms one of the significant elements of the VCLT rules on interpretation,[135] a final borderline case from regional treaty practice concerns those situations in which one or more interpretive methods are excluded from the interpretive process.

A pertinent example is the reluctance of the CJEU to have recourse to subsequent agreements and subsequent practice[136] as well as the *travaux préparatoires* when interpreting the foundational treaties of the EU.[137] While the failure to take the latter into consideration—representing merely 'supplementary means' in the sense of Article 32 of the VCLT—does not yet render the interpretation 'untenable',[138] subsequent agreements and practice under Article 31(3) represent 'authentic means' for elucidating the intention of the parties and are thus an integral part of the 'crucible'. Yet, it is here where Article 5 comes into play, according to which Articles 31 to 33 are 'without prejudice to any relevant rules of the organization' when interpreting the respective constituent instrument. A number of commentators have, for example, argued that the exclusion of subsequent practice by the CJEU may fall under Article 5.[139] While Article 5 limits the interpreter's—here

[132] See also *NATO Strategic Concept Case* (n 117) [139]: 'If commitments that are made in the 1999 Strategic Concept are, in an insurmountable and clearly discernible manner, inconsistent with the area of operation that is defined in the Treaty, or if they contain an expansion of the Treaty beyond the scope that has been binding to this point, this indicates the parties' consent to amend the Treaty.'

[133] *Cruz Varas and others v Sweden* App 15576/89 (ECHR, 20 March 1991) [100]: 'Subsequent practice could (. . .) not to create new rights and obligations which were not included in the Convention at the outset (. . .).'

[134] See also the definition of informal modification given by the ILC in its 1966 commentary on draft Article 38 (Modification of a treaty by subsequent practice): 'where the parties by common consent in fact apply the treaty in a manner which its provisions do not envisage. (. . .) a consistent practice, establishing the common consent of the parties to the application of the treaty in a manner different from that laid down in certain of its provisions, may have the effect of modifying the treaty' (ILC (1966) YBILC II (n 57) 236).

[135] Section 4.3.1.

[136] See ILC, Information received by the EU, 67th session of the International Law Commission (2015), 'Contribution by the European Union on the topic of subsequent agreements and subsequent practice in relation to treaty interpretation' https://legal.un.org/ilc/sessions/67/pdfs/english/sasp_eu.pdf (accessed 29 April 2026) 3; ILC Report 2018 (SASP) (n 76) Conclusion 12, 105–106.

[137] J Odermatt, 'The Use of International Treaty Law by the Court of Justice of the European Union' (2015) 17 Camb Yearb Eur Leg Stud 121, 136–38 for further references.

[138] The ICJ often even explicitly refrains from consulting 'supplementary means' under Article 32 VCLT if the meaning is clear (eg *Maritime Dispute (Peru v Chile)* (n 98) [66]).

[139] See eg Schmalenbach (n 51) 103 [9].

the CJEU's—interpretive freedom by linking it to an accepted practice by the member States, this requirement has arguably been met in this case as the exclusion of subsequent agreements and subsequent practice as means of interpretation of the EU founding instruments has been continuously confirmed in the case law of the CJEU and accepted by the members States over the last decades.[140]

By contrast, the approach taken by the CJEU in the 2016 *Front Polisario* case may be seen as an example where the threshold to an untenable interpretation was crossed. In this case, the CJEU, on appeal brought by the Council of the EU, set aside a judgment of the General Court of the EU rendered in December 2015. In that decision, the General Court had annulled the Council Decision approving the Euro-Mediterranean Agreement concluded between the EU and Morocco in so far that it applied to the territory of Western Sahara.[141] On appeal, the CJEU concluded in 2016 that the General Court had 'erred in law in holding that the subsequent practice (...) justified an interpretation of those agreements as meaning that they were legally applicable to the territory of Western Sahara'.[142] Instead, the CJEU stated that the requirements of Article 31(3)(b) VCLT were not present absent an 'agreement' between the Parties given that such an 'agreement' would have implied an intention to violate 'the principles of self-determination and of the relative effect of treaties, even though the European Union repeatedly reiterated the need to comply with those principles'.[143] This approach has been severely criticized as an 'excessive reliance'[144] on and a 'most troublesome'[145] application of Article 31(3)(c). Even commentators who otherwise defended the decision described this interpretive approach as 'unconvincing' and a 'methodological error';[146] even as entirely undermining the 'crucible-approach' underlying the VCLT.[147]

4.4 Towards third parties: the limits of external legal effects of regional treaties

The previous section focused primarily on the perspective of States within a given region and on the problems that idiosyncratic regional approaches to treaty interpretation may pose for them. A different question is how such regional treaties may implicate third parties. The main concern for third parties with respect to regional

[140] See Palchetti (n 106) 493; see also J Odermatt, *International Law and the European Union* (CUP 2021) 62–63.
[141] *Front Polisario v Council* Case T-512/12 (EGC, 10 December 2015).
[142] *Council v Front Polisario*, Case C-104/16 P (CJEU, 21 December 2016) [125].
[143] *Council v Front Polisario* (n 142) [122]–[123].
[144] E Kassoti, 'The Council v. Front Polisario Case: The Court of Justice's Selective Reliance on International Rules on Treaty Interpretation (Second Part)' (2017) 2 European Papers 23, 30.
[145] J Odermatt 'International Decisions' (2017) 111:3 AJIL 731, 735.
[146] E Cannizzaro, 'In Defence of Front Polisario: The ECJ as a Global Jus Cogens Maker' (2018) 55:2 CMLR 569, 578.
[147] See Kassoti (n 144) 31; Odermatt (n 145) 735–37.

treaties is not so much an idiosyncratic interpretation of a given regional treaty as such, but rather the imposition of unwanted 'spill-over' effects that infringe upon their own legal position. At first glance, this concern may seem surprising, given that the legal position of third parties should be safeguarded by the *pacta tertiis* principle, which provides that treaties do not bind non-parties. Yet, like most legal principles, *pacta tertiis* is not absolute: its scope has been subject to certain limitations. In practice, these exceptions have largely been tied to the distinct characteristics of regional treaties that were identified in Chapter 2.[148]

4.4.1 Status, function, and scope of the *pacta tertiis* principle

Third parties are protected by the principle of *pacta tertiis nec nocent nec prosunt* reflected in Articles 34 to 38 of the VCLT. According to this principle, a treaty constitutes *res inter alios acta* for those parties that have not expressed their consent to be bound by it.[149] This rule has been recognized by universal and regional bodies—in principle—as being either customary international law or as a general principle of law.[150] The function of the rule has evolved over time. During the drafting process of the 1969 VCLT, the ILC explained that what eventually became Article 34 VCLT 'does not rest simply on this general concept of the law of contract but on the sovereignty and independence of States'.[151] However, in the drafting process of the 1986 VCLT, the ILC seemed to have adopted a broader understanding of its function stating that it 'lays down . . . the expression of one of the fundamental consequences of consensuality' that 'has been adapted without difficulty to treaties to which one or more international organizations are parties'.[152] Thus, the rule ensures that any restriction or extension of a subject's existing rights and obligations under international law—its legal scope of manoeuvre—cannot be imposed without its consent.

However, several issues relating to the rule's scope remain controversial.[153] An important issue in the context of regional treaties is whether so-called 'indirect obligations' fall within the rule's scope *ratione materiae*. Regional treaties tend to impose 'indirect obligations' on third parties, which do not directly bind third parties but rather incidentally yet adversely affect their position. Such 'indirect

148 See Chapter 2, section 2.3.
149 A Proelss,'Article 34' in O Dörr and K Schmalenbach (eds), *Vienna Convention on the Law of Treaties: A Commentary* (2nd edn, Springer 2018) 655–56 [1].
150 See *Territorial and Maritime Dispute (Nicaragua v Colombia)* [2012] ICJ Rep 624 [162].
151 ILC (1966) YBILC II (n 57) 226.
152 ILC, 'Question of treaties concluded between States and international organizations or between two or more international organizations' (1982) YBILC II(2) UN Doc A/CN.4/SER.A/1982/Add.l, 42.
153 See on the controversial issue regarding the scope *ratione personae* of this rule A Proelss, 'Article 34' (n 149) 659–63, 693–94.

obligations' typically arise from regional treaties, such as regional mechanisms to manage illegal, unreported, and unregulated (IUU) fishing,[154] regional rules on environmental protection,[155] and treaty provisions that form the legal basis for sanctions taken by the parties to that treaty against third parties.[156]

Recalling the purpose of the *pacta tertiis* principle, the decisive criterion here is whether the treaty provision in question restricts the third party's *legal* scope of manoeuvre.[157] This purpose could easily be frustrated if the rule were confined to treaty provisions that bind third parties directly, as its effectiveness would then depend largely on the ingenuity of treaty drafting. At the same time, it would go too far to extend it to purely factual, incidentally unfavourable effects on third parties.[158] By their very nature, plurilateral or bilateral treaties disadvantage non-parties simply by depriving them of the benefits of membership, including legal privileges arising therefrom. If *pacta tertiis* was given such a broad scope *ratione materiae*, treaty-making below the universal level would be rendered impossible. Similarly, treaty provisions that simply require parties to conduct their relations with third parties in compliance therewith do not yet cross the threshold of an infringement of a third party's *legal* scope of manoeuvre.[159] In the same vein, the rule embodied in Article 34 cannot be understood to privilege a third party's legal position in the sense that it would protect it from legal effects that find a legal basis in general international law, for example, the right to collective self-defence.[160]

There is prima facie no indication that the *pacta tertiis* rule does not apply to regional treaties. Still, the question is whether certain types of such treaties—by virtue of the characteristics that render regional law legally distinct—may, in exceptional cases, impose rights or obligations on third parties that extend or limit their legal scope of manoeuvre without their (express) consent.

[154] See eg A Serdy, '*Pacta Tertiis* and Regional Fisheries Management Mechanisms: The IUU Fishing Concept as an Illegitimate Short-Cut to a Legitimate Goal' 2017 (48) OD&IL 345–64.

[155] Eg International Convention for the Prevention of Pollution from Ships, 1973 (signed 2 November 1973, entered into force 2 October 1983) 1340 UNTS 184 (MARPOL Convention), art 5(4). Kolb suggests avoiding any conflict of this provision with the *pacta tertiis* rule by interpreting it in a way that would limit its application to situations where the ship with the third State flag comes within the waters under the jurisdiction of the coastal State being a party to the MARPOL Treaty (R Kolb, *The Law of Treaties: An Introduction* (Edward Elgar Publishing 2023) 136).

[156] See for a critical assessment of the judicial review of the EU's restrictive measures: E Kassoti, 'Beyond Collective Countermeasures and Towards an Autonomous External Sanctioning Power? The General Court's Judgment in Case T-65/18 RENV, Venezuela v Council' (2024) 9 European Papers 247, 253.

[157] See Proelss, 'Article 34' in Dörr/Schmalenbach (n 149) 670 [26]: 'the intensity of the negative impact of a treaty rule on the third State must constitute the decisive factor.'

[158] Kolb (n 155) 134.

[159] C Chinkin, *Third Parties in International Law* (OUP 1993) 19; Proelss, 'Article 34' in Dörr/Schmalenbach (n 149) 664–65 [16].

[160] Kolb (n 155) 134.

4.4.2 Exceptions to the *pacta tertiis* principle for regional treaties: 'objective regimes'

As discussed above, it was the proposal on 'restricted multilateral treaties' that came closest to a 'law on regional treaties'. Yet, there has been a second, even more prominent concept that was designed to capture the specific nature of regional treaties in the context of the debate on *pacta tertiis*: the concept of 'objective regimes'.

The term 'objective regimes' traditionally designates certain territorial treaty regimes that also bind and entitle third States (effect *erga omnes*).[161] Building on previous case law, State practice, and academic works,[162] Special Rapporteur Waldock defined 'objective regimes' in draft Article 63(1) in his 1964 report as established by a treaty

> . . . when it appears from its terms and from the circumstances of its conclusion that the intention of the parties is to create in the general interest general obligations and rights relating to a particular region, State, territory, locality, river, waterway, or to a particular area of sea, sea-bed, or air-space; provided that the parties include among their number any State having territorial competence with reference to the subject-matter of the treaty, or that any such State has consented to the provision in question.[163]

Draft Article 63(2)(b) envisaged that a State 'which does not protest against or otherwise manifest its opposition to the regime . . . shall be considered to have impliedly accepted the regime'. The proposal met with some support,[164] but also with manifest criticism within the ILC, notably from members from socialist and newly independent States.[165] They were concerned that 'a certain groups of States might acquire a sort of legislative power over the rest of the world'.[166] Eventually, the ILC 'decided not to propose any special provision on treaties creating so-called objective regimes' '[s]ince to lay down a rule recognizing the possibility of the

[161] F Salerno, 'Treaties Establishing Objective Regimes' in E Cannizzaro (ed), *The Law of Treaties Beyond the Vienna Convention* (OUP 2011) 225 for further references.

[162] In particular: 'Report of the International Committee of Jurists entrusted by the Council of the League of Nations with the task of giving an advisory opinion upon the legal aspects of the Aaland Islands question' (1920) 3 League of Nations Official Journal, Special Supplement, 17, 18; A McNair, 'The Functions and Differing Legal Character of Treaties' (1930) 11 BYBIL 100, 114.

[163] ILC (1964) YBILC II (n 71) 26. See commentaries at 26–34 for examples from practice.

[164] ILC, 'Summary records of the sixteenth session' (1964) YBILC I UN Doc A/CN.4/SER.A/1964, 97 [34] (Paredes who, however, supported deletion later, see at 103 [44]); 99, [50]–[51] (Verdross); 99–100, [2]–[8] (de Luna); 100 [14] (Tsuruoka); 103 [48]–[51] (Briggs); 103–104 [54]–[64] (Rosenne, who held that Article 63 reflected *lex lata*); 107–108 [26]–[30] (Lachs, albeit cautiously).

[165] ILC (n 164) 97 [38] (Elias); 97–99 [39]–[47] (El-Erian); 100 [9]–[12] (Ruda); 100–101 [17]–[23] (Jiménez de Aréchaga); 101 [24]–[28] (Yasseen who, however, stated that the idea was not 'incompatible' with existing international law); 101–102 [28]–[34] (Castrén who, however, stated that the idea was 'defensible'); 102 [35]–[37] (Pal); 102 [38]–[40] (Amado); 103 [45]–[47] (Tunkin); 103 [52]–[53] (Bartos); 104 [65]–[66] (Tabibi); 105 [72]–[74] (Liu).

[166] ILC (n 164) 101 [22] (Jiménez de Aréchaga); see also Tunkin, 103 [46].

creation of objective regimes directly by treaty might be unlikely to meet with general acceptance' in 1966.[167]

4.4.3 The persistent impact of 'objective regimes'

Although the concept of 'objective regime' did not make it into the text of the VCLT, the idea that certain territorial treaty regimes do have legal effects beyond the treaty relationship proved to be rather persistent in subsequent practice. Apart from the fact that States still invoke (and reject) the concept of 'objective regimes' in their pleadings before international courts and tribunals,[168] it keeps re-emerging in various guises.

Firstly, Article 12 of the 1978 Vienna Convention on Succession of States in respect of Treaties stipulates that territorial treaty regimes remain unaffected by the succession of States.[169] The 1974 commentary of the ILC on Article 12 of the draft articles basically replicates the case law and practice cited by Special Rapporteur Waldock in support of 'objective regimes' and explained that the 'special rules' in territorial regimes are 'binding upon the territory'.[170] In its 1997 judgment in the *Gabčíkovo-Nagymaros Project*, the ICJ confirmed the status of Article 12 as a rule under customary international law.[171]

Secondly, regional treaties, despite being *res inter alios acta*, have occasionally been treated as a 'relevant circumstance' in the context of maritime delimitation between two States by international courts and arbitral tribunals.[172]

Thirdly, regional treaties have played a significant role in the interpretation of rules contained in universal and other regional treaties.[173] This notably concerns

[167] ILC (1966) YBILC II (n 57) 231.

[168] See eg *Passage through the Great Belt (Finland v Denmark)*, Memorial of Finland (December 1991) [382]; Counter-Memorial of Denmark (May 1992) [695]–[699]; *Arbitration Between the Republic of Croatia and the Republic of Slovenia (Final Award)* PCA Case No 2012-04 (29 June 2017) [804] and [810]–[814].

[169] Vienna Convention on Succession of States in respect of Treaties (22 August 1978 adopted, entered into force 6 November 1996) 1946 UNTS 3.

[170] ILC, 'Report of the ILC on the work of its twenty-sixth session' (1974) YBILC II(1), UN Doc A/CN.4/SER.A/1974/Add.l, 196.

[171] *Gabčíkovo-Nagymaros Project (Hungary/Slovakia)* [1997] ICJ Rep 7 [123]. See also, relatedly, the relevance that the Court attributed to the territorial character of treaties in their termination and interpretation: *Navigational and related rights* (n 70) [68]; *Territorial and Maritime Dispute (Nicaragua v Colombia)*, (Preliminary Objections) [2007] ICJ Rep 832 [89]; *Territorial Dispute (Libya/Chad)* (n 77) [72]–[73].

[172] See *Delimitation of the maritime boundary between Guinea and Guinea-Bissau* (Award) 14 February 1985, RIAA, Vol XIX, 149 [109]. See S Fietta and R Cleverly, *A Practitioner's Guide to Maritime Boundary Delimitation* (OUP 2016) at 91 and fn 118.

[173] See eg *Ahmadou Sadio Diallo (Republic of Guinea v Democratic Republic of the Congo)* (Merits) [2010] ICJ Rep 639 [68]; but see for a sceptical view: Counter-Memorial of the United Kingdom, MOX Plant Case (*Ireland v United Kingdom*) PCA Case 2002-01 (discontinued by Order No 6 of 6 June 2008) [7.46]–[7.47] arguing that regional agreements, such as the Convention for the Protection

the phenomenon of 'cross-referencing' regarding provisions with a comparable content and a broad understanding of 'systemic integration'.[174]

Finally, regional treaties have been relied upon to identify parallel customary rules which would also bind non-parties to the regional treaty.[175] In that sense, Article 38 of the VCLT provides that:

> Nothing in articles 34 to 37 precludes a rule set forth in a treaty from becoming binding upon a third State as a customary rule of international law, recognized as such.

What was stated to be a 'saving clause'[176] met with concerns and even suspicions within the ILC and among delegations during the Vienna Conference. It was feared that Article 38 would be used to introduce exceptions to the *pacta tertiis* rule through the back door, namely by alleging the existence of a parallel rule under regional or local custom that would bind third States.[177] This anxiety was exacerbated by what was perceived to be a lack of a 'precise definition of international custom' generally, and even more so with regard to the formation of regional custom.[178] Even though it would be inaccurate to perceive Article 38 as a 'Trojan Horse' for exceptions to *pacta tertiis* by way of regional custom, the category of 'objective regimes' was clearly on the drafters' mind as illustrated by the ILC's commentary[179] and a statement by Abdullah El-Erian from Egypt who argued that Article 38

> must be maintained because the decision not to include an article concerning objective regimes had been accepted by some members on the understanding that article 62 would at least partially fill the gap.[180]

Alfred Verdross' opposition to including regional customary law and his proposal to add the word 'general' to achieve an exclusion of unwritten regional law remained

of the Marine Environment of the North-East Atlantic (OSPAR) cannot be used in interpreting UNCLOS.

[174] See Chapter 7, section 7.3.3.

[175] Eg in the *Territorial and Maritime Dispute in the Caribbean Sea* case, Honduras argued that 'a regional practice of using lines of latitude and longitude as maritime boundaries and, specifically, that the 1928, 1986 and 1993 bilateral treaties concluded separately with Colombia, while *res inter alios acta* between Nicaragua and Honduras, nonetheless confirm the 15th parallel as the maritime boundary between Honduras and Nicaragua' (*Territorial and Maritime Dispute between Nicaragua and Honduras in the Caribbean Sea (Nicaragua v Honduras)* [2007] ICJ Rep 659 [246]). The Court, however, recalled Nicaragua's 'persistent objections' to the 1986 and 1993 treaties ([255]).

[176] UNCLOT I, 201 [43] (Waldock); see also UNCLOT II, 63 [38] (UK).

[177] See eg UNCLOT I, 197 [73] (Venezuela); 199 [11]–[12] (Czechoslovakia).

[178] See eg UNCLOT I, 199 [24] (DRC).

[179] ILC (1966) YBILC II (n 57) 230–31.

[180] ILC, 'Summary records of the eighteenth session from 4 May to 19 July 1966' (1966) YBILC I(2), UN Doc A/CN.4/SER.A/1966, 91 [87].

a minority position within the ILC.[181] During the Vienna Conference, a number of delegations expressed their scepticism and suggested, unsuccessfully, deleting the entire provision,[182] adding a reference to Article 38(1)(b) of the ICJ-Statute,[183] or inserting the word 'general' before 'international law' in order to exclude regional custom.[184]

Today, Article 38 is generally understood to encompass regional custom.[185] Nevertheless, as Giorgio Gaja observes:

> Article 38 does not make a distinction between universal customary rules and regional or local customary rules. This does not imply that the conditions for the formation of universal customary rules are necessarily identical to those of other customary rules.[186]

It is precisely the latter statement about the formation of regional custom, to which we will turn in the next chapter.

4.5 Conclusion

Regional treaties occupy a distinctive position in international law, yet this distinctiveness does not imply that their interpretation and application are governed by entirely separate secondary rules. There is no evidence in practice of a distinct 'law of regional treaties'. Efforts to establish separate regimes—whether in the form of 'restricted multilateral treaties' or 'objective regimes'—have not succeeded. Rather, the general law of treaties as codified in the VCLT is widely accepted across regions as a common starting point for interpreting and applying regional treaties. This common core of rules functions as a crucial safeguard against hegemonic impositions presented under the guise of treaty interpretation and application, while simultaneously disciplining overly activist regional judicial bodies and providing a framework to assess whether the organs of a regional organization have exceeded their mandate.

At the same time, these universal rules enable, channel, and limit the emergence of regional variations in treaty interpretation, and even leave some scope for what

[181] ILC (n 180) 91 [64]–[66] (Verdross).

[182] See eg as suggested by Finland and Venezuela during UNCLOT I and as supported by El Salvador and Iran (UNCLOT II, 65 [53] and 67 [17]).

[183] UNCLOT I, 198 [2] (Turkey).

[184] UNCLOT II, 70–71 by Greece and Switzerland. See also Spain: 'The fact that the adjective "general" had not been used might perhaps be intended to cover regional or local custom.' (UNCLOT II, 68 [29]).

[185] Proelss, 'Article 38' in O Dörr and K Schmalenbach (eds), *Vienna Convention on the Law of Treaties: A Commentary* (2nd edn, Springer 2018) 750–51 [15]; G Gaja, 'Article 38' in O Corten and others (eds), *The Vienna Conventions on the Law of Treaties* (2nd edn, OUP 2025) 1077 [7].

[186] Gaja (n 185).

might be termed 'regional laws of treaties'. In practice, the regional character of a treaty encourages States and regional bodies to pursue distinctive interpretative approaches. In turn, the reliance on universal rules by regional bodies ensures that these approaches gain recognition and acceptance by third parties, provided that the 'outer limits' set by the VCLT are respected.

5

Under what conditions do unwritten regional norms qualify as international law?

5.1 Unwritten regional international law: a perplexing legal category

Regional treaties represent a significant, but not the only—and perhaps not even the most challenging—category of regional law. The practice of international law is permeated by references to regional norms, the claimed legal validity and consequences of which are based not on regional treaties, but on common legal practices or shared values among States within a region.[1] Such 'unwritten' regional norms are not necessarily of a purely symbolic or rhetorical nature. They are often invoked by States and international organizations (IOs) as an independent basis for legal obligations[2] and as the primary justification for regional variations,[3] modifications,[4] reservations,[5] or exceptions[6] to the universal legal framework.

However, unlike the perhaps more tangible regional treaties, it is far more difficult to distinguish between 'unwritten' regional norms that qualify as regional *international* law, and regional legal doctrines, traditions, usages, policies, and practices that are non-binding under international law.[7]

[1] 'Norm' is used as a generic term to describe both binding and non-binding rules and principles (see also: *Obligations of States in respect of Climate Change* (Advisory Opinion of 23 July 2025) [287]). See on unwritten regional norms in Europe: J Barkholdt, 'Unwritten European Rules in International Law: From Eurocentric to Regional International Law?' (2026) 39 LJIL 149.

[2] See eg Request for an Advisory Opinion on Democracy and its protection before the Inter-American Human Rights System submitted by Guatemala before the Inter-American Court of Human Rights (6 December 2024) <https://jurisprudencia.corteidh.or.cr/en/vid/1074848299M> (accessed 10 May 2026) [25]–[27].

[3] See eg *Land and Maritime Delimitation and Sovereignty over Islands (Gabon/Equatorial Guinea)* (Judgment of 19 May 2025) (separate opinion of Judge Yusuf) [16].

[4] See eg ILC, 'Final consolidated report of the Co-Chairs of the Study Group on sea-level rise in relation to international law' (2025) UN Doc A/CN.4/783 [58]; *Chirinos Salamanca y otros v Venezuela* (Preliminary Objections) (21 August 2025) IACHR Series C No 562 [61]–[63].

[5] See eg reservations based on 'the Islamic *Shari'a*' by the majority of the Islamic States to arts 2 and 16 of the Convention on the Elimination of All Forms of Discrimination against Women (adopted 18 December 1979, entered into force 3 September 1981) 1249 UNTS 13.

[6] See eg P Grzebyk, 'Crime of Aggression Against Ukraine: The Role of Regional Customary Law' (2023) 21 J Int Crim Justice 435.

[7] See eg the ambiguous reference to 'one of the most firmly established traditions of Latin America, namely, non-intervention' by the ICJ in *Asylum (Colombia/Peru)* [1950] ICJ Rep 266, 285–86.

Regional and General International Law. Janina Barkholdt, Oxford University Press. © Janina Barkholdt 2026.
DOI: 10.1093/9780198953432.003.0005

One reason for this difficulty is that the existence, nature, and criteria for identifying 'unwritten' forms of regional international law, such as regional customary international law, general principles of law with a regionally confined scope (regional GPL), and regional *jus cogens*,[8] are controversial among States, IOs, and experts alike. While some embrace them as an integral expression of the normative plurality of international law, advocating flexible standards for their identification or even the recognition of distinct regional sources of international law,[9] others adopt a more sceptical stance, fearing normative fragmentation along regional lines, insist on strict criteria and high thresholds for their recognition, or even dismiss their relevance in practice altogether.[10] One telling symptom of this divide is reflected in the numerous compromises that the ILC ultimately felt compelled to make in its work on these issues. In its project on the 'Identification of customary international law', the International Law Commission (ILC) avoided recognizing regional custom as a distinct category and instead treated it as a subcategory of 'particular customary international law'.[11] As for regional GPL[12] and regional *jus cogens*,[13] the ILC was even unable to reach consensus on whether they exist in international law, hence leaving these issues unresolved.

There are sound reasons for exercising caution with respect to claims about unwritten regional norms. Historically, unwritten regional norms have been instrumentalized by powerful States for endorsing their hegemonial interests, for demarcating regional spheres of influences, and for the oppression of minorities.[14] Doctrinally, it is not easy to subsume unwritten regional international law under a set of universal secondary rules. While Article 38(1)(a) of the Statute of

[8] 'Unwritten' international law usually refers to customary international law, general principles of law, and peremptory norms of general international law (see also Statement of HE Abdulqawi Ahmed Yusuf, President of the International Court of Justice before the Sixth Committee of the UN General Assembly, 'The International Court of Justice and unwritten sources of international law' (New York, November 2019) <http://statements.unmeetings.org/media2/23328836/president-icj-e.pdf> (accessed 5 May 2026)).

[9] See eg O Amao, *African Union Law. The Emergence of a Sui Generis Legal Order* (Hart 2018) 22; A Buss, 'The Preah Vihear Case and Regional Customary Law' (2010) 9 Chin J Int Law 111, 121–22.

[10] See eg C Greenwood, 'Unity and Diversity in International Law' in M Andenas and E Bjorge (eds), *A Farewell to Fragmentation: Reassertion and Convergence in International Law* (CUP 2015) 37, 40; JR Gutiérrez Álvarez, 'A Melting Snowball—Difficulties in Identifying Particular Customary International Law' (2024) 73 ICLQ 1083, 1087–91.

[11] ILC, 'Draft conclusions on identification of customary international law, with commentaries' (2018) UN Doc A/73/10 ('ILC Report 2018 (CIL)'), Conclusion 16 ('Particular customary international law'), see also section 5.2.2.

[12] ILC, 'General principles of law: texts and titles of the draft conclusions adopted by the Drafting Committee on second reading' (2025) UN Doc A/CN.4/L.1018, draft conclusion 12 ('General principles of law with a limited scope of application'), see also section 5.3.1.

[13] ILC, 'Draft conclusions on identification and legal consequences of peremptory norms of general international law (*jus cogens*), with commentaries' (2022) UN Doc A/77/10 ('ILC Report 2022 (*Jus cogens*)'), draft Conclusion 1 ('Scope'), 17, see also section 5.4.1.

[14] See eg Barkholdt (n 1); A Becker Lorca and A Álvez Marín, 'Turning International Law against Indigenous Peoples' in A Chehtman, A Huneeus, and S Puig (eds), *Latin American International Law in the Twenty-First Century* (OUP 2025) 81–104; P Singh, 'A Custom's Nine Lives: Decolonial Continuities of *Opinio Juris* in Customary International Law' (2024) 23 Chin J Int Law 689–734.

the International Court of Justice (ICJ) clearly encompasses regional treaties as a sub-category of 'particular conventions', the provision remains silent with regard to regional customary international law and regional GPL. The fact that Article 38(1)(b) and (c) of the ICJ Statute as well as the provisions contained in the Vienna Convention on the Law of Treaties (VCLT) addressing *jus cogens* (Articles 53 and 64) refer to the 'general' character of unwritten rules of international law rather raises the question as to whether this effectively excludes 'regional' equivalents.[15] Methodologically, the identification of practice from which criteria for the recognition of the latter could be deduced is difficult. States and IOs rarely refer explicitly to concepts such as 'regional custom', 'regional GPL', or 'regional *jus cogens*'.

These challenges underscore the need to dispel the perplexity surrounding unwritten regional norms. To this end, the present chapter proceeds from three premises.

Firstly, the susceptibility of unwritten regional norms to be misused under the guise of legality for hegemonic or oppressive objectives originates in its inherently elusive legal nature.[16] Preventing such misuse requires the establishment of clear and universally accepted criteria that distinguish regional international law from non-binding regional policies, practices, or values.

Secondly, Article 38(1) of the ICJ Statute and the VCLT provide a point of departure for identifying the relevant criteria. The reference to a '*general* practice' in Article 38(1)(b) of the ICJ Statute has prevented neither the ICJ nor the ILC from recognizing that regional custom falls within the scope of the provision.[17] Thus, the term 'general' does not necessarily refer to the size of a legal community (ie generality in a quantitative sense), but may also refer to a certain level of normative cohesion within that community.[18] This understanding aligns with the function of unwritten international law: the protection and stabilization of mutual expectations arising from such normative cohesion.[19] The regulatory need to protect such expectations is neither confined to the universal level,[20] nor is it confined to expression through the category of customary international law.[21] Accordingly, the term 'general' does not exclude unwritten regional law per se, that is, as long as

[15] See Chapter 3. See also *North Sea Continental Shelf (Federal Republic of Germany/Denmark)* [1969] ICJ Rep 3, 39 [63]; GJH van Hoof, *Rethinking the Sources of International Law* (Kluwer Law and Taxation Publishers 1983) 67–68.

[16] See Chapter 2, section 2.4.2.

[17] *Asylum (Colombia/Peru)* (n 7) 276–77; ILC Report 2018 (CIL) (n 11) Conclusion 16(2), 156 [7].

[18] K Skubizewski, 'Elements of Custom and the Hague Court' (1971) 31 ZaöRV 810, 830. See also H Thirlway, *International Customary Law and Codification* (Sijthoff 1972) 68, 135. See also Chapter 3.

[19] See also M Mendelson, 'The Formation of Customary International Law' (1998) 272 RdC 155, 184–86, 188.

[20] See also TW Bennett, 'Comparative Law and African Customary Law' in M Reimann and R Zimmermann (eds), *The Oxford Handbook of Comparative Law* (2nd edn, OUP 2019) 652, 653.

[21] One may argue that customary international law serves to stabilize expectations regarding the conduct of other subjects; general principles of law, by contrast, stabilize expectations as to the internal functioning of the applicable legal order, whether regional or universal; *jus cogens* norms safeguard expectations concerning a shared minimum standard of legality.

it can be said to be 'general' in both a quantitative and qualitative sense: the qualitative dimension concerns the requisite normative cohesion among States within a region, while the quantitative dimension pertains to the acceptance—by third parties—of the way in which a particular category of unwritten regional international law is identified within that region.[22]

Thirdly, the fact that explicit references by States and IOs to 'regional custom', 'regional GPL', or 'regional *jus cogens*' are seldom made does not necessarily imply that unwritten regional international law cannot be identified in practice.[23] The apparent reluctance to use this exact terminology may, in part, be explained by uncertainty regarding the criteria employed for their identification. It may also reflect a desire to express or preserve regional autonomy by avoiding any impression that unwritten regional concepts are merely variants of universal ones. It is even conceivable that certain forms of unwritten regional international law exist without any direct equivalent at the universal level. Hence, the third premise is that unwritten regional norms—even if terminologically or substantively distinct from Article 38 of the ICJ Statute or the VCLT—may nonetheless be recognized as regional international law, provided that sufficient practice across regions supports such recognition.

It is against this background that the present chapter examines the conditions under which unwritten regional norms qualify as regional customary international law (5.2), regional GPL (5.4), and regional *jus cogens* (5.5).

5.2 Regional custom

Today, nobody seriously contests that regional customary international law falls within the scope of Article 38(1)(b) of the ICJ Statute despite the requirement of a '*general* practice'.[24] However, the threshold and criteria for its identification remain controversial.[25]

5.2.1 From twilight to respectability

Prior to the ICJ's judgment in the *Asylum* case of 1950, regional custom remained in twilight: whereas claims for recognition of customary rules particular to a region had been made well before the Court's judgment—notably in the contexts of

[22] See Chapter 3, section 3.5.1.
[23] See Barkholdt (n 1).
[24] See also M Wood, 'What Is Public International Law? The Need for Clarity about Sources' (2011) 2 Asian J Int Law 205, 214.
[25] See also G Gaja, 'Article 38' in O Corten and others (eds), *The Vienna Conventions on the Law of Treaties* (2nd edn, OUP 2025) 1077 [7].

proclamations of a 'Latin-American international law'[26] and in proceedings before the PCIJ[27]—the existence of regional custom was not addressed by the Advisory Committee of Jurists (ACJ) in 1920 during the debate on what was later to become Article 38(1)(b) of the PCIJ Statute. Interestingly, the term 'general' was not contained in the initial proposal submitted by Baron Descamps, which merely referred to 'practice between nations, accepted by them as law'.[28] A number of qualifiers were then suggested, such as 'recognized practice' by Elihu Root[29] and 'common practice' by the Root-Phillimore proposal,[30] until the ACJ changed the definition to 'international custom as evidence of a general practice'.[31]

At the San Francisco Conference in 1945, Costa Rica as well as Cuba suggested deleting the word 'general'.[32] Ecuador even went so far as to propose a further paragraph for Article 38, according to which '[i]nternational customs, and principles of law, either continental or regional, applicable to controversies between states belonging to the continent or region involved' would be added to the law applied by the ICJ.[33] None of these proposals was accepted. Instead, Article 38(2) PCIJ Statute was incorporated in identical terms into Article 38(1)(b) of the ICJ Statute. However, this does not necessarily imply that States thereby sought to exclude regional custom, given the general unwillingness to deviate from the text of Article 38 of the PCIJ Statute.[34] The controversies about the meaning of the term 'general', notably, its compatibility with the notion of 'regional custom', thus persisted,[35] dividing scholars into those who argued that 'general' was to be understood as 'universal', hence excluding regional custom,[36] and those who maintained

[26] The idea of a regional custom was prominently raised by Álvarez at the beginning of the twentieth century (see G Cohen-Jonathan, 'La coutume locale' (1961) 7 Annuaire français de droit international 119). See also American Institute of International Law, 'Project 2, Approved at the Havana Session of 1925' (1926) 20:4 AJIL 300, 302, 304–306.

[27] See also K Wolfke, *Custom in Present International Law* (2nd edn, Martinus Nijhoff Publishers 1993) 89, who understands the references of the PCIJ in its Advisory Opinions in *European Commission of the Danube* (Advisory Opinion) [1927] PCIJ Series B, No 14, 17 and *The Free City of Danzig and the International Labour Organization* (Advisory Opinion) [1930] PCIJ Series B, No 18, 13, as examples of particular custom. See, however, on the two opinions A Pellet and D Müller, 'Article 38' in A Zimmermann and others (eds), *The Statute of the International Court of Justice: A Commentary* (3rd edn, OUP 2019) fn 710, who regard them as subsequent practice in the sense of Article 31(3)(b) VCLT.

[28] Advisory Committee of Jurists, *Procès-verbaux of the Proceedings of the Committee June 16th to July 24th, 1920, with Annexes* (The Hague: Van Langenhuysen, 1920) 306.

[29] *Procès-verbaux* of the ACJ (n 28) 344.

[30] *Procès-verbaux* of the ACJ (n 28) 548.

[31] *Procès-verbaux* of the ACJ (n 28) 567.

[32] *Documents of the United Nations Conference on International Organization* (San Francisco 1945) (hereinafter: 'UNCIO') vol xiv, 170 (Costa Rica) and 435 (Cuba).

[33] UNCIO vol iii, 412.

[34] See also Pellet and Müller (n 27) [43]–[46], in particular at [46].

[35] For an overview of the debate in doctrine, see: Inter-American Juridical Committee, 'Final report on particular customary international law in the Americas', Annual report of the Inter-American Juridical Committee to the General Assembly (15 March 2024) OEA/Ser.Q CJI/doc.719/24 (hereinafter: 'Final Report of the IAJC (2024)') 19–35.

[36] See eg K Wolfke, *Custom in Present International Law* (Warsaw Scientific Society 1964) 89–90.

that 'general' was to be understood as 'uniform' and thus including regional custom.[37]

The 'seal of respectability'[38] was eventually conferred upon regional custom with the Court's judgments in the 1950 *Asylum* case, the 1952 *Nationals of the United States of America in Morocco* case and the 1960 *Right of Passage* case. In these cases, the Court indicated that Article 38(1)(b) did not preclude the existence of regional custom (*Asylum; Nationals in Morocco*)[39] and eventually applied this type of unwritten regional law (*Right of Passage*).[40] The fact that in the *Asylum* case the ICJ implicitly rejected Álvarez' claim—according to which regional custom might also bind States within and beyond the region which have not accepted it—is likely to have contributed to this 'respectability'.[41]

Yet, doubts as to the existence of regional custom persisted after these decisions and re-emerged during the drafting process of the VCLT, notably, in the debate of what was to become Article 38 of the VCLT. Roberto Ago, for instance, declared himself 'rather sceptical about local custom; it was frequently mentioned, but no really convincing example had been quoted so far'.[42] This view remained a minority position within the ILC and among States at the Vienna Conference.[43] However, the curious omission of the word 'general' in Article 38 of the VCLT once again fuelled the controversy as to whether, in Article 38(1)(b) of the ICJ Statute, regional custom was excluded by the word 'general'.[44]

In the years following the drafting of the VCLT, it became more common for States (in their pleadings) and international and domestic courts[45] as well as the ILC[46] to refer to regional custom. Yet, the notion that non-universal custom with geographic links may appear in many different shades would similarly gain currency during the same period, notably, as regional and local custom, and with several normative *doppelgängers*. This is illustrated by the criticism voiced by Judge

[37] See eg Basdevant, who, as early as 1936, argued that regional custom was not precluded by Article 38(1)(b) (J Basdevant, 'Règles générales du droit de la paix' (1936) 58 RdC 471, 486–89).

[38] Thirlway (n 18) 134 fn 27.

[39] *Asylum (Colombia/Peru)* (n 7) 276–78; *Rights of Nationals of the United States of America in Morocco (France v US)* [1952] ICJ Rep 176, 200.

[40] *Right of Passage over Indian Territory (Portugal v India)* [1960] ICJ Rep 6, 39, 44.

[41] *Asylum (Colombia/Peru)* [1950] ICJ Rep 290 (dissenting opinion Álvarez) 294.

[42] ILC, 'Summary records of the eighteenth session from 4 May to 19 July 1966' (1966) YBILC I(2), UN Doc A/CN.4/SER.A/1966, 91 [71]. See also 91 [64] (Verdross): '... the [ICJ] had recognized the existence of a local custom ... The existence of a regional custom, on the other hand, was very difficult to prove.'

[43] ILC (n 42) 91 [68] (Tunkin); 91–92 [74] (Waldock); 92 [77] (Jiménez de Aréchaga); 92 [79] (Rosenne); 92 [86] (Briggs); 92 [87] (El-Erian); 92–93 [88] (de Luna); UNCLOT I 199 [12] (Czechoslovakia); 200 [38] (Iraq); UNCLOT II 67–68 [20]–[21] (Guatemala); 70 [44] (Ukrainian Soviet Socialist Republic).

[44] See eg UNCLOT II 68 [29] (Spain).

[45] See Chapter 2, section 2.2.

[46] ILC, 'Draft Articles on most-favoured-nation clauses with commentaries' (1978) YBILC II(2), UN Doc A/CN.4/SER.A/1978/Add.l, art 7, 25; ILC, 'Draft Articles on Diplomatic Protection with commentaries' (2006) YBILC II(2), UN Doc A/61/10, art 14, 45 [8].

Sepúlveda-Amor in the 2009 *Navigational and Related Rights* case, where Costa Rica claimed that 'it is of little consequence whether we talk about a local custom, acquiescence, tacit agreement, a territorial *régime* or even the survival of a traditional right dating back to the colonial era which has never been curtailed'.[47] This lack of precision, in his view, had prevented the Court from basing its decision on 'a more solid legal foundation'.[48] Judge Sepúlveda-Amor suggested that it would have been preferable to resort to the concept of acquired rights, insofar as the requirements for (regional) custom had yet to be met.[49] While the existence of regional custom was no longer a matter of controversy, the debate focused on the criteria employed for its identification and distinction from non-universal custom.

5.2.2 Conclusion 16 of the ILC Conclusions on the identification of customary international law

It was not until 2015 that the ILC dealt with what it would eventually refer to as 'particular customary international law' in the project on 'Identification of customary international law'.[50] The interplay between States, the Court, and the Commission up until 2018 ultimately led to the general recognition of regional custom as being contained in Article 38(1)(b). Conclusion 16 of the ILC Conclusions on the 'Identification of customary international law', adopted by the Commission in 2018,[51] states that

1. A rule of particular customary international law, whether regional, local or other, is a rule of customary international law that applies only among a limited number of States.
2. To determine the existence and content of a rule of particular customary international law, it is necessary to ascertain whether there is a general practice among the States concerned that is accepted by them as law (*opinio juris*) among themselves.

The 2018 commentary on Conclusion 16 states, '[t]hat rules of customary international law that are not general in nature may exist is undisputed'.[52] Yet, the debate

[47] *Dispute regarding Navigational and Related Rights (Costa Rica v Nicaragua)* [2009] ICJ Rep 273 (separate opinion of Judge Sepúlveda-Amor) 279 referring to CR 2009/3 (3 March 2009) 62 [41] (Kohen).
[48] *Navigational and Related Rights* (n 47) [23].
[49] *Navigational and Related Rights* (n 47) [36].
[50] ILC, 'Third report on the identification of customary international law by Michael Wood, Special Rapporteur' (2015) UN Doc A/CN.4/682, 54–58.
[51] UNGA 'Identification of customary international law' (20 December 2018) UN Doc A/RES/73/203.
[52] See ILC Report 2018 (CIL) (n 11) 154 [1].

preceding and succeeding the adoption of Conclusion 16 showed that two questions were particularly controversial: firstly, whether particular custom can exist without an element of regional cohesion, and, secondly, whether the threshold for identifying regional custom was the same, higher, or indeed lower than that for identifying general custom.

5.2.2.1 Conclusion 16(1): does 'other' particular custom exist?

Whether custom among States bound by a minimum of geographic cohesion (regional or local custom) is only one form of particular custom,[53] the 'best known manifestation[s]' of particular custom,[54] or even the *only* recognized form of non-universal custom,[55] remains controversial. As ILC member Sean Murphy observed during the 2015 plenary debate within the Commission:

> a key issue was whether [particular custom] had to have a geographic nexus. The principal case law to date had been driven by geography. Some scholars had characterized the rules deriving from regional custom as being binding only upon States in a certain geographic area or region, constituting a regionalized exception permitted out of respect for regional legal traditions. Others, including the Special Rapporteur, had argued that a rule of customary international law could exist among any group of States, even if they were scattered across the globe. Since the Special Rapporteur did not provide any examples of such a rule, one might wonder if his argument was based more on theory than practice.[56]

Following a contentious debate, the ILC included 'other' particular custom, going on to explain in the commentaries that

> although particular customary international law is mostly regional, subregional or local, there is no reason in principle why a rule of particular customary international law could not also develop among States linked by a common cause, interest or activity other than their geographical position.[57]

[53] See eg ILC, 'Fifth report on the identification of customary international law by Michael Wood, Special Rapporteur' (2018) UN Doc A/CN.4/717 [114]. This might be related to the diverging definitions of 'regional'. For instance, Karl understands Arabic, communist, and commonwealth practice as being non-regional and also does not regard the territorial element in the *US Nationals in Morocco* case as sufficient (W Karl, *Vertrag und spätere Praxis im Völkerrecht* (Springer 1983) 93–96 and fn 470).

[54] ILA, 'Final Report of the Committee on Formation of Customary (General) International Law' (London 2000) [8].

[55] ILC, 'Topical summary of the discussion held in the Sixth Committee' (2018) UN Doc A/CN.4/724 [136].

[56] ILC, 3251 Meeting (15 May 2015) UN Doc A/CN.4/SR.3251, 3 (Murphy).

[57] ILC Report 2018 (CIL) (n 11) 155 [5].

The commentaries on Conclusion 16(1) do not contain any example of non-territorial custom in State practice.[58] Conversely, most of the case law cited in support of Conclusion 16(1) involves practice among States bound by a minimum of geographic cohesion.[59]

The absence of examples of non-territorial custom in the commentaries is not surprising. More broadly, looking beyond Conclusion 16 and the ILC's project on the 'Identification of customary international law', identifiable instances of non-territorial custom remain scarce. When considering the 1960s debates on what was later to become Article 38 of the VCLT, it is remarkable that ILC members and delegations emphasized the distinction between local and regional custom; the existence of non-territorial custom did not play a role.[60] Furthermore, the few examples for non-territorial particular custom found in the work of expert bodies fail to convincingly establish the existence of such a category. The 2000 ILA report on 'Customary international law', for example, treats the development of the rules on the continental shelf as an example for a particular customary rule when stating that

> [w]hat started out as, first, a unilateral claim and undertaking, next a bilateral set of obligations, and then a body of particular customary law restricted to a confined (though not regionally defined) group of States, gradually ramified into a rule of general law.[61]

Equally, the 2020 'First Issues Paper on Sea-level Rise' of the ILC Study Group suggests that a 'particular or regional' customary rule regarding the preservation of baselines and the outer limits of maritime zones measured from the baselines may emerge.[62] Importantly, however, it clarifies that 'the character of the potential customary rule'

> can stay regional if confined (only) to the Pacific and South-East Asia, or, if confirmed for other regions as well and depending on the number of States involved,

[58] ILC Report 2018 (CIL) (n 11). See also M Wood and O Sender, *Identification of Customary International Law* (OUP 2024) 294–96 referring to some examples for 'particular customary international law without a geographical relationship', including the *Nationals in Morocco* case. However, this case concerned the alleged existence of capitulatory rights of the US, ie the right to exercise extra-territorial jurisdiction, in the territory of Morocco. Although other examples listed by them may not be characterized by a pronounced geographical component, this does not mean that they would not qualify as 'regional' in line with the characteristics identified in Chapter 2, section 2.2. See further M Mendelson, 'The ICJ and Sources of International Law' in V Lowe and M Fitzmaurice (eds), *Fifty Years of the International Court of Justice: Essays in Honour of Sir Robert Jennings* (CUP 1996) 63, 71 considering this case as a case of local custom where the territory of a State was burdened with a particular customary rule benefitting another State.

[59] ILC Report 2018 (CIL) (n 11) 15515–6.

[60] See (nn 42–44) above.

[61] ILA, Report on Customary International Law (n 54) 21.

[62] ILC, 'First issues paper on Sea-level rise in relation to international law by Bogdan Aurescu and Nilüfer Oral' (2021) UN Doc A/CN.4/740, 42 [104].

it can be general or particular (including 'thematic'—meaning that it is linked to the specific issue of sea-level rise and it applies among a limited number of States).[63]

The ILC issues paper thus assumes that 'thematic' custom develops based on a rule of regional custom that is 'confirmed for other regions as well'. As in the case of the continental shelf, this example appears to be different from the proposition that a customary rule develops among States 'linked by a common cause, interest or activity other than their geographical position'. Instead, these ostensible examples of particular custom illustrate the development from a geographically confined bilateral or regional customary rule to a rule of general custom, possibly based on the practice of 'specially affected States'.[64]

5.2.2.2 Conclusion 16(2): the threshold for recognizing particular custom?

While the inclusion of a possible 'other' particular custom merely served to avoid being overly restrictive, the less restrictive approach taken in Conclusion 16(1), in turn, contributed to an arguably overly restrictive approach in Conclusion 16(2), which sets out the criteria for the identification of particular custom.

The ILC conclusions and commentaries on CIL draw no distinction between different forms of particular custom with respect to criteria employed for their identification. Moreover, the Commission emphasizes that 'the application of the two-element approach is stricter in the case of rules of particular customary international law' when contrasted with general customary international law.[65] Notably, the commentaries highlight that States 'among which the rule in question applies' must participate in the practice which needs to be accepted as law by 'each of these States'.[66]

Whether the same, stricter, or more flexible criteria apply to the identification of regional custom, on the one hand, and to general customary international law, on the other, has long preoccupied scholars.[67] The controversy pivots on the identification of the two elements of customary international law, and on the allocation of the burden of proof.

[63] ILC (n 62) fn 229.
[64] ILC Report 2018 (CIL) (n 11) Conclusion 8, 136.
[65] ILC Report 2018 (CIL) (n 11) 156.
[66] ILC Report 2018 (CIL) (n 11).
[67] See A Bleckmann, 'Völkergewohnheitsrecht trotz widersprüchlicher Praxis?' (1976) 36 ZaöRV 374, 404; Mendelson (n 19) 216; L Crema, 'The "Right Mix" and "Ambiguities" in Particular Customs: A Few Remarks on the Navigational and Related Rights Case' in N Boschiero and others (eds), *International Courts and the Development of International Law: Essays in Honour of Tullio Treves* (Springer 2013) 65, 72–74; GR Bandeira Galindo, 'Particular Customary International Law and the International Law Commission: Mapping Presences and Absences' (2021) 86 QIL Zoom-in 3, 17 and 20.

States,[68] ILC members,[69] and scholars[70] in favour of a stricter standard appear to be primarily concerned about undesirable encroachments on the *pacta tertiis* rule.[71] They tend to compare the legal nature of particular custom with 'latent treaty rules',[72] 'tacit agreements',[73] and 'acquiescence'[74] stressing that 'particular custom' frequently represents an 'exception to general customary international law'.[75] On this basis, the said members submitted proposals to raise the standard of recognition, including the requirement of a higher degree of uniformity and longer duration of the practice,[76] an *opinio juris regionis*,[77] and the allocation of the burden of proof on the State alleging a rule of regional custom.[78] The ILC's commentary on Conclusion 16 leans towards this view by pointing to a 'stricter' application of the two-element-approach regarding particular custom.[79]

At the same time, this restrictive approach arguably blurs the lines between tacit agreements and customary international law.[80] It also does not fully align with more recent case law of the ICJ in which the Court applied criteria for the recognition of local custom that differed from those adopted in the *Asylum* case.[81] The question as to whether a less restrictive standard for regional custom might be justified by the distinct characteristics of regional custom,[82] is left unaddressed.

5.2.3 Different shades of regional customary international law

The disagreement about whether to apply a more lenient or a more restrictive standard is rooted in the diverse forms particular customary law may assume. In

[68] See UNGA (26 October 2016) UN Doc A/C.6/71/SR.22 [12] (Greece).

[69] See ILC (15 May 2015) UN Doc A/CN.4/SR.3251, 9 (Park); (8 May 2018) UN Doc A/CN.4/SR.3397, 4 (Murase).

[70] See eg K Guliyev, 'Local Custom in International Law—Something in Between General Custom and Treaty' (2017) 19 ICLR 47, 52.

[71] ILC (8 May 2018) UN Doc A/CN.4/SR.3397, 4 (Murase).

[72] ILC (19 May 2015) UN Doc A/CN.4/SR.3252, 8 (Caflisch).

[73] See for a criticism Guliyev (n 70) 55.

[74] ILC (15 May 2015) UN Doc A/CN.4/SR.3251, 11 (Hmoud).

[75] ILC (15 May 2015) UN Doc A/CN.4/SR.3251, 9 (Park).

[76] ILC, 'Topical summary of the discussion held in the Sixth Committee' (2016) UN Doc A/CN.4/689 [26]; Guliyev (n 70) 52.

[77] According to this requirement, the relevant *opinio juris* must be limited *ratione personae* to the group of States in question, see eg ILC, 'Comments submitted by the United States of America' (2018) <https://legal.un.org/ilc/sessions/70/pdfs/english/icil_usa.pdf> (accessed 10 May 2026) 19. See also TV Ananthavinayagan, 'Breaking Bad Customs: Involving the Idea of *Opinio Juris Communis* in Asian State Practice' (2018) 24 Asian YBIL 24, 36–40.

[78] *Asylum (Colombia/Peru)* (n 7) 276–77; Wood and Sender (n 58) 298.

[79] ILC Report 2018 (CIL) (n 11) 156. See also Wood and Sender (n 58) 296–97.

[80] ILC (11 May 2018) UN Doc A/CN.4/SR.3400, 4 (Sturma).

[81] ILC (15 May 2015) UN Doc A/CN.4/SR.3251, 7 (Forteau) pointing to the 'liberal view adopted by the International Court of Justice in the *Dispute regarding Navigational and Related Rights (Costa Rica v Nicaragua)* in 2009 (para 141), in which the Court had adopted a less consensualistic definition of special custom than in its previous judgments'.

[82] Mendelson (n 19) 216–17 and fn 152.

other words, both positions may have their merits: the appropriate threshold and criteria may depend on the specific type of particular custom in question. While international courts and tribunals have not always been clear and consistent in the use of the terms 'regional custom' or 'local custom'—a fact that has been frequently criticized by Judges writing separately[83]—their jurisprudence as well as State practice suggests distinguishing between these two types of regional customary international law. Before proceeding, it should be noted that regional custom *stricto sensu* and local custom are the most common types of regional custom in the broader sense, but they do not exhaust the possible forms regionally limited custom may assume. Such other types may include 'historic rights',[84] 'indigenous laws',[85] and regional secondary rules.[86]

5.2.3.1 Regional customary law *stricto sensu*

Regional customary international law *stricto sensu* protects mutual expectations that originate in a certain degree of ideological cohesion within a region (arising from ideological interdependence).[87] Such custom may arise from a shared political or constitutional identity, a common institutional framework, or from a combination of the two.[88] Such custom, insofar as it is typically reflected in political and legal instruments at the domestic or regional level, is identifiable for States within the region as well as for third parties.

The threshold for identifying regional custom *stricto sensu* is usually considered to be rather high and the criteria restrictive.[89] This view has been based mainly on the approach adopted by the ICJ's 1950 judgment in the *Asylum (Colombia v Peru)* case.[90] However, a closer reading of that judgment suggests that it need not necessarily be interpreted as requiring a more demanding test for regional custom *stricto sensu* than for general custom.

[83] See *Navigational and Related Rights* (separate opinion of Judge Sepúlveda-Amor) (n 47); *Alleged Violations of Sovereign Rights and Maritime Spaces in the Caribbean Sea (Nicaragua v Colombia)* [2022] ICJ Rep 435 (dissenting opinion of Judge ad hoc McRae) [50]–[70].

[84] 'Historic rights' have been defined in the *South China Sea* case as 'rights deriving from historical processes (. . .) that would not normally arise under the general rules of international law, absent particular historical circumstances' (*The South China Sea Arbitration (The Republic of Philippines v The People's Republic of China) (Award)* PCA Case 2013-19 (12 June 2016) [225]). There is a significant overlap between historic rights relating to transboundary rights of non-State actors and local custom, see section 5.3.2.2.

[85] Distinguishing between indigenous laws and custom: AC Diala, 'Comparative Indigenous Law' in M Siems and PJ Yap (eds), *The Cambridge Handbook of Comparative Law* (CUP 2024) 693, 696.

[86] An example for regional customary secondary rules would be the Pan-American practice regarding reservations to treaties (*Reservations to the Convention on the Prevention and Punishment of Genocide* (Advisory Opinion) [1951] ICJ Rep 15, 25). See also Barkholdt (n 1) distinguishing between regional custom *stricto sensu*, local custom, and regional secondary rules.

[87] See section 2.3.2.1.

[88] See also Barkholdt (n 1).

[89] ILC Report 2018 (CIL) (n 11) 156.

[90] J Crawford, *Chance, Order, Change: The Course of International Law, General Course on Public International Law* (Brill 2013) 56, 247.

In the *Asylum* case, Haya de la Torre, the Peruvian leader of a group which had attempted a *coup d'état* in Peru, fled to the Colombian Embassy in Lima and requested diplomatic asylum as a 'political refugee' to evade criminal proceedings in Peru. Colombia granted such asylum, alleging the existence of a rule under regional law which gave the State granting asylum the right to unilaterally qualify the offence. That qualification, according to Colombia, was binding on the other State. Having unsuccessfully invoked the 1911 Bolivarian Agreement on Extradition, the 1928 Havana Convention on Asylum, and the 1933 Montevideo Convention on Political Asylum, Colombia relied on 'American international law in general'. Examining whether such 'alleged regional or local custom peculiar to Latin-American States'[91] existed, the Court famously stated that

> [t]he Party which relies on a custom of this kind must prove that this custom is established in such a manner that it has become binding on the other Party. The Colombian Government must prove that the rule invoked by it is in accordance with a constant and uniform usage practised by the States in question, and that this usage is the expression of a right appertaining to the State granting asylum and a duty incumbent on the territorial State. This follows from Article 38 of the Statute of the Court, which refers to international custom 'as evidence of a general practice accepted as law'.[92]

Colombia relied on several regional agreements and instances of regional practice to prove the existence of such a right to unilateral qualification under regional custom. However, the Court concluded that it was 'not possible to discern in all this any constant and uniform usage, accepted as law, with regard to the alleged rule of unilateral and definitive qualification of the offence'.[93] The Court pointed out that even if there was such a rule under regional customary international law among Latin American States, it was, in any event, not opposable to Peru which had refrained from ratifying the Montevideo Conventions of 1933 and 1939.[94] The Court, notably, did not attach decisive value to official communications by the Peruvian Government that indicated an ambiguous position of the latter.[95]

This judgment could be understood as the formulation of a 'three-element-test' for identifying a rule under regional custom, allocating the burden of proof on the State invoking such a rule. That State must demonstrate, firstly, the existence of 'a constant and uniform usage practised by the States in question', secondly, that such practice is 'accepted as law', and thirdly, that the practice and *opinio juris* of the State alleged to be bound by it correspond to that rule.

[91] *Asylum (Colombia/Peru)* (n 7) 276.
[92] *Asylum (Colombia/Peru)* (n 7) 276–77.
[93] *Asylum (Colombia/Peru)* (n 7) 277.
[94] *Asylum (Colombia/Peru)* (n 7) 277–78.
[95] *Asylum (Colombia/Peru)* (n 7) 278.

On closer inspection, however, it is doubtful whether this 'three-element-test' establishes a stricter standard for regional custom than it does for general custom.

To begin with, the Court's cautious stance may be attributed to the fact that, in 1950, the very notion of regional custom was subject to debate—both for doctrinal reasons (given the unclear meaning of 'general' in Article 38(1)(b)) as well as for policy reasons (given the controversial view, prominently advocated by Judge Álvarez, that States could be bound by such regional custom without being part of that region).

Furthermore, the allocation of the burden of proof on Colombia can be explained by factors other than the regional nature of the rule, such as the effect of the alleged rule (a derogation from the principle of territorial sovereignty).[96] The ICJ affirmed the strict evidentiary threshold established in the *Asylum* case only once more, namely, two years later when it rejected the claim by the US that parts of the capitulatory regime formerly applicable in the French zone of Morocco persisted as local custom.[97] Conversely, the ICJ did not refer to it in its *Right of Passage* case ten years later,[98] nor, 36 years later, in *Military and Paramilitary Activities in and against Nicaragua (Nicaragua v United States of America)*.[99] In a more recent judgment, *Alleged violations in the Caribbean Sea*, the ICJ combined the allocation of the burden of proof on the invoking State with a more lenient standard of proof.[100] Likewise, as reflected in the 2012 *Jurisdictional Immunities* judgment, the Court's application of a stringent test for identifying customary international law, especially where a party alleges the existence of a customary exception to an existing rule under general international law, extends beyond cases involving regional custom.[101]

With respect to the possible 'third element'—the requirement of evidence of corresponding practice and *opinio juris* by the State against which the regional rule is invoked—may just restate the (controversial) principle that persistent objectors are not bound.[102] In fact, Peru's conduct has been interpreted as the first instance in which the concept of 'persistent objector' was used in the context of general international law.[103] More precisely, the Court's judgment cannot be interpreted as requiring *active* participation in the regional practice by the State against which the regional custom is invoked. Accordingly, the Court left open the possibility

[96] S Talmon, 'Determining Customary International Law: The ICJ's Methodology between Induction, Deduction and Assertion' (2015) 26:2 EJIL 417, 428; Wolfke (n 27) 120.

[97] *Nationals in Morocco* (n 39) 199–201.

[98] See also Wolfke (n 27) 120.

[99] *Military and Paramilitary Activities in and against Nicaragua (Nicaragua v United States)* (Merits) [1986] ICJ Rep 14 [196]–[199]. See also Final Report of the IAJC (n 35) 9.

[100] See *Alleged Violations of Sovereign Rights and Maritime Spaces in the Caribbean Sea (Nicaragua v Colombia)* [2022] ICJ Rep 266 [218] and [221].

[101] *Jurisdictional Immunities of the State (Germany v Italy: Greece intervening)* (Judgment) [2012] ICJ Rep 99 [55]–[79].

[102] See eg Mendelson (n 58) 63, 71.

[103] See J Green, *The Persistent Objector Rule in International Law* (OUP 2016) 38–40.

that, once the existence of a regional customary rule is established, a State that belongs to that region but which has remained inactive or silent may, under regional custom, nonetheless be bound by that rule.[104]

These aspects may give rise to doubts as to whether the Court intended to establish a more restrictive approach for identifying regional custom *stricto sensu* and whether it actually maintained this approach in its subsequent decisions.[105] Its judgment in the *Asylum* case nevertheless continues to be used to support such a restrictive approach. Interestingly, the Inter-American Court of Human Rights has been particularly loyal to a restrictive understanding of the Court's approach in the *Asylum* case. While, in 1950, the ICJ was not asked to address the existence of the institution of diplomatic asylum under regional customary law as such, the Inter-American Court of Human Rights found in an Advisory Opinion requested by Ecuador—68 years later—that the right to diplomatic asylum does not qualify as regional customary law due to a lack of uniform practice among the 35 Member States of the OAS as well as the persistent opposition of the United States of America.[106]

Beyond the ongoing influence of a certain reading of the *Asylum* case, the caution with respect to regional custom *stricto sensu* can be explained by four characteristics of such custom. These determine the parameters for its identification.

Firstly, it is difficult for both States within the region and third parties to identify the scope *ratione personae* of 'ideological custom'. However, this, in turn, means that factors facilitating the identification of its scope *ratione personae*, such as membership in a regional organization, might lower the threshold for identifying such custom.[107]

Secondly, due to its potentially generalizable subject-matter, regional custom *stricto sensu* can give rise to the danger of normative 'spill-over' effects for third parties, which may explain the Court's insistence on the criterion of uniformity. In the *Asylum* case, the highly divergent treaty practice on diplomatic asylum did not establish the expectation that such a right to unilateral qualification would apply as a self-standing unwritten regional rule. Such uniformity is particularly difficult to achieve with respect to duties of conduct, such as the precautionary principle, or open-textured rights, for instance, the right to diplomatic asylum or the right to property, for which it may, at best, be possible to identify a minimum content. By

[104] See also Thirlway (n 18) 135–41; M Akehurst, 'Custom as a Source of International Law' (1975) 47 BYBIL 1, 30; M Bos, *A Methodology of International Law* (Elsevier Science Publishers 1984) 247; Mendelson (n 19) 217, fn 152.

[105] See also Final Report of the IAJC (n 35) 9.

[106] *The institution of asylum, and its recognition as a human right under the Inter-American System of Protection* (Advisory Opinion OC-25/18) (30 May 2018) IACHR Series A No 25 [157]–[163]. See also *Indefinite Presidential Re-election in Presidential Systems in the context of the Inter-American System of Human Rights* (Advisory Opinion OC-28/21) (7 June 2021) IACHR Series A No 28 [96]–[99]; Final Report of the IAJC (n 35) 14–16, 18.

[107] See eg *Fisheries Jurisdiction (United Kingdom v Iceland)*, Memorial of the United Kingdom (31 July 1973) 242.

contrast, uniformity of practice with respect to rules containing a duty of result or a prohibition, such as the prohibition of refoulement or of the death penalty, is easier to ascertain.[108]

Owing to its broad substantive scope, regional custom *stricto sensu* is, thirdly, more likely to depart from general international law and thereby contribute to its fragmentation.[109] Accordingly, rather than rejecting or acknowledging a regional custom as diverging from general international law, courts and tribunals tend to prefer subsuming such custom under a corresponding rule under general customary international law—an approach adopted by the ICJ in its 1986 judgment in *Nicaragua v United States*[110]—possibly motivated by concerns about the coherence of international law.

Finally, reluctance to identify certain rules as regional custom may also stem from uncertainty as to the circumstances under which States cease to be bound by a specific rule of regional custom.[111] This primarily concerns situations in which States terminate a regional treaty containing provisions allegedly reflecting regional—but not general—custom or where States adopt a contrary practice accompanied by statements expressing such a disengagement. In the context of general customary international law the possibility of a unilateral withdrawal—which essentially amounts to a belated 'persistent objection'—is generally rejected.[112] This does not mean that such general custom is set in stone, but its applicability and content can only be changed through a collective act, namely, by way of a special treaty or customary rule.[113] However, given the relative nature of regional custom, the treaty analogy—and thus the possibility of unilateral withdrawal—may be more plausible for regional custom than for general custom. Yet even assuming that such an analogy is apposite, the mere termination of a regional treaty is not enough to automatically terminate the obligation under a parallel rule of regional custom.[114]

This view has been confirmed by the 2020 Advisory Opinion of the Inter-American Court of Human Rights. It did not only confirm that a State denouncing

[108] See eg A Peters, 'Die Missbilligung der Todesstrafe durch die Völkerrechtsgemeinschaft' (1999) 26 Europäische Grundrechte 650, 655.

[109] See Cohen-Jonathan (n 26) 140.

[110] See *Nicaragua v United States* (n 99) [199].

[111] Wood and Sender (n 58) 297: 'The question may be asked whether, and if so under what circumstances, a State may cease to be bound by a rule of particular customary international law . . . The question was not dealt with expressly in the ILC Conclusions, and there would seem to be no relevant practice.'

[112] But see: CA Bradley and M Gulati, 'Customary International Law and Withdrawal Rights in an Age of Treaties' (2010) 21 DJCIL 1–30.

[113] A Roberts, 'Who Killed Article 38(1)(B)—A Reply to Bradley & Gulati' (2010) 21 DJCIL 173, 176; Akehurst (n 104) 19.

[114] On this, see *Obligations of States in respect of Climate Change* (Advisory Opinion of 23 July 2025) ICJ [310]; *Nicaragua v United States* (n 99) [178].

and withdrawing from regional treaties remains bound by its obligations under general international law,[115] but also

> reaffirm[ed] the regulatory and binding nature of the American Declaration for Member States of the OAS, which is currently a central rule of the inter-American *corpus iuris* that reflects the minimum standard of protection of human rights in the American continent.[116]

This decision implies that Venezuela remains bound by unwritten regional law. The question, then, is whether conduct by a single State which would amount to a 'persistent opposition' to that regional custom—as an '*actus contrarius*' so to speak—results in a State ceasing to be bound by that rule. This is unlikely. Even if it is assumed that regional custom resembles treaty law, treaties do not generally permit a unilateral withdrawal either.[117] Moreover, regional custom *stricto sensu* creates a web of mutual expectations among a group of States. The moment a specific rule develops into regional custom, the individual State which participated in its creation cannot unilaterally dispose over it. Therefore, as holds for general custom, a collective act or practice by more than one State is necessary to change its content or application.

5.2.3.2 Local custom

Local custom protects expectations arising from the conduct of States relating to a specific territory or geographic feature (arising from their functional interdependence).[118] Accordingly, local custom may be considered the customary equivalent of 'boundary regimes' and 'other territorial regimes' in treaty law as reflected in Articles 11 and 12 of the 1978 Vienna Convention on Succession of States in respect of Treaties.[119] State practice confirms that the secondary rules applicable to these types of treaties differ from other treaties with respect to the need for stability of the territorial regime created by these agreements.[120] The question is whether the same rationale applies to the customary equivalent of these types of treaties, that is, 'territorialized' custom.

The ICJ indeed appears more willing to accept the existence of a rule under local custom as opposed to regional custom *stricto sensu*. Having rejected the existence of regional custom in the 1950 *Asylum* case, it readily accepted Norway's use of straight baselines 'imposed by the peculiar geography of the Norwegian

[115] *Denunciation of the American Convention on Human Rights and the Charter of the Organization of American States and the consequences for State human rights obligations* (Advisory Opinion OC-26/20) (9 November 2020) IACHR Series A No 26 [94]–[97], [100]–[110], and [155]–[157].
[116] *Denunciation of the American Convention* (n 115) [96].
[117] See VCLT, arts 54–56.
[118] See Chapter 2, section 2.3.2.1.
[119] See also Guliyev (n 70) 63–66.
[120] See also Chapter 4, section 4.4.3.

coast [and] consolidated by a constant and sufficiently long practice' in its 1951 Judgment in the *Anglo-Norwegian Fisheries* case[121] and—some ten years later—Portugal's claim to a right of passage over Indian territory, as based on a 'long continued practice' in its 1960 Judgment in the *Right of Passage over Indian Territory (Portugal v India)* case.[122] In the *Navigational and related rights* case in 2009, the ICJ identified a customary rule establishing a right of the inhabitants of the Costa Rican bank of the San Juan River to fish in the river for subsistence purposes.[123] Relying on a 'practice which had continued undisturbed and unquestioned over a very long period', the Court accepted that 'Costa Rica has a customary right' on the basis of a comparatively modest practice. Moreover, it considered the inaction of the other State, Nicaragua, as relevant practice in favour of the existence of a local custom. Accordingly, the Court's approach in that case has been understood as a departure from the standard developed in the *Asylum* case, for instance, by Judge Sepúlveda-Amor in his separate opinion,[124] by ILC members in the debate on Conclusion 16,[125] in the 'Final report on particular customary international law in the Americas' adopted by the Inter-American Juridical Committee in 2024,[126] and by various commentators.[127]

The ICJ made no reference to the *Asylum* case in any of the cases cited above. In contrast to general custom and regional custom *stricto sensu*, the ICJ appears to adopt a more flexible standard of proof.[128] Regarding the objective element, case law suggests that what is of relevance is the duration rather than the uniformity of the practice.[129] With respect to the subjective element, the ICJ seems to be more willing to infer *opinio juris* from inaction or silence.[130]

Some authors account for these differing criteria by interpreting the above-cited examples as tacit agreements, acquiescence, or simply as the application of general international law to an idiosyncratic geographic feature, rather than as instances of local custom.[131] However, these differing criteria may also be explained by the

[121] *Fisheries (UK v Norway)* [1951] ICJ Rep 116, 133, 138–39. It is controversial whether this case represents an example for regional custom (see for this view: B McGarry, 'The Development of Custom in Territorial Dispute Settlement' (2017) 8 J Int Dispute Settl 339, 349) or for the application of general international law to a regional peculiarity (Crawford (n 90) 248).

[122] *Right of Passage (Portugal v India)* (n 40) 39–40.

[123] *Navigational and Related Rights* (n 47) 56–57 [141].

[124] *Navigational and Related Rights* (separate opinion of Judge Sepúlveda-Amor) (n 47) 278.

[125] See Forteau (n 81).

[126] Final Report of the IAJC (2024) (n 35) 10.

[127] Pellet and Müller (n 27) [248]; Crema (n 67) 72–73, who, however, argues that 'this point must not be emphasized for two reasons' pointing to the, in his eyes, more liberal way the Court assesses custom and the fact that 'the provision of evidence by the parties was not controversial because both had agreed during the trial on the practice forming the basis of the local custom'.

[128] In *Alleged Violations (Nicaragua v Colombia)* (n 100) [214] and [218].

[129] *Fisheries (UK v Norway)* (n 121) 139; *Right of Passage (Portugal v India)* (n 40) 39; 40; *Nkondo v Minister of Police and Another* (South African Supreme Court) [1980] (2) SA 894 (O) (7 March 1980) 82 ILR 358, 359.

[130] Final report of the IAJC (2024) (n 35) 10; see also *Fisheries (UK v Norway)* (n 121) 139; *Right of Passage (Portugal v India)* (n 40) 40.

[131] See Crawford (n 90) 248. But see Wolfke (n 27) 90.

fact that local custom entails a reduced risk of normative 'spill-over effects' on third parties, given that its scope *ratione personae, ratione loci*, and *ratione materiae* is confined to the use of a specific territory. Hence, its potential to fragment the international legal rules governing territorial use is equally minimal.

The same holds with even greater force when the relevant practice concerns transboundary conduct by non-state actors, above all, traditional practices involving the access and use of natural resources located in the territory or maritime zone of another State.[132] Unlike the classic form of local custom arising from the conduct of two or more States, such custom not only pertains to a certain territory or geographic feature but is also linked to the private or traditional practice of an identifiable group of non-State actors.[133] Thus, its scope *ratione personae* and *ratione materiae* is even more limited and identifiable and so also is the risk of 'normative spill-over effects', which explains the flexibility of courts and tribunals when considering evidence relating to such local custom.[134]

5.2.4 Identifying regional custom

Practice confirms that the identification of regional custom generally adheres to the two-element approach reflected in Conclusion 16(2) of the ILC Conclusions.[135] However, the above-mentioned analysis does not necessarily confirm a 'stricter' application of the two-element approach in the case of rules of particular customary international law.[136] Rather, it indicates the need for a more nuanced approach.

The reason for this is that the variants of particular customary law differ in the degree to which their scope of application *ratione materiae, ratione personae*, and *ratione loci* is specific, or even confined, to a certain group of States. The greater the specificity of a particular customary rule to a limited group of States—and

[132] The Court, when examining the existence of custom in these cases, neither referred to the *Right of passage* case nor used the term 'local custom' itself to describe the rule in question. Judges writing separately in these two cases indeed criticized the ICJ for refraining from indicating the legal basis of such custom and suggested recourse to other types of custom, such as 'vested rights' (*Navigational and Related Rights* (separate opinion of Judge Sepúlveda-Amor) (n 47) 281), 'traditional rights' (*Alleged Violations (Nicaragua v Colombia)* (n 100) 404 (declaration of Judge Xue) [2]) or 'indigenous peoples' rights' (dissenting opinion of Judge ad hoc McRae [69]).

[133] See also *Eritrea/Yemen (Territorial Sovereignty and Scope of the Dispute)* (1998) 22 UNRIAA 209, 329–30 [526]; *Eritrea/Yemen (Maritime Delimitation)* (1999) 22 UNRIAA 335, 361 [103]–[112]; *Government of Sudan v Sudan People's Liberation Movement/Army (Abyei Arbitration) (Final Award)* PCA Case 2008-07 (22 July 2009) 408–10 and 412 [753]–[760] and [766].

[134] On this, see *Navigational and Related Rights* (n 47); *Alleged violations (Nicaragua v Colombia)* (n 100); *The South China Sea Arbitration* (n 84) 805.

[135] See also Resolution adopted by the Inter-American Juridical Committee (2024), 'Particular customary international law in the context of the Americas' (15 March 2024) OEA/Ser.Q CJI/RES. 290(CIV-O/24), 2(b).

[136] ILC Report 2018 (CIL) (n 11) 113.

its consequent identifiability and non-generalizability beyond that group—the greater the willingness among third parties to accept lower thresholds and more flexible criteria for its identification (given the lower risk of normative spill-over effects). At the same time, such regional specificity may give rise to an expectation among States within the region that each State can be presumed to be aware of the practice, and that, consequently, its inaction may be interpreted as consent.[137] This does not mean that regional custom can be imposed on a State without the latter's consent.[138] In the context of general custom, however, it is generally accepted that inaction can, 'under certain circumstances', qualify as relevant State practice.[139] The silence of a State, namely, a '[f]ailure to react over time to a practice may serve as evidence of acceptance as law (*opinio juris*), provided that States were in a position to react and the circumstances called for some reaction'.[140] The identifiable and non-generalizable nature of regional practice typifies the kind of 'circumstances' in which a State meets the two criteria identified by the ILC for treating silence as *opinio juris*: firstly, that a reaction by that State is called for because its interests are affected (as is notably the case for States sharing the geographic feature concerned by the practice or for member States of a regional organization); and secondly, that the State in question may be expected to have knowledge of the practice and to have had sufficient time and ability to react—assumptions that may be more readily made in a regionally limited context.[141] The specific threshold may vary depending on whether the alleged rule pertains to mutual expectations relating to a particular territory or geographic feature (local custom), or to those arising from ideological cohesion within a region (regional custom *stricto sensu*). Nevertheless, both forms of regional practice give rise to a presumption of awareness of, and consent to, the practice in question, which is rebuttable where a State provides other explanations for its inaction.[142]

5.3 Regional (general) principles of law

With respect to regional principles of law, the question is not so much whether regional principles can be recognized as international law. They may, after all, derive from a regional treaty, constitute regional custom, or, possibly, represent an autonomous regional source of law. The more complex issue is whether these principles may also qualify as general principles of law with a regional scope of

[137] See further: Bleckmann (n 67) 404; O Elias, 'The Relationship Between General and Particular Customary International Law' (1996) 8 AJICL 67, 77. See also Chapter 2, section 2.3.2.
[138] See also *North Sea Continental Shelf (Federal Republic of Germany/Denmark)* [1969] ICJ Rep 101 (separate opinion of Judge Ammoun) 132.
[139] ILC Report 2018 (CIL) (n 11) Conclusion 6(1); see also paragraph 3 of the commentary (99).
[140] ILC Report 2018 (CIL) (n 11), Conclusion 10(3),
[141] ILC Report 2018 (CIL) (n 11) 104.
[142] ILC Report 2018 (CIL) (n 11).

application (regional GPL), thus falling in the scope of Article 38(1)(c) of the ICJ Statute .

The complexity of this question is rooted both in the historical legacy of this source of law (5.3.1) and in the challenge of distinguishing (regional) general principles of law from other sources of regional law (5.3.2). To the extent that a regional legal principle meets the requirements of a modified 'two-step-approach' as proposed by the ILC, it can be recognized as falling within the scope of Article 38(1)(c) of the ICJ Statute (5.3.3).

5.3.1 From European to universal to regional principles of law

In contrast to regional custom, it took nearly 90 years after the adoption of Article 38(3) of the PCIJ Statute—the identical precursor to what later became Article 38(1)(c) of the ICJ Statute—before the recognition of regional GPL emerged as a subject of broader debate. In a rather optimistic vein, the ILA Study Group on 'The Use of Domestic Legal Principles for the Development of International Law' stated in its 2018 report that

> [s]imilar to the existence of regional customary law, the possibility exists of the existence of regional general principles derived from the domestic laws of a specific region[143]

The issue of regional principles of law resurfaced a year later in the ILC and the Sixth Committee following the Special Rapporteur's 'First Report on General Principles of Law', sparking significant debate over whether Article 38(1)(c) includes regional GPL.[144] Given the deadlock on this issue, the ILC, in 2025, provisionally adopted a 'without prejudice' clause regarding 'General principles of law with a limited scope of application' (draft Conclusion 12).[145]

This draft Conclusion does not resolve the question as to whether Article 38(1)(c) encompasses regional GPL but rather leaves the matter open. It seeks instead to offer a compromise reconciling the two positions that have emerged over the course of the debate.[146]

On one side, several ILC members and States have indicated their openness to the view that regional general principles of law fall within the scope of Article

[143] ILA, 'Report of the Study Group on the use of domestic law principles in the development of international law' (Sydney 2018) [216].

[144] See MC de Andrade, 'Regional Principles of Law in the Works of the International Law Commission' (2021) 86 QIL, Zoom-in 3–46.

[145] See (n 12).

[146] See also ILC, 'Report of the International Law Commission to the General Assembly on the work of its seventy-sixth session' (2025) UN Doc A/80/10 [262]–[266] summarizing the debate on draft Conclusion 12.

38(1)(c).[147] They argue that the term 'general' in Article 38(1)(c) cannot be read such as to exclude regional GPL given its structural similarity to Article 38(1)(b), which has been understood to include regional custom. Others, however, have expressed scepticism as to whether regional GPL are covered by Article 38(1)(c).[148] Essentially, they rely on four arguments: firstly, the word 'general' had to be understood as 'universal'. Secondly, the expression 'recognized by civilized nations' required recognition by 'all States'. Thirdly, the lack of examples militated against the recognition of regional GPL under Article 38(1)(c). Fourthly, general principles with a regional scope of application were, for the most part, tailored to the specific context of a regional IO and thus not covered by Article 38(1)(c).[149]

The unease and reluctance to recognize regional GPL under Article 38(1)(c) is, to a large extent, rooted in the text and historical legacy of this source of law.

The formulation of Article 38(1)(c), 'general principles of law recognized by civilized nations', dates back to a draft introduced by Root in the 1920 ACJ as an amendment to the Root-Phillimore proposal.[150] The debate in the Committee did not make clear whether members meant 'general' in a quantitative sense.[151] Even more so than in the context of custom, the records of the debate suggest that 'general' refers to the nature and substance of a principle, rather than to the number of States recognizing it. The phrase 'recognized by civilized nations' supports this interpretation by indicating the actors whose recognition is required; this wording would add nothing if 'general' were already taken to require universal recognition *ratione personae*.

The phrase 'recognized by civilized nations' has been central to the debate on regional GPL. While it is unclear whether the members of the ACJ considered all nations civilized[152] or whether they considered 'civilized nations' to be limited to States with a 'sufficiently developed' municipal system,[153] during the 1950

[147] ILC (n 146) [262]. See also ILC (26 July 2019) UN Doc A/CN.4/SR.3491, 12–13 (Nguyen); 17 (Reinisch); (29 July 2019) UN Doc A/CN.4/SR.3492, 4 (Argüello Gómez); 12 (Ruda Santolaria). See the statements made at the 6th Committee in 2019: UNGA (6 November 2019) UN Doc A/C.6/74/SR.32 [55] (Micronesia). France (Déclaration de la République française (5 November 2019), 6th Committee of the UNGA <https://www.un.org/en/ga/sixth/74/pdfs/statements/ilc/france_3.pdf> 2–3).

[148] See ILC Report 2025 (n 153) [264]. See the statements of the following delegations made at the 6th Committee in 2019: UNGA (6 November 2019) UN Doc A/C.6/74/SR.32 [5] (The Philippines); [16] (UK); [43] (Chile); [106] (Czech Republic); UNGA (6 November 2019) UN Doc A/C.6/74/SR.33 [26] (US).

[149] Chile (UNGA (6 November 2019) UN Doc A/C.6/74/SR.32); ILC (26 July 2019) UN Doc A/CN.4/SR.3491, 17 (Reinisch).

[150] *Procès-verbaux* of the ACJ (n 28) 344.

[151] *Procès-verbaux* of the ACJ (n 28) 335: Philimore clarified that he understood GPL as 'maxims of law', whereas de Lapradelle required at least 'quasi-unanimous support'.

[152] According to Pellet and Müller, 'apparently, the members of the 1920 Committee themselves considered "all nations" to be civilized' (Pellet and Müller (n 27) [262]), with reference to de Lapradelle in fn 772 according to whom the phrase was 'superfluous, because law implies civilization' (ACJ (n 28) 335).

[153] H Thirlway, *The Law and Procedure of the International Court of Justice: Fifty Years Jurisprudence Volume I* (OUP 2013) 243–44: 'The category of "civilized nations" was not defined once and for all in 1920; it remains open, and subject (at least in theory) to fluctuation.'

and 60s, this formulation constituted the basis for the rejection of this source of international law, notably, by newly independent and other non-Western States. For the latter, Article 38(1)(c) represented a thinly veiled attempt to impose European domestic law—European regional law—on other States;[154] a claim fuelled by the reasoning applied in international case law, notably in the 1912 *Russian Indemnity* case and in the 1951 *Sheik of Abu Dhabi* award.[155] In his separate opinions in the 1969 *North Sea Continental Shelf* cases, Judge Ammoun argued that Article 38(1)(c)

> is inapplicable in the form in which it is set down, since the term 'civilized nations' is incompatible with the relevant provisions of the United Nations Charter, and the consequence thereof is an ill-advised limitation of the notion of the general principles of law.[156]

He elaborated further by pointing to

> the particularly docile line taken by international decisions, understood by 'civilized nations' those composing the 'Concert of Europe', from whose systems of law alone they avowedly borrowed general principles of law by way of analogy.[157]

Pursuing a similar line of argument, the Soviet Union, during the Vienna Conference on the Law of Treaties, declared that the formula

> reflected the unequal position of colonialized peoples; the sources of those general principles were not international treaties or international custom, but the internal law of the European powers, and even Roman law.[158]

The Soviet Union suggested that the phrase was to be understood as 'general principles of international law'. During the session of the 6th Committee in 1971, Guatemala and Mexico—unsuccessfully—proposed deleting the reference to 'civilized nations'.[159] In a speech before the 6th Committee in 2019, then President of the ICJ Abdulqawi Yusuf, argued the reference to 'civilized nations' was the reason why

[154] Criticizing the use of the term 'civilized': UNCLOT I 201 [52] (Mali).

[155] *Russian Claim for Interest on Indemnities (Russian Federation/Turkey)* (Award) PCA Case 1910-02 (11 November 1912) [5]; *Petroleum Development Ltd v Sheikh of Abu Dhabi* (Award of September 1951) 18 ILR 144, 250–51.

[156] *North Sea Continental Shelf* (separate opinion of Judge Ammoun) (n 138) 133.

[157] *North Sea Continental Shelf* (n 138) 134.

[158] UNCLOT II 69 [32]. See also the statements by the Ukrainian Soviet Socialist Republic (70 [45]) referring to a proposal by Mongolia to amend the wording accordingly.

[159] UNGA, 'Review of the Role of the International Court of Justice: Report of the Secretary-General' (15 September 1971) UN Doc A/8382, 24–25.

> [n]either the PCIJ nor the ICJ has ever explicitly based a decision on a rule or principle derived from the 'general principles of law recognized by civilized nations'. This is, in my view, a result of the use of the phrase 'civilized nations' in Article 38 and the negative historical connotations associated with it.[160]

In light of these 'historical connotations', it is unsurprising that the debate on regional custom and regional GPL evolved in opposite directions: whereas the 1950s and 1960s led to an affirmation of the existence of regional custom, the same period also prompted advocates of the 'third source' of international law contained in Article 38(1)(c) to demonstrate that GPL were not drawn from (European) regional law, but were instead universal in character.

5.3.2 Different normative underpinnings of regional principles of law

Given the troubled legacy of this source of law and, accordingly, a certain concern to revive the idea that principles recognized within a particular region might be imposed upon others under the guise of international law, practice expressly invoking Article 38(1)(c) of the ICJ Statute in relation to regional principles is scarce. At the same time, legal practice across several regions confirms that regional principles of law play a role in three types of legal contexts: they are applied in the interpretation of regional treaties (5.3.2.1); as sources of law within regional organizations (5.3.2.2); and as sources of law beyond the treaty context (5.3.2.3). The challenge lies in determining whether these regional principles fall within the scope of Article 38(1)(c) of the ICJ Statute. This task is particularly difficult since in each of these contexts in which regional principles are invoked, their legal relevance may equally be explained by reference to a means of interpretation or another source of (regional) law.

5.3.2.1 Regional principles in the interpretation of regional treaties

Regional principles of law derived from the domestic laws of regionally limited groups of States play a role in the interpretation of regional treaties across multiple regions. In this regard, the practices of the European Court of Human Rights (ECtHR) and the Inter-American Court of Human Rights (IACtHR) are particularly illustrative in this regard. Both referred to principles of law recognized in the domestic laws of States within the region when interpreting the European Convention on Human Rights (ECHR) and the American Convention on Human Rights (ACHR).

In its Advisory Opinion of 15 November 2017, for example, the IACtHR concluded that 'in the context of the protection of the rights to life and to personal

[160] Yusuf (n 8) [27].

integrity, the Court considers that States must act in keeping with the precautionary principle'.[161] This conclusion was preceded by a detailed examination of the domestic laws of Organization of American States (OAS) member States[162] and an identification of the principles' content based on 'the domestic laws of the region'.[163] As Tullio Treves observed, these references 'could allude to a kind of regional general principles to be imported from domestic law'.[164]

The ECtHR, for its part, frequently draws on principles derived from the domestic legal systems of member States of the Council of Europe. When interpreting Article 3 of Protocol No 1 to the ECHR, enshrining the right to free elections,[165] for instance, the Court stated that

> the common principles of the European constitutional heritage, which form the basis of any genuinely democratic society, enshrine within themselves the right to vote in terms of the opportunity to cast a vote in universal, equal, free, secret and direct elections held at regular intervals (see the Code of Good Practice in Electoral Matters, paragraph 196 above).[166]

In order to substantiate these 'common principles', the Court drew on a comparative analysis undertaken by the Venice Commission of the various domestic legal systems of member States of the Council of Europe.[167] In this regard, Andreas von Arnauld observed that

> [b]y building (on) a network of general principles underlying the ECHR the ECtHR has over time developed the Convention—irrespective of its roots in an inter-state treaty—into a pan-European constitutional document . . . often clandestinely, . . . follow[ing] an approach of *wertende Rechtsvergleichung*, drawing its inspiration from the domestic legal systems of the members of the Council of Europe, without limiting itself to a minimum consensus.[168]

More specifically, the ECtHR's concept of a 'European consensus', which it uses to determine the scope and limits of an evolutive interpretation of the ECHR, has raised the question as to whether this approach extends beyond mere rules

[161] *The Environment and Human Rights* (Advisory Opinion OC-23/17) (15 November 2017) IACHR Series A No 23 [180].
[162] *Environment and Human Rights* (n 161) [178].
[163] *Environment and Human Rights* (n 161) fn 425 and 426.
[164] T Treves, 'The Expansion of International Law' (2019) 398 RdC 37, 183–84 fn 404.
[165] (European) Convention for the Protection of Human Rights and Fundamental Freedoms (adopted 4 November 1950, entered into force 3 September 1953; as amended) 213 UNTS 221, art 3.
[166] *Davydov and others v Russia* App 75947/11 (ECtHR, 13 November 2017) [285].
[167] *Davydov and others v Russia* (n 166) [196] and [283].
[168] A von Arnauld, 'Harmonisation Through General Principles of Law' in K Ziegler, PJ Neuvonen, and v Moreno-Lax (eds), *Research Handbook on General Principles in EU Law* (Edward Elgar Publishing 2022) 40, 54.

of interpretation and instead constitutes an autonomous source, potentially amounting to a form of regional GPL.[169]

Accordingly, recourse to regional principles is typically used to determine the content of regional treaty provisions. The approach adopted by these regional courts may, of course, simply qualify as (evolutive) treaty interpretation based on Article 31(1) VCLT or as interpretation in the light of subsequent State practice in accordance with Article 31(3)(b) and 32 VCLT. At the same time, the manner in which the ECtHR and the IACtHR draw on a comparative analysis of the domestic laws of their member States closely resembles the method employed to identify GPL. Moreover, recourse to these regional principles often test the limits of treaty interpretation in that they are often ascribed a legal effect that comes close to a modification, that is, an implicit amendment of the text as originally understood.[170]

5.3.2.2 Regional general principles as a source of law within regional organizations

Across various regions, 'general principles of law' recognized by the respective States within a given region form part of the applicable law in regional organizations binding on the IO's organs and its member States.

Some regional treaties expressly mention the role of regional principles. The 1981 African Charter on Human and Peoples' Rights (AfCHPR), for instance, provides that 'general principles of law recognized by African States' are 'subsidiary measures to determine the principles of law'.[171] Their purpose has been described as 'a pragmatic solution to enable the [African] Commission [on Human and Peoples' Rights] to have some standards to refer to if there was no African human rights instrument.'[172] However, to date, these African GPL have played only a limited role in regional practice.[173]

[169] See von Arnauld (n 168); see also G Nolte, 'The European Court of Human Rights and the Sources of International Law' Seminar organized by the Ministry of Foreign Affairs of the Czech Republic in connection with the 59th Meeting of CAHDI (Prague, 23 September 2020) 4. Others have understood 'regional consensus' as a form of regional custom: I Ziemele, 'European Consensus and International Law' in A van Aaken and I Motoc (eds), *The European Convention on Human Rights and General International Law* (OUP 2018) 23, 39; VP Tzevelekos and K Dzehtsiarou, 'International Custom Making and the ECtHR's European Consensus Method of Interpretation' (2016) 16 EYHR 313–44.

[170] See eg Council of Europe, Committee of Ministers, Steering Committee for Human Rights (CDDH) (2020), 'Report on the Place of the European Convention on Human Rights in the European and International Legal Order' (Strasbourg, 26–29 November 2019) [95]. See also Chapter 7, section 7.3.2.

[171] African Charter on Human and Peoples' Rights (adopted 28 June 1981, entered into force 21 October 1986) 1520 UNTS 217, art 61.

[172] R Murray (author and editor), 'Articles 60 and 61: Applicable Principles' in R Murray, *The African Charter on Human and Peoples' Rights: A Commentary* (OUP 2019) 782.

[173] Murray (n 172) 791–92.

In other regional systems, regional GPL are referred to both in the relevant texts and in practice. The 1997 Rules of Procedure of the Court of the Commonwealth of Independent States, for example, refer to GPL recognized in the respective region as an independent source of law,[174] which have played a role in the jurisprudence of the CIS Court.[175]

Another body of regional rules that may provide an example for regional GPL that fall within the scope of Article 38(1)(c) are 'general principles of EU law'.[176] Since the 1992 Treaty of Maastricht, EU GPLs are explicitly recognized in the text of the EU treaties as concretizing the requirements for the liability of the EU[177] as well as being one of the sources of EU fundamental rights in the EU treaties.[178]

At the same time, the CJEU continues to apply unwritten 'general principles of EU law' alongside the EU treaties, notably to 'fill[] gaps and as an aid to interpretation'.[179] Although the reasoning of the CJEU tends to be rather opaque, the method applied by the CJEU for their identification appears to consist of two steps, combining a comparative with a teleological approach.[180] Firstly, the CJEU compares the domestic legal systems and constitutional traditions of its members. Secondly, it examines whether the principle is 'appropriate to the needs and specific features of the Community legal system'.[181] Here, the second step assumes a particularly prominent role in that it does not 'draw on more or less arithmetical "common denominators" between the different national solutions, but chooses from each of the Member States those solutions which, having regard to the objects of the Treaty, appear to it to be the best'.[182]

It remains a matter of controversy as to whether these 'EU GPL' qualify as GPL in the sense of Article 38(1)(c) of the ICJ Statute. In a recent statement delivered by the EU in the 6th Committee of the UNGA, the EU emphasized that EU principles

174 Article 29 of the Rules of Procedure by the Economic Court of the Commonwealth of Independent States (10 July 1997) ('general principles of law recognized in the member states of the Commonwealth' [translation by the author]).

175 GM Danilenko, 'The Economic Court of the Commonwealth of Independent States' (1999) 31 NYU J Int'l L & Pol 893, 910.

176 See eg ILA Report on Domestic Legal Principles (n 143) [216].

177 TFEU, art 340(2).

178 TEU, art 6(3).

179 *Audiolux SA ea v Groupe Bruxelles Lambert SA (GBL) and Others and Bertelsmann AG and Others Case* C-101/08 (opinion of Advocate General Trstenjak delivered on 30 June 2009) [68].

180 See G Martinico, 'General Principles of EU Law and Comparative Law' in Ziegler and others (n 168) 82, 93.

181 See the consistent line of opinions of advocate generals on which the CJEU relies: *AM & S Europe Limited v Commission of the European Communities* Case 155/79 (opinion of Mr Advocate General Sir Gordon Slynn delivered on 26 January 1982) 1649; *FIAMM and Fedon v Council and Commission* Joined cases C-120/06 P and C-121/06 P (opinion of Mr Advocate General Poiares Maduro delivered on 20 February 2008) [55]; *Akzo Nobel Chemicals and Akcros Chemicals v Commission and Others* Case C-550/07 P (opinion of Advocate General Kokott delivered on 29 April 2010) [94].

182 See *Hoogovens v High Authority* Case 14/61 (opinion of Mr Advocate General Lagrange delivered on 4 June 1962) 283–84.

of law stem from an 'autonomous source of law'.[183] Several scholars are equally reluctant to classify EU GPL under Article 38(1)(c). Bruno De Witte states that EU GPL 'is not a sub-category of the GPIL, but an EU-specific source.'[184] Imogen Saunders has argued that '[g]eneral principles of EU law are another creature altogether'.[185] By contrast, Beatrice Bonafé and Paolo Palchetti, as well as the 2018 ILA report, considered EU GPL as the paradigmatic example of regional GPL under Article 38(1)(c) of the ICJ Statute.[186]

Others, while reluctant to classify EU GPL explicitly as GPL under Article 38(1)(c), point to commonalities and overlaps of certain types of EU GPL with GPL under international law[187] or, in a similar vein, suggest distinguishing

> general principles of Community law in the narrow sense, namely those which are developed exclusively from the spirit and system of the EC Treaty and relate to specific points of Community law, and those general principles which are common to the legal and constitutional orders of the Member States.[188]

Thus, the question regarding the legal nature of EU GPL does not necessarily have to be answered in an 'either/or' fashion (namely, as considering EU GPL as being either of a *sui generis* character or as falling naturally within the scope of Article 38(1)(c)). To the extent that the function, method of identification and legal effect of EU principles are equivalent to those at the universal level and in other regions, they may be recognized as a source of international law, namely regional GPL within the meaning of Article 38(1)(c). Even where this is not the case, EU GPL are not necessarily of a *sui generis* nature. They can still qualify as distinct rules of interpretation applicable within the framework of the regional IO under Article 5 VCLT or as treaty interpretation under Article 31(1) of the VCLT.[189]

The only regional court that has explicitly linked regional GPL to Article 38(1)(c) is the CARICOM Court of Justice (CCJ).[190] In its 2009 decision in *Trinidad*

[183] Statement on behalf of the EU at the Sixth Committee, 78th session of the UNGA (23 October 2023) <https://www.eeas.europa.eu/delegations/un-new-york/eu-statement-%E2%80%93-un-general-assembly-6th-committee-work-international-law-commission_en> (accessed 5 May 2026).

[184] B de Witte, 'Sources and the Subjects of International Law: The European Union's Semi-Autonomous System of Sources' in J d'Aspremont and S Besson (eds), *The Oxford Handbook of the Sources of International Law* (OUP 2017) 769, 775.

[185] I Saunders, *General Principles as a Source of International Law* (Hart 2021) 207. However, she also identifies several similarities between EU GPL and GPL under Article 38(1)(c) at 199–201

[186] See ILA Report on Domestic Legal Principles (n 143); BI Bonafé and P Palchetti, 'Relying on General Principles in International Law' in C Brölmann and Y Radi (eds), *Research Handbook on the Theory and Practice of International Law-Making* (Edward Elgar Publishing 2016) 160, 165–67; von Arnauld (n 177) 41.

[187] E Castellarin, 'General Principles of EU Law and General International Law' in J Wouters and others (eds), *General Principles of Law and the Coherence of International Law* (Brill Nijhoff 2019) 131, 133.

[188] Opinion AG Trstenjak (n 179) [69].

[189] See also Chapter 4.

[190] See for an analysis: D Berry, *Caribbean Integration Law* (OUP 2014) 188–246.

Cement Limited v The Community, the Court—when asked about the standard of review for decisions by CARICOM organs—stated that

> [t]he Court may also consider 'the general principles of law recognized by civilized nations'. If one applies Article 217 of the Revised Treaty the principles of law common to the principal legal systems of the Community are a source of law for this Court, as it is for the International Court of Justice: see Article 38(1)(c) of the Statute of the International Court of Justice.[191]

It then further elaborated the methodology for identifying these principles:

> The search is for general principles of law common to Member States. It is not necessary for the principle to be expressed identically in all Member States. It is sufficient if the general principle is widely accepted: . . . If the general principle is widely accepted throughout the Community and relevant it may become part of Community law. These are tests that will have to be applied if this Court is asked to strike down the decisions authorizing suspension of the CET on grounds that derive from the domestic law applicable to judicial review in common law jurisdictions.[192]

This decision laid the foundation for the subsequent treatment of regional GPL by the CCJ and has been confirmed in a number of its decisions. The 2009 *Trinidad Cement* decision, for example, was cited in the 2017 judgment *SM Jaleel and Co Limited and Guyana Beverages Incorporated v Guyana*,[193] and in the 2018 decision *Trinidad Cement Limited and Arawak Cement Limited v State of Barbados*, for which the Court referred to regional GPL when identifying the law on interim relief, stating that

> the principles on which national or domestic law grant interim relief are not generally admissible or relevant unless they are reflective of 'general principles of law recognized by' the Member States of the Community.[194]

To date, the case law of the CCJ has provided a unique example of a regional court that draws on GPL with a regional scope and explicitly justifies this approach on the basis of Article 38(1)(c).

[191] *TCL v Caribbean Community* App No AR 3 of 2008, CCJ 2 (OJ) (CCJ, 5 February 2009) [41].
[192] *TCL v Caribbean* (n 191).
[193] *SM Jaleel and Co Limited and Guyana Beverages Incorporated v Guyana* App No TTOJ2016/001, CCJ 2 (OJ) (CCJ, 9 May 2017), where the CCJ referred to the 2009 decision in support of its statement in [29].
[194] *Trinidad Cement Limited and Arawak Cement Limited v State of Barbados* App No TTOJ2018/002, CCJ 1 (OJ) (CCJ, 17 July 2018) [25].

5.3.2.3 Regional principles as sources of law outside the treaty context

One of the arguments against a recognition of regional GPL falling within the scope of Article 38(1)(c) is the absence of examples of such principles that have developed outside the framework of a regional treaty regime.[195] One example that may refute this argument is the principle of *uti possidetis*.[196] In substance, as confirmed by numerous decisions of international courts and tribunals adjudicating territorial and maritime disputes, *uti possidetis* 'upgrade[s] former administrative delimitations, established during the colonial period, to international frontiers'.[197]

The legal nature of *uti possidetis* at the universal level remains notoriously controversial. The central question concerns whether it has evolved from a non-binding policy or method into a universally binding principle—either as a GPL or as a rule of customary international law.[198] Nonetheless, there is one point about which most courts and commentators concur: *uti possidetis* is rooted in regional law. *Uti possidetis* has been considered, for example, as an 'intra-American international law rule'[199] and 'an important principle recognized by African States as part of the African legal order'.[200]

The extent to which regional practice has contributed to the universalisation of *uti possidetis* is discussed in Chapter 7. The present discussion focuses rather on whether regional practice—particularly the variants developed in Latin America and Africa—may qualify as GPL with a regional scope of application within the meaning of Article 38(1)(c) of the ICJ Statute.

Courts have so far avoided clarifying the legal nature of these regional origins, especially as to whether *uti possidetis* amounts to a regional GPL under Article 38(1)(c). In its 1986 judgment in the *Frontier Dispute case (Burkina Faso/Mali)*, the ICJ seemed reluctant to rely on *uti possidetis* as an unwritten African principle of law. Instead, the ICJ stated that

> [t]he fact that the new African States have respected the administrative boundaries and frontiers established by the colonial powers must be seen not as a mere practice contributing to the gradual emergence of a principle of customary international law, limited in its impact to the African continent as it had previously

[195] See Chile and ILC member August Reinisch (n 149).

[196] See eg ILC, 'Third report on general principles of law of the Special Rapporteur, Mr. Marcelo Vázquez-Bermúdez' (18 April 2022) UN Doc A/CN.4/753 [91]. See also the subsequent debate in the ILC (26 July 2019) UN Doc A/CN.4/SR.3491: in favour Nguyen (13); sceptical Reinisch (19).

[197] *Frontier Dispute (Burkina Faso/Republic of Mali) (Judgment)* [1986] ICJ Rep 554 [23].

[198] See MN Shaw, 'The Heritage of States: The Principle of *Uti Possidetis Juris* Today' (1996) 67 BYBIL 75, 111; J Crawford, *Brownlie's Principles of Public International Law* (9th edn, OUP 2019) 224. But see: A Peters, 'The Principle of *Uti Possidetis Juris*' in C Walter and A von Ungern-Sternberg (eds), *Self-Determination and Secession in International Law* (OUP 2014) 95, 99.

[199] *Dispute between Argentina and Chile concerning the Beagle Channel (Argentina v Chile)* (Award of 18 February 1977) (1977) 21 UNRIAA 53, 192.

[200] *Kasikili/Sedudu Island (Botswana v Namibia)* [1999] ICJ Rep 1111 (declaration of Judge Koroma) 1111.

been to Spanish America, but as the application in Africa of a rule of general scope.[201]

Accordingly, the ICJ refrained from treating regional practice in Africa regarding the intangibility of frontiers and the Latin American concept of *uti possidetis* as distinct regional rules, but rather as evidence for the existence of a universally applicable concept.[202]

Six years after the ICJ's decision in *Burkina Faso/Mali*, in 1992, the Badinter Commission adopted a similar approach when extending the scope of the principle *ratione materiae* from a situation of decolonization to the dissolution of States stating that '*[u]ti possidetis*, though initially applied in settling decolonisation issues in America and Africa, is today recognized as a general principle'.[203] This approach was again confirmed by the PCA in its final award of 2017 in the *Croatia v Slovenia* case, in which the tribunal held that *uti possidetis* was 'a well-established principle of international law'.[204] Significantly, the tribunal emphasized that the scope of the principle had been extended from the context of decolonization in Latin-America, Africa, and Asia to the dissolution of States wherever it occurs.[205]

To date, the approach adopted by international courts and tribunals, that is as deriving *uti possidetis* from regional practice and claiming its universal status, is problematic for at least two reasons. Firstly, neither the ICJ nor other international courts have undertaken a comprehensive comparative analysis of the domestic legal systems of States within a region or of practice at the universal level with respect to the principle of *uti possidetis*. The existence of *uti possidetis* as a norm at the regional level has merely been asserted and its transfer to the universal level justified by functional considerations, notably its 'logical connection' with the phenomenon of attaining independence. Hence, such reasoning neither meets the requirements for demonstrating a 'general practice accepted as law', necessary for recognizing it as custom, nor for a 'recognition by the community of nations', the requirement for universal GPL. Secondly, in all cases in which international courts have so far applied the principle of *uti possidetis*, the application of this principle has also found an additional basis in the express prior consent of the states concerned.[206] For these reasons, the purported universal legal status of *uti possidetis* rests on fragile normative and methodological foundations.

[201] *Burkina Faso/Mali* (n 197) [21]; see also [24].
[202] *Burkina Faso/Mali* (n 197) [20].
[203] Opinion No 3 (Badinter Commission) (1992) 92 ILR 170, 171.
[204] *Arbitration Between the Republic of Croatia and the Republic of Slovenia* (Final Award) PCA Case No 2012-04 (29 June 2017) [256].
[205] *Arbitration Between the Republic of Croatia and the Republic of Slovenia* (n 204).
[206] *Burkina Faso/Mali* (n 197) [20]; *Land, Island and Maritime Frontier Dispute (El Salvador/Honduras; Nicaragua intervening)* [1992] ICJ Rep 351 [40]; *Frontier Dispute (Benin/Niger)* [2005] ICJ Rep 90 [45]; *Territorial and Maritime Dispute (Nicaragua v Colombia)* [2012] ICJ Rep 624 [39]; *Frontier Dispute (Burkina Faso/Niger)* [2013] ICJ Rep 44 [63].

Against this background, it appears that recognizing the regional variants of the principle of the intangibility of frontiers as regional GPL within the meaning of Article 38(1)(c) could offer a more methodologically and normatively coherent legal foundation.

In this regard, both individual judges and scholars appear increasingly inclined to attribute distinct legal status to the regional manifestations of *uti possidetis*. Notably, they often regard the legal status of these regional variants as being more clearly established than that of their universal counterpart. Judge Yusuf, writing separately in the 2013 *Frontier Dispute (Burkina Faso/Niger)*, for example, argued that

> the OAU/AU principle is specific to the African continent where it is considered as part of the public law of Africa applicable to all African States, but has no claim to being a general principle or a customary rule of international law.[207]

While thus treating the OAU/AU principle on the respect of boundaries as deriving from an autonomous regional source of law, he considers the principle of *uti possidetis*, as 'a "method" for determining the course of a boundary' the application of which, however, was based on an agreement between the States concerned.[208] He recently reaffirmed this view, namely, that

> the OAU/AU principle of respect for borders existing on achievement of independence is neither identical nor equivalent to the principle of *uti possidetis juris* applied by the Spanish-American Republics following their own decolonization a century earlier.[209]

However, even those judges and commentators who acknowledge the binding nature of these regional variants tend to characterize their legal source as something other than a GPL with a regional scope of application within the meaning of Article 38(1)(c). Instead, they refer to them, for instance, as part of the 'public law of Africa'[210] or as 'regional custom'.[211] Courts and scholars thus appear to concur in their reluctance to regard the regional variants of *uti possidetis* as regional GPL encompassed by Article 38(1)(c).

[207] *Frontier Dispute (Burkina Faso/Niger)* [2013] ICJ Rep 134 (separate opinion of Judge Yusuf) [29].
[208] [2013] ICJ Rep 134 [32].
[209] See (n 3).
[210] Yusuf (n 207).
[211] See eg Thirlway (n 153) 201; SR Ratner, 'Drawing a Better Line: *Uti Possidetis* and the Borders of New States' (1996) 90:4 AJIL 590, 598–99; GJ Naldi, 'The Case Concerning the Frontier Dispute (Burkina Faso/Republic of Mali): *Uti Possidetis* in an African Perspective' (1987) 36:4 ICLQ 893, 898; J Dugard, 'Walvis Bay: Decolonization and International Law' (1991) 85:4 AJIL 751, 753.

At the same time, two aspects suggest considering regional variants of *uti possidetis* as a regional GPL encompassed by Article 38(1)(c). Firstly, the *function* fulfilled by the regional variants of *uti possidetis* corresponds to the function of GPL in the sense of Article 38(1)(c), ie to protect and stabilize expectations of the way the legal order responds to 'gaps' and novel situations such as decolonization and the dissolution of States. Secondly, the manner in which the regional variants of *uti possidetis* emerge from an interweaving of domestic and international law closely corresponds to what is, in fact, envisaged by Article 38(1)(c).[212] This is illustrated by the fact that both scholars and judges have described these regional variants as forms of regional 'public law', noting that they are simultaneously rooted in domestic public law and in the body of international law applicable within the region. One may indeed question how the identification of a principle of regional 'public law' differs from the identification of a regional GPL in the sense of Article 38(1)(c), which would derive from a comparative analysis of the domestic—specifically public—laws of States within a region. The method by which the regional variants of *uti possidetis* have been identified therefore appears more closely aligned with the approach prescribed by Article 38(1)(c)—namely, a comparative analysis of domestic legal systems and other forms of State practice—than with the method employed by courts and tribunals to justify its universal scope of application, which tends to emphasize the universality of the principle's purpose while implicitly relying on the ad hoc consent of parties to its application expressed in the jurisdictional basis. It remains to be seen how the ICJ or any other international court or tribunal will approach this principle in a case in which the parties have not explicitly agreed on its application.

5.3.3 Distinguishing regional general principles of law from other regional principles

Regional principles of law are relevant in legal practice both within the framework of regional treaties and organizations, and beyond such contexts, across various regions. Recourse to these principles often tests the limits of treaty interpretation and of other sources of international law. In several of the above-mentioned cases, legal practice did not conform to the requirements, method, or legal effect envisaged by these other secondary rules. At the same time, there is a striking similarity across different regions in the manner in which certain regional principles are identified, and the functions they perform within their respective legal orders: regional principles are employed to bridge normative gaps and safeguard

[212] See also Martinico (n 180) 83–84.

legitimate expectations vis-à-vis that legal order—functions traditionally understood as crucial to the purpose of Article 38(1)(c) for preventing a denial of justice.[213] Furthermore, the method of identifying regional general principles—by way of a comparative analysis of the domestic laws of States within a given region—is applied consistently across regions and is thus structurally analogous to the method envisaged by Article 38(1)(c).[214]

Accordingly, there are good reasons to consider recognizing (only) those regional principles whose function and method of identification correspond to those attributed to GPL at the universal level as falling within the scope of Article 38(1)(c), thereby distinguishing them from other sources of law.

Due to the structural similarities with universal GPL, the test for identifying the existence and content of regional GPL could follow a modified 'two-step-approach' adopted by the ILC with respect to GPL derived from national legal systems, requiring the determination of: (a) the existence and content of a principle common to the various legal systems of the region; and (b) its transposition to the regional legal system.[215] In this regard, the 'regional' element pertains both to the delimitation of the relevant group of States (a) as well as to the question whether the principle in question is transposable to the regional legal system (b).

To identify the relevant 'region', legal practice confirms that such a region is characterized by a close nexus between domestic and regional law, a certain degree of 'embeddedness' of regional law within the domestic legal systems,[216] which is typically present in regional integration organizations, and regional treaties that establish obligations regarding the internal political order of a State, notably human rights treaties. Yet, it also includes groups of States the domestic laws and constitutions of which have been shaped by a common historical experience, such as being formerly administrative units of the same State or (de-) colonization. Ultimately, the defining criterion for the existence and scope of such a region is whether within a group of States an objective convergence of domestic laws exists that reflects a shared intention to entrench that convergence through a common legal order.

Recognizing these regional principles as regional GPL within the meaning of Article 38(1)(c) has the distinct advantage of providing a legal category that, on the one hand, protects the expectations of States on matters relating to the operation of their respective regional legal orders, while, on the other hand, avoiding both overstretching other sources of law and unwarranted proliferation of distinct regional *sui generis* sources of law.

[213] ILC, 'General principles of law: texts and titles of the draft conclusions' (n 12) draft Conclusion 10.
[214] ILC, 'General principles of law: texts and titles of the draft conclusions' (n 12), draft Conclusions 4 to 6.
[215] ILC, 'General principles of law: texts and titles of the draft conclusions' (n 12), draft Conclusion 4.
[216] See Chapter 2, section 2.3.3.1.

5.4 Regional *jus cogens*

In 1986, Arnold McNair remarked that '[i]t is difficult to imagine any society, whether of individuals or of States, whose law sets no limit whatever to freedom of contract'.[217] In international law, such limits to the freedom of contract are prescribed by peremptory norms of general international law, also known as *jus cogens*. According to Article 53 of the VCLT

> [a] treaty is void if, at the time of its conclusion, it conflicts with a peremptory norm of general international law. For the purposes of the present Convention, a peremptory norm of general international law is a norm accepted and recognized by the international community of States as a whole as a norm from which no derogation is permitted and which can be modified only by a subsequent norm of general international law having the same character.

Article 64 of the VCLT provides that

> [i]f a new peremptory norm of general international law emerges, any existing treaty which is in conflict with that norm becomes void and terminates.

The support of UN member States for Conclusion 3 of the ILC's 'Conclusions on identification and legal consequences of peremptory norms of general international law (*jus cogens*)', adopted in 2022, which largely follows Article 53 of the VCLT, demonstrates that this concept is widely accepted.[218] Moreover, as Conclusions 14 to 16 clarify, it not only limits the 'freedom of contract', but also applies to general international law, unilateral acts, and acts of international organizations the binding legal effect of which is subject to their compatibility with *jus cogens*.[219] The implications of universal *jus cogens* for the application of regional international law is examined in Chapter 6, while Chapter 7 considers how regional practice contributes to the identification of universal *jus cogens*. The present section focuses on whether certain unwritten regional norms may qualify as *jus cogens* with a regionally limited scope of application ('regional *jus cogens*').

In light of McNair's observation, the existence of regional *jus cogens* may appear consequential. Given the emergence of multiple regional legal systems—some exhibiting such a high degree of legal integration that they resemble States—it seems natural that they would establish their own specific limits to the freedom of contract. However, the very existence of regional *jus cogens* in international law is so controversial among States, ILC members, and commentators that, in its

[217] A McNair, *The Law of Treaties* (OUP 1986) 213–14.
[218] ILC Report 2022 (*Jus cogens*) (n 13) 27.
[219] ILC Report 2022 (*Jus cogens*) (n 13) 55–64.

conclusions on *jus cogens*, the ILC ultimately decided to exclude the issue from the scope of the topic; and thus left the question open.[220]

Some ILC members, including the Special Rapporteur, had even preferred to state in the conclusions' commentaries that regional *jus cogens* does not exist, pointing to the incompatibility of the texts in Articles 53 and 64 of the VCLT with the idea of regional *jus cogens*, a lack of State practice in support of such a concept, and several other conceptual problems, including difficulty in defining a region, the formation of regional *jus cogens sans consentement* of all the intra-regional States, the legal consequences arising from non-derogability for third States, and the 'exceptional' and 'inherently universal' character of *jus cogens*.[221] Even among those in favour of excluding the issue from the scope—rather than explicitly rejecting the concept—support was, at best, lukewarm. Only a few members of that group actually supported the theoretical possibility of regional *jus cogens*, and even they conceded the absence of supporting State practice.[222] The majority of those who favoured excluding the issue from the scope of the topic did so not out of a belief that regional *jus cogens* exists or should exist, but rather because they considered it beyond the ILC's competence to exclude its existence.[223]

The general unease about regional *jus cogens* also stems from a deeper source. In some sense, the idea of regional *jus cogens* appears to serve as the *Gretchenfrage* in the relationship between regional and general international law, readily exposing its proponents to the charge of jeopardizing the universality of international law.[224] Yet, to the extent that general international law itself—in the form of universal secondary rules emerging from State practice—recognizes the possibility of regional *jus cogens*, the tension between regional and general international law may be reconciled.

To this effect, this section examines whether the concept of regional *jus cogens* is compatible with the universal secondary rules reflected in the VCLT (5.4.1) before

[220] ILC Report 2022 (*Jus cogens*) (n 13).

[221] ILC, 'Fourth report on peremptory norms of general international law (*jus cogens*) by Dire Tladi, Special Rapporteur' (2019) UN Doc A/CN.4/727, 21 [47]; Murase (UN Doc A/CN.4/SR.3459, 12); Galvão Teles (UN Doc A/CN.4/SR.3460, 3); Oral (UN Doc A/CN.4/SR.3460, 5); Hassouna (UN Doc A/CN.4/SR.3460, 15); Nguyen (UN Doc A/CN.4/SR.3460, 16–17); Jalloh (UN Doc A/CN.4/SR.3461, 8); Huang (UN Doc A/CN.4/SR.3461, 11–12); Rajput (UN Doc A/CN.4/SR.3461, 13–14); Aurescu (UN Doc A/CN.4/SR.3462, 3); Saboia (UN Doc A/CN.4/SR.3462, 5); Petrič (UN Doc A/CN.4/SR.3462, 8–9); Argüello Gómez (UN Doc A/CN.4/SR.3462, 11–12); Ruda Santolaria (UN Doc A/CN.4/SR.3462, 17). See also D Costelloe, *Legal Consequences of Peremptory Norms in International Law* (CUP 2017) 19–20; see also A Orakhelashvili, *Peremptory Norms of General International Law* (OUP 2006) 38–39.

[222] See eg Park (UN Doc A/CN.4/SR.3459, 15–16); Nolte (UN Doc A/CN.4/SR.3461, 4); Cissé (UN Doc A/CN.4/SR.3462, 7–8).

[223] This position was adopted by: Wood (UN Doc A/CN.4/SR.3459, 6); Hmoud (UN Doc A/CN.4/SR.3460, 13); Reinisch (UN Doc A/CN.4/SR.3461, 6); the position taken by Escobar Hernández (UN Doc A/CN.4/SR.3462, 14–15) and Lehto (UN Doc A/CN.4/SR.3459, 19) was ambiguous.

[224] See also A Garrido-Muñoz, 'Patterns of Avoidance and Assimilation Peremptory Norms in European Union Law' in FL Bordin, AT Müller, and F Pascual-Vives (eds), *The European Union and Customary International Law* (CUP 2022) 148, 164.

examining if distinct universal rules have emerged in practice across regions that would support its existence (5.4.2). It concludes that the current state of practice does not support the existence of regional *jus cogens* (5.4.3).

5.4.1 Regional *jus cogens* in the drafting process of the VCLT

Some authors exclude the possibility of regional *jus cogens* arguing that universality is an inherent feature of *jus cogens*.[225] It is true that the scope of Articles 53 and 64 VCLT does not include regional *jus cogens*. The universal recognition of the norms referred to in Articles 53 and 64 VCLT was rather a *conditio sine qua non* for their acceptance by several States at the Vienna Conference.[226]

Yet, although the drafters did not include regional *jus cogens* in the scope of Articles 53 and 64 VCLT, nothing in the *travaux* suggests an agreement among States to reject the concept as such. The drafters thereby did not exclude the possibility that regional *jus cogens* could exist beyond the scope of Articles 53 and 64. The ILC report of 1963 suggests that the expression 'general international law' was not meant to rule out that regional *jus cogens* could exist, but 'to make it clear that the article was concerned with universal international law . . . to the exclusion of regional international law'.[227] The *travaux* of the VCLT further demonstrate that the possibility of regional *jus cogens* had been considered by certain States since the 1960s—without, however, any agreement among them. For example, Ecuador, in the debate on what was to become Article 51 (Coercion), claimed that certain Latin-American principles 'had the character of regional *jus cogens*',[228] while Yugoslavia remarked that '[i]t would be desirable also to determine the relationship between the universal *jus cogens* and a regional *jus cogens*'.[229] At the same time, Mali argued that '[t]he moral and spiritual values inherent in *jus cogens* could only assert themselves with the desired peremptory force if no geographical limits were placed on their applicability. Hence there could be no question of a regional *jus cogens*.'[230]

[225] See eg A Koagne Zouapet, 'To Be or Not to Be Imperative: *Jus Cogens* Between Universal Vocation and Regional Claims' (2021) 86 QIL, Zoom-in 47, 51–56.

[226] See, for instance, the debate triggered by the US proposal for replacing 'recognized by the international community as a whole' as suggested by the ILC with 'recognized in common by the national and regional legal systems of the world', where delegations opposing it claimed that it undermined universality, whereas the US and supporting delegations insisted that the whole purpose of the proposal was to ensure universality (UNCLOT I, 295–333).

[227] ILC, 'Summary records of the fifteenth session from 6 May to 12 July 1963' (1963) YBILC I, UN Doc A/CN.4/SER.A/1963, 214 [72].

[228] UNCLOT II, 91 [70].

[229] ILC, 'Documents of the second part of the seventeenth session and of the eighteenth session including the reports of the Commission to the General Assembly' (1966) YBILC II, UN Doc A/CN.4/SER.A/1966/Add.l, 360 (Yugoslavia).

[230] UNCLOT I, 327 [73].

Similarly, the *travaux* leading to the phrase 'international community as a whole' reveal that the drafters did not insert the terms 'as a whole' because they were of the view that regional *jus cogens* did not exist. On the contrary, the expression 'as a whole' was intended to lower the threshold for the formation of a norm of *jus cogens*.[231] Indeed, at the Vienna Conference, Belgium even emphasized that

> [c]learly, that [the requirement of recognition by the international community as a whole] did not preclude the existence of peremptory rules in a more limited geographical framework, for instance, in an organized regional community.[232]

5.4.2 Traces of non-derogable regional norms in State practice

While there is agreement that Articles 53 and 64 of the VCLT do not include regional *jus cogens*, ascertaining whether universal secondary rules have since developed that (positively) recognize regional *jus cogens* presents a far greater challenge. In its 2011 Guide to practice on reservations to treaties, the ILC acknowledged the possible existence of regional *jus cogens*—without, however, providing examples from State practice.[233]

Contrary to the argument put forward by several critics of regional *jus cogens*, it is not so much the lack of potential examples for regional *jus cogens* that cast doubts on its recognition as a category of international law. With respect to State practice, it is indeed possible to identify some instances of regional practice that designate certain regional norms as being of a fundamental character, hierarchically superior, or even non-derogable, a (if not the[234]) defining feature of universal *jus cogens*.[235] However, while some other authors apparently consider these instances as sufficient evidence to establish a recognition of regional *jus cogens*,[236] the decisive element for the development of modified or even distinct secondary rules is missing, that is their acceptance by States within the region and by third parties as a distinct category of regional law.

5.4.2.1 Socialist international law

The first example relates to the claim formulated by the Soviet Union in justification of its intervention in Czechoslovakia in 1968, according to which its actions

[231] UNCLOT I, 472 [12] (Yasseen).
[232] UNCLOT I, 233 [63].
[233] ILC, 'Guide to Practice on Reservations to Treaties, Report of the International Law Commission' (2011) UN Doc A/66/10/Add. 1, footnote 2324.
[234] R Kolb, *Peremptory International Law—Jus Cogens: A General Inventory* (Hart 2015) 97–99.
[235] See draft Conclusions 2 and 3 (n 13).
[236] See eg Garrido-Muñoz (n 224).

were justified on the basis of 'socialist principles'.[237] This argument was further developed by Grigory Tunkin, who claimed that the 'principles of socialist internationalism'—which, in his view, included the 'right to fraternal assistance', as the *Brezhnev Doctrine* was called in legal terms—formed

> a new, higher type of international law—a socialist international law, the basis of which is being formed in relations among states of the socialist system and which is coming to replace contemporary general international law.[238]

Given that Tunkin understood these principles as 'local international legal norms which by their social content are distinct from norms of general international law',[239] it is not unreasonable to assume that he even argued that such norms superseded universal *jus cogens*. In his 1975 Hague Lecture Tunkin also implied the existence of local norms of a higher nature when arguing that

> [i]f principles of *jus cogens* are to exist they cannot bar the establishment of general or local norms which go beyond them in promoting peaceful and friendly relations among nations, corresponding to higher stages of international integration. Principles of *jus cogens* can also not prohibit the establishment of local norms which are different from them in their social contents.[240]

Yet, it should be noted that such derogation from fundamental principles of international law, notably the UN Charter, based on socialist principles was outrightly rejected by third States in response to the intervention undertaken by the Soviet Union and other Warsaw Pact States in Czechoslovakia in 1968.[241] The *Brezhnev Doctrine* itself was explicitly given up by the USSR under President Gorbachev.[242] Notably, during a summit of the Warsaw Pact States in 1989, the USSR and four other Warsaw Pact States conceded that the intervention in Czechoslovakia had been unjustified.[243]

237 First Secretary of the Soviet Union L Brezhnev in a Speech at the Fifth Congress of the Polish United Workers' Party (13 November 1968) <https://www.files.ethz.ch/isn/125400/1162_brezhnevdoctrine.pdf> (accessed 5 May 2026).

238 GI Tunkin, *Theory of International Law* (translated with an introduction by WE Butler) (Harvard University Press 1974) 444; see also Fourth Report on *jus cogens* (n 221) 41–44.

239 Tunkin (n 238).

240 GI Tunkin, 'International Law in the International System' (1975) 147 RdC 9, 94.

241 See G Hafner, 'The Intervention in Czechoslovakia—1968', in T Ruys, O Corten, A Hofer (eds), *The Use of Force in International Law: A Case-Based Approach* (OUP 2018) 149–51.

242 C Gray, *International Law and the Use of Force* (4th edn, OUP 2018) 96.

243 See B Keller, 'Clamor in Europe: Warsaw Pact Condemns '68 Prague Invasion' The New York Times (5 December 1989) <https://www.nytimes.com/1989/12/05/world/clamor-in-europe-warsaw-pact-condemns-68-prague-invasion.html> (accessed 5 May 2026).

5.4.2.2 Europe

In Europe, several court decisions have referred to a 'European *ordre public*', in particular with regard to the right of access to justice in the context of UN sanctions.[244] Examples are the *Al-Dulimi v Switzerland* case before the ECtHR of 2016 as well as the *Kadi* cases before the CJEU,[245] but also decisions concerning the validity of reservations on the jurisdiction of the ECtHR.[246] In these cases, the courts did not only attribute hierarchical superiority to the regional norms that they considered to reflect fundamental values.[247] They also considered the legal effects of those norms that have been identified as typical for *jus cogens*. Nevertheless, it is important to note that they apparently deliberately refrained from designating it as 'regional *jus cogens*'. Moreover, some of the regional court decisions, notably the 2005 Judgment by the Court of First Instance of the EU,[248] the implied criticism of the lack of access to justice in the sanctions system contained in the 2005 World Summit Outcome document,[249] as well as the subsequent reform of the sanctions system at the UN level,[250] indicate that the insistence on access to justice by regional courts was not so much perceived as an idiosyncratic contestation of the UNSC's powers under the UN Charter, but that the core of the right of access to justice even reflects universal *jus cogens*.

5.4.2.3 Inter-American system

With respect to the inter-American system, at least two examples appear as possible candidates for a regional *jus cogens*.[251]

Firstly, the recognition of the prohibition of enforced disappearance as a norm of *jus cogens* 'has been particularly consistent in the inter-American system'.[252] Yet, this fact could merely refer to the role of regional practice as a 'building block' or

[244] See P Sturma, 'Is There Any Regional Jus Cogens in Europe? The Case of the European Convention on Human Rights' in D Tladi (ed), *Peremptory Norms of General International Law (jus cogens)* (Brill 2021) 302.

[245] See *Al-Dulimi and Montana Management Inc v Switzerland* App 5809/08 (ECtHR, 21 June 2016) [145]; *Kadi and Al Barakaat International Foundation v Council and Commission* Joined Cases C-402/05 P and C-415/05 P (CJEU, 3 September 2008) [281].

[246] In *Loizidou*, the ECtHR regarded 'the Convention as a constitutional instrument of European public order (*ordre public*)': *Loizidou v Turkey* App 15318/89 (ECtHR, 23 March 1995) [75].

[247] See for an extensive analysis of the peremptory nature of EU law Garrido-Muñoz (n 224) 148, 160–74, who concludes that '[t]he foundational elements of EU law reflect the existence of a sort of *lex specialis* in the field of peremptory norms that is not reflected in the universalistic features of general international law.'

[248] *Kadi v Council and Commission*, Case T-315/01 (CFI, 21 September 2005) [233].

[249] UNGA, 'World Summit Outcome' (16 September 2005) UN Doc A/RES/60/1 [109].

[250] Subsequent to the CFI's decision, the UNSC established the so-called Focal Point for receiving de-listing requests on 19 December 2006. Shortly after the ECJ's 2008 *Kadi* judgment, the UNSC replaced the focal point by way of introducing the Ombudsperson in 2009 who is authorized to receive information from listed persons and make suggestions to the committee. While the scope of the Ombudsperson was initially limited to selected sanctions procedures, it was soon extended to all the sanctions procedures established by UNSC resolutions. As of 2021, the sanctions committee published, inter alia, the names and reasons of listing, and has published Guidelines which explain its procedure and the criteria which it applies.

[251] On the role of (regional) *jus cogens* in Latin America: LC Lima and L Marotti, 'An Unlikely Duo? Regionalism and *Jus Cogens* in International Law' (2022) 12 Go JIL 219, 229–38.

[252] Fourth report on *jus cogens* (n 221) [126]–[127].

means of identification of a universally recognized peremptory norm, given that there are strong indications that the prohibition against enforced disappearance is recognized as such.[253]

Secondly, the prohibition of juvenile executions has been understood as an example of regional *jus cogens* by some, due to a rather ambiguous formulation by the Inter-American Commission in the 1987 decision in *Roach v Pinkerton* stating that

> [t]he Commission finds that in the member States of the OAS there is recognized a norm of *jus cogens* which prohibits the State execution of children. This norm is accepted by all the States of the inter-American system, including the United States.[254]

It is unclear whether this should be read as 'only' (ie, as establishing regional *jus cogens*) or as 'also' (ie, as evidence of universal *jus cogens*) member States of the OAS/the States of the inter-American system have recognized the *jus cogens* character of the prohibition of juvenile executions. The ambiguity continued in the Commission's decision in the *Domingues v United States* case, where the Commission recognized 'the existence of a particularly pervasive regional norm repudiating the application of the death penalty to persons under 18 years of age'[255] which 'has been recognized as being of a sufficiently indelible nature to now constitute a norm of *jus cogens*, a development anticipated by the Commission in its *Roach and Pinkerton* decision'.[256] However, the Commission also noted that

> [t]he acceptance of this norm crosses political and ideological boundaries and efforts to detract from this standard have been vigorously condemned by members of the international community as impermissible under contemporary human rights standards.[257]

Thus, it appears that the prohibition of juvenile executions was understood, by the Commission, as reflecting universal *jus cogens*.

5.4.2.4 Islamic *Shari'a*

Finally, the predominant role attributed to the *Shari'a* by member States of the OIC has been understood as an example of regional *jus cogens* rooted in natural law.[258]

[253] Fourth report on *jus cogens* (n 221) [30] and [123]. See also Chapter 7, section 7.4.3.
[254] *Roach and Pinkerton v United States* Case No 9647 (IACHR, 22 September 1987) Res No 3/87 [56].
[255] *Michael Domingues v United States* Case 12.285 (IACHR, 22 October 2002) Report No 62/02 [75].
[256] *Domingues v United States* (n 255) [85].
[257] *Domingues v United States* (n 255).
[258] R Hasmath, 'The Utility of Regional Jus Cogens', *Paper presented at the American Political Science Association Annual Meeting* (New Orleans, 30 August–2 September 2012) 11–12.

The 1990 Cairo Declaration on Human Rights in Islam adopted by the member States of the OIC, for instance, subjects, inter alia, in its Article 24 human rights to the *Shari'a*.[259]

The difference between this last example and the previous examples is that it does not concern a specific regional rule, but an entire body of regional rules from which no derogation is permitted. The question here is whether the Cairo Declaration represents merely a symbolic proclamation or do OIC member States indeed derogate in practice from other rules of international law if these are incompatible with *Shari'a* law.

The most prominent reflection of the *Shari'a* law based exception represents the practice of reservations of OIC member States to human rights treaties, notably to CEDAW, in those cases in which human rights guarantees are in conflict with the roles ascribed to women under Islamic law.[260] At first glance, this practice thus may prove that *Shari'a* law is indeed regarded as regional law from which no derogation is permitted. At closer inspection, however, the practice of OIC member States is anything but consistent in its insistence on *Shari'a* law. Instead, recourse to *Shari'a* law is marked by its selectivity.[261]

Moreover, even with respect to *Shari'a* law as pertains to gender equality, it should be noted that out of 23 OIC member States that initially submitted reservations to the core nine UN human rights treaties based on *Shari'a* law, all but four States have withdrawn at least one *Shari'a* reservation in the past 20 years.[262] In light of this practice, it is doubtful whether *Shari'a* law could serve as a convincing example for the existence of regional *jus cogens*.

5.4.3 Recognizing peremptory norms of regional law as a distinct legal category?

The examples outlined above may be considered the functional equivalent of *jus cogens* at the regional level. Each of the examples implies a set of unwritten norms regarded as reflecting the 'fundamental values' of the regional community, thereby safeguarding the latter's shared expectations of a common normative minimum. This is, however, where their functional equivalence ends. Ultimately, they do not suffice for supporting the existence of regional *jus cogens*.

In each example, the relevant regional practice was either rejected by third parties, where the claim of non-derogability was, ultimately, not sustained, or the

[259] Organization of the Islamic Conference, Cairo Declaration on Human Rights in Islam (adopted 5 August 1990), art 24.

[260] On this: N Salem, 'Sharia Reservations to Human Rights Treaties' in A Peters (ed), *Max Planck Encyclopedia of Public International Law* (OUP 2020) [23].

[261] Salem (n 260) [27].

[262] Salem (n 260) [28].

regional assertion was coupled to the argument that the rule in question also reflected universal *jus cogens*. The approach taken by European courts concerning UN sanctions, the practice regarding *Shari'a*-motivated reservations on human rights, and the *Brezhnev Doctrine*, for instance, have been largely rejected by third States and IOs.

In contrast to regional custom or regional general principles of law, these examples are also far more heterogeneous. It is not possible to discern a common method for identifying regional norms with *jus cogens* status—neither one analogous to the approach used for identifying universal *jus cogens*, nor a distinct method applied consistently at the regional level (which, by contrast, could be identified with respect to regional principles of law).[263] In some cases, the higher rank of the norm has been proclaimed *ex post facto* by scholars (for example, regarding the *Brezhnev Doctrine*) without evidence of near-unanimous acceptance by States within the region. In other instances, notably, the Latin American example, reference is made not only to the acceptance by Latin American States but also beyond the region, emphasizing that 'this norm crosses political and ideological boundaries'.

Finally, these examples do not even share a common understanding of the consequences issuing from the purportedly superior hierarchical status of such unwritten regional norms: Whether this regional 'non-derogability' is understood to apply to all rules pertaining to international law, whether it may be invoked against third parties, and whether it entails the same legal consequences as *jus cogens*—namely, the voidness of conflicting acts—or merely renders such conduct unlawful, remains unclear.

Thus, even if one accepts that *jus cogens* norms need not be universal and that the criteria for identifying regional *jus cogens* need not replicate the methods or effects associated with universal *jus cogens*, the existence of universal secondary rules recognizing regional *jus cogens* would require, at the very least, a consistent practice across multiple regions—both in how these norms are identified and in the legal consequences attributed to their status (which, in the author's view, would not even need not to include universal non-derogability). Such regional practice does not exist to date.

There are, however, two important caveats. Firstly, the absence, to date, of universal secondary rules that recognize regional *jus cogens* does not preclude the possibility that a universal rule of recognition could emerge in the future; this depends on whether a sufficiently accepted practice develops. Secondly, this finding does not imply that certain forms of higher regional law have not been generally recognized as possessing distinct normative significance for the identification of universal *jus cogens*, a matter addressed in Chapter 7.[264]

[263] Section 5.3.3.
[264] See Chapter 7, section 7.4.3.

5.5 Conclusion

This chapter concludes the first step of the three-step approach by identifying the criteria through which an unwritten regional norm can be translated into, and thereby recognized as, international law.

Three main conclusions may be drawn. Firstly, the identification of regional customary international law does not follow criteria distinct from those applicable to general customary international law or non-regional custom. However, the application of these criteria is determined by the extent to which the alleged rule is identifiable for States within the region and for third parties, and by its non-generalizability *ratione materiae*. Secondly, under certain conditions, regional principles of law are capable of falling within the scope of Article 38(1)(c) of the ICJ Statute and can be identified by using a method analogous to that proposed for the identification of universal GPL derived from national legal systems. Thirdly, while traces in State practice of regional norms considered of particular normative significance do indeed exist, there still remains insufficient practice supporting the existence of a universal secondary rule that recognizes the concept of regional *jus cogens*. This does not, however, preclude the possibility that where situations of conflict arise with other rules of international law, regional rules may still prevail. The conditions under which rules of regional international law may take precedence over other international rules are discussed in Chapter 6. Even unwritten regional norms that fail to qualify as regional international law, above all, as certain regional customs or regional GPL, are not normatively irrelevant. They continue to play a significant role as regional practice in the development of treaties, customary international law, general principles of law, and *jus cogens* with a general scope of application. These are taken up and further discussed in Chapter 7.

6

Does regional international law fragment general international law?

6.1 Fragmentation as an inevitable consequence of regional international law?

In 1920, the French member of the Advisory Committee of Jurists Albert de Lapradelle expressed concerns about regional conceptions of international law, particularly those emerging from the American continent, emphasizing that 'international law ought to be one and remain so'.[1] This chapter examines how international law can remain 'one' while simultaneously recognizing the existence of regional international law and allowing for its application alongside general international law. In other words, Chapter 6 explores how fragmentation along regional lines can be prevented. To this effect, it considers the methodological potential of secondary rules to avoid and resolve conflicts arising between regional and general rules under international law.[2] Accordingly, Chapter 6 elaborates on the second step of the 'three-step-approach' developed in Chapter 3: once it has been established that a regional claim indeed qualifies as regional international law (according to the first step as developed in Chapters 4 and 5), the subsequent challenge lies in understanding the universal secondary rules under which regional rules are accepted by third parties to prevail over competing rules. When a regional rule meets these conditions, it may be viewed as contributing constructively to, rather than corroding, the idea of international law as 'one'—and vice versa.

The first section addresses the distinct character of regional fragmentation (as opposed to functional fragmentation)[3] (6.2). It then turns to the role of secondary

[1] Advisory Committee of Jurists, *Procès-verbaux of the Proceedings of the Committee June 16th to July 24th, 1920, with Annexes* (The Hague: Van Langenhuysen, 1920) 200.

[2] The term 'conflict' is used here in a narrow sense, referring to situations in which a subject of international law can comply with one rule only by thereby failing to comply with another rule. See on this 'strict notion' of conflict: ILC, 'Fragmentation of International Law: Difficulties Arising from the Diversification and Expansion of International Law: Report of the Study Group of the International Law Commission—Finalized by Martti Koskenniemi' (2006) UN Doc A/CN.4/L.682 ('Fragmentation Report') [24], which itself, however, 'adopts a wide notion of conflict as a situation where two rules or principles suggest different ways of dealing with a problem' [25].

[3] Functional fragmentation is understood as fragmentation along 'functionally defined issue-areas' in international law which claim autonomy from either other specialized fields or from general international law itself (see J Pauwelyn, 'Fragmentation in International Law' in A Peters (ed), *Max Planck Encyclopedia of Public International Law* (OUP 2006) [2]).

Regional and General International Law. Janina Barkholdt, Oxford University Press. © Janina Barkholdt 2026.
DOI: 10.1093/9780198953432.003.0006

rules in preventing regional fragmentation (6.3). The chapter demonstrates the potential of secondary rules to reconcile regional and other rules of international law through harmonization (6.3.1), hierarchization (6.3.2), prioritization (6.3.3), and co-ordination (6.3.4).

6.2 The 2006 Fragmentation Report and regional fragmentation

It is not obvious that preventing fragmentation along regional lines requires an approach distinct from that used to address functional fragmentation. In its 2006 Fragmentation Report, the ILC Study Group did not consider regional fragmentation to differ from the challenges arising from functional fragmentation.[4] This assumption informed the approach taken throughout the report. Ultimately, the Study Group's conclusions made no reference to regionalism at all.[5]

The report's approach was supported by States in the 6th Committee of the United Nations General Assembly (UNGA)[6] and by several commentators.[7] Yet, it was not uncontroversial. The 2005 ILC report noted that '[w]hile members noted that "regionalism" generally fell under the problem of *lex specialis*, some still felt that this was not all that could be said about it'.[8] This view has also been articulated by scholars.[9] Sean Murphy, for instance, criticized in 2013 that 'the Report arguably fails to pay sufficient heed to fragmentation in the form of regionalism, viewing it as simply an example of a possible *lex specialis*, and thereby denying regionalism's rich cultural content'.[10] Similarly, Christopher Borgen observed that '[t]he ILC Study Group downplayed the role of geographic

[4] Fragmentation Report (n 2) [216]; see also ILC, 'Report of the Commission to the General Assembly on the work of its fifty-seventh session' (2005) YBILC II(2) UN Doc A/CN.4/SER.A/2005/Add.1, 86 [466].

[5] ILC, 'Conclusions of the work of the Study Group on the Fragmentation of International Law: Difficulties arising from the Diversification and Expansion of International Law' (2006) UN Doc A/61/10 [251].

[6] ILC, 'Topical summary of the discussion held in the Sixth Committee' (2005) UN Doc A/CN.4/560 [236].

[7] See M Wood, 'A European Vision of International Law: For What Purpose?' in H Ruiz Fabri, E Jouannet, and V Tomkiewicz (eds), *Select Proceedings of the European Society of International Law (2006)* (Hart 2008) 151, 152–54; M Forteau, 'Regional International Law' in A Peters (ed), *Max Planck Encyclopedia of Public International Law* (OUP 2006) [22].

[8] ILC Report 2005 (n 4) 85 [461].

[9] See also C Landauer, 'Regionalism, Geography, and the International Legal Imagination' (2011) 11:2 Chi J Int'l L 557, 560–61; J Finke, 'Regime-Collisions: Tensions Between Treaties (and How to Solve Them)' in CJ Tams, A Tzanakopoulos, and A Zimmermann (eds), *Research Handbook on the Law of Treaties* (Edward Elgar Publishing 2014) 415, 427–29.

[10] SD Murphy, 'Deconstructing Fragmentation: Koskenniemi's 2006 ILC Project' (2013) 27:2 Temp Int'l & Comp LJ 293, 302–303.

regionalism'.[11] However, these critics did not explain why, in their view, the approach adopted in the report was insufficient to address conflicts arising from regionalism.

This chapter shows that the Fragmentation Report's limitations stem from its underlying premise that functional differentiation (fragmentation *ratione materiae*) has historically replaced regional differentiation (fragmentation *ratione personae*) as the 'sociological root' and 'moving force' of fragmentation.[12] Accordingly, the ILC Study Group understood normative conflicts as being rooted in 'differing pursuits and preferences', and approached them as the outcome of distinct functional approaches to specific subject matters.[13] This assumption may work well for some forms of regional international law—those that resemble functional legal regimes. However, it does not sufficiently take into account that other forms of regional international law differ from such functional legal regimes,[14] challenging three core premises of the Fragmentation Report.

6.2.1 Regional identity and the fiction of a unitary legislator

Certain forms of regional international law represent an assertion of regional identity—that is, the existence of a distinct polity within international law.[15] Even though the Fragmentation Report claims that '[t]here is no single legislative will behind international law',[16] it is still implicitly based on the fiction of a unitary legislator, or at least of a unitary legal society.[17] It does not address polity-based differentiation *from* this society, a differentiation *ratione personae*. Yet, the suggested conflict resolution techniques, *lex specialis, lex posterior, lex superior*, and systemic integration, are based on the fiction of a unitary legislator—a fiction that stems from domestic law with a centralized legislator.[18] These techniques may work in cases of differentiation *ratione materiae*. Yet, it is far from clear whether they can be transposed, without modification, to instances of fragmentation *ratione personae* that are grounded in a desire for self-organization—and, at times, in resistance to the very idea of a unitary international society.

[11] CJ Borgen, 'Treaty Conflicts and Systemic Fragmentation' in DB Hollis (ed), *The Oxford Guide to Treaties* (2nd edn OUP 2020) 432, 436.
[12] Fragmentation Report (n 2) [20], [204], [133] footnote 168.
[13] Fragmentation Report (n 2) [16].
[14] See Chapter 2, sections 2.3 and 2.4.
[15] See Chapter 2, section 2.4.1.1.
[16] Fragmentation Report (n 2) [34].
[17] Fragmentation Report (n 2) [7], [16].
[18] See also A Peters, 'The Refinement of International Law: From Fragmentation to Regime Interaction and Politicization' (2017) 15:3 Int J Const Law 671, 692.

6.2.2 Regional alternativity and the presumption of non-derogation

Regional rules of international law frequently arise from a claim to normative alternativity.[19] The Fragmentation Report formulates a 'thumb-rule' according to which 'States are assumed not to *derogate* from their obligations'.[20] This 'thumb rule' purports to rely on the judgment of the International Court of Justice (ICJ) in the *Right of passage* case, where the ICJ considered that a State committing to a rule intends such a rule to 'produce effects in accordance with its existing legal obligations and not in violation of it'.[21]

However, the Study Group's 'non-derogation' rule goes far beyond the 'non-*violation* presumption' articulated by the ICJ in that case. Rather, it seems to be based on a rather negative view of alternative rules at the regional level. Yet, in certain cases, regional rules may derogate from general international law without violating their obligations thereunder. This is especially the case where regional rules condense experiences and practices with respect to a particular geographic feature,[22] reflect a normative compromise which has been achieved among only a limited number of States sharing a similar set of values,[23] or represent a more exclusive understanding of their respective *domaine réservé*.[24]

It is doubtful whether such regional rules—which may regulate non-generalizable subject-matters or even contain a 'trailblazing' approach—are necessarily regarded as an unwelcome derogation or a violation of other rules, particularly by third parties.[25]

6.2.3 Regional autonomy and the idea of a system

The Fragmentation Report assumes that '[i]nternational law is a legal system'[26] and that regionalism has not 'meant the emergence of isolated legal systems on a regional basis'.[27] Yet, some forms of regional law form part of a more holistic and all-embracing regional legal order[28] which shows, inter alia, in the existence

[19] See Chapter 2, section 2.4.1.2.

[20] Fragmentation Report (n 2) [38]. Italics by the author.

[21] *Right of Passage over Indian Territory (Portugal v India)* [1957] ICJ Rep 125, 142 as quoted in [39] of the Fragmentation Report.

[22] See eg *European Commission of the Danube* (Advisory Opinion) [1927] PCIJ Series B, No 14, 17; *Right of Passage over Indian Territory (Portugal v India)* [1960] ICJ Rep 6, 39–40; *Dispute regarding Navigational and Related Rights (Costa Rica v Nicaragua)* [2009] ICJ Rep 213 [141].

[23] See also Murphy (n 10) 301.

[24] See also A Lang, 'Twenty Years of the WTO Appellate Body's "Fragmentation Jurisprudence"' (2015) 14:3 J Int Trade Law Policy 116, 122.

[25] See also Chapter 2, sections 2.3.3 and 2.3.4.

[26] Conclusions of the Study Group (n 5) [1].

[27] Fragmentation Report (n 2) [221].

[28] G Teubner, *Constitutional Fragments: Societal Constitutionalism and Globalization* (OUP 2012) 156.

of unwritten regional norms and institutions that tend to resemble domestic law. Unlike other particular international law, such regional orders may claim a degree of autonomy which comes close to a dualist understanding of the regional and the international legal order. In such cases, recourse to techniques like harmonization, priority maxims, and systemic integration is more difficult.[29] Furthermore, the Fragmentation Report focuses mainly on conflicts which arise from a diversity of treaty regimes and does not systematically address conflicts arising from unwritten international law.[30] It also excluded institutional techniques for addressing competing claims of normative priority.[31] Yet, the absence of guidance on how to deal with conflicts involving unwritten regional law and regional institutions creates a problematic vacuum, in which such conflicts risk being 'resolved' according to the political power of the respective regional or universal body.[32]

6.3 Secondary rules and regional fragmentation

The three distinct characteristics of regional fragmentation identified above mirror the 'defects' which HLA Hart understood to be remedied by the existence of secondary rules.[33]

It is, firstly, difficult to understand the extent to which regional rules are indeed intended to deviate from other rules (or instead seek to vernacularize them—the 'defect' of uncertainty), whether such a *regional* deviation is considered inacceptable by third States (or a desirable change—evoking the 'defect' of *stasis*) and, eventually, how to confront and mitigate irreconcilable conflicts (the 'defect' of (in-)efficiency). Accordingly, the fact that regional fragmentation gives rise to these three 'defects' suggests that recourse to secondary rules of international law may offer a means to address the specific challenges in this context.

This is not to imply that the Fragmentation Report adopted an entirely different methodological approach. On the contrary, many of the techniques presented in the report—as derived from the VCLT provisions and general international law—can themselves be understood as secondary rules of international law. Indeed, the

[29] See also L Pasquet, 'De-Fragmentation Techniques' in A Peters (ed), *Max Planck Encyclopedia of Public International Law* (OUP 2018) [26]; R Michaels and J Pauwelyn, 'Conflict of Norms or Conflict of Laws? Different Techniques in the Fragmentation of Public International Law' (2012) 22 Duke J Comp & Int'l L 349, 353–54.

[30] Fragmentation Report (n 2) [6], [15], [17], and [493].

[31] Fragmentation Report (n 2) [13].

[32] On 'irresolvable norm conflicts', see also V Jeutner, *Irresolvable Norm Conflicts in International Law: The Concept of a Legal Dilemma* (OUP 2017), who argues that 'judicial actors should respond to undecided dilemmatic conflicts by issuing dilemmatic declarations and that dilemmas should then be decided by sovereigns' (at 149).

[33] See Chapter 3, section 3.2.4.

report frames the role of those secondary rules as that of providing a 'tool-box' for the 'efficient management' of conflicts arising from functional differentiation.[34]

However, the next sections adopt a slightly different approach to the role played by secondary rules in responding to the distinct character of polity-based fragmentation, fragmentation *ratione personae*. They are based on the idea that a crucial first step consists in understanding the relevant perspective before 'managing' dissonances.

In this sense, the role of secondary rules, as understood here, may be compared to that of a 'mediator' rather than a 'manager'. Such a reconceptualization is not merely a play with words but expresses a substantially different understanding of the role played by secondary rules: unlike a 'manager', a 'mediator' seeks long-term reconciliation between two or more parties instead of specific results. While a 'manager' seeks to increase the efficiency of attaining certain policy goals (adequate for fragmentation *ratione materiae*), the 'mediator's' primary aim is to ensure mutual recognition of the respective perspectives (more appropriate for fragmentation *ratione personae*). The 'mediator' also considers mutual expectations (which underlie unwritten international law) and not merely common goals (as expressed in written international law). Finally, the mediator does not take his or her position for granted, as being *the* decision-maker, but takes a humbler approach, providing guidance rather than directives. Such a mediating, yet no less important role has been attributed to universal secondary rules in recent scholarship on interactions between international law and domestic legal orders.[35] Given that regional orders often oscillate between these two approaches, this understanding appears particularly suitable for addressing the challenges posed by regional fragmentation.

Bearing this reconceptualization in mind, the following sections essentially entail a constant shifting of perspectives between States and IOs adopting a regional rule and third parties. In this sense, the first section deals with the extent to which regional rules can be harmonized with other rules under international law by assessing if a given regional rule truly deviates from another rule under international law through recourse to the secondary rules on interpretation reflected in the VCLT, notably its Article 31, and those that regulate the identification of unwritten regional law (6.3.1). To the extent that such harmonization is not possible, the question is then if the application of these regional rules *necessarily* implies non-compliance with other existing obligations under international law or if there are recognized legal grounds which allow the regional rule to prevail. To address

[34] Fragmentation Report (n 2) [493].

[35] See eg HP Aust, 'The Rules of Interpretation as Secondary Rules: The Perspective of Domestic Courts' in M Heupel and T Reinold (eds), *The Rule of Law in Global Governance* (Palgrave Macmillan 2016) 59, 60; A Nollkaemper, 'The Power of Secondary Rules to Connect the International and National Legal Orders' in T Broude and Y Shany (eds), *Multi-Sourced Equivalent Norms in International Law* (Hart 2011) 45, 47 (secondary rules as a 'help to moderate the divergence'), 67 (secondary rules as a 'normative penumbra'); see also O Ammann, *Domestic Courts and the Interpretation of International Law Methods and Reasoning Based on the Swiss Example* (Brill 2020), in particular 221–22.

this question, the perspective is shifted to that of third parties which are bound by other rules that may potentially conflict with the regional rule. The following sections thus analyse the conditions, reflected in Articles 53 and 64 of the VCLT as well as Article 103 of the UN Charter (*lex superior*), pursuant to which third parties limit the application of a regional rule (6.3.2). To the extent that the regional rule in question is compatible with these secondary rules setting out such *lex superior*, the question is then under which circumstances third parties also accept the priority of a given regional rule over other rules of international law, notably by recourse to *lex posterior*, *lex prior*, and *lex specialis* (6.3.3). Where these three stages do not yield a reconciliation of a given regional rule and one or more other rules under international law, their rapprochement may be achieved through those secondary rules that allow for a certain mutual recognition and co-ordination to avoid conflicts (6.3.4).

6.3.1 Harmonization of regional and other rules

A first step in preventing conflicts between regional and other rules under international law is to make use of all available methods for harmonizing their interpretation. In this context, the secondary rules of recognition play a crucial role, as they help determine whether States truly intend to derogate from existing international law by adopting the regional rule.

Many regional instruments explicitly envisage a consistent interpretation of their provisions with other rules under international law.[36] In the absence of specific guidance in the regional instruments, the 'generally recognized principle' applies, requiring 'that, when several rules bear on a single issue, they should, to the extent possible, be interpreted so as to give rise to a single set of compatible obligations'.[37] Three means of treaty interpretation concretize this principle and are key for harmonizing the meaning of the regional rule with that of otherwise applicable rules under international law: a 'good faith' interpretation of the regional rule, ie a presumption that such a rule does not seek to frustrate or violate other rules under international law (Article 31(1) of the VCLT), an interpretation of the regional rule in light of subsequent agreements and subsequent practice of the parties beyond the regional context, eg expressed in subsequently established obligations (Articles 31(3)(a) and (b) and 32 of the VCLT), and an interpretation of the regional rule which considers 'other relevant rules applicable between the parties' (Article 31(3)(c) of the VCLT).[38] Although these three means of treaty interpretation are dealt with

[36] See North American Free Trade Agreement (adopted 17 December 1992, entered into force 1 January 1994) (1993) 32 ILM 289, art 104; African Charter on Democracy, Elections, and Governance (adopted 30 January 2007, entered into force 15 February 2012), art 52.

[37] *Obligations of States in respect of Climate Change* (Advisory Opinion of 23 July 2025) ICJ [165].

[38] See also Chapter 7, section 7.3.2. and 7.3.3.

extensively in the Fragmentation Report,[39] the question is to what extent they can be employed in the context of regional fragmentation and whether they encounter specific limitations.

6.3.1.1 Harmonization of regional treaty provisions and other rules of international law

Both universal and regional courts and tribunals generally prefer to harmonize the meaning of regional and other treaty rules rather than declare one to prevail over the other, even though they have not always specified the exact interpretive methods guiding them in reaching this outcome. This approach is particularly common in the field of human rights. For example, in *Diallo*, the ICJ applied regional and universal treaty rules in parallel, even though the terms of the respective provisions were not entirely identical.[40] With respect to regional bodies, case law from the ECtHR,[41] the IAtCHR,[42] the African Commission on Human and Peoples' Rights (AfrComHPR),[43] and the African Court on Human and Peoples' Rights (AfrCHPR)[44] illustrates that these institutions usually seek to interpret their provisions in a manner consistent with the meaning attributed to corresponding provisions in universal treaties which demonstrates that conflict avoidance through harmonization is not confined to any particular region.[45]

Conflict avoidance through harmonization is also not confined to the field of human rights. Even though the ICJ was barred from directly applying the UN Charter and the OAS Charter in its 1986 *Nicaragua v United States* judgment, it concluded that

> [u]nlike the United Nations Charter, the Organization of American States Charter does not use the expression 'collective self-defence', but refers to the case of 'self-defence in accordance with existing treaties or in fulfilment thereof', one such treaty being the United Nations Charter. *Furthermore it is evident that if actions of the United States complied with all requirements of the United Nations*

[39] Fragmentation Report (n 2) [37]–[43].

[40] *Ahmadou Sadio Diallo (Republic of Guinea v Democratic Republic of the Congo)* (Merits) [2010] ICJ Rep 639 [64]–[65] and [74]–[75]; see also *Armed Activities on the Territory of the Congo (Democratic Republic of the Congo v Uganda)* [2005] ICJ Rep 168 [254].

[41] See eg *Hassan v the United Kingdom* App 29750/09 (ECHR, 16 September 2014) [102]–[104]; *Magyar Helsinki Bizottság v Hungary* App 18030/11 (ECtHR, 8 November 2016) [141]–[143].

[42] See eg *Massacres of El Mozote v El Salvador* (Preliminary Exceptions, Merits, Reparations, and Costs) (25 October 2012) IACHR Series C No 252 [141]; *Anzualdo Castro v Peru* (Preliminary Objections, Merits, Reparations, and Costs) (22 September 2009) IACHR Series C No 202 [90]–[101].

[43] See eg *Thomas Kwoyelo v Uganda* Comm No 431/12 (AfrComHPR, 17 October 2018) [150]. See also for references to other regional instruments: *Open Society Justice Initiative v Republic of Cameroon*, Comm No 290/04 (AfrComHPR, February–March 2019) [138]–[140] and [165].

[44] *Boubakar Sissoko et Autres v Republic of Mali* App No 037/2017 (Judgments on Merits and Reparations) (AfrCHPR, 25 September 2020) [94], [108], [121]–[130].

[45] But see section 6.3.1.3.

> *Charter so as to constitute the exercise of the right of collective self-defence, it could not be argued that they could nevertheless constitute a violation of Article 21 of the Organization of American States Charter.*[46]

The second part of the ICJ's conclusion was, however, not self-evident given that it was equally possible that Article 21 of the OAS Charter provides for stricter requirements for a recourse to self-defence than Article 51 of the UN Charter.[47] The ICJ also interpreted regional and universal rules harmoniously in the 2018 *Bolivia v Chile* case.[48]

The potential for harmonizing regional rules with 'equivalent' rules has equally been argued for the field of trade law.[49] This is illustrated by the 2016 decision of the Court of the EAEU in the *General Freight* case where the Court gave a broad interpretation of the rule on applicable law of its Statute (Article 50(2)) so as to include international agreements other than those enlisted provided that they relate to the field of EAEU common policy and that all members States are parties to it.[50]

Furthermore, the case law of the ECtHR indicates that even a regional norm which protects a different legal interest than another rule can be reconciled with the latter, as in the 2001 case *Al-Adsani,* where the Court, when interpreting Article 6 ECHR (right of access to court), held that

> [t]he Convention . . . cannot be interpreted in a vacuum. The Court must be mindful of the Convention's special character as a human rights treaty, and it must take the relevant rules of international law into account. The Convention should so far as possible be interpreted in harmony with other rules of international law of which it forms a part, including those relating to the grant of State immunity.[51]

[46] *Military and Paramilitary Activities in and against Nicaragua (Nicaragua v United States)* (Merits) [1986] ICJ Rep 14 [50]. Italics by the author.

[47] Despite the fact that Nicaragua in its Memorial stressed that the two provisions were 'coterminous' (*Military and Paramilitary Activities in und against Nicaragua (Nicaragua v United States of America),* Memorial of Nicaragua (30 April 1985) 85 [321]) and 'coextensive' (91, footnote 12), it also stressed that '[t]he OAS Charter represented a special law for the American States, colored by their history and tailored to their needs. Viewed in the abstract, the Charter's prohibitions of intervention and the use of force may seem only to reiterate universal norms of international law. However, seen against the backdrop of the history of the Western Hemisphere, they take on a pointed meaning and a particular relevance for this case.' (91–92 [345]).

[48] *Obligation to Negotiate Access to the Pacific Ocean (Bolivia v Chile)* [2018] ICJ Rep 507 [165]–[167].

[49] See L Hsu, 'Applicability of WTO Law in Regional Trade Agreements: Identifying the Links' in L Bartels and F Ortino (eds), *Regional Trade Agreements and the WTO Legal System* (OUP 2006) 525.

[50] *General Freight v Commission (Appeal)* Case SE-1-2/2-16-AP (EAEU, 21 June 2016) <http://courteurasian.org/page-24161> (accessed 10 May 2026) [5.1.1]; see on this case and the specific interpretation: V Tolstykh, 'Between a "Heavenly" Life and an "Earthly" Life: Jurisprudence of the Court of the EAEU from 2012–2019' (2019) 7:3 Russ Law J 194, 199, 217; M Karliuk, *The Emerging Autonomous Legal Order of the Eurasian Economic Union* (CUP 2023) 208, arguing that 'created a rule that, if certain conditions are met, the EAEU Court is bound by international agreements that do not fall under any of the categories of Union law'.

[51] *Al-Adsani v UK* App No 35763/97 (ECtHR, 21 November 2001) [55].

6.3.1.2 Harmonization of unwritten regional and universal law

With regard to the harmonization of unwritten regional rules and other rules of international law, practice suggests a tendency to treat them as equivalent or overlapping in substance, rather than as divergent. For example, in the *Nicaragua* case, the ICJ simply applied regional and universal custom in parallel.[52] It adopted a similar approach in the *Burkina Faso/Mali* case, where the Court recognized that the principle of *uti possidetis* was not merely a regional rule (be it of a customary nature or a regional GPL),[53] but had also matured into a rule with a universal scope of application.[54] This approach is equally found in the practice of regional bodies, for example, in the case law of the Inter-American Commission on juvenile executions,[55] and of the CJEU.[56]

6.3.1.3 Limits to harmonization

At the same time, there is a 'definite limit to harmonization'.[57] In this vein, the CAHDI Steering Committee stated in its 2020 report that:

> [i]n the light of significant differences between the regional and the universal systems of human rights protection, achieving absolute harmony in international human rights law is not a probability.[58]

As Joost Pauwelyn observed, interpretation 'may resolve apparent conflicts; it cannot resolve genuine conflicts'.[59] The limits of harmonization depend on the will of those States that established the rules in question.[60] In practice, the harmonization of a regional rule with other rules encounters its limits in three distinct scenarios.

Firstly, regional 'trailblazer' rules, that is, regional rules intended to be generalizable and applicable beyond their region, yet lacking a counterpart under general international law, test the limits of harmonization. A pertinent example for this

[52] *Nicaragua v United States* (n 46) [183] and [192].

[53] See on this Chapter 5, section 5.3.

[54] *Frontier Dispute (Burkina Faso/Republic of Mali) (Judgment)* [1986] ICJ Rep 554 [20] and [26]; see also J Crawford, *Chance, Order, Change: The Course of International Law, General Course on Public International Law* (Brill 2013) 248 [433].

[55] *Michael Domingues v United States* Case 12.285 (IACHR, 22 October 2002) Report No 62/02 [85].

[56] *Opel Austria GmbH v Council of the European Union* Case T-115/94 (CFI, 22 January 1997) [93]: '[T]he principle of good faith is the corollary in public international law of the principle of protection of legitimate expectations which forms part of the Community legal order.'

[57] Fragmentation Report (n 2) [42]: '[T]here is a definite limit to harmonization.'

[58] Council of Europe, Committee of Ministers, Steering Committee for Human Rights (CDDH) (2020), 'Report on the Place of the European Convention on Human Rights in the European and International Legal Order' (Strasbourg, 26–29 November 2019) [12]; see also *Correia de Matos v Portugal* App No 56402/12 (ECtHR, 4 April 2018) [135].

[59] J Pauwelyn, *Conflict of Norms in International Law: How WTO Law Relates to Other Rules of International Law* (CUP 2003) 272.

[60] Fragmentation Report (n 2) [42]: 'anything may be harmonized as long as the will to harmonization is present.'

group concerns the tension between the 'precautionary principle', argued to exist at the regional level, and the WTO rules, which emerged in the *EC—Beef Hormones* case.[61] Another example concerns the interpretation of the term 'national origin' in CERD in the case *Application of the International Convention on the Elimination of All Forms of Racial Discrimination (Qatar v United Arab Emirates)*, where the ICJ considered that '[t]he jurisprudence of regional human rights courts based on those [regional] legal instruments is … of little help for the interpretation of the term "national origin" in CERD' given that 'their purpose is to ensure a wide scope of protection of human rights and fundamental freedoms';[62] an approach that was, however, criticized by Judge Iwasawa in his separate opinion.[63]

Secondly, certain regional rules are deliberately conceived as alternative rules, that is, rules intended to establish norms specific to a group of States at the regional level that differ from those under general international law.[64] Here, a careful distinction must be made between regional rules that intend to establish a different normative approach (ie where there is no will to harmonization) and regional rules that are considered to reflect, clarify, or specify the legal status under general international law (ie where a will to harmonization may be present) but where the law under general international law is contested. The former category, alternative rules 'proper', includes, for example, the right to grant diplomatic asylum under Latin American international law, which, to the extent that it is applied by or towards third parties, stands in tension with Article 41 of the VCDR,[65] as well as the right to intervene in a State within the region in cases of unconstitutional changes of government or mass atrocities, which is difficult to reconcile the system of collective security established by chapters VII and VIII of the UN Charter.[66]

[61] See also Finke (n 9) 434–35. See also *Obligations of States in respect of Climate Change* (n 37) [294]: 'the precautionary approach or principle, where applicable, guides States in the determination of the required standard of conduct in fulfilling their customary duty to prevent significant harm.'

[62] *Application of the International Convention on the Elimination of All Forms of Racial Discrimination (Qatar v United Arab Emirates)* [2021] ICJ Rep 71 [104].

[63] *Application of the International Convention on the Elimination of All Forms of Racial Discrimination (Qatar v United Arab Emirates)* [2021] ICJ Rep 157 (separate opinion of Judge Iwasawa) [36].

[64] See also several examples of alternative regional rules to general rules under international law discussed by S Ranganathan, *Strategically Created Treaty Conflicts and the Politics of International Law* (CUP 2014) 6–7.

[65] See FJ Quintana and J Uriburu, 'Mexico and Ecuador at the ICJ: A Plea for Taking the Latin American Experience Seriously' (EJILTalk! 1 May 2024) <https://www.ejiltalk.org/mexico-and-ecuador-at-the-icj-a-plea-for-taking-the-latin-american-experience-seriously/> (accessed 10 May 2026); L Kleinert, 'Controversies in Caracas: Diplomatic asylum: regional customary law or treaty application?' (Völkerrechtsblog, 17 May 2019) <https://voelkerrechtsblog.org/controversies-in-caracas/> (accessed 10 May 2026).

[66] See Protocol relating to the Mechanism for Conflict Prevention, Management, Resolution, Peace-Keeping and Security (signed and provisionally entered into force 10 December 1999) ('Lomé Protocol'), ECOWAS Doc A/P10/12/99 (1999), Art 25(e); Constitutive Act of the African Union (adopted 11 July 2000, entered into force 26 May 2001) 2158 UNTS 3, art 4(h); Mutual Assistance Pact Between Member States of ECCAS (Malabo, 24 February 2000), art 7; Pact on Security, Stability and Development in the Great Lakes Region (adopted 15 December 2006, entered into force 21 June 2008) 46 ILM 175, art 4(8).

The second category may include rules defining a different scope of immunity for heads of State, such as Article 46A*bis* of the Malabo Protocol adopted under the auspices of the AU. This provision may be in tension with Article 27 of the Rome Statute regarding exceptions to the immunities of heads of State. However, Article 27 can be interpreted as reflecting the current state of general international law, and to the extent that it is applied only to non-parties to the Rome Statute after its entry into force, it is not necessarily in conflict with the Rome Statute.[67]

Thirdly, a conflict between a regional rule and other rules cannot be resolved through harmonization when the regional treaty regime is understood as providing for an 'autonomous' interpretation of its provisions. This dynamic has been particularly evident in substantive matters, as illustrated by the controversy between the ECtHR and the HRC concerning the legality of a veil ban.[68] Even more prominently, this tension has arisen in the context of procedural provisions. In *Achmea*, the CJEU held that Article 8 of the applicable BIT, which established an arbitral tribunal, was incompatible with EU law.[69] In *Loizidou*, the ECtHR emphasized the differences between Article 46 of the ECHR and Article 36 of the ICJ Statute when it came to the question of admissibility of reservations to the acceptance of jurisdiction. While it acknowledged that 'Article 46 of the Convention was modelled on Article 36 of the Statute',[70] it underlined that 'the context within which the International Court of Justice operates is quite distinct from that of the Convention institutions'.[71]

6.3.2 Compatibility of regional rules with *lex superior*

To the extent that harmonization between the regional rule in question and another rule of international law cannot be achieved, the second step is to determine whether, in accordance with the requirements established by the relevant universal secondary rules, the regional rule may nonetheless be applied. The first condition for such application is that the regional rule must be compatible with *lex superior*.[72] '*Lex superior*' is an umbrella term for those types of universally applicable rules from which derogation is not permitted.[73] These notably include *jus cogens* and

[67] Protocol on Amendments to the Protocol on the Statute of the African Court of Justice and Human Rights ('Malabo Protocol') (adopted 27 June 2014, not yet in force). See D Tladi, 'Immunities (Article 46Abis)' in G Werle and M Vormbaum (eds), *The African Criminal Court: A Commentary on the Malabo Protocol* (Springer 2017) 203, 210–16.

[68] See Report of Steering Committee (n 58) [282].

[69] *Slowakische Republic (Slovak Republic) v Achmea BV* Case C-284/16 (CJEU, 6 March 2018) [58]. The Court relied on relied on Article 4(3) TEU (the principle of sincere co-operation), Article 19(1)2 TEU (role of the EU Court of Justice), Article 267 TFEU (preliminary ruling procedure), and Article 344 TFEU.

[70] *Loizidou v Turkey* App 15318/89 (ECtHR, 23 March 1995) [83].

[71] *Loizidou v Turkey* (n 70) [84].

[72] See also Fragmentation Report (n 2) [324]–[379].

[73] Fragmentation Report (n 2) [326]–[327].

Article 103 of the UN Charter which set certain 'outer limits' to the priority given to regional rules. In cases in which the applicability of the regional rule is maintained despite its incompatibility with *jus cogens* or Article 103, third States are entitled and even obliged to treat this regional claim as being without legal effect. In practice, both *jus cogens* and Article 103 have operated less as a conflict resolution technique but rather channelled the process of interpretation to avoid a conflict between the regional rule and *jus cogens* or the UN Charter.[74]

6.3.2.1 Regional rules and *jus cogens*

According to Articles 53 and 64 of the VCLT, any agreement in violation of 'peremptory norms of general international law' is void. This legal consequence applies *mutatis mutandis* to conflicting rules of customary international law, general principles of law, unilateral acts, and secondary acts of IOs.[75]

Few, if any, regional rules contain explicit derogations from universally recognized peremptory norms formulated as prohibitions.[76] In practice, the potential for conflict between a regional rule and *jus cogens* has arisen in particular with respect to peremptory norms that are not framed as a prohibition, such as the principle of self-determination.[77] However, both the ICJ and regional courts have so far refrained from declaring a regional rule void on the grounds of incompatibility with *jus cogens.* Instead, they have either interpreted the regional rule so as to render it consistent with the right to self-determination or, conversely, construed the scope of that right in a manner compatible with the regional rule. In the *Burkina Faso/Mali* case, for example, the ICJ was faced with a potential conflict between (a regional variant of) *uti possidetis* and the principle of self-determination.[78] However, the ICJ concluded that

> [a]t first sight this principle [*uti possidetis*] conflicts outright with another one, the right of peoples to self-determination. In fact, however, the maintenance of the territorial *status quo* in Africa is often seen as the wisest course, to preserve what

[74] See for *jus cogens*: Fragmentation Report (n 2) [409]; J Klabbers, 'Beyond the Vienna Convention: Conflicting Treaty Provisions' in E Cannizzaro (ed), *The Law of Treaties Beyond the Vienna Convention* (OUP 2011) 192, 201–202.

[75] ILC, 'Draft conclusions on identification and legal consequences of peremptory norms of general international law (*jus cogens*), with commentaries' (2022) UN Doc A/77/10 ('ILC Report 2022 (*Jus cogens*)'), draft Conclusions 13 to 16.

[76] See for a 'non-exhaustive list' of peremptory norms: ILC (n 75), draft Conclusion 23. One example that may be considered in tension with peremptory norms of general international law is the applicability, under certain conditions, of the death penalty to juvenile offenders as envisaged by Article 7(1) of the 2004 Arab Charter on Human Rights (revised) (adopted 22 May 2004, entered into force 15 March 2008) ('Sentence of death shall not be imposed on persons under 18 years of age, unless otherwise stipulated in the laws in force at the time of the commission of the crime.').

[77] See eg RP Barnidge, 'Anti-Zionism, *Jus Cogens*, and International Law: The Case of the Banjul Charter and the Arab Charter' (2018) 9 J Middle East Afr 77.

[78] GJ Naldi, 'The Case Concerning the Frontier Dispute (Burkina Faso/Republic of Mali): *Uti Possidetis* in an African Perspective' (1987) 36:4 ICLQ 893, 902–903.

> has been achieved by peoples who have struggled for their independence, and to avoid a disruption which would deprive the continent of the gains achieved by much sacrifice. The essential requirement of stability in order to survive, to develop and gradually to consolidate their independence in all fields, has induced African States judiciously to consent to the respecting of colonial frontiers, and to take account of it in the interpretation of the principle of self-determination of peoples. Thus the principle of *uti possidetis* has kept its place among the most important legal principles, despite the apparent contradiction which explained its coexistence alongside the new noms implied. Indeed. it was by deliberate choice that African States selected, among all the classic principles, that of *uti possidetis*.[79]

In that case, the ICJ not only interpreted *uti possidetis* as a rule of universal scope but also construed the right of self-determination in a manner that allowed it to coexist with *uti possidetis*. In a more recent case before the AfrCHPR, a Ghanaian national had filed an application against several member States of the African Union (AU) arguing that the Sahrawi's right to self-determination as a *jus cogens* norm entailed a prohibition to admit Morocco to the AU without requesting it to stop its alleged occupation of the territory of Western Sahara.[80] Although the AfrCHPR confirmed the right of the Sahrawi people to self-determination, and considered the right to self-determination a peremptory norm of international law, it concluded that the respondent States had not breached their obligations under the African Charter on Human and Peoples' Rights, including the right to self-determination, by admitting the Kingdom of Morocco to be a member of the AU.[81] According to the AfrCHPR,

> the duty to assist the people of the SADR in their struggle to realize the full enjoyment of their right to self-determination [] does not require States to take a list of specific actions or measures of a particular nature. Therefore, it is up to the Respondent States to choose the kind of positive measures that they consider appropriate for the realisation of the right for the said people.[82]

Accordingly, the AfrCHPR granted a margin of appreciation to the States in how they would assist the Sahrawi people in their struggle for self-determination. The compatibility of regional law with the right to self-determination as a peremptory norm also came up in the *Brita*, *Western Sahara*, and *Front Polisario* cases before the CJEU. The central issue in those cases concerned the legality of agreements between the EU and Israel (*Brita*) and Morocco (*Western Sahara, Front Polisario*)

[79] *Burkina Faso/Mali* (n 54) [25]–[26].
[80] *Bernard Anbataayela Mornah v Republic of Benin and Others* App No 028/2018 (AfrCHPR, 22 September 2018) [274].
[81] *Bernard Anbataayela Mornah* (n 80) [343(v)].
[82] *Bernard Anbataayela Mornah* (n 80) [314].

given that in these cases, the relevant agreements appeared to apply to the occupied Palestinian territory (*Brita*) and to Western Sahara (*Western Sahara, Front Polisario*) and thus potentially infringing on the right of self-determination of the Palestinian people and Sahrawi people respectively.[83] However, in none of these cases the CJEU declared the EU agreements to be in violation of the right of self-determination. It rather interpreted the agreement consistent with the *pacta tertiis* principle (*Brita*; *Western Sahara*) to exclude the respective territory from the scope of application or based the invalidity of the act in question (solely) on an infringement of the *pacta tertiis* principle (*Front Polisario*).[84]

6.3.2.2 Regional rules and Article 103 of the UN Charter

The outer limits of applying regional rules are further defined by Article 103 of the UN Charter, which stipulates that

> [i]n the event of a conflict between the obligations of the Members of the United Nations under the present Charter and their obligations under any other international agreement, their obligations under the present Charter shall prevail.

So far, three recurring scenarios across all regions have raised questions about the compatibility of regional rules with the UN Charter.

Firstly, the competences of regional institutions entrusted with the peaceful settlement of disputes must be compatible with the UN Charter which means that such institutions cannot disregard or replace the functions of the ICJ or the UNSC. This was clarified by the ICJ in the 1984 *Nicaragua v US* judgment where the US claimed that the Court was barred from exercising its jurisdiction for as long as the regional dispute settlement mechanism, the Contadora Process, had not been exhausted. The Court rejected this contention stating that

> it is also important always to bear in mind that all regional, bilateral, and even multilateral, arrangements that the Parties to this case may have made, touching on the issue of settlement of disputes or the jurisdiction of the International Court of Justice, must be made always subject to the provisions of Article 103.[85]

[83] See A Garrido-Muñoz, 'Patterns of Avoidance and Assimilation Peremptory Norms in European Union Law' in FL Bordin, AT Müller, and F Pascual-Vives (eds), *The European Union and Customary International Law* (CUP 2022) 148, 153–60; E Kassoti, 'Between Sollen and Sein: The CJEU's Reliance on International Law in the Interpretation of Economic Agreements Covering Occupied Territories' (2020) 33 LJIL 371.

[84] *European Commission and Council of the European Union v Front Polisario* Joined Cases C-779/21 P and C-799/21 P (CJEU, 4 October 2024) [145]–[161], [175]; *Western Sahara Campaign UK v Commissioners for Her Majesty's Revenue and Customs, Secretary of State for Environment, Food and Rural Affairs* Case C-266/16 (CJEU, 27 February 2018) [63]–[73]; *Firma Brita GmbH v Hauptzollamt Hamburg-Hafen* Case C-386/08 (CJEU, 25 February 2010) [43]–[53].

[85] *Military and Paramilitary Activities in and against Nicaragua (Nicaragua v United States of America)* [1984] ICJ Rep 392 [107].

Secondly, regional organizations' rules that depart from the collective security framework established by the UN Charter have been understood as challenging the boundaries set by Article 103. In this regard, the compatibility of intervention clauses that allow for military interventions in cases of unconstitutional changes of government and mass atrocities with Article 103 of the UN Charter has been subject to debates as it implies the proclamation of a right of these regional organizations to intervene military without either the consent of the territorial State and a UNSC mandate.[86] So far, the AU has not relied on this reading of Article 4(h) to justify intervention, implying that Article 103 of the UN Charter has ensured its interpretation remains aligned with the Charter.[87] Another approach to reconciling these regional rules and interventions with Article 103 and general international law is to treat the regional treaty rule as merely reflecting the consent of the State whose territory is concerned by such an intervention.[88] In other words, it is not the regional rule that serves as the basis for such an intervention, but that State's consent, removing the tension with Article 2(4) and, accordingly, Article 103.[89]

Finally, regional challenges to the implementation of Security Council resolutions, particularly those involving regional human rights instruments, have prompted several decisions by European courts in which Article 103 of the UN Charter has played a central role. For example, in the 2016 Judgment in *Al-Dulimi v Switzerland*, the ECtHR emphasized

> that one of the basic elements of the current system of international law is constituted by Article 103 of the UN Charter, which asserts the priority, in the event of conflict, of the obligations deriving from the Charter over any other obligation arising from an international agreement, regardless of whether the latter was concluded before or after the UN Charter or was a purely regional arrangement.[90]

Similarly, the Court of First Instance of the EU in its 2005 *Kadi* decision acknowledged that

> Member States may, and indeed must, leave unapplied any provision of Community law, whether a provision of primary law or a general principle of that

[86] See the examples from regional instruments mentioned in (n 66). See on this: E de Wet, *Military Assistance on Request and the Use of Force* (OUP 2020) 226; JJ Niyo, 'More Stick and Less Carrot: ECOWAS, the Use of Force to Restore Democracy, and the Contest between Regional and International Normative Regimes' (2025) AJIL Unbound 254.

[87] But see de Wet (n 86) 226–27.

[88] See eg Niyo (n 86) 258.

[89] On this controversial issue: J Barkholdt, 'Intervention By Invitation' in A Peters (ed), *Max Planck Encyclopedia of Public International Law* (OUP 2024) [38]–[49].

[90] *Al-Dulimi and Montana Management Inc v Switzerland* App 5809/08 (ECtHR, 21 June 2016) [135].

> law, that raises any impediment to the proper performance of their obligations under the Charter of the United Nations.[91]

These three examples demonstrate how Article 103 of the UN Charter constrains regional rules, ensuring their interpretation aligns with the Charter.

At the same time, several avenues have been explored by scholars and pursued in practice to limit the scope of Article 103 of the UN Charter in favour of the priority of regional rules.

Firstly, unlike their member States, regional IOs are not parties to the UN Charter. This raises the question whether the conduct of regional IOs, including secondary law adopted by their organs, falls outside the scope of Article 103 of the UN Charter. In this regard, the Court of First Instance of the EU pointed out in 2005 that

> unlike its Member States, the Community as such is not directly bound by the Charter of the United Nations and that it is not therefore required, as an obligation of general public international law, to accept and carry out the decisions of the Security Council in accordance with Article 25 of that Charter. The reason is that the Community is not a member of the United Nations, or an addressee of the resolutions of the Security Council, or the successor to the rights and obligations of the Member States for the purposes of public international law.[92]

The principle of *pacta tertiis* suggests that the UN Charter should not be considered as creating directly binding obligations on regional international organizations themselves.[93] Furthermore, Articles 25 and 48(2) of the UN Charter, which refer to the implementation of UNSC decisions, are only addressed to UN Members. However, the member States of the regional IO remain bound by the UN Charter and cannot circumvent their obligations under the UN Charter by relying on their obligations arising from regional law.[94] Still, while several regional IOs have unilaterally accepted the priority of the UN Charter in their constituent instruments,[95] or have otherwise sought to identify, under general international

[91] *Kadi v Council and Commission* Case T-315/01 (CFI, 21 September 2005) [190].

[92] *Kadi v Council* (n 91) [192].

[93] See C Tomuschat, 'The Kadi Case: What Relationship is there between the Universal Legal Order under the Auspices of the United Nations and the EU Legal Order?' (2009) 28 Yearb Eur Law 654, 656.

[94] See *Nicaragua v United States of America* (n 85) [107]; see also: A Paulus and JR Leiss, 'Article 103' in B Simma and others (eds), *The Charter of the United Nations: A Commentary, Volume II* (4th edn, OUP 2024) [69].

[95] A number of regional IOs prescribe the compatibility with the UN Charter in their constituent instrument: Arts 3(5), 21(1), 42(1), 42(7) TEU; Art 131 OAS Charter; Art 7 NATO Treaty; Art 2(1) of the Charter of the Organization of the Islamic Conference (adopted 14 March 2008, entered into force 3 September 2009), replacing the Charter of the Islamic Conference (adopted 4 March 1972, entered into force 28 February 1973) 914 UNTS 110; Preamble of the Shanghai Cooperation Organisation Charter (signed in June 2002, entered into force on 19 September 2003) 2896 UNTS I-50517.

law or the respective regional law, ways to ensure the compatibility with the UN Charter, the issue remains particularly pertinent in those cases in which the regional rule is considered to reflect universal *jus cogens*[96] or has attributed priority under the regional treaty in question or by way of its status as an unwritten regional 'super norm'.[97]

Secondly, some regional courts and commentators put emphasis on the fact that Article 103 refers to 'any *international* agreement' whereas, in their view, certain regional rules belong to an 'autonomous legal order' or are of a 'domestic' or '*sui generis*' legal nature.[98] While in particular the legal nature of the EU is subject to controversy,[99] Chapter 2 demonstrated that the elusive legal nature is characteristic of regional law more broadly, that is, beyond the context of the EU.[100] Taking the EU as an example for a particularly idiosyncratic regional legal order, however, the registration of the Lisbon Treaty under Article 102 of the UN Charter indicates that its member States themselves understand the Lisbon Treaty as a 'treaty' or an 'international agreement'.[101] And even if the EU legal order is equated to a domestic legal order, this would not lead to a priority of EU law vis-à-vis the UN Charter: while Article 103 of the UN Charter may not be applicable, Article 27 of the VCLT (which reflects custom) clarifies that States cannot invoke their internal law to justify the violation of an international treaty.[102]

It is, finally, unclear to what extent Article 103 claims priority over unwritten (regional) international law given that it applies to conflicts between the UN Charter and 'any other international *agreement*'. The ordinary meaning of the text and the *travaux préparatoires* suggest limiting Article 103 to written agreements.[103] Article 59 ARSIWA appears to reflect this view as it stipulates that '[t]he focus of Article 103 is on treaty obligations inconsistent with obligations arising under the Charter'.[104] According to this view, unwritten regional law would not be encompassed by the scope of Article 103. However, an interpretation of Article 103 based on subsequent practice of member States and UN organs since its adoption in 1945

[96] For example, in *Kadi* [2005] (n 91), the Court interpreted the universal *jus cogens* rules in a way that corresponded to the requirements for access to courts under EU law ([226] and [238]).

[97] Klabbers (n 74) 201; see also with respect to 'OIC norms': KLH Samuel, *The OIC, the UN, and Counter-Terrorism Law-Making. Conflicting or Cooperative Legal orders?* (Hart 2013) 239–41, 240.

[98] See eg *Kadi and Al Barakaat International Foundation v Council and Commission* C-402/05 P and C-415/05 P (CJEU, 3 September 2008) [285]–[288]; see also *Kadi v Council of the European Union and Commission of the European Communities* Case C-402/05 P (Opinion of Mr Advocate General Maduro delivered on 16 January 2008) [24].

[99] See *Van Gend & Loos v Netherlands Inland Revenue Administration* Case 26/62 (ECJ, 5 February 1963) 12.

[100] See Chapter 2, section 2.4.2.

[101] Paulus and Leiss (n 94) [68].

[102] Paulus and Leiss (n 94).

[103] See eg R Liivoja, 'The Supremacy of the United Nations Charter' (2008) 57:3 ICLQ 583, 602–12; R Kolb, 'L'article 103 de la Charte des Nations Unies' (2013) 367 RdC 9, 209.

[104] See ILC, 'Articles on the Responsibility of States for Internationally Wrongful Acts' (2001) YBILC II(2) UN Doc A/56/10, 31, 143.

suggests that Article 103 extends to unwritten sources of international law.[105] The ILC, in its conclusions on the fragmentation of international law, stated that

> [g]iven the character of some Charter provisions, the constitutional character of the Charter and the established practice of States and United Nations organs, Charter obligations *may* also prevail over inconsistent customary international law.[106]

Regardless of whether general customary law falls within the scope of Article 103, there is little practice suggesting that States and IOs may deviate from the UN Charter based on unwritten regional international law.[107] For example, the Soviet Union's reliance on 'their own vital interests, their own obligations, including the obligation to protect their mutual security, and their own socialist principles of mutual relations based on brotherly assistance, solidarity and internationalism' to justify its intervention in Czechoslovakia in 1968[108] was overwhelmingly rejected in the UNGA.[109]

6.3.3 Priority of regional rules over other rules

To the extent that a regional rule is compatible with *lex superior*,[110] it may prevail over other rules under international law to the extent that the applicable secondary rules express a recognition by third States of such a priority through the principles of *lex posterior* and *lex specialis*.[111]

6.3.3.1 *Lex posterior*

Article 30 (regulating the application of successive treaties relating to the same subject-matter) and Article 41 of the VCLT (on *inter se* agreements to multilateral treaties) set out the conditions for the priority of a later treaty rule (*lex posterior*).

[105] See eg Fragmentation Report (n 2) [345]. See also in this direction: Paulus and Leiss (n 94) [74]–[75].

[106] See, Conclusions (n 5) 183. Italics by the author.

[107] See also Liivoja (n 103) 602: 'The clear meaning of "international agreements", as interpreted in the context, does not by any stretch of the imagination encompass customary international law (nor, for that matter, general principles of law). Even if bilateral or regional custom can be assimilated to some type of a tacit agreement, the same can hardly be said about general custom.'

[108] UNGA, Verbatim Record (3 October 1968) UN Doc A/PV.1679 [68] (Soviet Foreign Minister Gromyko); UNSC, Verbatim Record (21 August 1968) UN Doc S/PV.1441 [86]. See also G Hafner, 'The Intervention in Czechoslovakia—1968' in T Ruys, O Corten, A Hofer (eds), *The Use of Force in International Law: A Case-Based Approach* (OUP 2018) 149.

[109] Hafner (n 108) 149–51.

[110] See VCLT, art 30(1).

[111] See on the legal nature of these maxims: E Vranes, 'Lex superior, lex specialis, lex posterior—zur Rechtsnatur der 'Konfliktlösungsregeln' (2005) 65 ZaöRV 391, 392–94; Fragmentation Report (n 2) [46], [56], [104], [226].

Both provisions clarify that they are without prejudice to any special rules contained in the relevant treaties.[112] There is a wide variety of such clauses both in universal as well as in regional treaties: while some claim priority over a succeeding or preceding agreement,[113] others subordinate themselves under succeeding or preceding agreements.[114] Other clauses again make their priority or subordination conditional on the existence of certain requirements.[115] The admissibility of modification agreements *inter se* is often expressed by way of a 'without-prejudice-clause',[116] yet some also contain substantial requirements.[117] Such special rules may lead to a convergence of the intention of some States to derogate on a regional basis with the acceptance of such derogation by the third States which are bound to the conflicting rule.

However, Article 30(2) does not provide for a solution in cases in which two conflict clauses collide, either because both clauses claim priority or, alternatively, attribute priority to the other treaty.[118] Nor does Article 41(1)(a) assist in the resolution of a conflict between the earlier treaty and a later regional rule which does not conform to the modification requirements set out in the earlier treaty.

Here, the secondary rules reflected in Articles 30(5) and Article 41(1)(b) provide further guidance and require us to distinguish two situations.[119] We must first ascertain whether a regional treaty satisfies the requirements set out in Article 41 for a modification agreement *inter se*. If it does, the regional treaty is opposable to all States parties to the treaty it modifies. In this case, Article 30(5) implies that the rule reflected in Article 30(4) is no longer relevant. However, if the regional treaty does not meet the criteria of Article 41, Article 30(4) provides that the later regional treaty applies, in accordance with the *lex posterior* principle and subject to the *pacta tertiis* principle, with the consequence that its parties are internationally responsible toward States parties to the earlier treaty. In other words, neither provision renders the later regional treaty invalid; rather, its provisions are only opposable to the parties to the earlier treaty under the conditions established by Article 41.

[112] See VCLT, art 30(2) and 41(1)(a).

[113] NATO Treaty, art 8; UNCLOS, art 311; UN Charter, art 103; Covenant of the League of Nations, art 20.

[114] TFEU, arts 350 and 351.

[115] UN Charter, arts 52–54; International Coffee Agreement (adopted 31 March 1968, entry into force 1 October 1968) 647 UNTS 4, art 41, which provides that 'Regional and inter-regional price arrangements among exporting Members shall be consistent with the general objectives of the Agreement.'

[116] Treaty on Non-proliferation of Nuclear Weapons, art VII.

[117] GATT, art XXIV.

[118] See also K Von der Decken, 'Article 30' in O Dörr and K Schmalenbach (eds), *Vienna Convention on the Law of Treaties: A Commentary* (2nd edn, Springer 2018) [19] mentioning as one option that both clauses 'cancel out one another'.

[119] This derives from Articles 30(5) in conjunction with Article 30(4)(a). According to K von der Decken, 'Article 41' in O Dörr and K Schmalenbach (eds), *Vienna Convention on the Law of Treaties: A Commentary* (2nd edn, Springer 2018) [4].

For this reason, we will now focus on the conditions set out by Article 41. According to this provision, a later agreement among only certain parties to the earlier treaty is accepted as prevailing over the earlier treaty provided that the formal and substantive conditions set out in Article 41(1)(b), (2) are met. In substance, a modification *inter se* must neither affect the rights and obligations of the other parties (Article 41(1)(b)(i)), nor the object and purpose of the treaty (Article 41(1)(b)(ii)). As the 'gatekeeper' for the application of Article 41, this second requirement, the object and purpose test, marks the point at which the real difficulty arises. Traditionally, *inter se* agreements which seek to modify 'reciprocal' or 'bilateralizable' provisions of an earlier treaty are considered not to infringe upon the object and purpose of that treaty.[120] Modifications of provisions contained in 'interdependent' (eg disarmament conventions) or 'integral' treaties (eg human rights conventions), however, are a different issue.[121]

State practice suggests that regional agreements frequently test the limits of the 'object and purpose' test set out in Article 41(2)(b)(ii) of the VCLT. Apart from individual examples involving later regional treaty rules,[122] the EU practice of insisting on 'disconnection clauses' in multilateral (human rights and environmental) treaty regimes since the late 1980ies represents a structural challenge to Article 41 of the VCLT.[123] These 'disconnection clauses' are inserted in a multilateral treaty and stipulate that 'in their relations *inter se* certain of the parties to the multilateral convention would not apply the rules of the convention but specific rules agreed among themselves [that is, EU law]'.[124]

The permissibility and ambivalence of such clauses was addressed by the 2006 Fragmentation Report. The report pointed to risks for the integrity of the treaty regime, and of creating 'double standards', as well as for legal certainty given that 'disconnection clauses', notably those employed by the EU, often refer to the EU legal order which is a legal regime whose complexity makes it almost impossible for the other parties to assess the scope of the exception in advance.[125] The Fragmentation Report, however, also pointed to advantages of such clauses for the implementation of the more general treaty and proposed criteria for assessing the permissibility of these clauses on a case-by-case basis. The permissibility of these clauses

[120] Examples for these are the Vienna Convention on Diplomatic Relations (adopted 18 April 1961, entered into force 24 April 1964) 500 UNTS 95 (hereinafter: 'VCDR'), and the Marrakesh Agreement Establishing the World Trade Organization (adopted 15 April 1994, entered into force 1 January 1995) 1867 UNTS 154 (Von der Decken (n 119) [18)].

[121] Von der Decken (n 119) [18].

[122] See *Slivenko and others v Latvia* App No 48321/99 (ECtHR, 23 January 2002) [60]–[61].

[123] The case of 'disconnection clauses' has been understood as falling both under Article 30(2) as a type of conflict clause and as an *inter se* agreement under Article 41 (M Fitzmaurice and P Merkouris, 'Uniformity Versus Specialization (1): The Quest for a Uniform Law of inter-State Treaties' in CJ Tams, A Tzanakopoulos, and A Zimmermann (eds), *Research Handbook on the Law of Treaties* (Edward Elgar Publishing 2014) 341, 365–67).

[124] ILC Report 2005 (n 4) [463].

[125] Fragmentation Report (n 2) [293]–[294].

nevertheless continues to engage sceptical and cautious reactions.[126] The 2008 report by CAHDI on 'disconnection clauses', for example, warned that such practices 'inspire similar practices with regard to the relations *inter se* between States engaged in integration processes in other regions'.[127]

Due to the limits set by the 'object-and-purpose-test' for *inter se* agreements, States and IOs within a regionally confined setting have increasingly adopted non-legally binding agreements among themselves to advance a certain interpretation and application of the relevant multilateral treaty, for example, with respect to the interpretation of UNCLOS in the face of sea-level rise[128] and suspected attacks against submarine infrastructure.[129]

The VCLT rules reflecting the *lex posterior* maxim thus help identifying the conditions under which the priority of a later regional rule is acceptable to third States. This is clearly the case when third States have agreed to such a priority in an earlier treaty and the later regional rule complies with any requirements set out in that earlier treaty. Further, the priority of a regional treaty rule contained in an *inter se* agreement is acceptable as long as it complies with the conditions set out in Article 41, notably, if it does not infringe upon the object and purpose of the earlier treaty. However, the analysis has also revealed the considerable limitations of the *lex posterior* principle as expressed in the VCLT

For one, Article 41 only applies to *inter se* agreements, not to later agreements between some parties of the earlier treaty and non-parties. In the latter situation, Article 30(4)(b) alone is applicable which provides for the applicability of both treaties, and, accordingly, does not help to solve potential conflicts.[130] This scenario is particularly acute in situations in which an earlier regional treaty rule competes with a later treaty involving non-parties to that earlier treaty. As highlighted by the Fragmentation Report, there has been some support for the primacy of the earlier rule (*lex prior*). Notably, the two examples from case law that are mentioned in the report pertain to regional treaties: the 1917 decisions of the Central American Court of Justice in the cases concerning Costa Rica, El Salvador, and Nicaragua concerning the latter's conclusion of a subsequent treaty with the

[126] Council of Europe, Directorate of Legal Advice and Public International Law, Legal Opinion on Budapest Cyber Crime Convention, 'Use of a "Disconnection Clause" in the Second Additional Protocol to the Budapest Convention on Cybercrime' (Strasbourg, 29 April 2019) [25]–[32].

[127] Council of Europe, Committee of Legal Advisers on Public International Law, 'Report on the Consequences of the so-called "Disconnection Clause" in International Law in General and for Council of Europe Conventions, containing such a clause, in particular' (Strasbourg, 7 October 2008) CAHDI (2008) 1 rev 2 [9].

[128] Pacific Islands Forum, 'Declaration on Preserving Maritime Zones in the Face of Climate Change-related Sea-Level Rise' (12 August 2021) <https://forumsec.org/sites/default/files/2024-05/2021%20Declaration-on-Preserving-Maritime-Zones.pdf> (accessed 10 May 2026).

[129] H Ringbom, 'New Threats—Old Rules: Law of the Sea Issues Raised by Suspected Attacks on Submarine Infrastructure in the Baltic Sea' (2025) 56:3 Ocean Dev Int Law 390, 409.

[130] See on this: Ranganathan (n 64); Chapter 2.

United States,[131] and 'objective territorial regimes'.[132] As discussed in Chapter 4, the idea that regional treaties should be protected from subsequent deviations also motivated the French proposal regarding special rules for 'restricted multilateral treaties' during the VCLT conference.[133]

A further limitation of the VCLT rules is demonstrated by the example of 'disconnection clauses': it is often impossible for third parties to assess whether the object and purpose is infringed by an *inter se* agreement that seeks to preserve regional regulatory autonomy. Therefore, some scholars have even argued that Articles 30 and 41 are inapplicable to such forms of regional law which claim a separate status. They suggest considering them as being analogous to domestic law under Article 27 VCLT.[134] In light of these limitations, a number of commentators, including Sinclair, have raised doubts as to the adequacy of *lex posterior* in addressing conflicts involving regional treaty rules.[135]

6.3.3.2 *Lex specialis*

In contrast to the *lex posterior* principle, the *lex specialis* principle has not been codified in the VCLT. As the drafting history shows, any attempts to insert the *lex specialis* principle in the VCLT were absorbed by Articles 30 and 41: for example, de Luna argued in the ILC in 1963 that

> [i]n many instances States in a particular region which were parties to multilateral treaties had concluded among themselves regional agreements containing provisions that differed from those of the earlier treaties. For such States it was the regional agreements which had effect, by virtue of the principle *tractatus specialis derogat generali*.[136]

Similarly, the UK delegation unsuccessfully tried to integrate the *lex specialis* principle into what became Article 30.[137] The futile attempts to incorporate *lex specialis* in the VCLT do not mean that the principle does not play a significant role in the interpretation of treaties, including for the avoidance of a conflict between regional

[131] Fragmentation Report (n 2) [239], citing two decisions of the Central American Court of Justice: *Costa Rica v Nicaragua* (1917) 11:1 AJIL 181, 228; *El Salvador v Nicaragua* (1917) 11:3 AJIL 674, 674.

[132] Fragmentation Report (n 2) [240].

[133] See Chapter 4, section 4.2.

[134] See M Ličková, 'European Exceptionalism in International Law' (2008) 19:3 EJIL 463, 470–71; von der Decken (n 118) [10].

[135] I Sinclair, *The Vienna Convention on the Law of Treaties* (Manchester University Press 1984) 98 (referring to the high degree of trust underlying regional rules); Finke (n 9) 428 (relying on the complementary character of universal and regional rules).

[136] ILC, 'Summary records of the fifteenth session from 6 May to 12 July 1963' (1963) YBILC I, UN Doc A/CN.4/SER.A/1963, p 89.

[137] See also von der Decken (n 118) [12].

and general treaty rules. In its 2025 advisory opinion on *Obligations of States in respect of Climate Change*, the ICJ stated that

> [t]he principle of *lex specialis* is a maxim of interpretation that is used for determining which of several potentially applicable rules is to prevail or whether the rules simply coexist. It is generally accepted that, in some cases, a specific rule, or a specific set of rules, takes precedence over more general or less focused rules, while in other cases the specific rule should be seen as an elaboration of one or more general rules, the latter continuing to play an interpretative role in the background.[138]

However, when discussing the relationship between regional treaty rules and other rules under international agreements, the principle of *lex specialis* plays a fairly limited role due to, ironically, the nature of Article 41 of the VCLT as *lex specialis* vis-à-vis the *lex specialis* principle. In other words, the *lex specialis* principle cannot be used to circumvent the requirements for *inter se* agreements set out in Article 41, in particular, the 'object-and-purpose-test' as a basis to justify the application of a regional rule and thereby non-compliance with that other rule. Accordingly, *lex specialis* knows mainly two scenarios in which it can resolve a 'genuine conflict' between regional and other rules: first, where at least one of the two conflicting rules provide for the priority of the more special one;[139] and second, where a (regional) treaty rule is considered *lex specialis* vis-à-vis a general customary rule.[140]

6.3.3.3 Priority of regional custom?

The question of normative conflicts between regional custom and competing rules has been addressed by some States and members during the ILC's work on the 'Identification of customary international law'.[141] However, the Commission ultimately decided to exclude this question from the scope of the topic.[142]

Two normative relationships are distinguished and discussed in this section: first, the relationship and potential conflict between regional and general custom; and second, between regional custom and treaty rules.

Turning first to the relationship between regional and general custom, the priority of regional custom over general custom has been confirmed both by the ICJ and the ILC. In its 1960 *Right of Passage* case, the ICJ held that 'such a particular practice must prevail over any general rules'.[143] According to the Fragmentation

138 *Obligations of States in respect of Climate Change* (n 37) [166].
139 See eg UNCLOS, art 282.
140 *Nicaragua v United States* (n 46) [274]; Fragmentation Report (n 2) [79]–[83].
141 ILC, 'Written comments of New Zealand' (21 December 2017) UN Doc A/CN.4/716 [29]; ILC (20 May 2015) UN Doc A/CN.4/SR.3253, 9 (Petric); 12 (Huang).
142 ILC, 'Draft conclusions on identification of customary international law, with commentaries' (2018) UN Doc A/73/10, Commentary to Conclusion 1, 124 [6].
143 *Right of Passage* (n 22) 44.

Report 'it may be assumed (as is indeed suggested by the *Right of Passage* case) that local customs (if proven) have priority over general customary law'.[144] Accordingly, their relationship is governed by *lex specialis*.

By contrast, the second type of normative relationship, between regional customary law and treaty rules, is considerably more complex. In the absence of such a conflict clause in the treaty accommodating regional custom, the question is how to reconcile the rule of regional custom and the treaty rule. Due to the specific consent of States expressed in later treaty rules, it can be presumed, in the absence of contrary indications arising from an interpretation of the treaty, that these prevail over regional custom as *lex posterior*. Taking a rather restrictive position to this effect, the tribunal in the *South China Sea Arbitration* stated with respect to the question of whether unwritten regional rules existent prior to the adoption of UNCLOS continued to apply that 'the Tribunal does not consider it possible that the drafters of the Convention intended for traditional or artisanal fishing rights to survive the introduction of the exclusive economic zone'.[145]

The issue becomes more difficult when examining whether later emerging regional custom prevails over treaty rules. According to Michael Akehurst, 'in such cases the maxim *lex specialis derogat generali* causes the customary rule to prevail over the treaty'.[146] Hugh Thirlway, more cautiously, suggests applying the rules on *lex posterior* (on application, modification, and amendment) from the VCLT analogously.[147] Yet, it is doubtful whether either of these propositions corresponds to the nature of regional custom as a source of law which develops gradually and, to a certain extent, unconsciously. In practice, these cases suggest that the rule under regional custom does not override the application of the relevant treaty rule. However, it may inform the interpretation of the treaty or contribute to the development of general customary international law, and thus still effectively prevails, even if only in substance.[148] For example, the ECtHR has explicitly acknowledged 'evolutions' in the practice of member States of the Council of Europe, notably regarding the prohibition of the death penalty, the right of access to information, and the right to conscientious objection.[149] In these cases, the Court effectively departed from the original understanding at the adoption of the 1950 Convention and even from the literal terms of the relevant provisions. Still, its reasoning was grounded in treaty interpretation rather than in the recognition of regional

[144] Fragmentation Report (n 2) [84].

[145] *The South China Sea Arbitration (The Republic of Philippines v The People's Republic of China)* (Award) PCA Case 2013-19 (12 June 2016) [803].

[146] M Akehurst, 'The Hierarchy of the Sources of International Law' (1976) 47 BYBIL 273, 275.

[147] See also H Thirlway, *International Customary Law and Codification* (Sijthoff 1972) 142–43, who draws a parallel to the modification *inter se* based on a regional treaty rule.

[148] See also Chapter 7, sections 7.3.2 and 7.4.

[149] See eg *Al-Saadoon and Mufdhi v UK* App 61498/08 (ECHR, 2 March 2010) (prohibition of death penalty); *Bayatyan v Armenia* App No 23459/03 (ECtHR, 7 July 2011) (conscientious objection); and *Magyar Helsinki Bizottság v Hungary* App 18030/11 (ECtHR, 8 November 2016) (right of access to information).

custom. In their individual opinions, several judges argued that the Court should have relied on regional custom rather than evolutive treaty interpretation.[150] For example, Judge Ziemele asked in *Lalmahomed v The Netherlands*

> Should not the Chamber have tried to assess whether there might be a regional custom as concerns procedural guarantees for the leave to appeal in minor offences cases, and whether any effect might be discerned in relation to the scope of Article 6, . . . and in that sense the difference between the obligations under Article 6 of the Convention and Article 14 of the ICCPR is reduced?[151]

In her concurring opinion to the 2015 *Rohlena v The Czech Republic* case, Judge Ziemele stated even more explicitly that

> [t]his is yet another case in which the Court is tempted to engage in a discussion on the existence of a European consensus. The notion remains controversial . . . I have noted elsewhere that a more orthodox way for the Court to proceed would have been to rely on the tools that international law offers anyway . . . In my view this means that the Court, when it examines domestic laws and practices and the positions which European States may have expressed on the issue in question in other international fora, is in fact looking for a particular regional practice that the States consider it necessary to follow, in other words, regional custom. (Incidentally, the notion of custom has also evolved in international law and is most likely no longer as rigid as may have been the case some time ago.).[152]

While this example relates to the relationship of regional custom and a regional treaty rule, States are even more reluctant to accept the priority of regional custom vis-à-vis treaty rules binding upon States beyond the region, such as those contained in the UN Charter or UNCLOS.[153] While some authors appear to consider that later regional custom may be applied alongside such treaties,[154] practice by States or international courts and tribunals in support of such a proposition

[150] See Concurring Opinion of Judge Sicilianos, joined by Judge Raimondi in *Magyar Helsinki Bizottság v Hungary* (n 149) [16].

[151] *Lalmahomed v The Netherlands* App No 26036/08 (ECtHR, 22 February 2011) (Concurring Opinion of Judge Ziemele).

[152] *Rohlena v The Czech Republic* App No 59552/08 (ECtHR, 27 January 2015) (Concurring Opinion of Judge Ziemele) [2].

[153] See eg with respect to the impact of climate change induced sea-level rise on UNCLOS: Statement of the European Union and its Member States on Sea Level Rise in Relation to International Law (UNGA 6th Committee, 78th session, 2023) [8]: '[C]ertain possible emerging regional State practices regarding sea level rise should not lead to the recognition of a regional customary law of the sea rule.'

[154] See AA Yusuf, *Pan-Africanism and International Law* (Brill 2014) 191–92, who seems to suggest that under 'African Public law', the AU does not need a prior authorization by the UNSC. See also the discussion of regional custom as modifying the understanding of baselines set out in art 5 UNCLOS: ILC, 'First issues paper on Sea-level rise in relation to international law by Bogdan Aurescu and Nilüfer Oral' (2021) UN Doc A/CN.4/740, 42 [104].

is sparse.[155] However, where the other parties to the treaty (implicitly) agree to the application of such regional custom, there is no apparent reason to reject its operation alongside the treaty. This approach finds support in the 2016 award of the tribunal in the *South China Sea Arbitration*. Although the tribunal generally adopted a restrictive stance regarding the applicability of unwritten regional rules alongside UNCLOS, it nevertheless recognized that such rules may apply where the following three criteria are met:

> the assertion by a State of a right at variance with the Convention [the author: including a right under regional custom], acquiescence therein by the other States Parties, and the passage of sufficient time to establish beyond doubt the existence of both the right and a general acquiescence.[156]

Unless these criteria can be established, however, it seems that such regional rules may only retain legal significance for interpreting the content and scope of the competing rule.[157] In other words, regional custom does not prevail over the treaty rule per se yet represents a piece of a jigsaw that shapes the meaning given to the rules under general international law.

6.3.4 Co-ordination of regional and other rules

In some cases, it is neither possible to avoid a conflict (by denying a regional intention to derogate) nor to resolve the conflict (by affirming the (in-)acceptability of a regional derogation for third parties). Such situations notably arise when a regional rule purports to constitute an autonomous legal order, thereby inviting analogies with conflict-of-law techniques derived from private international law.[158] In these situations and in the absence of a *renvoi* to the other legal order,[159] certain secondary rules allow for a rapprochement of conflicting obligations.[160] These secondary rules neither focus on nor prioritize the perspective of the regional States,

[155] See *The South China Sea Arbitration* (n 145) [275]; see also J Barkholdt, 'Progress Through Preservation of the Legal Status Quo: Paradox or Prerequisite?' (2024) 4 ZaöRV 925, 943–48.

[156] *The South China Sea Arbitration* (n 145) [275].

[157] See Chapter 7, sections 7.3 and 7.4.

[158] See eg R Michaels, 'Global Legal Pluralism and Conflict of Laws' in P Schiff Berman (ed), *The Oxford Handbook of Global Legal Pluralism* (OUP 2020) 629, 646–48, and Jeutner (n 32) 68, discussing the application of the conflict-of-laws approach to the 'Kadi saga' in the European courts.

[159] See for such a *renvoi* eg the Protocol to the African Charter on Human and Peoples' Rights on the Rights of Women in Africa (adopted 11 July 2003, entered into force 25 November 2005) CAB/LEG/66.6 (2003), art 11(1); TEU, art 42(7); Convention (No 169) concerning indigenous and tribal peoples in independent countries (adopted 27 June 1989, entered into force 5 September 1991) 1650 UNTS 383, art 8(1).

[160] See on the concept of 'interface norms': N Krisch, *Beyond Constitutionalism: The Pluralist Structure of Postnational Law* (OUP 2010) 285–96; on 'linkage rules': D von Daniels, *The Concept of Law from a Transnational Perspective* (Routledge 2010) 158–66.

nor that of third parties.[161] Instead, they are designed to bridge the two perspectives by facilitating mutual recognition, whether through a decline of jurisdiction, deference to the assessment of another international body, or institutional dialogue. However, the application of these techniques is limited by the respective mandates as well as general procedural principles, notably the prohibition of a denial of justice.[162]

6.3.4.1 Decline of jurisdiction

An international body which is confronted with a conflict of mandates between a regional and a non-regional institution may, for example, consider declining to exercise its jurisdiction in favour of the other institution. This can be achieved, for example, by way of a narrow interpretation of the scope of application of the respective treaty. In the context of regional international law, the exercise of jurisdiction was declined by the arbitral tribunal in the *Mox Plant* Arbitration between Ireland and the UK in 2003.[163] Recently, the CJEU in the *Slovenia v Croatia* case declared Croatia's application for infringement proceedings against Croatia for not complying with a 2017 arbitral award to be inadmissible.[164] Yet, such an approach finds its limits in the prohibition of a denial of justice or where it is incompatible with the mandate of the respective institution. For example, the ICJ refused to decline its jurisdiction in favour of regional institutions in the 1984 *Nicaragua v US* case and in the 1998 *Nigeria v Cameroon* judgment.[165] Another example to this effect concerns Article 344 TFEU which explicitly prohibits member States of the EU from submitting a dispute concerning EU law to any other method of dispute settlement other than those provided for in the EU treaties.[166]

6.3.4.2 Dialogue and deference

Apart from mitigating frictions between regional and other rules by mutual cross-referencing (judicial dialogue),[167] the international institution or State may also consider deferring to the assessment of the competing international institution when applying a certain rule. For example, in cases relating to the compatibility of the individual sanctions regime imposed on the basis of UNSC resolutions with the ECHR, the ECtHR applied a presumption of a law-abiding intention

[161] See R Michaels, 'Tertiary Rules', in N Krisch (ed), *Entangled Legalities Beyond the State* (CUP 2021) 424, 425, 435, 434–35, who considers these rules 'tertiary' rather than 'secondary' rules.

[162] *Factory at Chorzów (Germany v Poland)* (Jurisdiction) [1927] PCIJ Series A, No 9, 30.

[163] *The MOX Plant Case (Ireland v United Kingdom)* (Order No 3) PCA Case 2002-01 (24 June 2003) [26].

[164] *Slovenia v Croatia* Case C-457/18 (CJEU, 31 January 2020) [104].

[165] *Nicaragua v United States of America* (n 85) [107]–[108]; *Land and Maritime Boundary between Cameroon and Nigeria (Cameroon v Nigeria)* [1998] ICJ Rep 275 [67]–[68].

[166] 'Member States undertake not to submit a dispute concerning the interpretation or application of the Treaties to any method of settlement other than those provided for therein.'

[167] See also Chapter 7, section 7.3.3.

with regard to the interpretation of the UNSC.[168] At the universal level, the ICJ in the 2010 *Diallo* decision deferred to the AfrComHPR.[169] However, the Court has also explicitly declined to defer to regional institutions—at times without giving reasons (as in the 2012 *Belgium v Senegal* case),[170] on other occasions, such as in the 2009 *Navigational and Related Rights* case, by distinguishing between the different provisions.[171]

6.4 Regional and general international law between harmonization and co-ordination

Today, it is almost taken for granted that the existence and application of regional international law, alongside other rules of international law, do not necessarily undermine the notion of international law as 'one'. Rather, the proliferation of regional institutions since de Lapradelle articulated his concerns has often served to vernacularize international law, embedding it more deeply in local contexts rather than fragmenting it. Nonetheless, the risk of regional fragmentation cannot be dismissed lightly or assumed to be manageable merely through the 'toolbox' provided by the VCLT. While the 2006 Fragmentation Report offers a useful point of departure for addressing regional fragmentation, it remains limited in certain situations involving regional international law, given its focus on conflicts arising from treaty obligations, its exclusion of institutional techniques, and its equation of regional and functional fragmentation. Chapter 6, having considered the role of secondary rules in resolving conflicts between regional and other rules, suggested that for such fragmentation *ratione personae*, these rules may be considered as mediators between different perspectives. To this effect, a sequential test has been proposed, comprising three stages. The first stage involves determining whether States or IOs intended to derogate from general rules when adopting regional ones. If this stage does not resolve the potential conflict, the second stage assesses, from the perspective of third parties, whether such derogations may be permissible. The third stage examines those secondary rules which encourage those interpreting and applying the rules to see the two perspectives, regional and general, together.

168 *Al-Dulimi* (n 90) [140]; *Nada v Switzerland* App No 10593/08 (ECtHR, 12 September 2012) [171]–[172] (even though the Court saw this presumption as being rebutted in that case); *Al-Jedda v UK* App No 27021/08 (ECtHR, 7 July 2011) [102].

169 *Diallo* (n 40) [67].

170 *Questions relating to the Obligation to Prosecute or Extradite (Belgium v Senegal)* (Judgment) [2012] ICJ Rep 422 [111]; but see dissenting opinion of Judge Xue [43].

171 *Navigational and Related Rights* (n 22) [49].

7

Does regional practice reform or deform international law?

7.1 Is all international law regional law?

In 1997, Shirley Scott observed that '[v]irtually all international law is "regional" in the sense of having been developed by a sub-set of the international legal community'.[1] While Scott's observation may appear sweeping, it is hard to dispute that regional practice has shaped and continues to shape rules under international law, including general international law.[2] Many rules of contemporary international law, now enshrined in quasi-universal treaties or reflected in general international law, owe their existence to regional precursors and 'trailblazers', which inspired and paved the way for the adoption of universal counterparts.[3] At the same time, it is equally difficult to dispute that, throughout the history of international law, certain regions, especially Europe, have imposed their regional laws on others and, ultimately, on the universal plane, thereby displacing pre-existing regional normative systems.[4] The influence of such rules persists to this day,[5] as do attempts by States to act through regional institutions to shape international law in ways that align with their own particular interests or values, which are not necessarily shared universally.[6]

This final chapter focuses on the pervasive yet ambivalent role of regional practice in the evolution of international law over time. It argues that the universal secondary rules governing the formation, identification, and interpretation of international law perform a dual function in this process. On the one hand, they channel the trailblazing role of regional practice toward adapting international law to emerging global challenges such as technological innovation and climate change. On the other hand, they act as a safeguard, ensuring the equal

[1] S Scott, 'Universalism and Title to Territory in Antarctica' (1997) 66 Nord J Int Law 33, 37.
[2] On the term 'general international law', see Chapter 3, section 3.2.1.
[3] See eg *Asylum (Colombia/Peru)* [1950] ICJ Rep 290 (dissenting opinion of Judge Álvarez) 294.
[4] See Y Onuma, 'When Was the Law of International Society Born—An Inquiry of the History of International Law from an Intercivilizational Perspective' (2000) 2 JHIL 1.
[5] See eg *Land and Maritime Delimitation and Sovereignty over Islands (Gabon/Equatorial Guinea)* (Judgment of 19 May 2025) (separate opinion of Judge Yusuf) [1].
[6] See eg L Khasanova and A Simonyan, '(Geo)politicizing International Law of Cyberspace in Post-Soviet Eurasia' (2025) 24 Chin J Int Law 1.

Regional and General International Law. Janina Barkholdt, Oxford University Press. © Janina Barkholdt 2026.
DOI: 10.1093/9780198953432.003.0007

participation of States in the development of international law, irrespective of size or power, thereby protecting against regional imbalance, imposition, and exceptionalism. Accordingly, this chapter explores how regional practice—even where it does not attain the status of regional international law (Chapters 4 and 5) or when the application of regional international law is constrained by conflicting international rules (Chapter 6)—nonetheless shapes the corpus of universally applicable rules. In doing so, the chapter completes the 'three-step approach' introduced in Chapter 3. The first part of this chapter defines the notion of regional practice and considers its ambivalent role in the evolution of international law (7.2). The second part examines how regional practice contributes to changes in written international law (7.3), while the third part focuses on its influence on unwritten international law (7.4).

7.2 Regional practice in the evolution of international law

Unlike the previous three chapters, which focused on regional international *law*, this chapter takes a broader approach and concentrates on regional *practice*. Disregarding regional practice that falls short of qualifying as international law would provide an incomplete account of its legal significance. Even when such practice does not attain the status of regional international law, it plays a significant role in the evolution of general international law.

7.2.1 What is 'regional practice'?

Regional practice encompasses, but is not limited to, regional international law. Although the term 'practice' is often understood as referring to the conduct of a variety of actors, including non-State actors, the understanding of 'practice' adopted here is narrower. It focuses on conduct which is attributable to States, acting individually or together with other States, or to intergovernmental organizations (IOs), as well as pronouncements of judicial and expert bodies established by an international agreement.[7] Conduct by non-State actors is considered to the extent

[7] Both the ILC conclusions on CIL and SASP recognize that the practice of member States can be identified based on the practice of IOs (ILC, 'Draft conclusions on subsequent agreements and subsequent practice in relation to the interpretation of treaties, with commentaries' (2018), UN Doc A/73/10 (hereinafter: 'ILC Report 2018 (SASP)'), Conclusion 5, 40; ILC, 'Draft conclusions on identification of customary international law, with commentaries' (2018) UN Doc A/73/10 (hereinafter: 'ILC Report 2018 (CIL)'), Conclusion 12(2) and (3).) See also J Barkholdt, 'The Contribution of International Organizations to the Formation, Interpretation and Identification of International Law: Questions Arising from the Work of the International Law Commission' (2021) 18 IOLR 1, 26–38 on the distinction between State practice and IO practice and the legal relevance of IO practice 'as such' in the formation, identification, and interpretation of international law.

that it is either attributable to States, or recognized by States or IOs as relevant to the identification, interpretation, or formation of international law. The term practice is further understood to include a wide range of conduct, notably 'both physical and verbal acts' and 'under certain circumstances, ... inaction'.[8]

Practice is considered 'regional' when it has a 'regional nexus', that is, when it arises from a State's or IO's affiliation with a region, distinguishing it from unilateral practice rooted solely in domestic or national policy preferences, and from conduct linked to a State's or IO's affiliation with a non-regionally defined group of States.[9] Practice with a regional nexus typically encompasses conduct of organs of regional IOs and of regional bodies established by such an agreement, notably regional courts and tribunals, as well as conduct of States in connection with the interpretation and application of an agreement with a regional scope of application. The distinction between regional and other practice tends to be more blurred with regard to the conduct of individual States or groups of States in universal—or potentially universal—institutions, their interactions with third States (eg, in concluding bilateral treaties), and domestic conduct, including a State's treatment of its own nationals. Determining whether such practice exhibits a regional nexus requires a case-by-case analysis, considering whether the conduct responds to a specific geographic feature, results from co-ordination within a regional group of States, reflects a pattern common among geographically proximate States (particularly if it is less prevalent elsewhere), or corresponds to a declared intention by the State to pursue a regional approach.

7.2.2 Reforming international law: regional practice as a catalyst for change

The term 'reform' is usually understood to refer to changes to the existing legal framework aimed at improving it.[10] Whether the existing legal framework should be improved, and what qualifies as an improvement in substance, are largely matters of political choice. How such changes are made and, in particular, whether any alleged changes conform to the procedures prescribed by the legal system, is a question subject to legal assessment. In this more legal sense, reform is understood here to refer to 'an evolution [of the existing law] brought about by virtue of the juridical order itself'.[11]

[8] See also ILC Report 2018 (CIL) (n 7) Conclusions 5 and 6; ILC Report 2018 (SASP) (n 7) Conclusion 5.

[9] See also the definition of a 'region' and 'regional international law' in Chapter 2, section 2.2.2.

[10] See also R Ivory, 'The Concept of International Law Reform and the Case of Negotiated Settlements in Foreign Bribery Matters' (2024) 35:4 EJIL 867, 877; T Rensmann, 'Reform' in B Simma and others (eds), *The Charter of the United Nations: A Commentary, Volume I* (4th edn, OUP 2024) [1]: '[C]hange for the better.'

[11] JL Kunz, 'The Law of Nations, Static and Dynamic' (1933) 27 AJIL 628, 631.

The significant role of regional practice in the evolution of general international law rests on the absence of a central legislator at the universal level.[12] Change in international law occurs in a largely decentralized manner and is structured around the duality of formal mechanisms—change brought about by procedures designed to create, amend, or terminate rules—and mechanisms that allow the meaning and scope of a rule to evolve informally through practice.[13] Both modes of change, however, face certain limitations. Successful recourse to formal mechanisms depends on the ability of States and other subjects of international law to build consensus around a given normative project. Given the large number and diversity of States, these formal processes are often protracted—or may not even be feasible.[14] The challenge arising from informal changes brought about by practice lies in the difficulty of determining whether such practice crosses the threshold from mere practice to legal change.

Regional practice catalyses change in international law because it directly addresses the challenges of both formal and informal change and is particularly responsive to the requirements set by universal secondary rules due to its distinctive characteristics.[15] As we will see below, regional practice can help build the consensus necessary to meet the threshold required for changing international law through formal mechanisms. Regional practice often emerges from a well-tested and mature legal approach that has proven effective at the international level within a limited group of States.[16] Regional practice thereby pre-structures the consensus-building in a smaller group of States and often provides a model—or at least a point of departure—for universal regulation.[17] Regional practice also facilitates identifying State practice. Such practice is presumed to represent a certain part of the international community and thus carries particular weight for the identification, interpretation, and formation of general international law.[18] It is also typically easier to identify regional practice than other forms of collective

[12] See also BS Chimni, 'Epilogue: Fragmentary Thoughts on Change' in N Krisch and E Yildiz (eds), *The Many Paths of Change in International Law* (OUP 2023) 335; CW Jenks, 'The Conflict of Law-Making Treaties' (1953) 30 BYBIL 401; ILC, 'Fragmentation of International Law: difficulties arising from the Diversification and Expansion of International Law: Report of the Study Group of the International Law Commission–Finalized by Martti Koskenniemi' (2006) UN Doc A/CN.4/L.682 ('Fragmentation Report') [5].

[13] See also Rensmann (n 10) [13]–[19], who divides avenues for reforming the UN Charter into formal and informal mechanisms; S Vöneky, 'Article 108' in B Simma and others (eds), *The Charter of the United Nations: A Commentary, Volume II* (4th edn, OUP 2024) [12] distinguishes between formal amendments and informal modifications/transformations.

[14] See also Chimni (n 12) 335–36; FL Bordin, 'Interpreting Constituent Instruments to Justify the Evolving Powers of International Organizations' in G Marceau and H Gött (eds), *International Organization Initiatives: How and Why Organizations Adapt and Change* (OUP 2025) 73.

[15] See also Jenks (n 12) 403.

[16] See Chapter 2, section 2.3.3.

[17] See section 7.3 below. See also Chapter 2, section 2.3.3.

[18] See section 7.4 below. See also Chapter 2, section 2.3.2.

practice due to the existence of regional institutions which aggregate, reflect, and publish the view and practice of their member States.[19]

7.2.3 Deforming international law: risks arising from recourse to regional practice

The very factors that underpin the distinctive role of regional practice in reforming international law, its legal maturity, identifiability, and presumed representativeness, also create the risk that one or more regions exert a disproportionate influence in asserting changes to the existing legal framework, thereby 'deforming' general international law. To mitigate these risks, three limits define the extent to which secondary rules accommodate regional practice in the evolution of international law.

First, where a particular regional practice reflects a legal approach that is entrenched in a regional legal system and may, in that sense, assume a privileged role in the evolution of international law,[20] it can readily tip over into 'regional exceptionalism'—that is, the insistence by a regionally defined group of States on applying a distinct legal approach at the universal level, even where it may conflict with existing general international law.[21] The distinction between a regional 'trailblazer' and a 'trespasser' is a fine one. It is inherently connected to the larger question of whether and to what extent practice which deviates from, or even violates, an existing rule can change it and if so, within which limits.[22] Classic examples illustrating this tension include military interventions by regional organizations in States within their region, purportedly justified by regional rules.[23] Secondary rules determine the extent to which such practice reflects or contributes to changes in the existing legal framework, and when it instead constitutes mere non-compliance with the rules.

Second, the representative role attributed to regional practice is limited by the principle of consent, prominently reflected in the *pacta tertiis* principle, which serves as a safeguard against the imposition of normative understandings that

[19] See ILC, 'Memorandum by the UN Secretariat, Ways and means for making the evidence of customary international law more readily available' (2018) UN Doc A/CN.4/710/Rev.1 for various regional resources, and on the potential of regional institutions [65], [73], [98], [107], [120].

[20] See section 2.3.3.

[21] See on the EU: T Cabrita, 'The Integration Paradox: an ILC View on the EU Contribution to the Codification and Development of Rules of General International Law' (2021) 5 EWLR 1, 3; see further examples in Chapter 2, section 2.4.1.

[22] In its 1997 judgment, the ICJ recalled that according to the 'principle of *ex injuria jus non oritur*' 'facts which flow from unlawful conduct [must not] determine the law' (*Gabčíkovo-Nagymaros Project (Hungary/Slovakia)* [1997] ICJ Rep 7 [133]).

[23] See eg JJ Niyo, 'More Stick and Less Carrot: ECOWAS, the Use of Force to Restore Democracy, and the Contest between Regional and International Normative Regimes' (2025) AJIL Unbound 254. See also the examples mentioned in section 1.1 and at the end of section 7.3.

may prevail in one or more regions but are not universally shared.[24] For instance, despite criticisms of exporting its own rules globally,[25] it is notable that the European Union (EU), in the context of sea-level rise and its impact on the interpretation of the United Nations (UN) Convention on the Law of the Sea (UNCLOS), cautioned

> regarding the consideration of regional State practices together with the respective *opinio juris* in this context, because universally applicable provisions and principles such as the United Nations Convention on the law of the Sea need to be applied in a uniform way in all regions of the world.[26]

Secondary rules help determine whether the presumptive role ascribed to regional practice accurately reflects the consent of all States concerned.

Third, while regional practice can help identify State practice, it must not produce regional imbalances.[27] Such regional imbalance may arise from the uneven availability of regional practice.[28] Moreover, differing levels of State integration into regional institutions, across and within regions,[29] risk a 'double-counting' of practice—as both State and institutional practice—thereby distorting the picture of State practice to the disadvantage of less integrated States and regions.[30] The use of secondary rules ensures a careful attribution and equal consideration of State practice.

7.3 Regional practice and written international law

Although regional practice is, by its very nature, limited in scope, such practice plays a significant role in shaping the evolution of multilateral treaties with near-universal membership (hereinafter 'universal treaties'), including the UN Charter, often referred to as the 'constitution of the international community',

[24] See eg during the debates on Article 38 of the VCLT during the Vienna Conference: UN Conference on the Law of Treaties 'Official Records: Summary Records of the Plenary Meetings and of the Meetings of the Committee of the Whole (Second Session)' (9 April–22 May 1969) UN Doc A/CONF.39/11.Add.1 ('UNCLOT II'), Guatemala (67–68), and the USSR (69).

[25] A Bradford, *The Brussels Effect: How the European Union Rules the World* (OUP 2020).

[26] Statement of the European Union and its Member States on Sea Level Rise in Relation to International Law (UNGA 6th Committee, 78th session, 2023) [7].

[27] See also JHF Van Panhuys, 'Regional or General International Law? A Misleading Dilemma' (1961) 8 NILR 146, 161–62.

[28] ILC, Memorandum CIL (n 19) [76], [83]–[84], [89].

[29] In contrast to Africa, the Americas, and Europe, there is, for example, no regional human rights court in Asia. See further: A Saidov, 'Regionalism and Human Rights: Towards an Asian Human Rights Protection System' (2025) 24 Chin J Int Law 1.

[30] See, for a more detailed discussion of the problem of double-counting and potential approaches to avoid it: Barkholdt (n 7) 26, 33, 39.

and UNCLOS, the 'constitution for the Oceans'.[31] The drafting and negotiation of universal agreements are frequently guided by regional initiatives and informed by established regional practice.[32] The concept of the Exclusive Economic Zone (EEZ) in Part V of UNCLOS, for example, drew directly on the practice of Latin American and African States.[33] Articles 19–23 of the 1969 Vienna Convention on the Law of Treaties (VCLT), governing reservations to treaties, reflect the substantial influence of Pan-American practice.[34] Furthermore, some universal agreements emulate approaches previously adopted in regional agreements, such as the 1997 Convention on the Law of the Non-navigational Uses of International Watercourses.[35] In some instances, regional groups of States have successfully advocated for the incorporation of language originating from a particular regional context. Notable examples include Article 20(3) of the 1989 Convention on the Rights of the Child[36] and Article 41(3) of the 1961 Vienna Convention on Diplomatic Relations.[37] Finally, most universal treaties seek to accommodate regional particularities by including rules that assign a special role to regional institutions and regional norms.[38]

Nonetheless, universal agreements frequently encounter regional contestation, whether for reflecting an outdated regulatory approach, for having been shaped by one or more regions to the detriment of others (creating a 'regional imbalance'), or for failing to accommodate a particular regional practice or rule (resulting in

[31] See B Fassbender, *The United Nations Charter as the Constitution of the International Community* (Brill 2009); TB Koh, 'Remarks', reproduced in *UN The Law of the Sea: Official Text of the UNCLOS* (London 1983) xxxiii.

[32] See eg the role played by Latin-American States during the San Francisco Conference (M Akehurst, 'Enforcement Action by Regional Agencies, with Special Reference to the Organization of American States' (1967) 42 BYBIL 175, 175–76); the active participation of African States in the negotiation of the 1966 ICSID Convention (A Hankings-Evans, 'The Africanization of International Investment Disputes—from Past to Present' (*Verfassungsblog*, 23 July 2020) <https://verfassungsblog.de/the-africanization-of-international-investment-disputes-from-past-to-present/> (accessed 8 May 2026).

[33] See M Tsamenyi and K Ali, 'African States and the Law of the Sea Convention: Have the Benefits Been Realized' (2012) 26 Ocean Yearbook 113; A Proelss, 'Article 55' in A Proelss (ed), *United Nations Convention on the Law of the Sea. A Commentary* (CH Beck, Hart, Nomos 2017) 413–14.

[34] ILC, 'Guide to Practice on Reservations to Treaties, Report of the International Law Commission' (2011) UN Doc A/66/10/Add. 1, 209; C Walter, 'Article 19' in O Dörr and K Schmalenbach (eds), *The Vienna Convention on the Law of Treaties: A Commentary* (2nd edn, Springer 2018) 266–68, 272–73.

[35] L Boisson de Chazournes, *Interactions Between Regional and Universal Organizations—A Legal Perspective* (Brill 2017) 31.

[36] UN Convention on the Rights of the Child (adopted 20 November 1989, entered into force 2 September 1990) 1577 UNTS 3: 'Such care could include, inter alia, foster placement, kafalah of Islamic law, adoption or if necessary placement in suitable institutions for the care of children.'

[37] E Denza, 'Article 41' in *Diplomatic Law: Commentary on the Vienna Convention on Diplomatic Relations* (4th edn, OUP 2016) 384.

[38] See eg UN Charter, arts 33, 52–54; 1994 GATT, art XXIV; 1968 Non-Proliferation Treaty, art VII; UNCLOS, art 282; Convention on the Rights of Persons with Disabilities (adopted 13 December 2006, entered into force 3 May 2008) 2515 UNTS 3, art 44; Convention on Biological Diversity (adopted 5 June 1992, entered into force 29 December 1993) 1760 UNTS 79, art 34.

'regional exceptionalism').[39] Such contestation often takes the form of regional resistance to universal agreements, with both its manifestation and legal implications under the secondary rules of international law depending on whether the States concerned are already bound by the agreement.

In certain cases, regional resistance has directly obstructed the adoption of universal agreements. The projects of the International Law Commission (ILC) on the 'Protection of Persons in the Event of Disaster' and on the 'Expulsion of Aliens', for instance, did not result in the conclusion of treaties, largely because States pointed to existing regional treaties or emphasized regional specificities.[40] Regional resistance has also hindered the widespread ratification of international agreements with universal aspirations, such as the 1990 International Convention on the Protection of the Rights of All Migrant Workers and Members of Their Families,[41] which has been ratified by only 56 States, primarily from Africa and Latin America, while many States from Asia, Europe, and North America have refrained from doing so. In other cases, regional resistance has led to a regionally diverging application of universal agreement, for example, where a regional group of States become parties to an agreement but insist on limiting or conditioning its application, notably through reservations that restrict the application of certain treaty provisions.[42] Some universal agreements have also faced collective withdrawal by regional groups of States. Two prominent examples in recent history include the withdrawal of several Latin American countries from the Convention on the Settlement of Investment Disputes between States and Nationals of Other States (ICSID Convention) in 2007[43] and the withdrawal of African Union (AU) member States from the 1998 Rome Statute.[44]

States are, of course, free not to enter into international agreements,[45] to submit reservations,[46] or to withdraw from such agreements[47] in accordance with the

[39] See eg TV Ananthavinayagan, 'Breaking Bad Customs: Involving the Idea of *Opinio Juris Communis* in Asian State Practice' (2018) 24 AYIL 24, 34–35, arguing that UNCLOS was shaped by Western powers.

[40] See S Sivakumaran, 'Techniques in International Law-Making: Extrapolation, Analogy, Form and the Emergence of an International Law of Disaster Relief' (2017) 28 EJIL 1097, 1100–101; States in the Sixth Committee of the UNGA expressed reluctance with respect to 'identify[ing] general rules of international law on the expulsion of aliens, since there already existed detailed regional rules on the subject' (ILC, 'Topical summary of the discussion held in the Sixth Committee' (2013) UN Doc A/CN.4/657 [4]).

[41] International Convention on the Protection of the Rights of All Migrant Workers and Members of Their Families (adopted 18 December 1990, entered into force on 1 July 2003) 2220 UNTS 3.

[42] See eg on the practice of Arab States with respect to CEDAW: M Bydoon, 'Reservations on the "Convention on the Elimination of All Forms of Discrimination against Women (CEDAW)" Based on Islam and its Practical Application in Jordan: Legal Perspectives' (2011) 25 Arab LQ 51.

[43] On this, see A Tzanakopoulos, 'Denunciation of the ICSID Convention under the General International Law of Treaties' in R Hofmann and CJ Tams (eds), *International Investment Law and General International Law From Clinical Isolation to Systemic Integration?* (Nomos 2011) 75.

[44] See C McLachlan, 'The Assault on International Adjudication and the Limits of Withdrawal' (2019) 68 ICLQ 499, 506–507.

[45] See also *The Case of the SS 'Lotus'* (Judgment) [1927] PCIJ Series A, No 10, 18.

[46] VCLT, arts 19–23.

[47] VCLT, art 56.

rules reflected in the VCLT. Accordingly, the most difficult form of regional resistance to a universal treaty involves regionally co-ordinated, idiosyncratic interpretations and applications of its provisions, which raise doubts whether those still fall within the treaty's scope or cross the line to collective non-compliance. There are numerous examples of regional practice which challenge arguably orthodox understandings of provisions contained in universal treaties. For instance, the understanding of Article 5 UNCLOS as allowing for 'fixed baselines' in the face of climate change-induced sea-level rise as put forward, inter alia, by the Pacific Islands Forum (PIF) challenged the long-standing view of Article 5 as providing for 'ambulatory baselines'.[48] In response to alleged activities of the 'Shadow fleet' in the Baltic Sea, several States in the Baltic region have, through their conduct, indicated a 'possible willingness to reinterpret, inter alia, UNCLOS Articles 56, 79, and 221 in favour of broader coastal State competence'.[49] Another example concerns the interpretation of Articles 27(2) and 98(1) of the Rome Statute by the AU and the League of Arab States as leaving unimpaired the immunity *ratione personae* of heads of States of non-parties to the Rome Statute before the International Criminal Court (ICC).[50] Regional trade agreements have been considered as challenging the conditions set out in Article XXIV of the General Agreement on Tariffs and Trade (GATT).[51] Since the establishment of the UN Charter, regional arrangements have frequently tested the limits for regional military actions contained in chapters VII and VIII of the UN Charter.[52]

Regional contestation through diverging practice is particularly difficult to address due to its ambivalent character. As famously stated by the International Court of Justice (ICJ) in its 1986 *Nicaragua v US* judgment, not every prima facie

[48] See Pacific Islands Forum, 'Declaration on Preserving Maritime Zones in the Face of Climate Change-related Sea-Level Rise' (12 August 2021) <https://forumsec.org/sites/default/files/2024-05/2021%20Declaration-on-Preserving-Maritime-Zones.pdf> (accessed 11 May 2026). On the 'ambulatory' understanding, see eg ILA, 'Final Report of the ILA Committee on baselines under the international law of the Sea' (Sofia 2012) 31. See section 7.3.2.5 for a discussion of how this debate evolved, as reflected particularly in the advisory opinion on *Obligations of States in respect of Climate Change* delivered by the ICJ in 2025.

[49] J Hartmann and A Lott, 'The Prosecution "Gap" for Attacks on Subsea Cables and Pipelines' (EJILTalk! 13 November 2025) <https://www.ejiltalk.org/the-prosecution-gap-for-attacks-on-subsea-cables-and-pipelines/> (accessed 11 May 2026).

[50] See eg 'The League of Arab States' Observations on the Hashemite Kingdom of Jordan's appeal' (16 July 2018) ICC-02/05-01/09-367 [17]–[19], [26]–[32]; 'The African Union's Submission in the 'Hashemite Kingdom of Jordan's Appeal' (16 July 2018) ICC-02/05-01/09-370 [9], [18].

[51] See G Marceau and C Reimann, 'When and How is a Regional Trade Agreement Compatible With the WTO?' (2001) 28 LIEI 297; MQ Zang, 'When the Multilateral Meets the Regionals: Regional Trade Agreements at WTO Dispute Settlement' (2019) 18 World Trade Rev 33.

[52] See eg the role of regional institutions and treaties in numerous examples discussed in T Ruys, O Corten, A Hofer (eds), *The Use of Force in International Law: A Case-Based Approach* (OUP 2018), including the military interventions involving the Warsaw Pact Treaty in Hungary (1956) and in Czechoslovakia (1968), the OAS in the Dominican Republic (1965), the OECS in Grenada (1983), ECOWAS in Liberia (1990), Sierra Leone (1997–99), and The Gambia (2016), as well as by NATO members States in Kosovo (1999), Afghanistan (2001), and Libya (2011).

instance of non-compliance necessarily undermines the rule in question. Instead, the ICJ emphasized that

> [i]f a State acts in a way *prima facie* incompatible with a recognized rule, but defends its conduct by appealing to exceptions or justifications contained within the rule itself, then whether or not the State's conduct is in fact justifiable on that basis, the significance of that attitude is to confirm rather than to weaken the rule.[53]

The ICJ even acknowledged that '[r]eliance by a State on a novel right or an unprecedented exception to the principle might, if shared in principle by other States, tend towards a modification of customary international law'.[54]

This raises the question of the parameters, the secondary rules, that decide whether regional practice—whether compliant or non-compliant—serves to confirm the rule contained in a universal agreement or even to 'reform' it, or instead 'deforms' and weakens it.

7.3.1 Amendment and modification of universal treaties and regional practice

The parameters for the amendment or modification of an international agreement are set out in Articles 39 to 41 of the VCLT,[55] which reflect both the general rules on amendments (Articles 39, 40) and on modifications *inter se* (Articles 39, 41) of multilateral treaties.[56] However, they are of a purely residual nature. Many universal agreements contain special provisions on amendments and modifications. Framework agreements tend to be particularly permissive in this regard, often allowing for *inter se* modifications, including through regional agreements, which then effectively introduce *ex post* exceptions specifically for regional institutions into the universal treaty.[57] In his third report on the law of treaties of 1964 Humphrey Waldock highlighted the pivotal role of limited groups of States parties to a multilateral treaty in its reform observing that

> reliance on the *inter se* technique for the revision of general multilateral treaties is almost inevitable owing to the improbability that all the Parties to the original

[53] *Military and Paramilitary Activities in and against Nicaragua (Nicaragua v United States)* (Merits) [1986] ICJ Rep 14 [186].

[54] 1986] ICJ Rep 14 [207].

[55] On Article 41, see also chapter 6, section 6.3.3.1.

[56] See M Fitzmaurice and P Merkouris, *Treaties in Motion: The Evolution of Treaties from Formation to Termination* (CUP 2020) 182–83, 187–88, 227, on the blurred distinction between amendment, modification, and revision.

[57] See Chapter 6, section 6.3.3.1.

> treaties will take the necessary steps to ratify or otherwise give their consent to the new treaty.[58]

However, many universal agreements do not contain provisions allowing for *inter se* modification. Instead, they provide for amendment procedures, which establish high procedural hurdles, such as Articles 108–109 of the UN Charter[59] and Articles 312–16 of UNCLOS[60]. Regional initiatives can exert pressure for the amendment of these agreements by taking the lead in reform initiatives. However, securing sufficient cross-regional support among member States for an amendment of a multilateral treaty is typically difficult. The UN Charter, for example, has been amended only five times in the almost 80 years since its conclusion.[61] As a result, mechanisms for informal change are central to how multilateral agreements evolve in practice.[62]

7.3.2 Change through regional practice: between modification and interpretation

Many examples of regional practice under a universal agreement ultimately boil down to the seemingly simple question of how to distinguish between divergent regional practice that reflects, or even brings about informal change to a universal agreement and regional practice that merely violates its provisions.

Although informal change of a treaty's text through practice may be considered as an alternative to its amendment, this does not necessarily imply that the threshold for establishing the consent of States parties to any such informal change is lower, or that consent can be dispensed with.[63] The secondary rules governing such informal change simply determine the existence of such consent differently—that is, by assessing whether a particular development in State practice is sufficient to change the meaning given to a treaty's text. For determining whether a certain practice informally changes the text of a treaty, different rules apply depending on whether that practice implies merely an interpretation of the text (ie, a changed

[58] ILC, 'Third Report on the Law of Treaties, by Sir Humphrey Waldock, Special Rapporteur' (1964) YBILC II, UN Doc A/CN.4/167, 49.

[59] See S Vöneky, 'Article 108' (n 13); S Vöneky, 'Article 109' in B Simma and others (eds), *The Charter of the United Nations: A Commentary, Volume II* (4th edn, OUP 2024).

[60] See A Boyle, 'Further Development Of The Law Of The Sea Convention: Mechanisms For Change' (2005) 54 ICLQ 563, 564.

[61] See Vöneky, 'Article 108' (n 13) [3].

[62] See Institut de droit international, Resolution on 'Limits to Evolutive Interpretation of the Constituent Instruments of the Organizations within the United Nations System by their Internal Organs' (adopted 4 September 2021); ILC, 'Study Group under the Chairmanship of G Nolte, Treaties Over Time, in Particular: Subsequent Agreement and Practice' (2008) UN Doc A/63/10 ('ILC, Treaties over Time (2008)'); Boyle (n 60).

[63] See also Vöneky, 'Article 108' (n 13) [13].

understanding of the provision that can still be grounded in the (presumed) intention of the parties to the treaty at the time of its conclusion)[64] or an informal modification of the text (ie, an understanding that changes the meaning given to the text by the parties to the treaty at the time of its conclusion). However, 'the dividing line between the interpretation and the amendment or modification of a treaty is in practice sometimes "difficult, if not impossible, to fix."'[65] As stated by the ILC commentaries on 'Subsequent agreements and subsequent practice in relation to the interpretation of treaties' (SASP), a modification of a treaty through practice is not to be presumed.[66]

The subsequent sections illustrate that secondary rules considerably restrict the role of regional practice in the informal *modification* of universal agreements (7.3.2.1 to 7.3.2.2). At the same time, they show that regional practice has, in certain cases, been recognized as pushing the limits of what still constitutes an admissible *interpretation* further than other forms of collective practice; thereby allowing for a certain trailblazing role of regional practice without necessarily crossing the line to regional exceptionalism (7.3.2.3 and 7.3.2.4).

7.3.2.1 Tacit amendment

Subsequent conduct of States that deviates from the provisions of the universal agreement, can, in theory, amount to a (tacit) agreement to amend the treaty pursuant to Article 39 of the VCLT.[67] Article 39 provides that

> [a] treaty may be amended by agreement between the parties. The rules laid down in Part II apply to such an agreement except insofar as the treaty may otherwise provide.

However, the proposition that regional practice may constitute a tacit agreement to informally amend a universal agreement is problematic in several respects.

Firstly, most universal agreements contain specific amendment procedures that supersede Articles 39 and 41 of the VCLT.[68] For the latter to remain applicable, these special amendment provisions would have to be interpreted as leaving intact the possibility of subsequent amendment through a 'simple' agreement between the parties, in accordance with the principle of *lex specialis*. Unless such an intention can be clearly established, any modification by way of an 'agreement' would effectively circumvent the special procedures prescribed in the treaty.

[64] See Chapter 4, section 4.3.1.

[65] ILC Report 2018 (SASP) (n 7) 60 citing, inter alia, I Sinclair, *The Vienna Convention on the Law of Treaties* (Manchester University Press 1984) 13 and others.

[66] See ILC Report 2018 (SASP) (n 7) commentary on conclusion 7(3), 55; Fitzmaurice and Merkouris (n 56) 231.

[67] V Koutroulis, 'Article 39' in O Corten and others (eds), *The Vienna Conventions on the Law of Treaties* (2nd edn, OUP 2025) [37]–[44].

[68] See Fitzmaurice and Merkouris (n 56) 195–202.

Secondly, the *travaux préparatoires* of the VCLT cast doubt on whether the term 'agreement' in Article 39 of the VCLT encompasses tacit agreements arising from the subsequent conduct of States parties. During the Vienna Conference, many States rejected draft Article 38 ('Modification of treaties by subsequent practice'), which provided that '[a] treaty may be modified by subsequent practice in the application of the treaty establishing the agreement of the parties to modify its provisions'.[69] Draft Article 38 was ultimately not adopted, precisely because many States did not wish to address the complex relationship between customary and treaty law and pointed to the risk for the stability of treaties.[70]

Thirdly, viewed in its normative context, there is little support for an amendment of *multilateral* agreements through a *tacit* agreement based on Article 39 of the VCLT. Article 40 of the VCLT contains additional requirements for the amendment of multilateral treaties, which suggests that Article 39 applies as *lex generalis* mainly to bilateral treaties. The ILC's proposal for draft Article 38 was indeed inspired by the practice of modification of bilateral, not multilateral, agreements, notably by the 1963 Award in the Air Transport Services agreement between the US and France, and territorial treaties.[71] Caution regarding tacit amendment of multilateral treaties through subsequent custom is also reflected in the approach of the ICJ in this regard. Rather than determining, in a given case, whether subsequent custom tacitly amends such a treaty, the Court has consistently held that the rule under the treaty and the rule under customary international law 'retain a separate existence'[72] and 'should, to the extent possible, be interpreted so as to give rise to a single set of compatible obligations'.[73]

Fourthly, specifically with respect to the possibility of amending multilateral agreements through *regional* practice, caution is warranted in light of historical experience. The drafting of Articles 39 to 41 was heavily influenced by the negative experiences of many States with the practice of the 'Concert of Europe', which frequently modified multilateral treaties without involving the other parties.[74]

Thus, as the next sections show, States, presumably to avoid (the impression of) circumventing the procedures established for amending and modifying treaties set out in the respective treaties, in the VCLT, and in customary international law,

[69] ILC, 'Documents of the second part of the seventeenth session and of the eighteenth session including the reports of the Commission to the General Assembly' (1966) YBILC II, UN Doc A/CN.4/SER.A/1966/Add.l ('ILC 1966 (II) YBILC') 236.

[70] UNCLOT I 207–15 (debate of delegations on draft Article 38); see also Fitzmaurice and Merkouris (n 56) 220–21.

[71] ILC 1966 (II) YBILC (n 69) 236; see also Fitzmaurice and Merkouris (n 56) 218.

[72] *Nicaragua v United States* (n 53) [178].

[73] *Obligations of States in respect of Climate Change* (Advisory Opinion of 23 July 2025) [165] and [310]; see also *Legal Consequences for States of the Continued Presence of South Africa in Namibia (South West Africa) notwithstanding Security Council Resolution 276 (1970)* (Advisory Opinion) [1971] ICJ Rep 16 [53].

[74] ILC, 'Third Report on the Law of Treaties' (n 58) 48 [4], Fitzmaurice and Merkouris (n 56) 189.

rather base such alleged changes on more specific and narrowly defined mechanisms for informal change.

7.3.2.2 *Desuetudo* and obsolescence

The first two more narrowly defined mechanisms for change through practice concern the concepts of *desuetudo* and obsolescence. *Desuetudo* refers to the termination of treaty rules because of continuous non-application (non-enforcement or non-compliance) over a substantial period of time, accompanied by *vacatio legis*.[75] *Desuetudo* should be distinguished from obsolescence, whereby a provision is terminated because events occurring since its adoption render its execution unjust or senseless.[76] Although the ILC Study Group on 'Treaties over Time', regarded the concept of obsolescence as 'particularly significant with regard to law-making treaties',[77] it did not pursue this potential avenue of informal treaty reform any further. In relation to the UN Charter, the prevailing view among commentators seems to be that the persistent non-application of the so-called 'enemy State' clauses contained in Articles 53, 77, and 107 of the UN Charter 'may affect its normative validity'.[78] Similarly, Article 46 of the UN Charter has been described as 'the most obsolete of all those provisions of Chapter VII which have been overtaken by historical events and replaced with more flexible peacekeeping arrangements'.[79]

However, States and commentators are hesitant to declare the provisions definitively inapplicable without a formal amendment of the UN Charter. The inconclusive practice thus suggests that the threshold for assuming the termination of certain provisions is high. This aligns with the view that the rules governing the termination of treaties, as set out by the treaties themselves and in the VCLT, should not be circumvented, lest the stability of treaty relations be undermined. In practice, moreover, it is often difficult to draw a clear distinction between mere non-application due to a temporary lack of opportunity—regardless of its duration—and a definitive loss of purpose that renders the provision's revival entirely improbable. In the context of regional practice, the relevance of these two concepts is even more limited, as it would have to be demonstrated that, across regions, certain provisions have consistently not been applied or complied with.

7.3.2.3 Established practice

To the extent that regional practice relates to a universal agreement that also serves as the constituent instrument of an IO, such practice may be evidence for

[75] Vöneky (n 13) [13] with further references. See also W Karl, *Vertrag und spätere Praxis im Völkerrecht. Zum Einfluß der Praxis auf Inhalt und Bestand völkerrechtlicher Verträge* (Springer 1983) 257–68.

[76] Vöneky (n 13) [13].

[77] ILC, Treaties over Time (n 62) 153 [10].

[78] Rensmann (n 10) [17].

[79] G Novak and A Reinisch, 'Article 46' in B Simma and others (eds), *The Charter of the United Nations: A Commentary, Volume I* (4th edn, OUP 2024) [3].

an 'established practice'. 'Established practice' has been defined as the 'customary law of the organization'.[80] As their 'most dynamic component',[81] 'established practice' forms part of the 'rules of the organization' (Article 2(1)(j) of the 1986 VCLT). The 'rules of the organization', for their part, continue to apply to the interpretation and modification of constituent instruments of IOs alongside the general rules on the law of treaties reflected in the VCLT (Article 5 of the 1969 VCLT).[82] The precise meaning and scope of such 'established practice' remains, however, unclear, as does the extent to which it must be accompanied by some form of acceptance by member States.[83] According to Shabtai Rosenne,

> the practice of the organization does not operate in the same way as the subsequent conduct of the parties to a treaty as a guide to interpretation, though there may be a certain functional similarity between the two processes . . . [I]t is the ensemble of the action of the organ in question, or indeed of the Organizations as a whole . . . that constitutes the living interpretation of the constituent instrument, the 'established practice of the organization' in the words of the 1986 Vienna Convention.[84]

Christopher Peters has argued that the term 'established practice' has a double function. On the one hand, it amounts to 'quasi-custom' which does not only serve to interpret but can also modify the secondary rules embodied in the general law of treaties for constituent instruments. In this regard, it can even lower the requirements for subsequent practice under Article 31(3)(b) of the VCLT[85] to the extent that 'an express or implied agreement of all Member States would not be necessary'.[86] On the other hand, 'established practice' as 'autonomous organ practice' can also substantively modify the provisions contained in the constituent instrument.[87] Although the scope and legal effect of 'established practice' is, to date, unclear, regional practice may be considered as 'established practice' where, firstly, it can be considered as the practice of an organ of the IO set up by that universal agreement, secondly, where such practice relates to the procedure on the basis of the organ fulfils its mandate under the constituent instrument, thirdly, where such practice is of a certain duration and, fourthly, where such practice does not meet with protest by member States or other organs of the IO. Accordingly, 'established

[80] N Blokker, 'Legal Facets of the Practice of International Organizations' (2024) 435 RdC 73, 125–26.
[81] Blokker (n 80) 122.
[82] See generally: Blokker (n 80) 95–130; Barkholdt (n 7) 36.
[83] Bordin (n 14) 73, 75–75, fn 12.
[84] S Rosenne, *Developments in the Law of Treaties 1945–1986* (CUP 1989) 241.
[85] C Peters, *Praxis Internationaler Organisationen—Vertragswandel und völkerrechtlicher Ordnungsrahmen* (Springer 2016) 181.
[86] C Peters, 'Subsequent Practice and Established Practice of International Organizations: Two Sides of the Same Coin' (2011) 3 GOJIL 617, 642.
[87] Peters (n 85) 181; Peters (2011) (n 86).

practice' might also apply to practice attributable to regional institutions that are integrated within the constituent instrument and endowed with a specific function by the constituent instrument of the IO with a view to fulfilling the IO's mandate. In this regard, their institutional role is hybrid: on the one hand, they function as a quasi-organ of the IO; on the other hand, they operate as a third party, often not even a member of the IO in question.[88] To the extent that the practice of those regional institutions pertains to their function as an organ of that institution, notably with respect to its methods of work or procedural provisions, its practice may consolidate into an 'established practice' which can—like 'quasi-custom'—lead to an interpretation of the provisions set out in the constituent instrument that comes close to their modification.

Examples for such practice may include the practice of regional arrangements regarding the non-application of the reporting obligation under Article 54 of the UN Charter which envisages that regional arrangements keep the UNSC 'fully informed of activities undertaken or in contemplation'. According to Walter, 'the practice of notification . . . still does not correspond to the intention of Art. 54' while

> the SC has never criticized a regional arrangement or agency for not fulfilling its reporting obligation under Art. 54. Thus, it has so far been left to the regional arrangements and agencies to determine which type of information they convey to the SC. The SC seems to have acquiesced to the rather restricted reporting practice.[89]

7.3.2.4 Subsequent practice

Where the regional practice cannot be regarded as 'established practice', it may nonetheless be considered as 'subsequent practice' under Articles 31(3)(b) or 32 of the VCLT. Although both provisions concern subsequent practice,[90] they differ in three important respects: the extent to which such (here: regional) practice must or, alternatively, may be considered in the interpretation of a given treaty, its interpretive weight in interpreting the treaty, and the criteria that such practice must satisfy to be considered.

Only regional practice that falls within the scope of Article 31(3) of the VCLT must be considered in the interpretation of a treaty. This follows from the text of the *chapeau* of Article 31(3) of the VCLT, which provides that 'subsequent agreements' (Article 31(3)(a)), 'subsequent practice' (Article 31(3)(b)) and 'any relevant

[88] This hybrid role of regional IOs mirrors the hybrid nature, both conventional and institutional, of constituent instruments establishing international organizations, see *Legality of the Use by a State of Nuclear Weapons in Armed Conflict* (Advisory Opinion) [1996] ICJ Rep 66 [19].

[89] C Walter, 'Article 54' in B Simma and others (eds), *The Charter of the United Nations: A Commentary, Volume II* (4th edn, OUP 2024) [24]–[25].

[90] See also ILC Report 2018 (SASP) (n 7) Conclusion 2(1); *Right to Strike under ILO Convention No. 87* (Advisory Opinion of 21 May 2026) ICJ [112]–[115].

rules of international law' (Article 31(3)(c))[91] 'shall be taken into account, together with the context' in the interpretation of a treaty. With respect to regional practice, Article 31(3)(a) seems to be less relevant given that the ILC stated, in 2018, that this provision was 'limited to a common act or undertaking between all the parties'.[92] At the same time, the ILC also clarified that

> [d]ifferent later agreements between a limited number of parties that, taken together, establish an agreement between all the parties regarding the interpretation of a treaty constitute subsequent practice under article 31, paragraph 3(b).[93]

Accordingly, several subsequent regional agreements concluded by parties to a universal treaty may, taken together, constitute subsequent practice under Article 31(3)(b). As 'objective evidence of the understanding of the parties as to the meaning of the treaty',[94] subsequent practice under Article 31(3)(b) constitutes an 'authentic means' of interpretation and requires that such practice is taken into account.[95] In this regard, subsequent practice that falls within the scope of Article 31(3)(b) differs from subsequent practice under Article 32 VCLT as a 'supplementary means' of interpretation, to which recourse 'may be had'.[96]

Depending on whether regional practice qualifies as subsequent practice under Article 31(3)(b) or Article 32, the interpretive weight accorded to it differs significantly. Both 'contribute, in their interaction with other means in the process of interpretation, to the clarification of the meaning of a treaty'.[97] The *chapeau* of Article 31(3), 'shall be taken into account, *together with the context*' underlines that such an agreement or practice is not 'necessarily conclusive in the sense that it overrides all other means of interpretation'.[98] However, while subsequent practice under Article 31(3) serves to 'determine' the meaning of a text, Article 32 serves to 'confirm a meaning arrived at under article 31'.[99]

In light of the two preceding points, it is unsurprising that the threshold for regional practice to qualify under Article 31(3)(b) is higher than that required for its consideration under Article 32. The term 'parties' as used in Article 31(3)(b) refers to the practice of 'all parties'.[100] By contrast, subsequent practice under Article 32 also includes 'conduct by one or more parties in the application of the treaty'.[101]

[91] See section 7.3.3.1 infra.
[92] ILC Report 2018 (SASP) (n 7) Commentary on Conclusion 4, 30.
[93] ILC (n 92).
[94] ILC (n 92), Conclusion 3.
[95] ILC (n 92) 25–26; see also ILC 1966 (II) YBILC (n 69) 221 [14]–[15].
[96] ILC (n 92), Conclusion 2(4). See also on Article 32 section 7.3.3.3.
[97] ILC (n 92) 48.
[98] ILC (n 92) 25.
[99] ILC (n 92) 50.
[100] ILC Report 2018 (SASP) (n 7) Commentary on Conclusion 4(1), 31.
[101] ILC Report 2018 (SASP) (n 7), Conclusion 4(3).

Still, this does not mean that regional practice cannot give rise to subsequent practice under Article 31(3)(b). Article 31(3)(b) does not require that an agreement between all parties is based on 'positive acts' by every single party to the treaty.[102] Already in 1966, the ILC made clear that '[i]t omitted the word 'all' merely to avoid any possible misconception that every party must individually have engaged in the practice where it suffices that it should have accepted the practice'.[103] This was confirmed in Conclusion 10(2) of the ILC Conclusions on SASP in 2018, which states that

> [t]he number of parties that must actively engage in subsequent practice in order to establish an agreement under article 31, paragraph 3 (b), may vary. Silence on the part of one or more parties may constitute acceptance of the subsequent practice when the circumstances call for some reaction.

Thus, although regional practice, as such, does not amount to the practice of 'all parties', it can still be considered as subsequent practice under Article 31(3)(b) where such practice gives rise to 'circumstances' that 'call for some reaction' by the other parties, and those parties fail to react to the regional practice.

This is supported, for example, by the 2014 decision of the International Tribunal for the Law of the Sea (ITLOS) in *M/V 'Virginia G' (Panama/Guinea-Bissau)*, in which the Tribunal considered the extent to which the coastal State, Guinea-Bissau, was permitted to regulate the bunkering (refuelling) of foreign vessels fishing in its EEZ and, for that purpose, interpreted Articles 56 and 62(4) of UNCLOS.[104] The Tribunal concluded that

> the regulation by a coastal State of bunkering of foreign vessels fishing in its exclusive economic zone is among those measures which the coastal State may take in its exclusive economic zone to conserve and manage its living resources under article 56 of the Convention read together with article 62, paragraph 4, of the Convention. This view is also confirmed by State practice which has developed after the adoption of the Convention . . . the national legislation of several States, not only in the West African region, but also in some other regions of the world, regulates bunkering of foreign vessels fishing in their exclusive economic zones in a way comparable to that of Guinea-Bissau. The Tribunal further notes that there is no manifest objection to such legislation and that it is, in general, complied with.[105]

[102] G Nolte, 'Treaties and Their Practice: Symptoms of their Rise or Decline' (2017) 392 RdC 205, 344.

[103] ILC 1966 (II) YBILC (n 69) 222 [15].

[104] *The M/V 'Virginia G' Case (Panama/Guinea-Bissau)* (Judgment of 14 April 2014) ITLOS Reports 2014, 4.

[105] *The M/V 'Virginia G' Case* (n 104) [217]–[218].

Although the tribunal did not expressly refer to Article 31(3)(b) of the VCLT, and its use of the term 'confirm' suggests recourse under Article 32, the way in which it considered regional practice essentially mirrored the two criteria for considering regional practice as subsequent practice under Article 31(3)(b), that is, the existence of regional practice under the treaty and a failure to react by the other parties to that treaty.

Another example concerns the interpretation of UNCLOS in light of climate change induced sea-level rise, in particular its impact on States' baselines and maritime entitlements.[106] This issue was addressed by the ICJ in its 2025 advisory opinion on the *Obligations of States in Respect of Climate Change*. Prior to the Court's opinion, the point of contention among States and commentators had included, inter alia, whether Article 5 of UNCLOS provides for ambulatory baselines or, in the context of sea-level rise, allows States to 'fix' their baselines.[107] In its advisory opinion, the ICJ 'observe[d] that UNCLOS does not contain provisions requiring States parties to update normal baselines that have been marked (Article 5)'.[108] In support of this interpretation, the ICJ 'consider[ed] relevant for the purposes of the interpretation of UNCLOS'

> regional and cross-regional declarations, such as, among others, the 2021 Declaration of the Pacific Islands Forum on Preserving Maritime Zones in the Face of Climate Change-Related Sea-Level Rise, supported in 2022 by the member States of the Organization of African, Caribbean and Pacific States[109]

and

> a convergence of views among States across all regions in support of the absence of an obligation of States parties to UNCLOS to update charts or lists of geographical co-ordinates relating to their maritime zones once they have been duly established.[110]

Some have understood this finding of the Court as implicitly confirming that Article 5 of UNCLOS allows States to fix their baselines and thereby preserve their maritime entitlements.[111] However, given that the Court confined itself to noting the absence of an obligation to update charts and lists of co-ordinates, and

[106] See also ILC, 'Report of the International Law Commission to the General Assembly on the work of its seventy-sixth session' (2025) UN Doc A/80/10 [60] referring to Article 31(3)(b) as a means for interpreting the law of the sea relating to climate change.

[107] ILC, 'Additional paper to the first issues paper on sea-level rise in relation to international law by Bogdan Aurescu and Nilüfer Oral' (2023) UN Doc A/CN.4/761 [17]–[98]; ILA, 'Final report of the ILA Committee on international law and sea-level rise' (Athens 2024) 41–45.

[108] *Climate Change* (n 73) [359].

[109] *Climate Change* (n 73) [360].

[110] *Climate Change* (n 73) [361].

[111] See eg *Climate Change* (n 73) (separate opinion of Judge Aurescu) [5]; N Khng, 'The World Court on Law of the Sea and Statehood in the Context of Climate Change-Related Sea-Level Rise' (EJILTalk!

considering that these arguably do not, as such, constitute the source of maritime entitlements,[112] the opinion could also be read as if this question was left open by the Court. For present purposes, it is, in any event, not necessary to determine the full extent of the Court's substantive finding. Whether the interpretation relates solely to the obligation to update charts and lists, or extends further, this example illustrates the two criteria discussed above for considering regional practice under Article 31(3)(b): the Court relied on widespread regional practice to determine the existence of an obligation to update charts or lists of co-ordinates under UNCLOS. Although the Court did not explicitly refer to the absence of protest by States that did not actively engage in such practice, such lack of protest was noted by Judge Aurescu in his separate opinion.[113]

Article 31(3)(b) of the VCLT may also provide a basis for explaining the significant evolution of the scope of Article XXIV of the GATT 1994.[114] In 2000, a note by the WTO Secretariat argued that

> a further re-interpretation of the rules drafted 50 years ago would not suffice to take into account the fundamental changes observed in the nature and scope (both geographical and in terms of coverage) of RTAs and their increasingly overlapping membership.[115]

Since then, such regional practice has, however, continued. Alberta Fabbricotti, for example, observed that 'RTAs systematically disobey Article XXIV's requirements in a disguised or indirect manner'.[116] The evolution of Article XXIV in light of such practice can, to some extent, be considered under Article 31(3)(b). For one, all WTO member States are party to at least one regional trade agreement (RTA); thus, participate in regional practice under the GATT 1994.[117] At the same time, they are kept informed of the existence and content of these RTAs entered into by other member States. As Michelle Zang points out, WTO members are required to notify RTAs in which they participate pursuant to the RTA transparency mechanism and that

17 November 2025) <https://www.ejiltalk.org/the-world-court-on-law-of-the-sea-and-statehood-in-the-context-fo-climate-change-related-sea-level-rise/> (accessed 11 May 2026).

[112] *North Sea Continental Shelf (Federal Republic of Germany/Denmark)* [1969] ICJ Rep 3 [96]; see on the role of maps in the context of territorial disputes: *Frontier Dispute (Burkina Faso/Republic of Mali) (Judgment)* [1986] ICJ Rep 554 [54].

[113] *Climate Change* (n 73) (separate opinion of Judge Aurescu) [6] and [11].

[114] On this issue: Marceau and Reimann (n 51); Zang (n 51).

[115] WTO Committee on Regional Trade Agreements, Synopsis of 'Systemic' Issues Related to Regional Trade Agreements—Note by the Secretariat (2 March 2000) WT/REG/W/37 [5].

[116] A Fabbricotti, 'The Interplay Between the WTO and the RTAs: Is It A Question of Interrelation Between Different Sources of International Law?', Inaugural Conference of the Society of International Economic Law (Geneva, 15–17 July 2008) <https://ssrn.com/abstract=1151386> (accessed 11 May 2026) 2.

[117] Zang (n 51) 50.

> [t]hrough such institutional establishment, WTO membership is assumingly well informed of RTA policies that deviate from the standard WTO commitments and is offered a number of occasions and opportunities to comment or even object before it becomes necessary to initiate a formal complaint at the dispute settlement.[118]

Nonetheless, disputes over obligation conflict between RTAs and the WTO are relatively rare.[119] Accordingly, such practice could be considered as a form of subsequent practice under Article 31(3)(b) adapting the text of Article XXIV through the combination of regional practice under the RTAs and the absence of protest by other parties to the WTO Covered Agreements.

At the same time, universal agreements have also withstood pressures for change arising from subsequent regional practice. This includes multiple attempts by some regional groups of States to extend the scope of Article 51 of the UN Charter to attacks by non-State actors.[120] However, since such regional practice has met with protest from several other parties, including other regional groups of States that are parties to the UN Charter,[121] it does not (yet) constitute regional practice that could give rise to subsequent practice under Article 31(3)(b).

7.3.3 Cross-referencing of regional rules: between representation and imposition

A related, but distinct issue from cases in which regional practice tests the limits of permissible interpretation or modification of a universal agreement concerns the use of regional rules, and their interpretation, in construing such agreements. International courts and tribunals frequently draw on regional practice, particularly the rules of regional counterparts and their interpretation by competent regional institutions. However, they rarely clarify the legal basis for such cross-referencing. Providing such justification, especially when referring to regional rules, can help prevent allegations of regional imbalance or the imposition of normative concepts that are not universally shared.[122]

[118] Zang (n 51) fn 64.

[119] See eg Appellate Body Report, *Turkey—Restrictions on Imports of Textile and Clothing Products* (22 October 1999) WT/DS29/AB [58]; Report of the Appellate Body, *Peru—Additional Duty on Imports of Certain Agricultural Products* (20 July 2015) WT/DS457/AB [5.115]–[5.117].

[120] See eg ILA, 'Final Report on Aggression and the Use of Force' (Sydney Conference 2018), 15.

[121] See eg Letter of the Permanent Mission of Mexico to the United Nations addressed to the Secretary-General and the President of the Security Council on Mexico's position paper on the interpretation and application of Article 51 of the Charter of the United Nations (10 January 2025) UN DocA/79/719 [20]. See also J Brunnée and S Toope, 'Self-Defence Against Non-State Actors: Are Powerful States Willing But Unable to Change International Law?' (2018) 67:2 ICLQ 263, 277.

[122] This section focuses on the extent to which the rules reflected in the VCLT provide a basis for referring to regional rules in the interpretation of a treaty. However, to the extent that decisions by regional courts or by courts in region are considered, these may also constitute subsidiary means in

7.3.3.1 Regional rules and systemic integration (Article 31(3)(c) VCLT)

Only in very limited cases does Article 31(3)(c) provide a basis for applying regional provisions when interpreting a universal treaty.

This provision requires, firstly, that regional rules qualify as 'rules under international law'. Whether this is indeed the case, however, is less clear than the text of Article 31(3)(c) might suggest. During the debates within the ILC in 1964, a number of members tried to limit the term 'any relevant rules of international law' to 'general rules'[123] or 'general principles of international law'.[124] The Commission eventually adopted the expression 'in the light of the general rules of international law in force at the time of its conclusion' on a provisional basis in 1964.[125] This formulation met with scepticism by Special Rapporteur Waldock himself[126] and seems to have resulted from the need to find a compromise given the insistence of Tunkin on the formulation 'basic principles of international law';[127] a formulation that was opposed by Castrén, de Luna, Jiménez de Aréchaga, and Yasseen.[128] Apart from Yasseen, these members argued that Tunkin's formulation would lead to an undesirable exclusion of regional law. This argument eventually convinced Tunkin in 1966 who stated that

> there were arguments for and against qualifying the rules of international law as 'general'. Mr. Castrén had rightly pointed out the need to take into account rules of a regional character that were binding on the parties.[129]

Furthermore, the United States criticized that 'the use of the term "general" before "international law" could add an element of confusion and should be eliminated'.[130] The ILC draft articles of 1966 suggested the formulation 'any relevant rules of international law', which met with agreement by States during the Vienna Conference.[131] This broader approach has been confirmed in later practice, eg, in the 2005 *Iron Rhine Arbitration* award where the tribunal understood 'European law' (EU secondary law, such as EU directives and regulations) as falling under

the sense of Article 38(1)(d) of the ICJ Statute. On this, see the on-going projection of the ILC on 'Subsidiary means for the determination of rules of international law'.

[123] ILC, 'Summary records of the sixteenth session' (1964) YBILC I UN Doc A/CN.4/SER.A/1964 ('(1964) YBILC I') 312 [32] (Verdross).

[124] ILC (n 123) 310 [9] (Ago).

[125] ILC, 'Documents of the sixteenth session including the report of the Commission to the General Assembly' (1964) YBILC II, UN Doc A/CN.4/SER.A/1964/ADD.1, 199–202 (draft Article 69(1)(b)).

[126] (1964) YBILC I (n 123) 310–11 [10], [26] (Waldock).

[127] (1964) YBILC I (n 123) 310 [8].

[128] (1964) YBILC I (n 123), Yasseen 310 [11], de Luna 310 [13]; ILC, 'Summary records of the eighteenth session from 4 May to 19 July 1966' (1966) YBILC I(2), UN Doc A/CN.4/SER.A/1966 ('(1966) YBILC I(2)'): Castrén 188 [49]; Jiménez de Aréchaga 190 [70].

[129] (1966) YBILC I(2) (n 128) 190 [64].

[130] ILC 1966 (II) YBILC (n 69) Annex A, 359.

[131] ILC 1966 (II) YBILC (n 69) 222 (draft Article 27(3)(c)).

'relevant rules of international law' when interpreting the (bilateral) Treaty of Separation between Belgium and the Netherlands of 1839.[132] The decision of the Tribunal to include (binding) resolutions of a regional IO, EU secondary law, further confirms that the term 'rules' is not restricted to the three traditional sources explicitly mentioned in Article 38(1) of the ICJ Statute. Yet, the extent to which the term 'rules' also encompasses binding decisions of international bodies, non-binding resolutions of IOs, and 'soft law' is less clear.[133] The ECtHR, for instance, has adopted a very broad understanding in the *Mamatkulov* decision.[134] In light of the purpose of Article 31(3)(c) VCLT to reflect a presumption of non-derogation, however, it appears more convincing to limit the term 'rule' to binding rules and decisions of international bodies.[135]

Article 31(3)(c) requires, secondly, that a given 'rule under international law' is 'applicable in relations between the parties' for it to be taken into account in the interpretation of a treaty. However, if 'between the parties' were construed as referring to '*all* the parties', the possibility of considering regional rules under Article 31(3)(c) in the interpretation of a universal agreement would be effectively precluded.

A textual and systematic interpretation of Article 31(3)(c) VCLT does not provide a definite answer in this regard. In contrast to Article 31(2)(a) VCLT, Article 31(3)(c) does not refer to 'all the parties', but only to 'parties'. Dörr and Villiger nonetheless favour a restrictive understanding of Article 31(3)(c) VCLT, according to which the rule in question needs to be applicable between all parties to the interpreted treaty.[136] Dörr points to a systematic understanding of Article 31(3) arguing that

> it would be incongruous to allow the interpretation of a treaty to be affected by rules of international law that are not applicable between all parties to the treaty, but not by a subsequent practice, which does not establish the agreement of all parties regarding the meaning of that treaty.

In a similar vein, the WTO panel in its 2006 Panel Report *EC—Biotech* held that

> it makes sense to interpret Article 31(3)(c) as requiring consideration of those rules of international law which are applicable in the relations between all parties

[132] *Iron Rhine Arbitration (Belgium/Netherlands)* (Award) PCA Case 2003-02 (24 May 2005) 28 [58].
[133] See examples from practice cited by O Dörr, 'Article 31' in O Dörr and K Schmalenbach (eds), *Vienna Convention on the Law of Treaties: A Commentary* (2nd edn, Springer 2018) [100]–[101].
[134] *Mamatkulov and Askarov v Turkey* App 46827/99 and 46951/99 (ECtHR, 4 February 2005) [111]–[120], where the ECtHR referred to decisions of other bodies on applications for interim measures, including the ICJ (and its Rules of Court), the UNHRC, the UNCAT, and the IACtHR.
[135] See P Merkouris, *Article 31(3)(c) VCLT and the Principle of Systemic Integration* (Brill Nijhoff 2015) 19–20, who, however, excludes judicial decisions.
[136] Dörr (n 133) [103]–[104]; M Villiger, *Commentary on the 1969 Vienna Convention on the Law of Treaties* (Martinus Nijhoff 2009) 'Article 31' [25].

> to the treaty which is being interpreted. Requiring that a treaty be interpreted in the light of other rules of international law which bind the States parties to the treaty ensures or enhances the consistency of the rules of international law applicable to these States and thus contributes to avoiding conflicts between the relevant rules.[137]

A similarly restrictive approach was adopted by the tribunal in the 2003 *OSPAR* award, which involved interpreting the regional 1992 Convention for the Protection of the Marine Environment of the North-East Atlantic ('OSPAR Convention'), in particular Article 9(2) concerning 'environmental information'.[138] Even though Ireland had argued that this expression should be interpreted, inter alia, in light of the Aarhus Convention under Article 31(3)(c) VCLT,[139] the tribunal refused to take this instrument into account, be it under Article 31(3)(c) or under other rules of interpretation, stating that

> Ireland has sought to rely upon treaties that are as yet unratified and not in force as between the Parties or regional legislative initiatives that have not been finalized nor entered into force for the Parties. Although, it is arguable—but in the view of the Tribunal not conclusive—that Ireland's claim might have succeeded under some of these drafts, the Tribunal is not empowered to apply legally unperfected instruments.[140]

A more nuanced position has been adopted by Campbell McLachlan. He identifies two scenarios in which treaty rules not binding on all parties to the interpreted treaty may still be considered under Article 31(3)(c). The first is where the treaty rule reflects a customary international law rule binding on all parties to the interpreted treaty.[141] The second scenario arises where, 'on its proper construction, a particular obligation in the treaty is owed in a synallagmatic way between pairs of parties, rather than *erga omnes partes* (even if contained within a multilateral treaty)'.[142] Under this view, regional rules cannot be taken into account under Article 31(3)(c) VCLT when interpreting 'interdependent' or 'integral' treaties, such as universal agreements on collective security and human rights.

The 2006 Fragmentation Report seems to take an even more liberal approach than McLachlan, suggesting that rules could 'in addition' be taken into account as

137 Panel Report, *EC—Measures Affecting the Approval and Marketing of Biotech Products* WT/DS293/R (29 September 2006) 334 [7.70].

138 *OSPAR Arbitration (Ireland v United Kingdom)* (Award) PCA Case 2001-03 (2 July 2003).

139 *OSPAR Arbitration* (n 138) [150]; *OSPAR Arbitration (Ireland v United Kingdom)*, Memorial of Ireland (7 March 2002) [100]–[101].

140 *OSPAR Arbitration* (n 138) [180]. But see the dissenting opinion of Gavan Griffith [7]–[10], [19].

141 C McLachlan, 'The Principle of Systemic Integration and Article 31(3)(C) of the Vienna Convention' (2005) 54 ICLQ 279, 314.

142 McLachlan (n 141) 315.

long as these 'have been 'implicitly' accepted or at least tolerated by the other parties'.[143] The report also criticizes the requirement of perfect congruence in membership, contending that such a restrictive interpretation effectively precludes the use of 'regional or other particular implementation agreements—including *inter se* agreements—that may have been concluded under a framework treaty, as interpretative aids to the latter'.[144] In this regard, the Fragmentation Report leans towards the view expressed by Isabelle Van Damme and Joost Pauwelyn who have—in the context of the relationship between the WTO Covered Agreements and RTAs—adopted a liberal approach with respect to the understanding of 'parties', provided that the regional rule in question is 'relevant' in order to establish the common understanding of all parties to the interpreted treaty.[145] In this vein, the 1998 Appellate Body decision in *US—Shrimps* relied heavily on the 1996 Inter-American Convention for the Protection and Conservation of Sea Turtles—arguably under Article 31(3)(c) of the VCLT—when interpreting Article XX of GATT.[146] Similarly, Alan Boyle, after having warned that '[i]f the integrity and global character of the Convention [UNCLOS] are to be preserved, courts must necessarily approach interpretation by reference to Article 31(3)(c) with some caution', still appears to see room for reliance on that provision when stating that

> if such a [regional] treaty were representative of a pattern of regional treaties, spread across different regions, and possibly giving effect to UN policy endorsed by consensus at a global level, its evolutionary value as an interpretative guide would be significantly enhanced.[147]

Panos Merkouris suggests an even 'more flexible approach'. According to him, it is sufficient if merely the parties to the dispute are bound by the rule since

> the term 'parties' of Article 31(3)(c) was of a 'generic' nature and far from the most important piece of the puzzle. Its scope is relative and dependent on another critical element. That element that determines the meaning to be given to the terms 'relevance', 'applicability' and 'parties' is one singular criterion: the proximity criterion.[148]

[143] Fragmentation Report (n 12) [472]. See for the caution expressed by McLachlan (n 141) 314.

[144] Fragmentation Report (n 12) [471].

[145] I Van Damme, 'What Role is There for Regional International Law in the Interpretation of the WTO Agreements?' in L Bartels and F Ortino (eds), *Regional Trade Agreements and the WTO Legal System* (OUP 2006) 553, 559; J Pauwelyn, *Conflict of Norms in Public International Law* (CUP 2003) 259–63.

[146] Appellate Body Report, *US—Import Prohibition of Certain Shrimp and Shrimp Products* WT/DS58/AB/R (6 November 1998) [169]–[171]. See reference to art 31(3)(c) in [157] footnote 157.

[147] Boyle (n 60) 569.

[148] Merkouris (n 135) 100–101.

In his view, the case law does not support a restrictive view but rather exhibits that 'four manifestations' of the criterion of proximity has led judges to take other rules of international law into account.[149] At the same time, he concedes that '[s]uch an extremely expansive interpretation seems to go against the very text of Article 31(3)(c)' arguing that cross-referencing should rather be considered under Article 32 of the VCLT.[150]

In its 2026 advisory opinion in *Right to Strike*, the majority of ICJ judges appeared to lean towards a more flexible approach, when stating that Article 31(3)(c) 'does not necessarily require all parties to the treaty under interpretation to be bound by the "relevant rules of international law" in order for those rules to be taken into account.'[151] Still, with respect to the cross-referencing of regional rules and in the absence of a *renvoi* to regional rules in the universal agreement that is being interpreted, recourse to Article 31(3)(c) is problematic in several respects. An expansive recourse to regional treaties in the interpretation of universal rules bears the risk of either an inconsistent application of that treaty, or of imposing a certain regional understanding on all parties to the universal treaty. In this light, the Tribunal in *Eskosol* rightly highlighted that

> [t]he text of a multilateral treaty must have a consistent and objective meaning, not different meanings determined separately and subjectively for each different subset of States that may be involved in a particular future dispute.[152]

Although case law frequently refers to regional rules in treaty interpretation, courts and tribunals have generally exercised caution in taking such rules into account under Article 31(3)(c) of the VCLT when interpreting treaties concluded by a larger group of States. Such caution in practice aligns with the rationale underlying Article 31(3)(c). Article 31(3)(c) mandates the consideration of 'any relevant rule of international law' based on the presumption of non-derogation, according to which a State committing to a rule intends such a rule to 'produce effects in accordance with its existing legal obligations and not in violation of it'.[153] However, the presumption does not apply when a universal agreement is interpreted with reference to a regional rule, since it cannot be assumed that third parties, bound by the

[149] Merkouris (n 135) 101.
[150] Merkouris (n 135) 100.
[151] *Right to Strike* (n 90)

[90]. See for diverging views on the correct understanding of Article 31(3)(c) (separate opinion of President Iwasawa [2]–[14]; dissenting opinion of Judge Tomka [65]–[72]; declaration of Judge Bhandari [7]–[8]; separate opinion of Judge Nolte [23]–[30].

[152] *Eskosol SpA v Italy* (Decision on Termination Request and Intra-EU Objection) ICSID Case No ARB/15/50 (7 May 2019) [125].
[153] *Right of Passage over Indian Territory (Portugal v India)* [1957] ICJ Rep 125, 142 as quoted in [39] of the Fragmentation Report.

universal agreement but not by the regional rule, intended the former to conform to the latter. A broad interpretation of the term 'parties' risks infringing upon the legal positions of third States by imposing on them a legal understanding adopted by one or more regions that those States do not necessarily share. A narrow interpretation of the term 'parties' is also consistent with the understanding of 'parties' in the context of the other 'authentic means of interpretation'—Articles 31(3)(a) and (b)—which refer to 'all parties'.

Accordingly, regional rules should not be taken into account under Article 31(3)(c) when interpreting a universal treaty, except where the parties to the dispute are bound by the regional rules and either the other parties to the universal agreement have expressed their consent to the consideration of these regional rules in the interpretation of the universal agreement, or the provisions in question are 'bilateralizable'.[154] These two exceptions are supported by way of an *argumentum a fortiori*, insofar as they mirror the conditions under which the VCLT authorizes *inter se* agreements among parties to *modify* a multilateral treaty pursuant to Article 41.[155]

7.3.3.2 Regional practice as evidence for the object and purpose (Article 31(1) VCLT)

Reference to regional rules in interpreting a provision of a universal agreement may be justified under Article 31(1) to the extent that they assist in determining the object and purpose of the treaty and thus serve as 'evidence of the common understanding of the parties as to the meaning of the term used'.[156]

From the ICJ's jurisprudence, three key criteria can be identified for the consideration of regional rules in interpreting a universal agreement. First, the regional rules must be 'close in substance' to the universal rule under interpretation, as highlighted by the ICJ in its 2010 *Diallo* judgment when interpreting the ICCPR in parallel with its African counterpart.[157] In that case, the Court held that

> [t]he interpretation by the European Court of Human Rights and the Inter-American Court of Human Rights, respectively, of Article 1 of Protocol No. 7 to the (European) Convention for the Protection of Human Rights and Fundamental Freedoms and Article 22, paragraph 6, of the American Convention on Human Rights—the said provisions being close in substance to those of the Covenant and the African Charter which the Court is applying in the present

[154] McLachlan (n 141) 314. See also Chapter 6, section 6.3.3.1.

[155] See Chapter 6, section 6.3.3.1.

[156] McLachlan (n 141) 315 referring to the dissenting opinion of Arbitrator Griffith in the *Mox Plant* case.

[157] *Ahmadou Sadio Diallo (Republic of Guinea v Democratic Republic of the Congo)* (Merits) [2010] ICJ Rep 639 [67]–[68].

> case—is consistent with what has been found in respect of the latter provisions in paragraph 65 above.

Secondly, the regional instruments should be comparable in scope and purpose to the universal instrument under interpretation. In this regard, the ICJ, in its 2021 *Qatar v UAE* judgment, rejected reliance on regional agreements and jurisprudence when interpreting Article 1 of CERD, arguing that

> [w]hile these legal instruments all refer to 'national origin', their purpose is to ensure a wide scope of protection of human rights and fundamental freedoms. The jurisprudence of regional human rights courts based on those legal instruments is therefore of little help for the interpretation of the term 'national origin' in CERD.[158]

In this vein, some scholars have generally expressed scepticism about interpreting the 1951 Refugee Convention in light of regional counterparts in Africa or Latin America, pointing to the differing contexts and approaches reflected in these regional conventions.[159]

Thirdly, as emerges from the cases cited above, in interpreting a universal agreement, the ICJ refrains from relying on rules from only one region, preferring instead regional rules that represent multiple regions. Similarly, in its 2014 decision in *Virginia G*, the ITLOS Tribunal relied on various regional and sub-regional fishing agreements from different regions when interpreting UNCLOS.[160]

7.3.3.3 Regional rules as supplementary means (Article 32 VCLT)

To the extent that neither Article 31(3) nor Article 31(1) VCLT allows for recourse to regional rules in the interpretation of a universal agreement, such rules can still be considered as a supplementary means of interpretation in accordance with Article 32 of the VCLT.[161] The line between the 'authentic means' of interpretation contained in Article 31 and the 'supplementary means' reflected in Article 32 VCLT has often been blurred in practice.[162] However, when considering regional practice in the interpretation of universal instruments, this distinction is crucial to avoid any appearance of regional imbalance or exceptionalism. Therefore, to the extent that regional practice cannot be taken into account under

[158] *Application of the International Convention on the Elimination of All Forms of Racial Discrimination (Qatar v United Arab Emirates)* [2021] ICJ Rep 71 [104]. See also section 6.3.1.3.

[159] See eg D Yu, 'With Our Feet to the Fire: Regional Agreements as Mechanisms of Changing International Law to Include Persons Displaced by Climate Change' (2021) 35 Emory Int Law Rev 517.

[160] *The M/V 'Virginia G' Case (Panama/Guinea-Bissau)* (n 104) [216].

[161] See also ILC Report 2018 (SASP) (n 7) draft Conclusion 4, 30; draft Conclusion 12(1) and commentary, 97; *Right to Strike* (n 90) [112]–[115]; specifically referring to regional instruments in [120]–[137]. On the role of Article 38(1)(d), see n 122.

[162] See ILC Report 2018 (SASP) (n 7) draft Conclusion 4(3), 36.

Article 31, recourse to regional practice under Article 32 VCLT should be limited to 'confirm[ing] the meaning resulting from the application of article 31'. For example, the ICJ, in its 2022 judgment in the case *Armed Activities on the Territory of the Congo (Democratic Republic of the Congo v Uganda),* relied, inter alia, on General Comment No 4 adopted by the AfrCommHPR, to confirm

> that rape and other acts of sexual violence committed in the context of armed conflict may amount to grave breaches of the Geneva Conventions or violations of the laws and customs of war, and that they may also constitute a form of torture and inhuman treatment.[163]

At the same time, it must be ensured that regional practice, which may not represent the practice of other regions, is not given undue weight—even where such practice may assist in determining the meaning of the treaty text 'where interpretation under Article 31 is ambiguous, obscure, or leads to a manifestly absurd or unreasonable result' (see Article 32).

The explosive force of a blurred distinction between Articles 31(3)(b) and 32 is illustrated in the 2020 judgment of the ICJ in the case between *Equatorial Guinea v France.* In this case, the Court gave significant weight to the practice of a number of States in interpreting Articles 22 and 1(1)(i) of the VCDR stating that

> [t]he Court does not consider that this practice necessarily establishes 'the agreement of the parties' within the meaning of a rule codified in Article 31, paragraph 3 (b), of the Vienna Convention on the Law of Treaties ... Nevertheless, the practice of several States which clearly requires the prior approval of the receiving State before a building can acquire the status of 'premises of the mission'—and the lack of any objection to such practice—are factors which weigh against finding a right belonging to the sending State under the Vienna Convention unilaterally to designate the premises of its diplomatic mission.[164]

This approach, and the blurred distinction it entails, was criticized by several judges in their separate or dissenting opinions, who pointed to the distorted outcomes of the interpretative process.[165]

In sum, regional practice can play a meaningful role in shaping the interpretation of treaties with a universal scope over time and thus adapting them to

[163] *Armed Activities on the Territory of the Congo (Democratic Republic of the Congo v Uganda)* [2022] ICJ Rep 13 [188].

[164] See *Immunities and Criminal Proceedings (Equatorial Guinea v France)* [2020] ICJ Rep 300 [69].

[165] See *Immunities and Criminal Proceedings* (n 163) (separate opinion of President Yusuf 340 [24], [29]–[31]; dissenting opinion of Judge Bhandari 390 [50]–[53]; dissenting opinion of Judge Robinson 415 [30]–[37]; dissenting opinion of Judge ad hoc Kateka 442 [18]). See also *Right to Strike* (n 90) (separate opinion of Judge Nolte) [49]–[50].

changing circumstances. However, because regional practice is inherently limited, it is essential that such practice be equally identified and considered across multiple regions. When an interpretation relies primarily on practice from a single region, it becomes especially important to attribute and explain the weight of that practice in accordance with the secondary rules of interpretation, so as to avoid introducing regional imbalances into the treaty.

7.4 Regional practice and unwritten international law

The previous section explained how secondary rules channel the influence of regional practice on the development of written international law, particularly in the interpretation of quasi-universal treaties. However, regional practice contributes not only to the development of written international law, but also to the development of unwritten international law, that is, general customary international law, general principles of law (GPL), and *jus cogens*.[166]

This section examines, for each of the three categories of unwritten international law, three overarching issues concerning the contribution of regional practice to their formation and identification. First, it assesses whether the relevant secondary rules accord regional practice a distinct role as compared to other forms of collective conduct. Second, whether the practice of one or more regions may, in certain cases, be given particular weight in this process. Third, whether the existence of 'regional equivalents', such as regional custom, regional principles of law, and regional 'super norms', supports or undermines the claim to universality of a rule of unwritten international law.

7.4.1 Regional practice and customary international law

The significant influence of regional practice on the evolution of customary international law is exemplified by Article 1 of the 1933 Montevideo Convention. Although the Convention has been ratified by only 17 States in the Americas, it is widely regarded as a reference point for identifying the criteria for Statehood under general customary international law.[167] This section thus takes a closer look at the conditions that determine the influence of regional practice in the formation and identification of general customary international law under Article 38(1)(b) of the ICJ Statute.

[166] This section does not address the controversial question of the conditions under which regional practice constitutes unwritten regional international law. See on this: Chapter 5.

[167] Convention on the Rights and Duties of States, Montevideo (26 December 1933) 165 LNTS 19; J Crawford, *The Creation of States in International Law* (2nd edn, OUP 2007) 97.

7.4.1.1 Regional practice as evidence of a general practice

Regional practice, despite its inherently limited scope, is critical for assessing the generality of State practice. As reflected in both the work of the ILC and the jurisprudence of international courts and tribunals, this is because regional practice is presumed to represent the practice of distinct parts of the international community.[168]

Conclusion 8 of the ILC Conclusions on the 'Identification of customary international law' defines a 'general practice' as being 'sufficiently widespread and representative, as well as consistent'.[169] Whether a practice is 'representative', according to the ILC commentary, 'needs to be assessed in light of all the circumstances, including the various interests at stake and/or the various geographical regions'.[170]

The ILC's approach finds support in the case law of international courts and tribunals, notably that of the ICJ. In its 1996 advisory opinion on the *Legality of the Threat or Use of Nuclear Weapons*, for instance, the ICJ based its analysis of customary international law on a careful assessment of the various regional agreements dealing with nuclear weapons.[171] Similarly, the 2012 judgment in the *Jurisdictional Immunities of the State* case contains a comprehensive analysis of practice across many regions before pronouncing on the state of general customary international law.[172] The idea that regional practice typically represents (only) a part of the international community of was implied in the declaration by Judge Donoghue to the Court's 2012 judgment in *Belgium v Senegal*. She emphasized that

> [i]n *Jurisdictional Immunities of the State* . . . two States from a single region, with a common legal tradition, agreed on many aspects of the law governing foreign State immunity. Because its conclusions had implications for other States, however, the Court conducted its own analysis of customary international law.[173]

The relevance of regional practice for assessing the existence and scope of the right to a healthy environment is further illustrated by the approach taken by the ICJ in its 2025 Advisory Opinion on the *Obligations of States in respect of Climate Change*. While the Court did not take a clear position on whether it considers the right to a healthy environment a self-standing right under customary

[168] See Chapter 2, section 2.3.2.

[169] ILC Report 2018 (CIL) (n 7) 135.

[170] ILC Report 2018 (CIL) (n 7) Conclusion 8, 136.

[171] *Legality of the Threat or Use of Nuclear Weapons* (Advisory Opinion) [1996] ICJ Rep 226 [59]–[63].

[172] *Jurisdictional Immunities of the State (Germany v Italy: Greece intervening)* (Judgment) [2012] ICJ Rep 99 [59], [61], and [89] where the Court refers to the European Convention and the draft Inter-American Convention on State immunity.

[173] *Questions relating to the Obligation to Prosecute or Extradite (Belgium v Senegal)* (Judgment) [2012] ICJ Rep 584 (declaration of Judge Donoghue) [21].

international law—which was addressed by several judges in their opinions[174]—it considered several regional human rights instruments recognizing such a right[175] before concluding that 'under international law, the human right to a clean, healthy and sustainable environment is essential for the enjoyment of other human rights'.[176] The judges who criticized the majority for not explicitly recognizing the right as a self-standing right under customary international law emphasized, in particular, that 'there is widespread, cross-regional recognition' of such a right.[177]

Conversely, the practice of one or more regions can also halt, prevent, or redirect the emergence of a specific rule of customary international law, notably by adopting a different practice. This is illustrated by the ICJ's 1951 Advisory Opinion on *Reservations to the Convention on the Prevention and Punishment of the Crime of Genocide*. In assessing whether a State could become a party to the Convention despite making reservations to certain provisions to which other parties objected, the Court examined State practice on reservations. It found that

> [i]t must also be pointed out that there existed among the American States members both of the United Nations and of the Organization of American States, a different practice which goes so far as to permit a reserving State to become a party irrespective of the nature of the reservations or of the objections raised by other contracting States.[178]

The relevance of cross-regional practice in the identification of customary international law is illustrated, moreover, when considering the legality of the practice adopted by the EU regarding third-party countermeasures. Such practice has been consistently protested by regional groups of States,[179] and thus raises significant doubts as to the extent to which such practices have led to the emergence of a right to adopt such countermeasures under (customary) international law.[180] Another example to this effect concerns the identification of customary international in the work of the ILC on the topic 'Immunity of State officials from foreign criminal jurisdiction'. During the debate in the 6th Committee in 2025, Cameroon, on behalf of the African Group in the UN, for instance, encouraged

[174] *Climate Change* (n 73) (declaration of Judge Tladi) [24]–[33]; (separate opinion of Judge Aurescu) [28]; (separate opinion of Judge Bhandari) [3]; but see (separate opinion of Judge Charlesworth) [8].

[175] *Climate Change* (n 73) [390].

[176] *Climate Change* (n 73) [393].

[177] *Climate Change* (n 73) (declaration of Judge Tladi) [30]; (separate opinion of Judge Aurescu) [29].

[178] *Reservations to the Convention on the Prevention and Punishment of Genocide* (Advisory Opinion) [1951] ICJ Rep 15, 25.

[179] As illustrated, eg by AALCO, 'Extraterritorial Application of National Legislation: Sanctions Imposed Against Third Parties' (2021) AALCO/59/HONG KONG/2021/SD/S6 [61].

[180] See also A Hofer, 'Third-Party Countermeasures: Making Custom Out of Ambiguous Practice?' (2025) 74 ICLQ 287.

> the Commission to incorporate evidence of state practice, expressions of *opinio juris*, and caselaw from all regions, including Africa. Indeed, several members of the Commission have noted that the case law and practice cited in the report were not necessarily representative, and that there were insufficient references to caselaw from regions such as Africa.[181]

By way of a final note of caution on this point, it should be emphasized that regional practice is an important, but not the only, means of assessing the generality of State practice. In particular, the practice of UN organs is often regarded as representative of the practice of those States, especially when the UNGA adopts a resolution without a vote on a topic for which the UN has been specifically mandated by States, such as decolonization and self-determination,[182] or where the UN and regional organizations fulfil complementary functions, such as collective security.[183]

7.4.1.2 Privileged forms of regional practice?

Two types of regional practice may assume a particularly important role when assessing the representative character of a practice. In both cases, the relevant practice relating to the specific subject-matter is, to some extent, exclusive to, or otherwise confined within, a regionally defined group of States.

The first type relates to the practice of regional IOs. Conclusion 4(2) of the ILC Conclusions on customary international law clarifies that the practice of IOs can contribute, in certain cases, 'as such' to the 'formation, or expression, of rules of customary international law'.[184] These 'certain cases' concern practice in subject-matters exclusive to IOs, where States typically do not act individually but rather consent to exclusive action by an IO.[185] This is notably the case in regional integration organizations, where IOs have been conferred exclusive competences by their member States, for example in the fields of trade or the management of shared resources, or with respect to 'IO-specific' practice, for example relating to jurisdictional immunities of IOs.[186] The privileged role of these forms of IO practice, allowing them to be considered 'as such' in the identification of customary

[181] Statement delivered on behalf of the African Group by Cameroon (27 October 2025) <https://www.un.org/en/ga/sixth/80/pdfs/statements/ilc/26mtg_african_group_1.pdf> (accessed 7 May 2026) [14].

[182] See, for example, the Court's 2019 *Chagos* Advisory Opinion and its 1971 *Namibia* Advisory Opinion, where the Court relied on UN General Assembly resolutions (*Legal Consequences of the Separation of the Chagos Archipelago from Mauritius in 1965* (Advisory Opinion) [2019] ICJ Rep 95 [155]; *Namibia* (n 73) [52]–[53]).

[183] See the Court's reliance on UNGA resolutions in *Nicaragua v United States* [1986] (n 53) [188]; *Legality of the Threat or Use of Nuclear Weapons* (n 171) [70]–[73].

[184] ILC Report 2018 (CIL) (n 7) draft Conclusion 4(2).

[185] Identifying four types of exclusive practice: Barkholdt (n 7) 35–38; see also ILC Report 2018 (CIL) (n 7) draft Conclusion 4(2), 131.

[186] On this, see RA Wessel, 'Jurisdictional Immunity of Regional Organisations—Substantive Unity in Instrumental Diversity?' in T Ruys and N Angelet (eds), *The Cambridge Handbook of Immunities and International Law* (CUP 2019) 214.

international law, derives from the absence of State practice in the relevant fields, as States have agreed to act exclusively through the IO rather than individually. However, where such 'exclusive' practice stems from regional IOs, its consideration must not result in regional imbalance in the identification of customary international law. Such imbalance may arise where the practice of regional IOs and that of their member States is effectively counted twice ('double-counting'),[187] or where States in certain regions are more reluctant to engage in densely integrated forms of regional co-operation.[188] It should therefore be avoided by carefully attributing and weighing the relevant practice of the regional IOs and its member States, and by ensuring that the practice of less integrated States is duly taken into account.

The second type of practice concerns the controversial concept of 'specially affected States', the origins of which date back to the ICJ's 1969 *North Sea Continental Shelf* judgments, where the Court emphasized that

> an indispensable requirement would be that within the period in question, short though it might be, State practice, including that of States whose interests are specially affected, should have been both extensive and virtually uniform.[189]

The concept of 'specially affected States' has faced substantial criticism for being obscure and for disadvantaging less powerful States.[190] After a substantial debate within the ILC in 2018 as well as among States in the Sixth Committee and scholars, the ILC Conclusions ultimately did not mention this concept in a separate conclusion. Instead, the commentary to Conclusion 8 clarifies that

> an indispensable factor to be taken into account [in assessing generality] is the extent to which those States that are particularly involved in the relevant activity or are most likely to be concerned with the alleged rule ('specially affected States') have participated in the practice.[191]

It continues that

> [a] relatively small number of States engaging in a certain practice might thus suffice if indeed such practice, as well as other States' inaction in response, is generally accepted as law (accompanied by *opinio juris*).[192]

[187] Barkholdt (n 7) 26, 33, 39.
[188] Saidov (n 29).
[189] *North Sea Continental Shelf (Federal Republic of Germany/Denmark)* [1969] ICJ Rep 3 [74].
[190] For a critical perspective: GR Bandeira Galindo and C Yip, 'Customary International Law and the Third World: Do Not Step on the Grass' (2017) 16 Chin J Int Law 251, 256–61. According to KJ Heller, AALCO accepts the existence of this concept (KJ Heller, 'Specially-affected States and the Formation of Custom' (2018) 112 AJIL 191, 200 fn 55).
[191] ILC Report 2018 (CIL) (n 7) draft Conclusion 8, 136–37.
[192] ILC Report 2018 (CIL) (n 7) 136.

While the commentary underlines that this statement 'should not be taken to refer to the relative power of States',[193] it remains unclear how those 'specially-affected States' are defined. The Court's pronouncement in the *North Sea Continental Shelf* cases can be understood as referring to the practice of States in relation to certain non-generalizable subject-matters, such as rights and obligations arising from a State's specific geographic position. The emergence of customary rules in such contexts would be nearly impossible if, for example, the practice of States that do not share a particular geographic disposition were required to carry equal weight to that of coastal States. Non-generalizability, in turn, is a defining feature of regional practice.[194] Therefore, such regional practice may coincide with the group of 'specially affected' States. The concept of 'specially affected States' has, for example, emerged in a case before domestic courts in Hong Kong that concerned the customary status of the principle of non-refoulement. In this case, the courts suggested that the practice of States in regions 'specially affected' by refugees was particularly relevant for the determination of its customary status.[195] The concept has also been explored in relation to the impact of sea-level rise on the universal law of the sea in the 'First issues paper' of the ILC Study Group on sea-level rise. The paper accords significant weight to that regional practice as the practice of 'specially affected States', noting that

> [t]he Pacific Island States would of course be among those 'States whose interests are specially affected', a significant attribute regarding the establishment of a general practice in the formation of a new rule of customary international law. . .[196]

However, this statement does not imply that the practice of Pacific Islands States suffices to establish a customary rule. Indeed, to avoid the imposition of certain regional practices on other States, there are good reasons to understand the 'specially affected' status of a regional group of States merely as giving rise to a duty on the part of third States to react to that practice if they wish to prevent the emergence of a customary rule. If they remain silent, such silence or inaction may be taken as acceptance.[197]

7.4.1.3 Regional custom as evidence for *opinio juris*

The existence of regional custom is widely recognized.[198] What is less clear, however, is the role regional custom plays in the formation and identification

[193] ILC Report 2018 (CIL) (n 7).
[194] See Chapter 2, section 2.3.4.
[195] *C v Director of Immigration* (High Court of Hong Kong) (Judgment of 21 July 2011) CACV 132–37/2008 [60]–[65]; *C v Director of Immigration* [2008] HKEC 281 (2008) (Hartmann J) [115].
[196] ILC, 'First issues paper on Sea-level rise in relation to international law by Bogdan Aurescu and Nilüfer Oral' (2021) UN Doc A/CN.4/740 [103] quoting ILA, 'Final Report of the ILA Committee on baselines under the international law of the Sea' (Sofia 2012), 887.
[197] ILC Report 2018 (CIL) (n 7) draft Conclusion 6(1) and draft Conclusion 10(3).
[198] See also Chapter 5, section 5.2.

of customary rules with a universal scope of application. According to the ILC Special Rapporteur on customary international law, '[t]he possibility is not to be excluded that such rules may evolve into rules of general customary international law over time'.[199] During the debate within the ILC, several members asked the Special Rapporteur to 'clarify how a particular customary rule might evolve into a rule of general customary international law over time or, indeed, might contradict such a rule'.[200]

Given that the purpose of regional custom consists in protecting mutual expectations within a limited, relatively cohesive community,[201] it is not self-evident that States are willing to extend this legal bond to a wider circle of States reflecting diverse political systems and ideological views.[202] Accordingly, regional custom constitutes a building block for the identification of general custom only to the extent that a willingness to generalize its content can be identified, either among States within the region or by third States. This may occur, for example, when States within the region act in accordance with, or invoke the rule towards States outside the region,[203] or when regional customary rules develop in parallel, as has been alleged with respect to *uti possidetis*, to address the same phenomenon (here, independence following decolonization) with a similar regulatory approach (here, the intangibility of colonial boundaries).[204]

7.4.2 Regional practice and general principles of law

While many issues relating to the identification of GPL are controversial,[205] it is generally understood that it comprises two criteria, namely the determination of the existence of a principle common to the various legal systems of the world; and its transposition to the international legal system.[206] Regional practice is relevant to the assessment of both criteria.

[199] ILC, 'Third report on the identification of customary international law by Michael Wood, Special Rapporteur' (2015) UN Doc A/CN.4/682 [82]; J Barboza, 'The Customary Rule: From Chrysalis to Butterfly' in CA Armas Barea and others (eds), *Liber Amicorum In Memoriam of Judge José María Ruda* (Kluwer Law International 2000) 1, 14.

[200] See also ILC, 'Summary records' (13 to 21 May 2015): Hassouna (UN Doc A/CN.4/SR.3252, 7); Park (UN Doc A/CN.4/SR.3396, 15); Hmoud (UN Doc A/CN.4/SR.3251, 11).

[201] See Chapter 5, section 5.2.3.1.

[202] JR Gutiérrez Álvarez, 'A Melting Snowball—Difficulties in Identifying Particular Customary International Law' (2024) 73 ICLQ 1083, 1091, who argues that 'a State adhering to a particular customary norm concerning ideological principles that are only accepted by a specific group of States must be aware of its particular status, rather than believing it to be general custom'.

[203] See by analogy: ILC Report 2018 (CIL) (n 7) commentary on draft Conclusion 9, 139.

[204] See eg H Thirlway, *The Law and Procedure of the International Court of Justice: Fifty Years Jurisprudence Volume I* (OUP 2013), 201. See also Chapter 5, section 5.3.2.3, including the criticism by Judge Yusuf in this regard.

[205] ILC, 'First report [on general principles of law] of the Special Rapporteur, Mr. Marcelo Vázquez-Bermúdez' (2019) UN Doc A/CN.4/732 [11].

[206] ILC, 'General principles of law: texts and titles of the draft conclusions adopted by the Drafting Committee on second reading' (2025) UN Doc A/CN.4/L.1018, draft Conclusion 4.

7.4.2.1 Regional practice as evidence of recognition

The first criterion, the existence of a principle common to the various legal systems worldwide, is defined in draft Conclusion 5 of the ILC Draft Conclusions, provisionally adopted in 2025.[207] According to draft Conclusion 5(1), the identification of a GPL requires 'a comparative analysis of national legal systems'. Draft Conclusion 5(2) clarifies that '[t]he comparative analysis must be wide and representative, including the different regions of the world'. This approach has found support by States in the Sixth Committee.[208] In 2025, Sierra Leone, for example,

> welcome[d] this effort to ensure balance and representativeness in the identification of general principles and support the continued recognition of African customary law and the legal experiences of least developed countries as integral to understanding State practice and adherence to shared legal principles.[209]

In its 2018 report on 'The use of domestic law principles in the development of international law', the ILA Study Group similarly stated that

> [I]t is also not enough to 'identify' a general principle among the main legal systems if there is not enough geographical representation, e.g., a general principle shared by Civil Law countries in Europe should also be identified in other Civil Law countries located in different geographical areas and belonging to different civilizations.[210]

The central role of regional practice in the 'comparative analysis' for identifying a GPL is reflected in the case law of both international and domestic courts and tribunals. In a judgment of 2016, the Supreme Court of the Philippines, for instance, referred to 'at least sixty countries in Asia, North and South America, and Europe [that] have passed legislation recognizing foundlings as its citizen' to establish 'a generally accepted principle of international law to presume foundlings as having been born of nationals of the country in which the foundling is found' under Article 38(1)(c) of the ICJ Statute.[211] Conversely, the lack of representative practice relating to the 'polluter pays' principle beyond Europe and specific treaty regimes appears to have been decisive in sustaining the scepticism of the ILC,

[207] ILC (n 207), draft Conclusion 5.

[208] See eg El Salvador, Guatemala, India, Israel, Lebanon, Peru, and Uganda (ILC, 'Fourth report [on general principles of law] of the Special Rapporteur, Mr. Marcelo Vázquez-Bermúdez' (2025) UN Doc A/CN.4/785 [94]).

[209] Statement by Sierra Leone (27 October 2025) <https://www.un.org/en/ga/sixth/80/pdfs/statements/ilc/26mtg_sierra_leone_1.pdf> (accessed 7 May 2026) [28].

[210] ILA, 'Report of the Study Group on the use of domestic law principles in the development of international law' (Sydney 2018) [214].

[211] *Mary Grace Natividad S Poe-Llamanzares* [2016] PHSC 84 (2016) WL, 21.

courts, and tribunals regarding its status as a GPL.[212] At the same time, some tribunals, in their comparative analysis, occasionally tend to consider certain regions in greater detail than others. Illustrative is that the protection of legitimate expectations was considered a GPL by several ICSID tribunals, relying mainly on practice from Europe and Latin America.[213] By contrast, the ICJ, in its 2018 judgment in *Obligation to Negotiate Access to the Pacific Ocean (Bolivia v Chile)*

> note[d] that references to legitimate expectations may be found in arbitral awards concerning disputes between a foreign investor and the host State that apply treaty clauses providing for fair and equitable treatment. It does not follow from such references that there exists in general international law a principle that would give rise to an obligation on the basis of what could be considered a legitimate expectation.[214]

Accordingly, an imbalanced reliance on regional practice risks asserting the existence of GPL with a content that is not universally accepted, thus potentially 'deforming' general international law.

7.4.2.2 Regional international organizations as 'nations'?

While the ILC Conclusions on the 'Identification of customary international law' provide that the practice of IOs, thus including that of regional IOs, can, in certain cases, contribute 'as such' to the identification of customary international law,[215] it is unclear to what extent the same applies to the identification of GPL.

In his fourth report of 2025, the ILC Special Rapporteur on the topic 'General principles of law', Marcelo Vázquez-Bermúdez, suggested mirroring the approach adopted by the ILC in the project on customary international law and including, in draft Conclusion 2, another paragraph providing that '[i]n certain cases, the recognition by international organizations may also contribute to the formation of general principles of law'.[216] Although this proposal was rejected by the ILC Drafting Committee, the statement by its Chair, Mario Oyarzábal, clarified that the term 'recognition by the community of nations' contained in draft Conclusion

[212] ILC, 'Draft Principles on the Allocation of Loss in the Case of Transboundary Harm arising out of Hazardous Activities' (2006) YBILC II(2), UN Doc A/61/10, 75 [15]; *Case concerning the audit of accounts between the Netherlands and France in application of the Protocol of 25 September 1991 Additional to the Convention for the Protection of the Rhine from Pollution by Chlorides of 3 December 1976* (2004) 25 UNRIAA 267, 312 [102]–[103]; *Climate Change* (n 73) [160]; see also in that case: Written Comments of the United States of America (15 August 2024) 4.33.

[213] See eg *Gold Reserve Inc v Bolivarian Republic of Venezuela* (Award) ICSID Case No ARB(AF)/09/1 (22 September 2014) [576]; see also *Total SA v Argentine Republic* (Decision on Liability) ICSID Case No ARB/04/1 (27 December 2010) [128]–[130].

[214] *Obligation to Negotiate Access to the Pacific Ocean (Bolivia v Chile)* [2018] ICJ Rep 507 [162].

[215] See section 7.4.1.2.

[216] ILC, 'Fourth report on general principles of law of the Special Rapporteur, Mr. Marcelo Vázquez-Bermúdez' (2025) UN Doc A/CN.4/785 [56].

2 'is intended to capture the possibility that international organizations may also contribute to the recognition of general principles of law'.[217] Although some States in the 6th Committee supported this approach, others rejected a role for IOs in this regard.[218]

It appears that, in principle, the same reasons that justify a role for IOs in identifying customary international law would also support their role in identifying GPL, particularly where they have been granted exclusive competences by their member States. To exclude the practice of such IOs would effectively exclude the conduct of States that, pursuant to the IO's constituent instrument, are legally prevented from acting independently in the relevant area. Such an exclusion could therefore undermine the principle of sovereign equality in the identification of GPL or even create an incentive for States to withdraw from IOs. Practice further suggests that references to IOs, including regional IOs, are considered relevant for identifying GPL.[219] Nevertheless, the caution expressed by some States is not without merit, given that most of these examples involve the practice of a single regional IO, the EU, which may create a regional imbalance in cases where the practice of its member States is effectively counted twice, while the practice of States outside such regional IOs is disregarded. However, there is no reason why only the EU should have this role. The decisive point here would not be to exclude the possibility of considering regional practice 'as such', but rather to define the circumstances under which such practice may contribute to the identification of GPL. To the extent that the constituent instrument of a regional IO confers to its organs the power to adopt decisions which are binding on its members States or to act, within a certain area, on behalf of its members, such practice may be relevant 'as such' for the identification of a GPL.[220] Examples may include the identification of the existence and content of GPL governing the judicial process, such as the existence and scope of the principles of judicial propriety, procedural fairness, and equality of the parties at the international level,[221] based on the practice of judicial and administrative bodies of regional IOs. With respect to GPL applicable to the inter-State context, this is supported by Article 33(1) of the UN Charter, which attributes a special role to 'regional agencies or arrangements' in the peaceful

[217] Statement of the Chair of the Drafting Committee on 'General principles of law', Mr Mario Oyarzábal (27 May 2025) 3.

[218] See ILC, 'Fourth Report on GPL' (n 216) [39]–[42].

[219] See eg Statement on behalf of the European Union and its Member States at the 80th Session of the UNGA Sixth Committee on the report by the ILC: 'General Principles of Law' (27 October 2025) [6] and [8]; *Questions relating to the Seizure and Detention of Certain Documents and Data (Timor-Leste v Australia)* Memorial of Timor-Leste (28 April 2014) fn 148; *Total SA v Argentine Republic* (n 214) [130].

[220] See also ILC (14 July 2021) UN Doc A/CN.4/SR.3539, 5 (Jalloh).

[221] On these principles: *Allegations of Genocide under the Convention on the Prevention and Punishment of the Crime of Genocide (Ukraine v Russian Federation: 32 States intervening)* (Preliminary Objections) [2024] ICJ Rep 360 [105]; *Legality of Use of Force (Yugoslavia v Belgium) (Provisional Measures)* [1999] ICJ Rep 124 [44].

settlement of international disputes, suggesting a particular relevance of their practice for identifying GPL applicable in this context.

7.4.2.3 Transposition of regional principles to the (universal) international legal system

The second criterion for the identification of general principles of law is contained in draft Conclusion 6, which provides that '[a] principle common to the various legal systems of the world may be transposed to the international legal system insofar as it is compatible with that system'. The compatibility of regional principles with the international legal system cannot be presumed given that these typically arise within distinct institutional legal frameworks in that region. In the case of EU principles of law, the issue is even more complicated due to the insistence by the CJEU on the unique character of certain regional principles.[222] The ICJ, in its 2007 *Bosnian Genocide* judgment, refused to recognize the existence of a GPL on the basis of other international instruments and the practice of international courts, notably the ECtHR, stating that these

> do not support the view that there exists a general principle which would apply to the Court, whose Statute not merely contains no such provision, but declares, in Article 60, the *res judicata* principle without exception. . . . [I]n the view of the Court, these . . . , being based on their particular facts, and the nature of the jurisdictions involved, do not indicate the existence of a principle of sufficient generality and weight to override the clear provisions of the Court's Statute, and the principle of *res judicata*.[223]

This does not mean, however, that a principle's regional character precludes its compatibility with the international legal system. As the ICJ's 1986 *Burkina Faso/Mali* judgment indicates, a regional principle can, in certain cases, be compatible with the international legal system. In that case, the ICJ, having established that 'the principle of *uti possidetis* seems to have been first invoked and applied in Spanish America',[224] justified its transposition to the universal level by arguing that

> the principle is not a special rule which pertains solely to one specific system of international law. It is a general principle, which is logically connected with the phenomenon of the obtaining of independence, wherever it occurs.[225]

[222] See also Chapter 5, section 5.3.
[223] *Application of the Convention on the Prevention and Punishment of the Crime of Genocide (Bosnia and Herzegovina v Serbia and Montenegro)* [2007] ICJ Rep 43 [119].
[224] *Frontier Dispute (Burkina Faso/Republic of Mali) (Judgment)* [1986] ICJ Rep 554 [20].
[225] [1986] ICJ Rep 554.

The approach adopted by the ICJ to justify the transposition of a regional principle to the universal level has been strongly criticized by Judge Yusuf, although his critique appears to focus on the Court's application of the first criterion for the identification of a GPL rather than the second.[226] While the ICJ's reasoning on this point is relatively sparse, the test emerging from this case appears to assume the transposition of *uti possidetis* where there is a 'logical connection' between the principle and a purpose or function of such a principle that is capable of universal application. Taking the Court's approach as a starting point, the relevant test for determining the transposability of a regional principle is therefore one of functional equivalence:[227] the closer the similarity between the legal relationship and the subject matter regulated at the regional and international levels, the stronger the presumption that States regulate the matter in a comparable manner internationally and regard the principle as transposable.

7.4.3 Regional practice and *jus cogens*

Regional practice contributes to the formation and identification of peremptory norms of general international law as reflected in Articles 53 and 64 of the VCLT. Regional practice from the African continent has, for instance, played a pivotal role in the process leading to the recognition of the principle of self-determination and the principle of non-refoulement as peremptory norms.[228] However, as the following section will show, the influential role that regional practice would later come to play was not foreseen during the Vienna Conference on the Law of Treaties.

7.4.3.1 Regional practice as evidence of universal acceptance

Compared to the identification of customary international law and GPL, the relevance of regional practice as evidence for the identification of a norm as *jus cogens* has, for a long time, been rather controversial. The *travaux préparatoires* leading to the adoption of Articles 53 and 64 of the VCLT indicate that the role of regional practice for identifying *jus cogens* divided States during the Vienna Conference. The division emerged subsequent to a proposal, submitted by the US, to replace, in

[226] But see for criticism in this regard: *Frontier Dispute (Burkina Faso/Niger)* [2013] ICJ Rep 134 (separate opinion of Judge Yusuf).

[227] On this: R Michaels, 'The Functional Method of Comparative Law' M Reimann and R Zimmermann (ed), *The Oxford Handbook of Comparative Law* (OUP 2012) 373.

[228] On this: T Maluwa, 'African State Practice and the Formation of Some Peremptory Norms of General International Law' in D Tladi (ed), *Peremptory Norms of General International Law (Jus Cogens)* (Brill 2021) 259, 261–62. See on the *jus cogens* status of this principle: *Bernard Anbataayela Mornah v Republic of Benin and Others* App No 028/2018 (AfrCHPR, 22 September 2018) [298]; *Legal Consequences arising from the Policies and Practices of Israel in the Occupied Palestinian Territory, including East Jerusalem* (Advisory Opinion of 19 July 2024) [233].

the text of the two draft articles, the phrase 'a norm accepted and recognized by the international community of States as a whole' with 'recognized in common by the national and regional legal systems of the world'.[229] This proposal was supported mainly, but not exclusively, by Western States.[230] States in support of this proposal argued that the reference to 'regional legal systems' constituted an 'objective criterion' (France) and 'safeguards' (Switzerland) to prevent abuses of the concept of *jus cogens*.[231]

However, the US amendment was vehemently opposed by newly independent States, Socialist States, Latin American States, and by the Special Rapporteur, Humphrey Waldock, himself.[232] Some States pointed out that the term 'regional legal systems' was not well-defined.[233] Others were concerned that this reference would weaken the concept of *jus cogens*. Poland, for example, argued that

> [t]he reference to 'national and regional legal systems' would make it extremely difficult in practice to determine the contents of many peremptory norms. Moreover, the amendment seemed to be based on the notion of the supremacy of the national over the international legal order and of the regional international over the general international legal order.[234]

In a similar vein, the Byelorussian Soviet Socialist Republic emphasized that

> [t]here might be, in the relations between States of a given geographical region, apart from the generally recognized norms of international law, norms which were peculiar to that group of States, but those norms could not be in contradiction with the fundamental principles of international law laid down in the United Nations Charter.[235]

Uruguay expressed similar concerns that the reference to regional systems might lead to a weakening of *jus cogens*, '[f]or example, if a regional international

[229] UN Conference on the Law of Treaties 'Official Records: Documents of the Conference' (First and Second Session) UN Doc A/CONF.39/11/Add.2 (hereinafter: 'UNCLOT III'), 174, [462]; UNCLOT I 295.

[230] See UNCLOT I 295–328.

[231] See in support: UNCLOT I 302 (Chile); 309–10 (France); 323 (Canada); 324, 326 (Malaysia); 307 (Sweden); 310 (Israel); 311 (Italy); 312 (New Zealand); 318 (Japan); 319 (Germany); 320 (Belgium).

[232] See, in addition to the statements mentioned in the text: UNCLOT I 298 (Nigeria); 302 (Poland); 303–304 (Uruguay); 307 (Byelorussian Soviet Socialist Republic); 308 (India); 311 (Hungary); 314 (Bulgaria); 315 (Ethiopia); 315 (Spain); 318 (Czechoslovakia); 319 (Ceylon); 320 (Ecuador); 321 (Ivory Coast); 322 (Tanzania); 322 (Ukrainian Soviet Socialist Republic); 322 (Zambia); 323 (Philippines); 327 (Trinidad and Tobago); 328 (Waldock).

[233] UNCLOT I 322 (Tanzania); 307 (Byelorussian Soviet Socialist Republic), 314 (Bulgaria).

[234] UNCLOT I 302.

[235] UNCLOT I 307.

organization embarked upon a policy of aggression, that would not mean that the rule prohibiting the use of force ceased to be a rule of jus cogens . . . lacking an element of general recognition'.[236] Eventually, the proposal by the US was rejected by 57 votes to 24, with seven abstentions.[237]

Despite the drafting history leading to the adoption of Articles 53 and 64, notably the caution expressed regarding a special role for 'regional legal systems' in its identification, regional practice plays a significant role in the identification of *jus cogens*. Draft Conclusion 7(2) of the ILC draft Conclusions on *jus cogens* adopted in 2022 states that

> [a]cceptance and recognition by a very large and representative majority of States is required for the identification of a norm as a peremptory norm of general international law (*jus cogens*); acceptance and recognition by all States is not required.

The accompanying commentaries of the ILC confirm the important role of regional practice in representing the international community 'as a whole'. In its explanation of draft Conclusion 7(3), the Commission noted that the determination of a 'very large majority of States'

> was not . . . a mechanical exercise in which the number of States is to be counted. . . . The idea that what is required is a qualitative assessment is also captured by the word 'representative' to qualify 'majority of States'. The acceptance and recognition by the international community of States as a whole requires that the acceptance and recognition be across regions, legal systems and cultures.[238]

Thus, regional practice constitutes evidence for establishing whether a peremptory norm is recognized by a representative majority of States. This approach is also reflected in case law of regional courts, such as the decision of the Inter-American Commission in *Michael Domingues v United States*, according to which

> [t]he acceptance of this norm crosses political and ideological boundaries and efforts to detract from this standard have been vigorously condemned by members of the international community as impermissible under contemporary human rights standards.[239]

[236] UNCLOT I 303–304.

[237] UNCLOT I 465.

[238] ILC, 'Draft conclusions on identification and legal consequences of peremptory norms of general international law (jus cogens), with commentaries' (2022) UN Doc A/77/10 ('ILC Report 2022 (Jus cogens)'), 40.

[239] *Michael Domingues v United States* Case 12.285 (IACHR, 22 October 2002) Report No 62/02 [85].

Another interesting example concerns the 2025 advisory opinion on *Climate Emergency and Human Rights* by the Inter-American Court of Human Rights. In its advisory opinion, the Court asserted the existence of a 'recognition of the peremptory prohibition to generate massive and irreversible damage to the environment'.[240] In support of its finding, the Court argued, inter alia, that

> State practice, the elaboration of multilateral environmental treaties, the resolutions of the United Nations General Assembly and the case law of regional courts constitute a process of progressive consolidation that should be interpreted as an emerging juridical recognition of the non-derogable prohibition of irreversible environmental damage.[241]

Both examples illustrate that practice of regional bodies may serve as indicative evidence for recognition of a norm as *jus cogens*, notably as subsidiary means under Article 38(1)(d) of the ICJ Statute.[242] Yet, without further support, such as explicit or implicit endorsement by the States themselves, such decisions cannot substitute the requisite recognition. As the IACHR did not refer to specific practice in its reasoning, it remains to be seen to what extent its finding will contribute to the emergence of regional and, eventually, universal recognition of the prohibition of irreversible environmental damage as *jus cogens*. A certain convergence between the universal and regional courts in this regard may be reflected by the fact that the ICJ, in its *Climate Change* Advisory Opinion, considered that 'certain rules of international law relating to global common goods, such as the climate system, may produce *erga omnes* obligations'.[243] The role of regional practice in the identification of *jus cogens* also assumes a particularly important role when it comes to preventing the recognition of a norm as *jus cogens*. For example, the decision by the ILC to include racial discrimination but not gender discrimination in the list of peremptory norms annexed to the ILC Conclusions was based on 'the significant number of reservations that are attached to the principal instrument on gender discrimination', mainly based on Shari'a law.[244]

7.4.3.2 Regional organizations as members of the 'international community'?

Nevertheless, by contrast to customary international law and, according to the view taken here, GPL, the practice of regional IOS 'as such' does not constitute

[240] See eg *Climate Emergency and Human Rights* (Advisory Opinion AO-32/25) (29 May 2025) IACHR Series A No 32 [294].

[241] *Climate Emergency and Human Rights* (n 240) [293].

[242] See on Article 38(1)(d) (n 122).

[243] *Climate Change* (n 73) [440].

[244] ILC, 'Fourth report on peremptory norms of general international law (*jus cogens*) by Dire Tladi, Special Rapporteur' (2019) UN Doc A/CN.4/727, fn 411. See for criticism of that decision: P Viseur Sellers, '*Jus Cogens*: Redux' (2022) 116 AJIL Unbound 281.

acceptance or recognition of a norm for it to qualify as *jus cogens*.[245] In this regard, the ILC, in its 2022 draft Conclusions, decided to retain the limited formulation contained in the 1969 VCLT (and which was confirmed in the 1986 VCLT), explaining in the commentary that

> [a]cts and practice of international organizations may provide evidence for the acceptance and recognition of States when determining whether a norm has a peremptory character. Ultimately, however, the positions of entities other than States are not, of themselves, sufficient to establish the acceptance and recognition required for the elevation of a norm of general international law to peremptory status.[246]

Given the more liberal approach towards the relevance of IO practice 'as such' in the project on customary international law, this position appears, at first glance, overly restrictive. However, the approach adopted by the ILC does not exclude considering the practice of regional IOs as evidence for the identification of *jus cogens*. Draft Conclusion 8(2) *does* recognize the role of IO resolutions as evidence for acceptance and recognition by States and thus caters to the significant role the practice of regional IOs assumes in the identification of *jus cogens*.[247] Above all, it is doubtful whether the reasoning justifying the distinct role of IO practice in the context of customary international law and GPL can be easily transposed to the context of *jus cogens*. The argument that (regional) IOs may, in certain cases, contribute to the formation of customary international law (and GPL) is rooted in them being conferred exclusive competences with respect to a certain field of international law. Yet, the acceptance of a norm as being of a peremptory character is based on an absolute form of recognition, that is, as constituting a norm from which no derogation is permitted. Such recognition cannot be limited to, or derived from, just one area of international law, where a regional IO might exercise exclusive competences. Such a more cautious approach also helps avoid regional imbalances in recognizing norms as having *jus cogens* character, especially given that some regional bodies are more willing to pronounce on the *jus cogens* status of certain norms than others.[248]

[245] See eg UNGA (5 December 2016) UN Doc A/C.6/71/SR.27 [9] (Canada). See further: ILC, 'Topical summary of the discussion held in the Sixth Committee' (2017) UN Doc A/CN.4/713, 15, [60].
[246] ILC Report 2022 (*Jus cogens*) (n 238) 39.
[247] ILC Report 2022 (*Jus cogens*) (n 238), draft Conclusion 8(2).
[248] See on the practice in the Inter-American system: JJ Ruda Santolaria, 'The Treatment of Peremptory Norms of General International Law (Jus Cogens) in the Inter-American Human Rights System' in D Tladi (ed), *Peremptory Norms of General International Law (Jus Cogens)* (Brill 2021) 319.

7.4.3.3 Regional 'super norms' as evidence of non-derogability

As discussed in Chapter 5, there is currently insufficient evidence to establish the existence of regional *jus cogens*, even though some instances of regional practice suggest that certain rules are accorded a hierarchically superior status within a given region.[249] Such practice may be considered as evidence for the recognition of a rule as *jus cogens*, reflecting the position of States in the region.[250] However, such regional practice can only be considered where the special status of such regional rules is not limited to a specific regional legal system (such as rules concerning the institutional relationship between the regional institutions and its members, as is the case with certain 'constitutional' EU principles) or otherwise confined to States within the region (as was the case, for example, with the *Brezhnev Doctrine* or with the supremacy of *Shari'a* law). By contrast, regional practice relating to the prohibitions of enforced disappearance and the juvenile death penalty, as well as the right of access to courts may indicate the recognition of States within the respective regions of those rules as peremptory norms of general international law.[251]

7.5 Conclusion

As the final stage of the three-step approach grounded in secondary rules, this chapter examined the conditions under which regional practice—whether or not it crystallizes into regional international law—nonetheless shapes the evolution of general international law.

It demonstrated that regional practice plays a central role in adapting both written and unwritten general international law over time. The important role of regional practice in shaping general international law is based both on the absence of a central lawmaker at the universal level and the distinct attributes often associated with regional practice: its presumed representativeness, its relative legal maturity, and its greater identifiability. These features enable regional practice to act as a catalyst for legal change, thus to 'reform' general international law, through the formal and informal mechanisms international law provides for its own adaptation over time. At the same time, the inherent exclusivity of regional practice carries the risk that one or more particularly powerful regions may exert disproportionate influence in steering legal change, thereby 'deforming' general international law. In balancing the ambivalent role of regional practice in the evolution of general international law, the universal secondary rules governing its formation, identification, and interpretation serve a dual function: they channel the trailblazing role

[249] See Chapter 5, section 5.4.3.
[250] See section 7.4.3.1.
[251] See also: ILC (n 244) [30].

of regional practice in adapting international law to emerging global challenges, while ensuring the equal participation of all States in that process, thereby safeguarding against regional imbalance, imposition, and exceptionalism.

The manner in which secondary rules perform this dual function—both enabling and constraining change driven by regional practice—has been illustrated by numerous examples from State practice. These include the contribution of regional practice to the gradual adaptation of several quasi-universal treaties, notably universal human rights treaties, the collective security system of the UN Charter; the evolution of UNCLOS, particularly in response to sea-level rise; and the adaptation of the WTO Covered Agreements in light of the unprecedented expansion of RTAs. The analysis has also shown how secondary rules channel the influence of regional practice in the emergence of unwritten international law, such as the right to a healthy environment, while preventing the imposition of purportedly universal unwritten rules without adequate support by all States.

While regional practice thus plays an important role in shaping general international law, this does not imply that the practice of universal institutions, in particular of organs of the UN, is any less significant. Rather, in areas where States have agreed to universalize the pursuit of a common objective, State practice suggests that the relative influence of regional practice is reduced, and the role of universal institutions correspondingly becomes more prominent.

8
Conclusion

8.1 International law as the interplay of regional and general international law

In recent years, the discourse on the relationship between regional and general international law has undergone a remarkable shift. For much of the post-Cold War period and as prominently captured in the ILC Fragmentation Report, regional international law was seen as having no distinct legal significance, while the integrative role of general international law, even if only loosely defined, was largely taken for granted. Two decades later, the pendulum appears to be swinging in the opposite direction. Several institutions and rules established in the aftermath of two world wars, long regarded as the epitome of general international law, face existential challenges, including accusations of being regionally biased by design. Meanwhile, the idea of regionally defined spheres of influence within which certain rules under international law may be modified, set aside, or replaced by regional rules appears to be gaining traction (again). Although the two paradigms diverge fundamentally in their understanding of the relationship between regional and general international law, both ultimately cast it as a binary choice in which one must be subordinated to the other. This book points in a different direction. It concludes that the international legal order is not based on the primacy of either regional or general international law, but rather on their equal and mutually constitutive relationship, confirming that

> [t]he particular and the universal are related through paradox: the articulation of the particular can be carried out only by reaching towards the universal. In this way, the universal also remains inseparable from the particular claims from which it emanates.[1]

While the secondary rules of international law do not resolve this paradox, the book shows that they provide a means of addressing it. In this sense, the book contains a plea for the value of a 'culture of formalism', especially during periods of geopolitical transformation.[2]

[1] M Koskenniemi, *The Gentle Civilizer of Nations: The Rise and Fall of International Law 1870–1960* (5th edn, CUP 2008) 505.
[2] Koskenniemi (n 1) 494–509.

Regional and General International Law. Janina Barkholdt, Oxford University Press. © Janina Barkholdt 2026.
DOI: 10.1093/9780198953432.003.0008

8.2 Regional international law shapes the evolution of (general) international law

The observation that 'the universal ... remains inseparable from the particular claims from which it emanates' reflects a key conclusion of this book: regional international law plays a determinative role in shaping international law, including the rules applicable across all regions (general international law). Regional international law is widely recognized, both by States within a given region and by third parties, as carrying distinct legal significance for the evolution of (general) international law, which sets it apart from non-regional particular international law.

This first main conclusion rests on three pillars.

First, Chapter 2 shows that the 'region', much like the 'State', is a social phenomenon with legal implications and therefore qualifies as a legal concept. States and IOs attach specific legal consequences to the 'regional' quality of a practice, rule, or institution in practice. Analogous to a State, a region can be defined according to three criteria that can be discerned from such practice. The use of the term 'region' in legal practice is narrower than in other contexts. In this narrower sense, a region refers to a grouping of two or more States that: (1) can be objectively identified by third parties, typically on the basis of geographic proximity (criterion of identifiability); (2) exhibits a minimum degree of normative cohesion (criterion of normative cohesion); and (3) is thereby distinguishable from other groups of States (criterion of distinctiveness). Accordingly, the term 'region[al]' defines a state of normative cohesion which typically arises from geographic proximity among a group of States distinguishing it from third parties. 'Regional international law' describes rules of international law which arise from this form of normative cohesion (section 2.2).

Second, Chapters 2 and 4 to 7 demonstrate that it is precisely these three defining features of regions that give regional international law legal significance, setting it apart from non-regional particular international law. Importantly, this distinct significance does not rest solely on unilateral assertions by a State or a group of regional States regarding the special or even *sui generis* character of a regional rule. It is grounded in, and conditioned by, the convergence between the normative claim articulated at the regional level and its acceptance by third parties (section 2.3). The book shows that third parties are willing to accord distinct legal significance to practices, rules, and institutions that emanate from regions fulfilling the three criteria of identifiability, normative cohesion, and distinctiveness identified above:

The criterion of identifiability facilitates the identification, both by States within the region and by third parties, of a uniform legal approach among a regionally defined group of States (section 2.3.2). This, in turn, translates into, inter alia, a more prominent role for implicit forms of consent, such as a duty to react or protest, in the interpretation of regional treaties in light of subsequent regional practice (section 4.3) and in the formation of regional custom

(section 5.2). It also underlies the presumption that such regional practice is representative for a part of the international community of States for purposes of interpreting universal agreements by way of subsequent practice (section 7.3) and the identification of a rule under general customary international, a general principle of law, or a peremptory norm of general international law (section 7.4).

The criterion of normative cohesion forms the basis of a privileged role of regional practice in the interpretation, identification, and formation of international law. To the extent that regional law is embedded within a cohesive and comprehensive legal order, it enjoys a heightened (though not unlimited) level of regulatory autonomy based on the respect for the self-determination of political communities and supported by practice (section 2.3.3). This is illustrated by the fact that third parties, within the outer limits of treaty interpretation, defer to region-specific interpretive approaches that differ from the general law of treaties (section 4.3). Moreover, third parties may recognize regional rules as valid within the region, even when the processes by which they emerge differ somewhat from those under general international law. This is illustrated, for example, by general principles of law with a regional scope of application (section 5.3). By contrast, such recognition has not yet extended to *jus cogens* norms with a regional scope of application (section 5.4). Practice further suggests that regional rules receive limited deference when they coexist with other applicable rules of international law that point in different directions (section 6.2). Several universal treaties assign a particular role to regional rules and institutions in the pursuit of the treaty's object and purpose, resulting in a particularly relevant role of regional practice in the interpretation of those treaties (section 7.3).

The criterion of distinctiveness typically corresponds to a lack of generalizability of a particular normative approach beyond the region. A lack of generalizability typically exists where the regional rule relates to a specific geographic situation, the political self-organization of States in that region, or the activities of a regional organization relating to that region. Such non-generalizability is significant for the extent to which third parties accept the deviation of such regional rules from general international law. The more a regional rule is limited in its personal, substantive, and territorial scope to the region, the more willing third parties are to recognize regional exceptions from general international law. This is because the risk of unfavourable spill-over effects of such non-generalizable regional law, that fall outside the scope of the protection afforded to third parties by the *pacta tertiis* principle and thus infringe their own legal position, is relatively low (section 2.3.4). Accordingly, practice suggests a greater tolerance on the part of third parties with respect to regional rules diverging from general rules, for example, in the interpretation of the constituent instrument of a regional organization (section 4.3) or in the formation of distinct regional rules regulating the use of a certain geographic feature located in a specific region ('local custom') (section 5.2).

Third, the flip side of the distinct legal significance of regional international law lies in a 'triple challenge' it poses to the international legal order (section 2.4). Regional international law presents a challenge to the evolution of international law precisely because of the features that distinguish it from non-regional particular international law. This triple challenge comprises an analytical challenge due to the ambivalent legal effects of regional law (section 2.4.1), a methodological challenge given its elusive legal nature (section 2.4.2), and a normative challenge, relating to the difficulty of determining a substantive common denominator shared across all regions (section 2.4.3). At its core, this triple challenge concerns the question how to assess whether regional idiosyncrasies in the law of treaties (4.1), unwritten regional norms (5.1), regional deviations from other international law rules (6.1), and regional practice under universal rules (7.1) advance the constructive development of international law or, conversely, whether they undermine it.

8.3 General international law ensures regional plurality in international law

The second main conclusion of this book is that general international law is indispensable for protecting regional plurality. In this sense, it confirms that 'the articulation of the particular can be carried out only by reaching towards the universal'.[3]

Although the term 'general international law' lacks a precise definition, this book concludes that the various interpretations converge on a single idea: they designate the rules, which are shared by, and applicable to, all subjects across all regions (section 3.2). The body of general international law, however, is not a fixed set of rules; it is continuously adapted and renegotiated by the subjects of international law. The rules that determine this process of continuous adaptation and renegotiation represent a distinct type of general international law, namely the secondary rules of international law (section 3.2.4). These secondary rules of international law have the methodological (section 3.3), normative (section 3.4), and analytical potential (section 3.5) to overcome the triple challenge posed by regional international law. On that basis, the book develops a 'three-step approach' for assessing the validity and the effects of regional practice and rules within the international legal system. This approach not only helps accommodate but also ensures regional plurality in international law.

First, the secondary rules governing the identification and interpretation of international law help to determine whether a regional rule or practice qualifies as regional *international* law (rather than as a mere regional policy, doctrine, or tradition) whether under the law of treaties (Chapter 4) or as a form of unwritten regional international law (Chapter 5). When a regional rule is recognized as a rule of international law, it becomes part of the body of international legal rules that are applicable and opposable to the subjects within that region. Conversely, where a regional legal claim does not meet the threshold of international law, it cannot bind

[3] See (n 1).

or confer rights on any subject under international law. Accordingly, this first step not only acknowledges the regulatory autonomy of regional communities but also serves as a safeguard against normative impositions by regional hegemons seeking to cloak their conduct in idiosyncratic regional legal arguments.

Second, where a regional claim qualifies as regional international law, the secondary rules governing the interpretation and application of international law assist in determining which rule prevails when both a rule of regional international law and another rule under international law apply to a particular situation and compliance with one rule entails a failure to comply with the other rule (Chapter 6). If the regional rule successfully satisfies this second step (meaning it may be applied despite competing rules under international law), the entity asserting the regional legal claim is entitled to do so. Accordingly, this second step recognizes that regional rules may, in certain cases, pursue alternative regulatory approaches and thus a certain regional autonomy, while distinguishing such cases from instances of regional non-compliance.

Third, when a regional claim fails to succeed either at the first or second step of the three-step-approach, the secondary rules governing the formation, identification, and interpretation of international law assist in evaluating whether such regional practice nonetheless constitutes a constructive contribution to the development of international law (its 'reform') rather than its deformation (Chapter 7). In this regard, the third step acknowledges that regional practice may act as a trailblazer in shaping the common framework of international law, while secondary rules provide a method to prevent regional imbalances and exceptionalism.

Accordingly, the book concludes that regional practice that fails any of the three steps yet continues to be followed by a State, or group of States, undermines not only general international law but also, ultimately, the role of regional international law. This is because the three-step approach is designed not to suppress, but to safeguard regional plurality within the common framework of international law. It thus functions both as an instrument to enrich and adapt the common legal framework through regional practices and rules and as a warning system against regional imbalances, impositions, and exceptionalism that threaten to usurp the common framework of international law, ultimately undermining regional plurality within it.

8.4 Regional and general international law: normative ownership through secondary rules

The coexistence of regional and general international law reflects a core problem of international law: who determines the rules based on which States, regardless of their size, power, and interests, interact? Which rules are applicable among all States given their diversity in political systems and ideological beliefs? Such questions become particularly urgent during periods of geopolitical transformation, where they manifest themselves in the tension between regional and general international law. Some States and other relevant actors may feel tempted to use the apparent shift to a more multipolar world and the actual and alleged regional imbalance reflected in international law as a justification to discard certain—perhaps inconvenient—rules, or even the entire concept of 'general international law', as outdated and to replace such general rules by regional rules. Others, by contrast, may feel compelled to assert even more forcefully the existence of universally applicable rules, without, however, considering ways to respond to or integrate such regional rules. A shared assumption underlying these otherwise opposing perspectives is that this situation ultimately requires a choice between regional *or* general international law.

In contrast, this book shows that the secondary rules of international law provide all States, regardless of whether they belong to a certain region or not, an equal opportunity to participate in and control the formation, identification, interpretation, and application of both regional *and* general international law. Hence, the secondary rules of international law confer normative ownership on all States with respect to both regional and general international law. As the ultimate safeguard against regional fragmentation and the usurpation of international law by regional hegemons, they are key for ensuring that international law remains both adaptive and resilient over time.

Bibliography

Abass A, 'Historical and Political Background to the Malabo Protocol' in G Werle and M Vormbaum (eds), *The African Criminal Court: A Commentary on the Malabo Protocol* (Springer 2017) 11

Abass A, *Regional Organisations and the Development of Collective Security: Beyond Chapter VIII of the UN Charter* (Hart 2004)

Abi-Saab G, 'Cours général de droit international public' (1987) 207 RdC 198

Acharya A, 'Norm Subsidiarity and Regional Orders: Sovereignty, Regionalism, and Rule-Making in the Third World' (2011) 55:1 Int Stud Q 95

Akehurst M, 'Custom as a Source of International Law' (1975) 47 BYBIL 1

Akehurst M, 'Enforcement Action by Regional Agencies, with Special Reference to the Organization of American States' (1967) 42 BYBIL 175

Akehurst M, 'The Hierarchy of the Sources of International Law' (1976) 47 BYBIL 273

Amao O, *African Union Law. The Emergence of a Sui Generis Legal Order* (Hart 2018)

Ammann O, *Domestic Courts and the Interpretation of International Law Methods and Reasoning Based on the Swiss Example* (Brill 2020)

Ananthavinayagan TV, 'Breaking Bad Customs: Involving the Idea of *Opinio Juris Communis* in Asian State Practice' (2018) 24 AYIL 24

Anghie A, 'Identifying Regions in the History of International Law' in B Fassbender and A Peters (eds), *The Oxford Handbook of the History of International Law* (OUP 2012) 1058

Anghie A, *Imperialism, Sovereignty, and the Making of International Law* (CUP 2004)

Anghie A, 'The Injustices of Reparation' (2025) 119:3 AJIL 423

Aral I, 'Russia's Expulsion: The Council of Europe as the Guardian of European Imperialism' (2025) 38:2 LJIL 113

Aust HP, 'Between Universal Aspiration and Local Application: Concluding Observations' in HP Aust and G Nolte (eds), *The Interpretation of International Law by Domestic Courts* (OUP 2016) 333

Aust HP, 'The Rules of Interpretation as Secondary Rules: The Perspective of Domestic Courts' in M Heupel and T Reinold (eds), *The Rule of Law in Global Governance* (Palgrave Macmillan 2016) 59

Azaria D, '"Codification by Interpretation": The International Law Commission as an Interpreter of International Law' (2020) 31:1 EJIL 171

Azaria D, 'The International Law Commission's Return to the Law of Sources of International Law' (2019) 13:6 FIU Law Review 989

Baetens F, 'First to Rise and First to Fall The Court of Cartago (1907–1918)' in I de la Rasilla and JE Viñuales (eds), *Experiments in International Adjudication: Historical Accounts* (CUP 2019) 211

Bandeira Galindo GR and Yip C, 'Customary International Law and the Third World: Do Not Step on the Grass' (2017) 16 Chin J Int Law 251

Bandeira Galindo GR, 'Particular Customary International Law and the International Law Commission: Mapping Presences and Absences' (2021) 86 QIL Zoom-in 3

Barboza J, 'The Customary Rule: From Chrysalis to Butterfly' in CA Armas Barea and others (eds), *Liber Amicorum In Memoriam of Judge José María Ruda* (Kluwer Law International 2000) 1

Barkholdt J, 'Intervention by Invitation' in A Peters (ed), *Max Planck Encyclopedia of Public International Law* (OUP 2024)

Barkholdt J, 'Is the International Law Commission Taking Regionalism Seriously (Enough)?' (2022) 12 GoJIL 155
Barkholdt J, 'Progress Through Preservation of the Legal *Status Quo*: Paradox or Prerequisite?' (2024) 4 ZaöRV 925
Barkholdt J, 'The Contribution of International Organizations to the Formation, Interpretation and Identification of International Law: Questions Arising from the Work of the International Law Commission' (2021) 18 IOLR 1
Barkholdt J, 'Unwritten European Rules in International Law: From Eurocentric to Regional International Law?' (2026) LJIL (forthcoming)
Barnidge RP, 'Anti-Zionism, *Jus Cogens*, and International Law: The Case of the Banjul Charter and the Arab Charter' (2018) 9 J Middle East Afr 77
Bartels L, 'Regional Trade Agreements' in A Peters (ed), *Max Planck Encyclopedia of Public International Law* (OUP 2013)
Becker Lorca A and Álvez Marín A, 'Turning International Law Against Indigenous Peoples' in A Chehtman, A Huneeus, and S Puig (eds), *Latin American International Law in the Twenty-First Century* (OUP 2025) 81
Becker Lorca A, *Mestizo International Law. A Global Intellectual History 1842–1933* (CUP 2014)
Bennett TW, 'Comparative Law and African Customary Law' in M Reimann and R Zimmermann (eds), *The Oxford Handbook of Comparative Law* (2nd edn, OUP 2019) 652
Berman F, 'Why do we need a law of treaties?—Inaugural Lecture' (2017) 385 RdC 19
Berry D, *Caribbean Integration Law* (OUP 2014)
Besson S and Kassoti E, 'The International Law of Regional Organizations—Mapping the Issues' (2024) 21:1 IOLR 1
Besson S, 'Sources of International Human Rights Law: How General is General International Law?' in J d'Aspremont and S Besson (eds), *The Oxford Handbook of the Sources of International Law* (OUP 2017) 769
Besson S, 'The Politics of Regional International Organizations: A New Dawn for the Political Legitimacy of International Law' (2024) 21:1 IOLR 87
Bjorge E, 'Opposability and Non-opposability in International Law' (2021) BYBIL 1
Bleckmann A, 'Völkergewohnheitsrecht trotz widersprüchlicher Praxis?' (1976) 36 ZaöRV 374
Blokker N, 'Legal Facets of the Practice of International Organizations' (2024) 435 RdC 73
Boisson de Chazournes L and Campanelli D, 'Neighbor States' in A Peters (ed), *Max Planck Encyclopedia of Public International Law* (OUP 2006)
Boisson de Chazournes L, *Interactions Between Regional and Universal Organizations—A Legal Perspective* (Brill 2017)
Bonafé BI and Palchetti P, 'Relying on General Principles in International Law' in C Brölmann and Y Radi (eds), *Research Handbook on the Theory and Practice of International Law-Making* (Edward Elgar Publishing 2016) 160
Bordin FL and Odermatt J, 'International Law of Regional Organizations: A Comparative Perspective' (2024) 21:1 IOLR 19
Bordin FL, 'Interpreting Constituent Instruments to Justify the Evolving Powers of International Organizations' in G Marceau and H Gött (eds), *International Organization Initiatives: How and Why Organizations Adapt and Change* (OUP 2025)
Borgen CJ, 'Treaty Conflicts and Systemic Fragmentation' in DB Hollis (ed), *The Oxford Guide to Treaties* (2nd edn, OUP 2020) 432
Börzel TA and Risse T, 'Introduction: Framework of the Handbook and Conceptual Clarifications' in TA Börzel and T Risse (eds), *The Oxford Handbook of Comparative Regionalism* (OUP 2016) 3
Bos M, *A Methodology of International Law* (Elsevier Science Publishers 1984)
Boyle A, 'Further Development Of The Law Of The Sea Convention: Mechanisms For Change' (2005) 54 ICLQ 563
Bradford A, *The Brussels Effect: How the European Union Rules the World* (OUP 2020)
Bradley CA and Gulati M, 'Customary International Law and Withdrawal Rights in an Age of Treaties' (2010) 21 Duke J Comp & Int'l L 1

Brölmann C, 'Regional Organizations in International Law: Exploring the Function-Territory Divide' (2024) 21:1 IOLR 132

Brölmann C, 'Typologies and the "Essential Juridical Character" of Treaties' in MJ Bowman and D Kritsiotis (eds), *Conceptual and Contextual Perspectives on the Modern Law of Treaties* (CUP 2018) 79

Brunnée J and S Toope, 'Self-Defence Against Non-State Actors: Are Powerful States Willing but Unable to Change International Law?' (2018) 67:2 ICLQ 263

Brunnée J and Toope S, 'International Law and the Practice of Legality: Stability and Change' (2018) 49:4 VUW L Rev 429

Buga I, *Modification of Treaties by Subsequent Practice* (OUP 2018)

Bull H, *The Anarchical Society. A Study of Order in World Politics* (3rd edn, Palgrave 2002)

Buss A, 'The Preah Vihear Case and Regional Customary Law' (2010) 9 Chin J Int Law 111

Buxbaum HL, 'Territory, Territoriality, and the Resolution of Jurisdictional Conflict' (2009) 57:3 Am J Comp L 631

Buzzini GP, 'La "généralité" du droit international général: réflexions sur la polysémie d'un concept' (2004) 2 RGDIP 381

Bydoon M, 'Reservations on the "Convention on the Elimination of All Forms of Discrimination against Women (CEDAW)" Based on Islam and its Practical Application in Jordan: Legal Perspectives' (2011) 25 Arab Law Q 51

Cabrita T, 'The Integration Paradox: an ILC View on the EU Contribution to the Codification and Development of Rules of General International Law' (2021) 5 Europe and the World: A Law Review 1

Cannizzaro E, 'In defence of Front Polisario: The ECJ as a global *jus cogens* maker' (2018) 55:2 CMLR 569.

Caserta S, 'Regional Integration through Law and International Courts – the Interplay between De Jure and De Facto Supranationality in Central America and the Caribbean' (2017) 30:3 LJIL 579

Castellarin E, 'General Principles of EU Law and General International Law' in M Andenas and others (eds), *General Principles of Law and the Coherence of International Law* (Brill Nijhoff 2019) 131

Chalmers D, 'The Distinctiveness of Regional International Organization Law' (2024) 21:1 IOLR 43

Charney JI, 'Universal International Law' (1993) 87:4 AJIL 529

Chesterman S, 'An International Rule of Law?' (2008) 56:2 AJIL 331

Chimni BS, 'Epilogue: Fragmentary Thoughts on Change' in N Krisch and E Yildiz (eds), *The Many Paths of Change in International Law* (OUP 2023) 335

Chimni BS, 'International Institutions Today: An Imperial Global State in the Making' (2004) 15:1 EJIL 1

Chimni BS, 'Is there an Asian Approach to International Law? Questions, Theses and Reflections' (2008) 14 Asian Yearbook of International Law 249

Chimni BS, 'The Articles on State Responsibility and the Guiding Principles of Shared Responsibility: A TWAIL Perspective' (2020) 31:4 EJIL 1211

Chinkin C, *Third Parties in International Law* (OUP 1993)

Choudhry S, 'Group Rights in Comparative Constitutional Law: Culture, Economics, or Political Power?' M Rosenfeld and A Sajó (eds), *The Oxford Handbook of Comparative Constitutional Law* (OUP 2016) 1099

Cohen-Jonathan G, 'La coutume locale' (1961) 7 Annuaire français de droit international 119

Cooley A and Schaaf M, 'Grounding the Backlash: Regional Security Treaties, Counternorms, and Human Rights in Eurasia' in S Hopgood, J Snyder, and L Vinjamuri (eds), *Human Rights Futures* (CUP 2017) 159

Costelloe D, *Legal Consequences of Peremptory Norms in International Law* (CUP 2017)

Crawford J, 'Continuity and Discontinuity in International Dispute Settlement: An Inaugural Lecture' (2010) 1:1 J Int Dispute Settl 3

Crawford J, 'The ILC's Articles on Responsibility of States for Internationally Wrongful Acts: A Retrospect' (2002) 96:4 AJIL 874
Crawford J, 'Universalism and Regionalism from the Perspective of the Work of the International Law Commission. *International Law on the Eve of the 21st Century* (New York, 1997) (UN Publication (No E/F 97.V.4)) 99
Crawford J, *Brownlie's Principles of Public International Law* (9th edn, OUP 2019)
Crawford J, *Chance, Order, Change: The Course of International Law, General Course on Public International Law* (Brill 2013)
Crawford J, *The Creation of States in International Law* (2nd edn, OUP 2007)
Crema L, 'The "Right Mix" and "Ambiguities" in Particular Customs: A Few Remarks on the Navigational and Related Rights Case' in N Boschiero and others (eds), *International Courts and the Development of International Law: Essays in Honour of Tullio Treves* (Springer 2013) 65
Cuyvers A, 'Comparing Regional Law' in M Siems and PJ Yap (eds), *The Cambridge Handbook of Comparative Law* (CUP 2024) 655
d'Aspremont J, 'Customary International Law Symposium: Rules Everywhere and At All Times (Whether You Like It or Not)' (OpinioJuris, 8 July 2020)
d'Aspremont J, 'The Idea of Rules in International Law' (2014) 84 BYBIL 103
d'Aspremont J, 'The International Court of Justice and the Irony of System-Design' (2017) 8:2 J Int Dispute Settl 366
d'Aspremont J, 'The International Court of Justice as the Master of the Sources' in C Espósito and K Parlett (eds), *The Cambridge Companion to the International Court of Justice* (CUP 2023) 165
Danilenko GM, 'The Economic Court of the Commonwealth of Independent States' (1999) 31 NYU J Int'L L & Pol 893
Danilenko GM, *Law-Making in the International Community* (Martinus Nijhoff Publishers 1993)
Davenport K, *The Nuclear Nonproliferation Treaty* (Morgan & Claypool Publishers 2019)
David E, 'Primary and Secondary Rules' in J Crawford and others (eds), *The Law of International Responsibility* (OUP 2012) 27
de Andrade MC, 'Regional Principles of Law in the Works of the International Law Commission' (2021) 86 QIL, Zoom-in 3
de Búrca G, 'The European Court of Justice and the International Legal Order after Kadi' (2010) 51 Harv Int Law J 1
de Hoogh A, Regionalism and the Unity of International Law from a Positivist Perspective. Conference Paper No 3/2012 of the ESIL 5th Biennial Conference (Valencia, 13–15 September 2012) 1
de Silva N and M Amadi, 'Renewed State Backlash Against the African Court: Tunisia is the Fifth State to Withdraw Individual and NGO Access' (EJILTalk!, 23 May 2025)
de Visscher C, 'La codification du droit international' (1925) 6 RdC 325
de Wet E, 'Regional Organizations and Arrangements: Authorization, Ratification, or Independent Action' in M Weller (ed), *The Oxford Handbook of the Use of Force in International Law* (OUP 2015) 314
de Wet E, 'The Emergence of International and Regional Value Systems as a Manifestation of the Emerging International Constitutional Order' (2006) 19:3 LJIL 611
de Wet E, *Military Assistance on Request and the Use of Force* (OUP 2020)
de Witte B, 'European International Law' in R Schütze (ed), *Globalisation and Governance: International Problems, European Solutions* (CUP 2018) 227
de Witte B, 'Sources and the Subjects of International Law: The European Union's Semi-Autonomous System of Sources' in J d'Aspremont and S Besson (eds), *The Oxford Handbook of the Sources of International Law* (OUP 2017) 769
Dellmuth LM and Tallberg J, 'Why National and International Legitimacy Beliefs are Linked: Social Trust as an Antecedent Factor' (2020) 15 Rev Int Organ 311
Denza E, 'Article 41' in *Diplomatic Law: Commentary on the Vienna Convention on Diplomatic Relations* (4th edn, OUP 2016)

Diala AC, 'Comparative indigenous law' in M Siems and PJ Yap (eds), *The Cambridge Handbook of Comparative Law* (CUP 2024) 693

Díaz de Valdés JM and Verdugo S, 'The ALBA Constitutional Project and Political Representation' (2019) 17:2 ICON 479

Donald A and Forde A, 'Reinforce, Reform or Rupture? The Future of the European Convention on Human Rights' (EJILTalk!, 29 October 2025)

Dörr O, 'Article 31' in O Dörr and K Schmalenbach (eds), *Vienna Convention on the Law of Treaties: A Commentary* (2nd edn, Springer 2018)

Dörr O, 'Article 32' in O Dörr and K Schmalenbach (eds), *Vienna Convention on the Law of Treaties: A Commentary* (2nd edn, Springer 2018)

Dugard J, 'Walvis Bay: Decolonization and International Law' (1991) 85:4 AJIL 751

Dugard JA, 'The choice before us: International law or a 'rules-based international order'?' (2023) 36:2 LJIL 223

Duguit L, *Traité de droit constitutionnel, Tome 1* (Paris 1911)

Dupuy P-M, '2000–2020: Twenty Years Later, Where Are We in Terms of the Unity of International Law?' (2020) 9 Camb Int Law J 6

Dupuy P-M, 'A Doctrinal Debate in the Globalisation Era: On the "Fragmentation" of International Law' (2007) 1 Eur J Leg Stud 1

Dupuy P-M, 'L'unité de l'ordre juridique international: Cours général de droit international public' (2000) 297 RdC 9

Dupuy P-M, 'The Danger of Fragmentation or Unification of the International Legal System and the International Court of Justice' 31 (1999) NYU J Int'L L & Pol 791

Dworkin R, *Taking Rights Seriously* (Harvard University Press 1977)

Elias O, 'The Relationship Between General and Particular Customary International Law' (1996) 8 AJICL 67

Fabbricotti A, 'The Interplay Between the WTO and the RTAs: Is It A Question of Interrelation Between Different Sources of International Law?', Inaugural Conference of the Society of International Economic Law (Geneva, 15–17 July 2008) https://ssrn.com/abstract=1151386

Fassbender B, *The United Nations Charter as the Constitution of the International Community* (Brill 2009)

Fietta S and Cleverly R, *A Practitioner's Guide to Maritime Boundary Delimitation* (OUP 2016)

Finke J, 'Regime-collisions: Tensions between treaties (and how to solve them)' in CJ Tams, A Tzanakopoulos, and A Zimmermann (eds), Research Handbook on the Law of Treaties (Edward Elgar Publishing 2014) 415

Fitzmaurice G, 'Some problems regarding the formal sources of international law' in FM van Asbeck and others (eds), *Symbolae Verzijl* (Martinus Nijhoff 1958) 153

Fitzmaurice G, 'The General Principles of International Law Considered from the Standpoint of the Rule of Law' (1957) 92 RdC 1

Fitzmaurice M and Merkouris P, 'Uniformity Versus Specialization (1): The Quest for a Uniform Law of Inter-State Treaties' in CJ Tams, A Tzanakopoulos, and A Zimmermann (eds), *Research Handbook on the Law of Treaties* (Edward Elgar Publishing 2014) 341

Fitzmaurice M and Merkouris P, *Treaties in Motion: The Evolution of Treaties from Formation to Termination* (CUP 2020)

Føllesdal A, 'The Principle of Subsidiarity as a Constitutional Principle in International Law' (2013) 2:1 Global Constitutionalism 37

Forteau M, 'Regional International Law' in A Peters (ed), *Max Planck Encyclopedia of Public International Law* (OUP 2006)

Franck T and Prows P, 'The Role of Presumptions in International Tribunals' (2005) 4:2 The Law and Practice of International Courts and Tribunals 197

Franck TM, 'Legitimacy in the International System' (1988) 82:4 AJIL 751

Franck TM, *The Power of Legitimacy Among Nations* (OUP 1990)

Friedmann W, *The Changing Structure of International Law* (Steven & Sons 1964)

Gaja G, 'Article 38' in O Corten and others (eds), *The Vienna Conventions on the Law of Treaties* (2nd edn, OUP 2025)

Gardiner R, 'The Vienna Convention Rules on Treaty Interpretation' in DB Hollis (ed), *The Oxford Guide to Treaties* (2nd edn, OUP 2020) 459

Gardiner R, *Treaty Interpretation* (2nd edn, OUP 2015)

Garrido-Muñoz A, 'Patterns of Avoidance and Assimilation Peremptory Norms in European Union Law' in FL Bordin, AT Müller, and F Pascual-Vives (eds), *The European Union and Customary International Law* (CUP 2022) 148

Gautron J-C, 'Le fait régional dans la société internationale' in Société Française pour le Droit International (ed), *Colloque de Bordeaux, Régionalisme et universalisme dans le droit international contemporain* (Pedone 1977) 4

Gaver CD, 'What are the Riyadh Agreements?' (*EJILTalk!*, 1 July 2020)

Gestri M, 'Sanctions Imposed by the European Union: Legal and Institutional Aspects' in N Ronzitti (ed), *Coercive Diplomacy, Sanctions and International Law* (Brill 2016) 70

Ginsburg T, 'Authoritarian International Law?' (2019) 114:2 AJIL 221

Gourgourinis A, 'General/Particular International Law and Primary/Secondary Rules: Unitary Terminology of a Fragmented System' (2011) 22:4 EJIL 993

Gray C, *International Law and the Use of Force* (4th edn, OUP 2018)

Green J, *The Persistent Objector Rule in International Law* (OUP 2016)

Greenwood C, 'Unity and Diversity in International Law' M Andenas and E Bjorge (eds), *A Farewell to Fragmentation: Reassertion and Convergence in International Law* (CUP 2015) 37

Grzebyk P, 'Crime of Aggression Against Ukraine: The Role of Regional Customary Law' (2023) 21 J Int Crim Justice 435

Guliyev K, 'Local Custom in International Law—Something in Between General Custom and Treaty' (2017) 19 ICLR 47

Gutiérrez Álvarez JR, 'A Melting Snowball—Difficulties in Identifying Particular Customary International Law' (2024) 73 ICLQ 1083

Habermas J, 'Making Sense of the EU: Toward a Cosmopolitan Europe' (2003) 14:4 Journal Democr 86

Hafner G, 'The Intervention in Czechoslovakia—1968' in T Ruys, O Corten, A Hofer (eds), *The Use of Force in International Law: A Case-Based Approach* (OUP 2018) 143

Hakimi M, 'Making Sense of Customary International Law' (2020) 118:8 Mich Law Rev 1487

Hankings-Evans A, 'The Africanization of International Investment Disputes—from Past to Present' (Verfassungsblog, 23 July 2020)

Hart HLA, *The Concept of Law* (3rd edn, OUP 2012)

Hartmann J and Lott A, 'The Prosecution "Gap" for Attacks on Subsea Cables and Pipelines' (EJILTalk! 13 November 2025) <https://www.ejiltalk.org/the-prosecution-gap-for-attacks-on-subsea-cables-and-pipelines/>

Hasmath R, 'The utility of regional jus cogens', Paper presented at the American Political Science Association Annual Meeting (New Orleans, 30 August–2 September 2012)

Heller KJ, 'Customary International Law Symposium: The Stubborn Tenacity of Secondary Rules' (*OpinioJuris*, 7 July 2020)

Heller KJ, 'Specially-affected States and the Formation of Custom' (2018) 112 AJIL 191

Hofer A, 'Third-Party Countermeasures: Making Custom Out of Ambiguous Practice?' (2025) 74 ICLQ 287

Hoffmeister F and Kleinlein T, 'International Public Order' in A Peters (ed), *Max Planck Encyclopedia of Public International Law* (OUP 2019)

Hsien-Li T, 'No Longer Hard Law's 'Poor Relative': The Growing Respect for Soft, Non-Binding Legal Instruments in the International Order' (EJILTalk! 6 June 2025)

Hsu L, 'Applicability of WTO Law in Regional Trade Agreements: Identifying the Links' in L Bartels and F Ortino (eds), *Regional Trade Agreements and the WTO Legal System* (OUP 2006) 525

Hurrell A, *On Global Order—Powers, Values, and Institutions of the International Society* (OUP 2008)

I Saunders, *General Principles as a Source of International Law* (Hart 2021)

Ikenberry GJ, 'Three Worlds: the West, East and South and the competition to shape global order' (2024) 100 International Affairs 121

Ivory R, 'The Concept of International Law Reform and the Case of Negotiated Settlements in Foreign Bribery Matters' (2024) 35:4 EJIL 867

Jellinek G, *Allgemeine Staatslehre* (3rd edn, Verlag von O. Haring 1914)

Jenks CW, 'The Conflict of Law-Making Treaties' (1953) 30 BYBIL 401

Jennings R and Watts A, *Oppenheim's International Law, Vol I* (9th edn, OUP 2008)

Jennings R, 'The Commonwealth and International Law' (1953) 30 BYBIL 320

Jennings R, 'Universal International Law in a Multicultural World' in M Bos and I Brownlie (eds), *Liber Amicorum for Lord Wilberforce* (OUP 1987) 39

Jessup PC, 'Non-Universal International Law' (1973) 12:3 Columbia J Transnatl Law 415

Jeutner V, *Irresolvable Norm Conflicts in International Law: The Concept of a Legal Dilemma* (OUP 2017)

Jorgensen M, 'Equilibrium & Fragmentation in The International Rule of Law: The Rising Chinese Geolegal Order' (2018) 21 KFG Working Paper Series

Jorgensen M, 'The Jurisprudence of the Rules-Based Order: The Power of Rules Consistent with but Not Binding Under International Law' (2021) 22 MJIL 221

Jouannet E, 'Universalism and Imperialism: The True-False Paradox of International Law?' (2007) 18:3 EJIL 379

Kajtár G, Çalı B, and Milanovic M, 'Introduction' in *Secondary Rules of Primary Importance in International Law* (OUP 2022) 1

Karl W, *Vertrag und spätere Praxis im Völkerrecht. Zum Einfluß der Praxis auf Inhalt und Bestand völkerrechtlicher Verträge* (Springer 1983)

Karliuk M, *The Emerging Autonomous Legal Order of the Eurasian Economic Union* (CUP 2023)

Kassoti E, 'Between Sollen and Sein: The CJEU's Reliance on International Law in the Interpretation of Economic Agreements covering Occupied Territories' (2020) 33 LJIL 371

Kassoti E, 'The *Council v. Front Polisario* Case: The Court of Justice's Selective Reliance on International Rules on Treaty Interpretation (Second Part)' (2017) 2 European Papers 23

Kassoti E, 'The European Union and Other Regional International Organizations: Tales of Solidarity' (2024) 21:1 IOLR 190

Keene A (ed), 'Outcome Paper for the Seminar on the International Court of Justice at 70: In Retrospect and in Prospect' (2016) 7 J Int Dispute Settl 238

Keller B, 'Clamor in Europe: Warsaw Pact Condemns '68 Prague Invasion' *The New York Times* (5 December 1989) <https://www.nytimes.com/1989/12/05/world/clamor-in-europe-warsaw-pact-condemns-68-prague-invasion.html>

Kelsen H, *The Law of the United Nations. A Critical Analysis of Its Fundamental Problems* (Steven and Sons Limited 1951)

Kembayev Z, 'Eurasian Economic Union (EAEU)' in A Peters (ed), *Max Planck Encyclopedia of Public International Law* (OUP 2018)

Khasanova L and Simonyan A, '(Geo)politicizing International Law of Cyberspace in Post-Soviet Eurasia' (2025) 24 Chin J Int Law 1

Khng N, 'The World Court on Law of the Sea and Statehood in the Context of Climate Change-Related Sea-Level Rise' (EJILTalk! 17 November 2025) <https://www.ejiltalk.org/the-world-court-on-law-of-the-sea-and-statehood-in-the-context-fo-climate-change-related-sea-level-rise/>

Klabbers J, 'Beyond the Vienna Convention: Conflicting Treaty Provisions' in E Cannizzaro (ed), *The Law of Treaties beyond the Vienna Convention* (OUP 2011) 192

Klabbers J, 'Contending approaches to international organizations: Between functionalism and constitutionalism' in J Klabbers and A Wallendahl (eds), *Research Handbook on the Law of International Organizations* (Edward Elgar Publishing 2011) 3

Klabbers J, 'Virtuous Interpretation' in M Fitzmaurice, O Elias, and P Merkouris (eds), *Treaty Interpretation and the Vienna Convention on the Law of Treaties: 30 Years on* (Brill Nijhoff 2010) 17

Klabbers J, 'The Soft Phenomenology of the Regional International Organization' in Kassoti E, Cabrita T, and Idriz N (eds), *The European Union and Regionalism: Conceptual and Contextual Perspectives* (Brill 2025) 21
Kleinert L, 'Controversies in Caracas: Diplomatic asylum: regional customary law or treaty application?' (Völkerrechtsblog, 17 May 2019)
Koagne Zouapet A, 'States and Regional International Organizations' (2024) 21(1) IOLR 147
Koagne Zouapet A, 'To be or not to be imperative: Jus cogens between universal vocation and regional claims' (2021) 86 QIL, Zoom-in 47
Koh TB, 'Remarks', reproduced in *UN The Law of the Sea: Official Text of the UNCLOS* (London 1983)
Kolb R, 'L'article 103 de la Charte des Nations Unies' (2013) 367 RdC 9
Kolb R, 'Le Droit International Comme Corps de Droit Privé et de Droit Public' (2021) 419 RdC
Kolb R, 'Peremptory Norms as a Legal Technique Rather than Substantive Super- Norms' in D Tladi (ed), *Peremptory Norms of General International Law (Jus Cogens)* (Brill 2021) 21
Kolb R, *Peremptory International Law—Jus Cogens: A General Inventory* (Hart 2015)
Kolb R, *The Law of Treaties: An Introduction* (Edward Elgar Publishing 2023)
Kolb R, *Theory of International Law* (Hart 2016)
Koskenniemi M, *The Gentle Civilizer of Nations: The Rise and Fall of International Law 1870-1960* (5th edn, CUP 2008)
Koutroulis V, 'Article 39' in O Corten and others (eds), *The Vienna Conventions on the Law of Treaties* (2nd edn, OUP 2025)
Krezdorn FJ, *Les Nations Unies et les Accords Régionaux* (Jägersche Buchdruckerei 1954)
Krieger H and Nolte G, 'The International Rule of Law—Rise or Decline?—Approaching Current Foundational Challenges' in H Krieger and others (eds), *The International Rule of Law: Rise or Decline?* (OUP 2019) 3
Krisch N, 'International Law in Times of Hegemony: Unequal Power and the Shaping of the International Legal Order' (2005) 16:3 EJIL 369
Krisch N, 'The Dynamics of International Law Redux' (2021) 74 Current Legal Problems 269
Krisch N, *Beyond Constitutionalism: The Pluralist Structure of Postnational Law* (OUP 2010)
Kulick A and Waibel M, 'General international law in international investment law' in *General International Law in International Investment Law: A Commentary* (OUP 2024) 1
Kunz JL, 'The Law of Nations, Static and Dynamic' (1933) 27 AJIL 628
Landauer C, 'Regionalism, Geography, and the International Legal Imagination' (2011) 11:2 Chic J Int Law 557
Lang A, 'Twenty Years of the WTO Appellate Body's "Fragmentation Jurisprudence"' (2015) 14:3 J Int Trade Law Policy 116
Lange F, 'Challenging the Paris Peace Treaties, State Sovereignty, and Western-Dominated International Law—The Multifaceted Genesis of the Jus Cogens Doctrine' (2018) 31:4 LJIL 821
Lauterpacht H, *The Development of International Law by the International Court* (Steven & Sons 1958, reprinted by Grotius Publications Ltd 1982)
Ličková M, 'European Exceptionalism in International Law' (2008) 19:3 EJIL 463
Liivoja R, 'The Supremacy of the United Nations Charter' (2008) 57:3 ICLQ 583
Lima LC and Marotti L, 'An Unlikely Duo? Regionalism and *Jus Cogens* in International Law' (2022) 12 GoJIL 219
Lixinski L, 'Treaty Interpretation by the Inter-American Court of Human Rights: Expansionism at the Service of the Unity of International Law' (2010) 21:3 EJIL 585
Luhmann N, *Das Recht der Gesellschaft* (Suhrkamp 1995)
Luhmann N, *Die Gesellschaft der Gesellschaft, Vol I* (Suhrkamp 1997)
Mackenzie-Gray Scott R, 'Due Diligence as a Secondary Rule of General International Law' (2021) 34 LJIL 343
Mahaseth H, 'Binding or Non-binding: Analysing the Nature of the ASEAN Agreements' (2021) 21 ICLR 100

Mälksoo L, 'International Legal Theory in Russia: A Civilizational Perspective, or Can Individuals be Subjects of International Law?' in A Orford and F Hoffmann (eds), *The Oxford Handbook of the Theory of International Law* (OUP 2016) 257

Maluwa T, 'African State Practice and the Formation of Some Peremptory Norms of General International Law' in D Tladi (ed), *Peremptory Norms of General International Law (Jus Cogens)* (Brill 2021) 259

Maluwa T, 'Reassessing Aspects of the Contribution of African States to the Reassessing Aspects of the Contribution of African States to the Development of International Law Through African Regional Multilateral Treaties' (2020) 41:2 Mich J Int Law 327

Manley S, Moslemzadeh Tehrani P, and R Rasiah R, 'The (Non-)Use of African Law by the International Criminal Court' (2023) 34 EJIL 555

Marceau G and Reimann C, 'When and How is a Regional Trade Agreement Compatible with the WTO?' (2001) 28 Leg Issues Econ Integr 297

Marschik A, 'Too Much Order? The Impact of Special Secondary Norms on the Unity and Efficacy of the International Legal System' (1998) 9 EJIL 212

Martinico G, 'General Principles of EU Law and Comparative Law' in K Ziegler, PJ Neuvonen, and V Moreno-Lax (eds), *Research Handbook on General Principles in EU Law* (Edward Elgar Publishing 2022) 82

Mayer FC, 'Auf dem Weg zum Richterfaustrecht. Zum PSPP-Urteil des BVerfG' (Verfassungsblog, 7 May 2020) <https://verfassungsblog.de/auf-dem-weg-zum-richterfaustrecht/>

McDougal MS and Lasswell HD, 'The Identification and Appraisal of Diverse Systems of Public Order' (1959) 53:1 AJIL 1

McDougal MS, 'The International Law Commission's Draft Articles upon Interpretation: Textuality Redivivus' (1967) 61:4 AJIL 992

McGarry B, 'The Development of Custom in Territorial Dispute Settlement' (2017) 8 J Int Dispute Settl 339

McLachlan C, 'On the Interface Between Public and Private International Law' (2025) 446 RdC

McLachlan C, 'The Assault on International Adjudication and the Limits of Withdrawal' (2019) 68 ICLQ 499

McLachlan C, 'The Principle of Systemic Integration and Article 31(3)(C) of the Vienna Convention' (2005) 54 ICLQ 279

McNair A, 'The functions and differing legal character of treaties' (1930) 11 BYBIL 100

McNair A, *The Law of Treaties* (OUP 1986)

McRae D, 'Treaty Interpretation by the WTO Appellate Body: The Conundrum of Article 17(6) of the Anti-Dumping Agreement' in E Cannizzaro (ed), *The Law of Treaties Beyond the Vienna Convention* (OUP 2011)

Mendelson M, 'The Formation of Customary International Law' 272 (1998) RdC 155

Mendelson M, 'The ICJ and Sources of International Law' in V Lowe and M Fitzmaurice (eds), *Fifty Years of the International Court of Justice: Essays in Honour of Sir Robert Jennings* (CUP 1996) 63

Merkouris P, *Article 31(3)(c) VCLT and the Principle of Systemic Integration* (Brill Nijhoff 2015)

Michaels R and Pauwelyn J, 'Conflict of Norms or Conflict of Laws? Different Techniques in the Fragmentation of Public International Law' (2012) 22 DJCIL 349

Michaels R, 'Global Legal Pluralism and Conflict of Laws' in P Schiff Berman (ed), *The Oxford Handbook of Global Legal Pluralism* (OUP 2020) 629

Michaels R, 'Tertiary Rules' in N Krisch (ed), *Entangled Legalities Beyond the State* (CUP 2021) 424

Michaels R, 'The Functional Method of Comparative Law' M Reimann and R Zimmermann (ed), *The Oxford Handbook of Comparative Law* (OUP 2012) 373

Miéville C, 'The Commodity-Form Theory of International Law: An Introduction' (2004) 17 LJIL 271

Mitchell R, 'Hegemony in a Multipolar World Order: Global Constitutionalism and the Großraum' (2019) 1 Jus Cogens 129

Murphy SD, 'Deconstructing Fragmentation: Koskenniemi's 2006 ILC Project' (2013) 27:2 TICLJ 293
Murray R and Oteng Kufuor K (eds), 'The Judicial Power of Africa's Supranational Courts' (2020) 28 AJICL 1–158
Murray R, *The African Charter on Human and Peoples' Rights: A Commentary* (OUP 2019)
Naldi GJ, 'The Case Concerning the Frontier Dispute (Burkina Faso/Republic of Mali): Uti Possidetis in an African Perspective' (1987) 36:4) ICLQ 893
Neuvonen PJ, 'Transforming Membership? Citizenship, Identity and the Problem of Belonging in Regional Integration Organizations' (2019) 30:1 EJIL 229
Nicholson R, *Statehood and the State-Like in International Law* (OUP 2019)
Niyo JJ, 'More Stick and Less Carrot: ECOWAS, the Use of Force to Restore Democracy, and the Contest between Regional and International Normative Regimes' (2025) 119:1 AJIL Unbound 254
Nollkaemper A, 'The Power of Secondary Rules to Connect the International and National Legal Orders' in T Broude and Y Shany (eds), *Multi-Sourced Equivalent Norms in International Law* (Hart 2011) 45
Nolte G and Aust HP, 'European Exceptionalism?' (2013) 2:3 Glob Const 407
Nolte G, 'From Dionisio Anzilotti to Roberto Ago: The Classical International Law of State Responsibility and the Traditional Primacy of a Bilateral Conception of Inter-state Relations' (2002) 13:5 EJIL 1083
Nolte G, 'The European Court of Human Rights and the Sources of International Law' Seminar organized by the Ministry of Foreign Affairs of the Czech Republic in connection with the 59th Meeting of CAHDI (Prague, 23 September 2020)
Nolte G, 'Treaties and Their Practice: Symptoms of their Rise or Decline' (2017) 392 RdC 205
Novak G and Reinisch A, 'Article 46' in B Simma and others (eds), *The Charter of the United Nations: A Commentary, Volume I* (4th edn, OUP 2024)
Nußberger A, 'Was ist Willkür? Auf der Suche nach europäischen Standards' (2021) 76 Juristenzeitung 965
Nye JS (ed), *International Regionalism* (Little, Brown and Co 1968)
O'Hara C and Vázquez Guevara V, '"We, the Peoples of the Earth": ALBA, Populism and the Making of an Alternative International Law' (2025) 13:2 London Review of International Law 201
Obregón L, 'Regionalism Reconstructed: A Short History of Latin American International Law' ESIL Conference Paper No 5/2012
Obydenkova AV and Libman A, *Authoritarian Regionalism in the World of International Organizations: Global Perspective and the Eurasian Enigma* (OUP 2019)
Odermatt J, 'International Decisions' (2017) 111:3 AJIL 731
Odermatt J, 'The Use of International Treaty Law by the Court of Justice of the European Union' (2015) 17 Camb Yearb Eur Leg Stud 121
Odermatt J, 'Unidentified Legal Object: Conceptualising the European Union in International Law' (2018) 33:2 Conn J Int Law 215
Odermatt J, *International Law and the European Union* (CUP 2021)
Onuma Y, 'A Transcivilizational Perspective on International Law' (2010) 342 RdC
Onuma Y, 'When Was the Law of International Society Born—An Inquiry of the History of International Law from an Intercivilizational Perspective' (2000) 2 JHIL 1
Onuma Y, *International Law in a Transcivilizational World* (CUP 2017)
Orakhelashvili A, *Peremptory Norms of General International Law* (OUP 2006)
Orakhelashvili A, *The Interpretation of Acts and Rules in Public International Law* (OUP 2008)
Oral N, 'Sea-Level Rise and Maritime Boundaries: From Uncertainty to Clarity?' (2025) 74 ICLQ 163
Orford A, 'Regional Orders, Geopolitics, and the Future of International Law' (2021) Curr Leg Probl 149
Paasi A, 'The Institutionalisation of Regions: A Theoretical Framework for Understanding the Emergence of Regions and the Constitution of Regional Identity' (1986) 164:1 *Fennia* 105

Pahuja S, *Decolonizing International Law* (CUP 2011)

Palchetti P, 'Halfway Between Fragmentation and Convergence: The Role of the Rules of the Organization in the Interpretation of Constituent Treaties' in M Andenas and E Bjorge (eds), *A Farewell to Fragmentation: Reassertion and Convergence in International Law* (CUP 2015) 486

Paulus A and Leiss JR, 'Article 103' in B Simma and others (eds), *The Charter of the United Nations: A Commentary, Volume II* (4th edn, OUP 2024)

Pauwelyn J, 'Bridging Fragmentation and Unity: International Law as a Universe of Inter-Connected Islands' (2004) 25:4 Mich J Int Law 903

Pauwelyn J, 'Fragmentation in International Law' in A Peters (ed), *Max Planck Encyclopedia of Public International Law* (OUP 2006)

Pauwelyn J, *Conflict of Norms in Public International Law: How WTO Law Relates to Other Rules of International Law* (CUP 2003)

Payandeh M, 'The Concept of International Law in the Jurisprudence of H.L.A. Hart' (2010) 21:4 EJIL 967–95

Peat D, 'Disciplining Rules? Compliance, the Rules of Interpretation, and the Evaluative Dimension of Articles 31 and 32 of the VCLT' (2022) 69 NILR 221

Peat D, *Comparative Reasoning in International Courts and Tribunals* (CUP 2019)

Pellet A and Müller D, 'Article 38' in A Zimmermann and others (eds), *The Statute of the International Court of Justice: A Commentary* (3rd edn, OUP 2019)

Pernice R, *Die Sicherung des Weltfriedens durch regionale Organisationen und die Vereinten Nationen. Eine Untersuchung zur Kompetenzverteilung nach Kapitel VIII der UN-Charta* (Hansischer Gildenverlag 1972)

Peters A, 'Die Missbilligung der Todesstrafe durch die Völkerrechtsgemeinschaft' (1999) 26 Europäische Grundrechte 650

Peters A, 'The Principle of *Uti Possidetis Juris*' in C Walter and A von Ungern-Sternberg (eds), *Self-Determination and Secession in International Law* (OUP 2014) 95

Peters A, 'The Refinement of International Law: From Fragmentation to Regime Interaction and Politicization' (2017) 15:3 Int J Const Law 671

Peters C, 'Subsequent Practice and Established Practice of International Organizations: Two Sides of the Same Coin' (2011) 3 GOJIL 617

Peters C, *Praxis Internationaler Organisationen: Vertragswandel und völkerrechtlicher Ordnungsrahmen* (Springer 2016)

Powell JE, *Islamic Law and International Law: Peaceful Resolution of Disputes* (OUP 2020)

Proelss A, 'Article 34' in O Dörr and K Schmalenbach (eds), *Vienna Convention on the Law of Treaties: A Commentary* (2nd edn, Springer 2018)

Proelss A, 'Article 38' in O Dörr and K Schmalenbach (eds), *Vienna Convention on the Law of Treaties: A Commentary* (2nd edn, Springer 2018)

Proelss A, 'Article 55' in A Proelss (ed), *United Nations Convention on the Law of the Sea. A Commentary* (CH Beck, Hart, Nomos 2017)

Prost M, *The Concept of Unity in Public International Law* (Hart 2012)

Quintana FJ and Uriburu J, 'Mexico and Ecuador at the ICJ: A Plea for Taking the Latin American Experience Seriously' (EJILTalk! 1 May 2024) <https://www.ejiltalk.org/mexico-and-ecuador-at-the-icj-a-plea-for-taking-the-latin-american-experience-seriously/>

Ranganathan S, *Strategically Created Treaty Conflicts and the Politics of International Law* (CUP 2014)

Ratner SR, 'Drawing a Better Line: *Uti Possidetis* and the Borders of New States' (1996) 90:4 AJIL 590

Raz J, 'The Identity of Legal Systems' (1971) 59 California Law Review 795

Raz J, 'Why the State?' in N Roughan and A Halpin (eds), *In Pursuit of Pluralist Jurisprudence* (CUP 2018) 136

Reinold T and Zürn M, '"Rules about Rules" and the Endogenous Dynamics of International Law: Dissonance Reduction as a Mechanism of Secondary Rule-making' (2014) 3:2 Glob Const 236

Rensmann T, 'Article 48' in O Dörr and K Schmalenbach (eds), *Vienna Convention on the Law of Treaties: A Commentary* (2nd edn, Springer 2018)
Ringbom H, 'New Threats—Old Rules: Law of the Sea Issues Raised by Suspected Attacks on Submarine Infrastructure in the Baltic Sea' (2025) 56:3 Ocean Dev Int Law 390
Roberts A, 'Who Killed Article 38(1)(B)—A Reply to Bradley & Gulati' (2010) 21 DJCIL 173
Roberts A, *Is International Law International?* (OUP 2017)
Romano CPR, 'Mirage in the Desert Regional Judicialization in the Arab World' in I de la Rasilla and JE Viñuales (eds), *Experiments in International Adjudication: Historical Accounts* (CUP 2019) 169
Rosenne S, *Developments in the Law of Treaties 1945-1986* (CUP 1989)
Rosenne S, *The Law of Treaties: A Guide to the Legislative History of the Vienna Convention* (AW Sijthoff 1970)
Ross A, *Constitution of the United Nations* (Rinehart 1950)
Roughlin N, 'Plurality of Laws and Conflict of Laws: Reconciling through Recognition?' in MS Green, R Michaels, and R Banu (eds), *Philosophical Foundations of Private International Law* (OUP 2024) 217
Ruda Santolaria JJ, 'The Treatment of Peremptory Norms of General International Law (Jus Cogens) in the Inter-American Human Rights System' in D Tladi (ed), *Peremptory Norms of General International Law (Jus Cogens)* (Brill 2021) 319
Saidov A, 'Regionalism and Human Rights: Towards an Asian Human Rights Protection System' (2025) 24 Chin J Int Law 1
Salem N, 'Sharia Reservations to Human Rights Treaties' in A Peters (ed), *Max Planck Encyclopedia of Public International Law* (OUP 2020)
Salerno F, 'Treaties Establishing Objective Regimes' in E Cannizzaro (ed), *The Law of Treaties Beyond the Vienna Convention* (OUP 2011) 225
Salter M and Yin Y, 'Analysing Regionalism within International Law and Relations: The Shanghai Cooperation Organisation as a Grossraum?' (2014) 13 Chin J Int Law 819
Samuel KLH, *The OIC, the UN, and Counter-Terrorism Law-Making. Conflicting or Cooperative Legal orders?* (Hart 2013)
Saul B, 'The Council of Europe's Proposed Definition of Terrorism Infringes Human Rights' (EJILTalk! 18 February 2025) <The Council of Europe's Proposed Definition of Terrorism Infringes Human Rights – EJIL: Talk!>
Schmahl S, 'Das Verhältnis der deutschen Rechtsordnung zu Regeln des Völkerrechts' (2013) 52:11 Juristische Schulung 961
Schmalenbach K, 'Article 5' in O Dörr and K Schmalenbach (eds), *Vienna Convention on the Law of Treaties: A Commentary* (2nd edn, Springer 2018)
Schmalenbach K, 'Article 53' in Ö Dörr and K Schmalenbach (eds), *Vienna Convention on the Law of Treaties: A Commentary* (2nd edn, Springer 2018)
Schmitt C, *The Concept of the Political*, G Schwab, trans (University of Chicago Press 2007)
Schmitt C, *Völkerrechtliche Großraumordnung mit Interventionsverbot für raumfremde Mächte* (3rd edn in the version of 1941, Duncker & Humblot 2009)
Schreuer C, 'Regionalism v. Universalism' (1995) 6 EJIL 477
Schütze R, *From Dual to Cooperative Federalism: The Changing Structure of European Law* (OUP 2009)
Schwarzenberger G, 'The Standard of Civilization in International Law' (1955) 8 Curr Legal Probl 212
Scott S, 'Universalism and Title to Territory in Antarctica' (1997) 66 Nord J Int Law 33
Sender O, *International Law-Making by the International Court of Justice and International Law Commission* (CUP 2024)
Serdy A, 'Article 282' in A Proelss (ed), *United Nations Convention on the Law of the Sea: A Commentary* (CH Beck/Hart/Nomos 2017)
Serdy A, '*Pacta Tertiis* and Regional Fisheries Management Mechanisms: The IUU Fishing Concept as an Illegitimate Short-Cut to a Legitimate Goal' (2017) 48 Ocean Development & International Law 345

Shapiro SJ, *Legality* (The Belknap Press of Harvard University Press 2011)
Shaw M, *International Law* (8th edn, CUP 2017)
Shaw MN, 'The Heritage of States: The Principle of *Uti Possidetis Juris* today' (1996) 67 BYBIL 75
Simma B, 'From Bilateralism to Community Interests in International Law' (1994) 250 RdC 217
Simma B, 'Universality of International Law from the Perspective of the Practitioner' (2009) 20:2 EJIL 265
Sinclair GF, *To Reform the World: International Organizations and the Making of Modern States* (OUP 2017)
Sinclair I, *The Vienna Convention on the Law of Treaties* (Manchester University Press 1984)
Sinclar Gf, 'Between Functionalism and Hegemony: Regional International Organizations in the History of International Law' (2024) 21:1 IOLR 65
Singh P, 'A Custom's Nine Lives: Decolonial Continuities of Opinio Juris in Customary International Law' (2024) 23 Chin J Int Law 689
Sivakumaran S, 'Techniques in International Law- Making: Extrapolation, Analogy, Form and the Emergence of an International Law of Disaster Relief' (2017) 28 EJIL 1097
Skordas A, 'Authoritarian Global Governance? The Russian-Chinese Joint Statement of March 2021' (2021) 81 ZaöRV 293
Skordas A, "Supranational Law' Law' in A Peters (ed), *Max Planck Encyclopedia of Public International Law* (OUP 2014)
Skubizewski K, 'Elements of Custom and the Hague Court' 31 (1971) ZaöRV 810
Sorel J-M and Boré Eveno V, 'Article 31' in O Corten and others (eds), *The Vienna Conventions on the Law of Treaties* (2nd edn, OUP 2025)
Sturma P, 'Is There Any Regional Jus Cogens in Europe? The Case of the European Convention on Human Rights' in D Tladi (ed), *Peremptory Norms of General International Law (Jus Cogens)* (Brill 2021) 302
Talmon S, 'Determining Customary International Law: The ICJ's Methodology between Induction, Deduction and Assertion' (2015) 26:2 EJIL 417
Talmon S, '*Jus Cogens* after *Germany v. Italy*: Substantive and Procedural Rules Distinguished' (2012) 25:4 LJIL 979
Tams CJ, 'Meta-Custom and the Court: A Study in Judicial Law-Making' (2015) 14 LAPE 51
Tan EEG and Ang B, 'ASEAN Ambiguity on International Law and Norms for Cyberspace' (2022) 20 Balt Yearb Int Law Online 133
Teubner G, *Constitutional Fragments: Societal Constitutionalism and Globalization* (OUP 2012)
Thirlway H, *International Customary Law and Codification* (Sijthoff 1972)
Thirlway H, *The Law and Procedure of the International Court of Justice: Fifty Years Jurisprudence Volume I* (OUP 2013)
Thirlway H, *The Sources of International Law* (2nd edn, OUP 2019)
Tladi D, 'Immunities (Article 46Abis)' in G Werle and M Vormbaum (eds), *The African Criminal Court: A Commentary on the Malabo Protocol* (Springer 2017) 203
Tladi D, 'Of Heroes and Villains, Angels and Demons: The ICC-AU Tension Revisited' (2017) 60 GYIL 43
Tolstykh V, 'Between a "Heavenly" Life and an "Earthly" Life: Jurisprudence of the Court of the EAEU from 2012–2019' (2019) 7:3 Russ Law J 194
Tomuschat C, 'The Kadi Case: What Relationship is there between the Universal Legal Order under the Auspices of the United Nations and the EU Legal Order?' (2009) 28 Yearb Eur Law 654
Treves T, 'The Expansion of International Law' 398 (2019) 398 RdC 37
Tsamenyi M and Ali K, 'African States and the Law of the Sea Convention: Have the Benefits Been Realized' (2012) 26 Ocean Yearbook 113
Tunkin GI, 'Co-existence and International Law' 1958 (95) RdC 5
Tunkin GI, 'International Law in the International System' (1975) 147 RdC 9
Tunkin GI, *Theory of International Law (translated with an introduction by WE Butler)* (Harvard University Press 1974)

Tzanakopoulos A, 'Denunciation of the ICSID Convention under the General International Law of Treaties' in R Hofmann and CJ Tams (eds), *International Investment Law and General International Law From Clinical Isolation to Systemic Integration?* (Nomos 2011) 75
Tzevelekos VP and Dzehtsiarou K, 'International Custom Making and the ECtHR's European Consensus Method of Interpretation' (2016) 16 EYHR 313
van Damme I, 'What Role is there for Regional International Law in the Interpretation of the WTO Agreements?' in L Bartels and F Ortino (eds), *Regional Trade Agreements and the WTO Legal System* (OUP 2006) 553
van Hoof GJH, *Rethinking the Sources of International Law* (Kluwer Law and Taxation Publishers 1983)
van Langenhove L, 'What is a Region? Towards a Statehood Theory of Regions' (2013) 19:4 Contemporary Politics 474
van Panhuys JHF, 'Regional or General International Law? A Misleading Dilemma' (1961) 8:2 NILR 146
Veber MT, 'The Notion of Regionalism in the Context of Sanctions Adopted by Regional International Organizations in the Defence of the General Interest' in Kassoti E, Cabrita T, and Idriz N (eds), *The European Union and Regionalism: Conceptual and Contextual Perspectives* (Brill 2025) 142
Villiger M, *Commentary on the 1969 Vienna Convention on the Law of Treaties* (Martinus Nijhoff 2009)
Virally M, 'Les relations entre organisations régionales et organisations universelles' in *Régionalisme et universalisme* in Société Française pour le Droit International (ed), *Colloque de Bordeaux, Régionalisme et universalisme dans le droit international contemporain* (Pedone 1977)
Viseur Sellers P, '*Jus Cogens*: Redux' (2022) 116 AJIL Unbound 281
Vogenauer S, 'Sources Of Law and Legal Method in Comparative Law' in M Reimann and Zimmermann (eds), *The Oxford Handbook of Comparative Law* (2nd edn, OUP 2019) 876
von Arnauld A, 'Harmonisation Through General Principles of Law' in K Ziegler, PJ Neuvonen, and V Moreno-Lax (eds), *Research Handbook on General Principles in EU Law* (Edward Elgar Publishing 2022) 40
von Daniels D, *The Concept of Law From a Transnational Perspective* (Routledge 2010)
von der Decken K, 'Article 30' in in O Dörr and K Schmalenbach (eds), *Vienna Convention on the Law of Treaties: A Commentary* (2nd edn, Springer 2018)
von der Decken K, 'Article 41' in O Dörr and K Schmalenbach (eds), *Vienna Convention on the Law of Treaties: A Commentary* (2nd edn, Springer 2018)
Vöneky S, 'Article 108' in B Simma and others (eds), *The Charter of the United Nations: A Commentary, Volume II* (4th edn, OUP 2024)
Vöneky S, 'Article 109' in B Simma and others (eds), *The Charter of the United Nations: A Commentary, Volume II* (4th edn, OUP 2024)
Vranes E, 'Lex superior, lex specialis, lex posterior—zur Rechtsnatur der 'Konfliktlösungsregeln' (2005) 65 ZaöRV 391
Waibel M, 'Demystifying the Art of Interpretation' (2011) 22:2 EJIL 571
Waibel M, 'Uniformity Versus Specialization (2): A Uniform Regime of Treaty Interpretation?' in CJ Tams, A Tzanakopoulos, and A Zimmermann (eds), *Research Handbook on the Law of Treaties* (Edward Elgar Publishing 2014) 375
Waldron J, 'International Law: "A Relatively Small and Unimportant" Part of Jurisprudence?' in L Duarte d'Almeida and others (eds), *Reading HLA Hart's 'The Concept of Law'* (Hart 2013) 209
Walter C, 'Article 19' in O Dörr and K Schmalenbach (eds), *The Vienna Convention on the Law of Treaties: A Commentary* (2nd edn, Springer 2018)
Walter C, 'Article 52' in B Simma and others (eds), *The Charter of the United Nations: A Commentary, Volume II* (4th edn, OUP 2024)
Weil P, 'Towards Relative Normativity in International Law' (1983) 77:3 AJIL 413
Weiler J, 'Cancelling Carl Schmitt?' (EJILTalk! 13 August 2021)

Wellens KC, 'Diversity in Secondary Rules and the Unity of International Law: Some Reflections on Current Trends' (1994) 15 Netherlands Yearbook of International Law 3
Werle G and Vormbaum M, 'African States, the African Union, and the International Criminal Court: A Continuing Story' (2017) 60:1 German Yearbook of International Law 17
Wessel RA, 'Jurisdictional Immunity of Regional Organisations—Substantive Unity in Instrumental Diversity?' in T Ruys and N Angelet (eds), *The Cambridge Handbook of Immunities and International Law* (CUP 2019) 214
Wiebusch M, *A Theory on Africanizing International Law* (Pretoria University Law Press 2024)
Wolfke K, *Custom in Present International Law* (2nd edn, Martinus Nijhoff Publishers 1993)
Wolfke K, *Custom in Present International Law* (Warsaw Scientific Society 1964)
Wolfrum R, 'Sources of International Law' in A Peters (ed), *Max Planck Encyclopedia of Public International Law* (OUP 2011)
Wood M and Sender O, *Identification of Customary International Law* (OUP 2024)
Wood M, 'A European Vision of International Law: For what Purpose?' in H Ruiz Fabri, E Jouannet, and V Tomkiewicz (eds), *Select Proceedings of the European Society of International Law (2006)* (Hart 2008) 151
Wood M, 'International Law in Practice. Courses of the Summer School on Public International Law' (2022) XI International and Comparative Law Research Center
Wood M, 'Method and Style in International Law, and the International Court of Justice's Contribution' in P Galvão Teles and M Almeida Ribeiro (eds), *Case-Law and the Development of International Law Contributions by International Courts and Tribunals* (Brill Nijhoff 2021) 14
Wood M, 'The International Tribunal for the Law of the Sea and General International Law' (2007) 22 Int'l J Marine and Coastal Law 351
Wood M, 'What Is Public International Law? The Need for Clarity about Sources' (2011) 2 Asian J Int Law 205
Yee S, 'Article 38 of the ICJ Statute and Applicable Law: Selected Issues in Recent Cases' (2016) 7 J Int Dispute Settl 472
Yee S, 'The Role of Law in the Formation of Regional Perspectives in Human Rights and Regional Systems for the Protection of Human Rights: The European and Asian Models as Illustrations' (2004) 8 Singap Year B Int Law 157
Yu D, 'With Our Feet to the Fire: Regional Agreements as Mechanisms of Changing International Law to Include Persons Displaced by Climate Change' (2021) 35 Emory Int Law Rev 517
Yusuf AA, *Pan-Africanism and International Law* (Brill 2014)
Zang MQ, 'When the Multilateral Meets the Regionals: Regional Trade Agreements at WTO Dispute Settlement' (2019) 18 World Trade Rev 33
Zarbiyev F, 'The "Cash Value" of the Rules of Treaty Interpretation' (2019) 32 LJIL 33
Ziemele I, 'European Consensus and International Law' in A van Aaken and I Motoc (eds), *The European Convention on Human Rights and General International Law* (OUP 2018) 23

Index

For the benefit of digital users, indexed terms that span two pages (e.g., 52–53) may, on occasion, appear on only one of those pages.